Chapter 74:

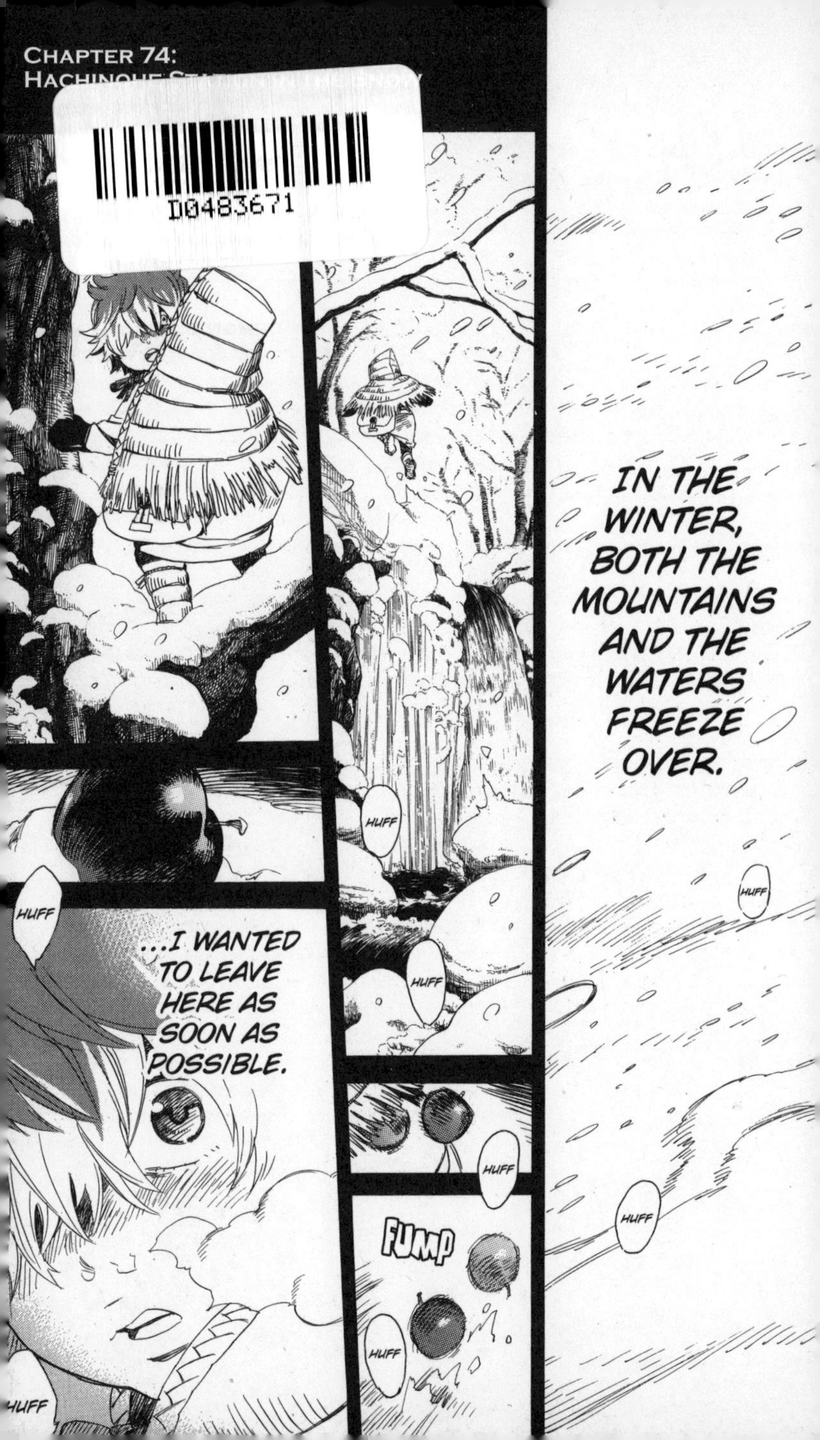
IN THE WINTER, BOTH THE MOUNTAINS AND THE WATERS FREEZE OVER.
HUFF
HUFF
HUFF
HUFF
HUFF
FUMP
HUFF
HUFF
...I WANTED TO LEAVE HERE AS SOON AS POSSIBLE.
HUFF

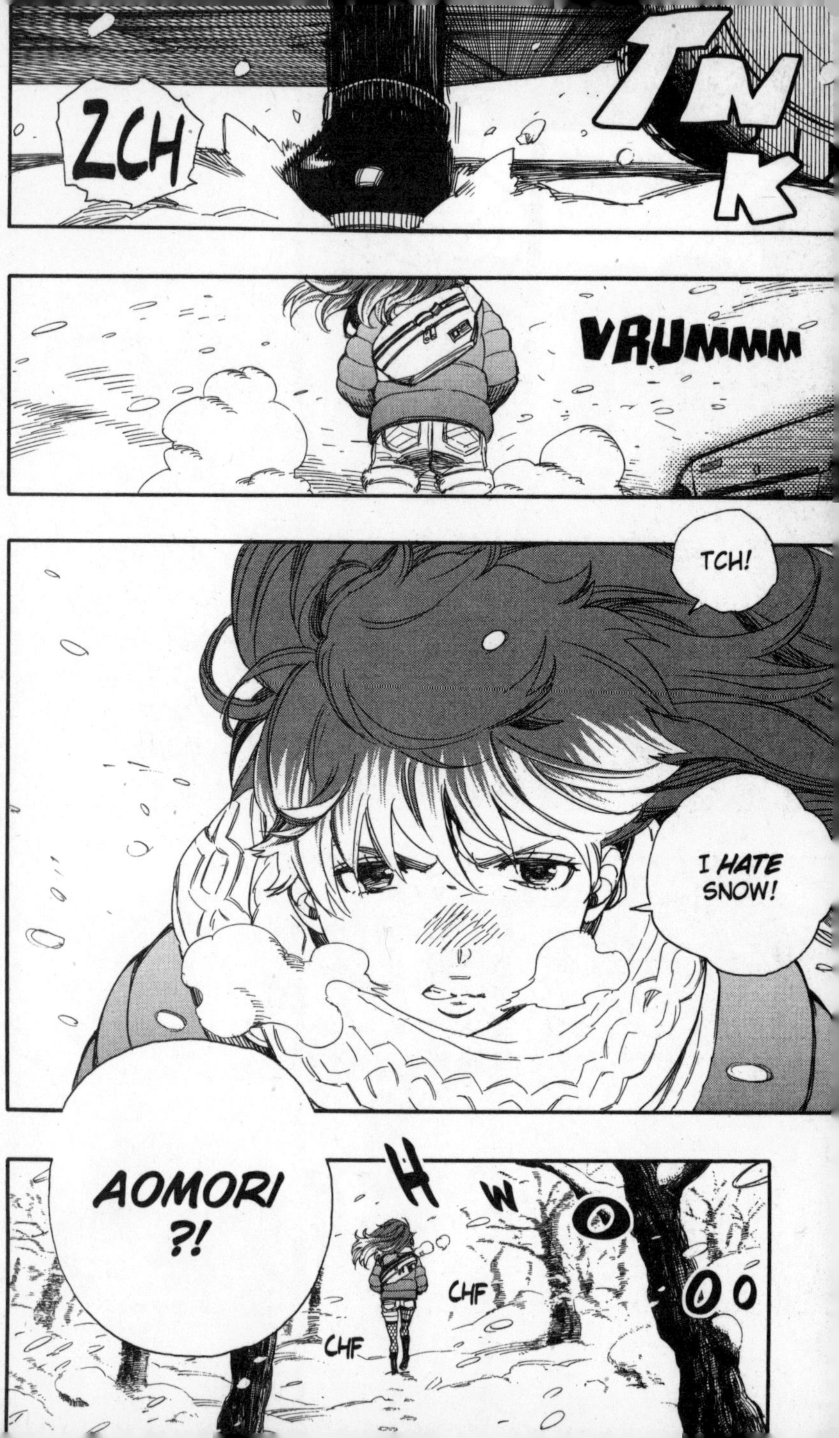
TINK
ZCH
VRUMMM
TCH!
I HATE SNOW!
HWOOO
AOMORI ?!
CHF
CHF

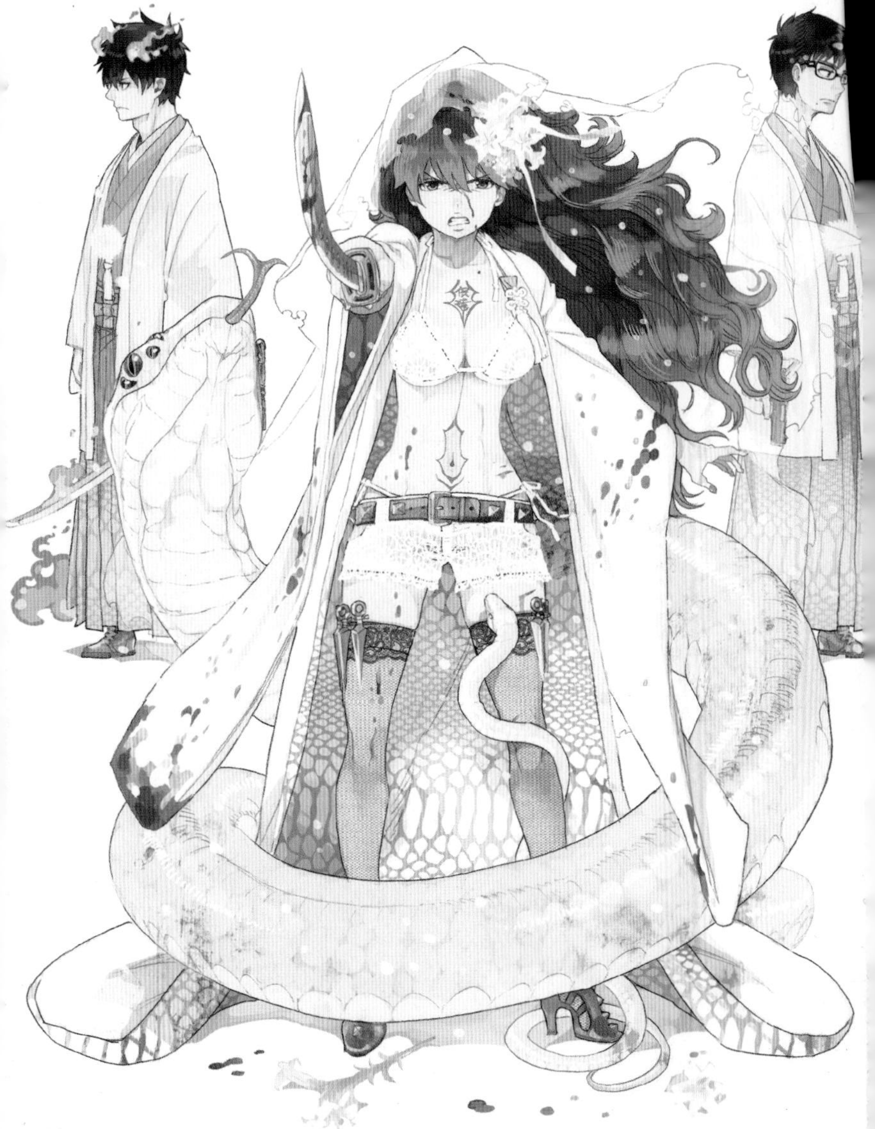

BLUE EXORCIST 17

KAZUE KATO

BLUE EXORCIST

Contents 17

I AM 18

CAST OF CHARACTERS

RIN OKUMURA

Born of a human mother and Satan, the God of Demons, Rin Okumura has powers he can barely control. After Satan kills Father Fujimoto, Rin's foster father, Rin decides to become an Exorcist so he can someday defeat Satan. Now a first-year student at True Cross Academy and an Exwire at the Exorcism Cram School, he hopes to someday become a Knight. When he draws the Koma Sword, he manifests his internal power in the form of blue ames. He succeeded in defeating the Impure King and affirmed his determination to live with his flame.

YUKIO OKUMURA

Rin's brother. Hoping to become a doctor, he's a genius who is the youngest student ever to become an instructor at the Exorcism Cram School. An instructor in Demon Pharmaceuticals, he possesses the titles of Doctor and Dragoon. Todo told him that his true nature is that of a demon.

SHURA KIRIGAKURE

An upper-rank special investigator dispatched by Vatican Headquarters to True Cross Academy. She's a Senior Exorcist First Class who holds the titles of Knight, Tamer, Doctor and Aria. She used to be Father Fujimoto's pupil.

MEPHISTO PHELES

President of True Cross Academy and head of the Exorcism Cram School. He was Father Fujimoto's friend, and now he is Rin and Yukio's guardian. The number two power in Gehenna and known as Samael, King of Time.

SHIRO FUJIMOTO

The man who raised Rin and Yukio. He was a priest at True Cross Cathedral. He held the rank of Paladin and once taught Demon Pharmaceuticals. Satan possessed him and he gave his life defending Rin.

◉ THE STORY SO FAR ◉

UNKNOWN TO RIN OKUMURA, BOTH HUMAN AND DEMON BLOOD RUNS IN HIS VEINS. IN AN ARGUMENT WITH HIS FOSTER FATHER, FATHER FUJIMOTO, RIN LEARNS THAT SATAN IS HIS TRUE FATHER. SATAN SUDDENLY APPEARS AND TRIES TO DRAG RIN DOWN TO GEHENNA BECAUSE RIN HAS INHERITED HIS POWER. FATHER FUJIMOTO FIGHTS TO DEFEND RIN, BUT DIES IN THE PROCESS. RIN DECIDES TO BECOME AN EXORCIST SO HE CAN SOMEDAY DEFEAT SATAN AND BEGINS STUDYING AT THE EXORCISM CRAM SCHOOL UNDER THE INSTRUCTION OF HIS TWIN BROTHER YUKIO, WHO IS ALREADY AN EXORCIST.

RIN AND THE OTHERS SUCCEED IN DEFEATING THE IMPURE KING, AWAKENED BY THE FORMER EXORCIST, TODO. MEANWHILE, YUKIO FIGHTS TODO, AND AS THE BATTLE RAGES, HE SENSES THE SAME FLAME IN HIS OWN EYES AS HIS BROTHER. AFRAID, HE KEEPS IT A SECRET.

LATER, MYSTERIOUS EVENTS BEGIN OCCURRING AROUND THE GLOBE. A SECRET SOCIETY KNOWN AS THE ILLUMINATI IS BEHIND THESE INCIDENTS, AND SHIMA IS THEIR SPY. ON MEPHISTO'S ORDERS, SHIMA HAD INFILTRATED THE ILLUMINATI TO WORK AS A DOUBLE AGENT AND WAS SUPPLYING INFORMATION TO BOTH SIDES.

WHEN SHIMA ASKS YUKIO ABOUT HIS MEETING WITH LUCIFER, YUKIO BRUSHES IT OFF. BUT YUKIO NOW GROWS INCREASINGLY UNEASY ABOUT THE POWER IN HIS EYES. HE DESIGNS DANGEROUS TESTS FOR HIMSELF TO AWAKEN THE FEAR OF DEATH AND KICK-START HIS POWER.

THEN MEPHISTO INFORMS RIN AND YUKIO THAT SHURA HAS DISAPPEARED AND ORDERS THEM TO FIND HER!

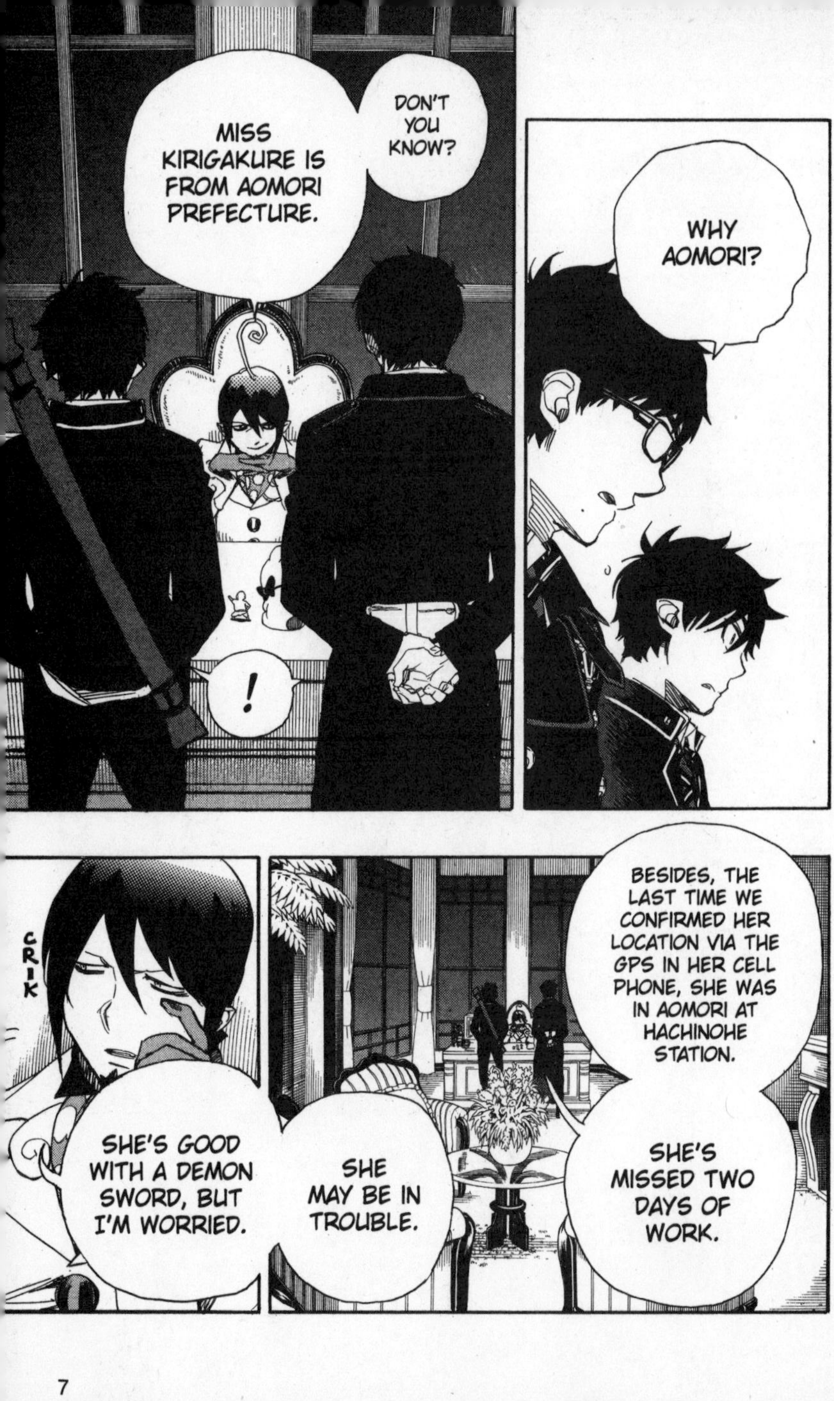
WHY AOMORI?
DON'T YOU KNOW?
MISS KIRIGAKURE IS FROM AOMORI PREFECTURE.
!
BESIDES, THE LAST TIME WE CONFIRMED HER LOCATION VIA THE GPS IN HER CELL PHONE, SHE WAS IN AOMORI AT HACHINOHE STATION.
SHE'S MISSED TWO DAYS OF WORK.
SHE MAY BE IN TROUBLE.
CRIK
SHE'S GOOD WITH A DEMON SWORD, BUT I'M WORRIED.

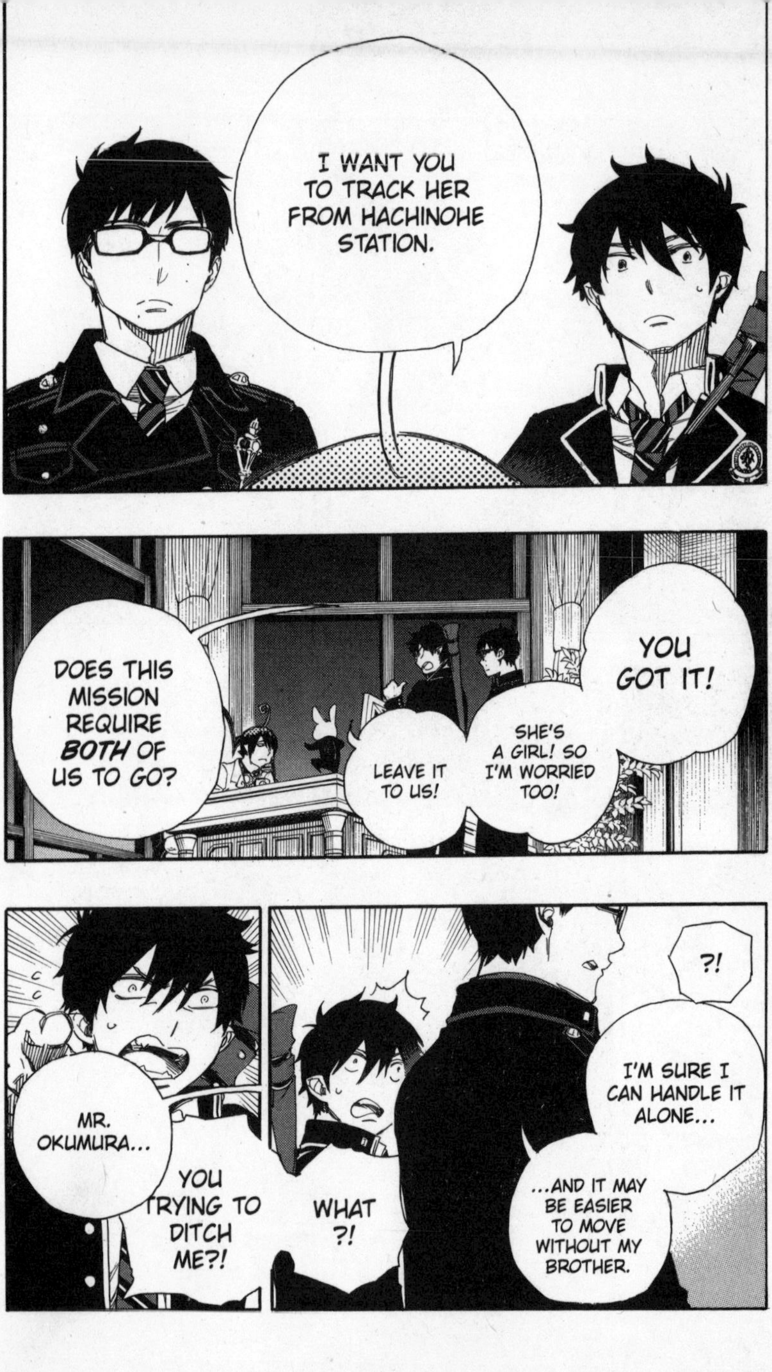
I WANT YOU TO TRACK HER FROM HACHINOHE STATION.
YOU GOT IT!
SHE'S A GIRL! SO I'M WORRIED TOO!
LEAVE IT TO US!
DOES THIS MISSION REQUIRE *BOTH* OF US TO GO?
?!
I'M SURE I CAN HANDLE IT ALONE...
...AND IT MAY BE EASIER TO MOVE WITHOUT MY BROTHER.
WHAT?!
MR. OKUMURA...
YOU TRYING TO DITCH ME?!

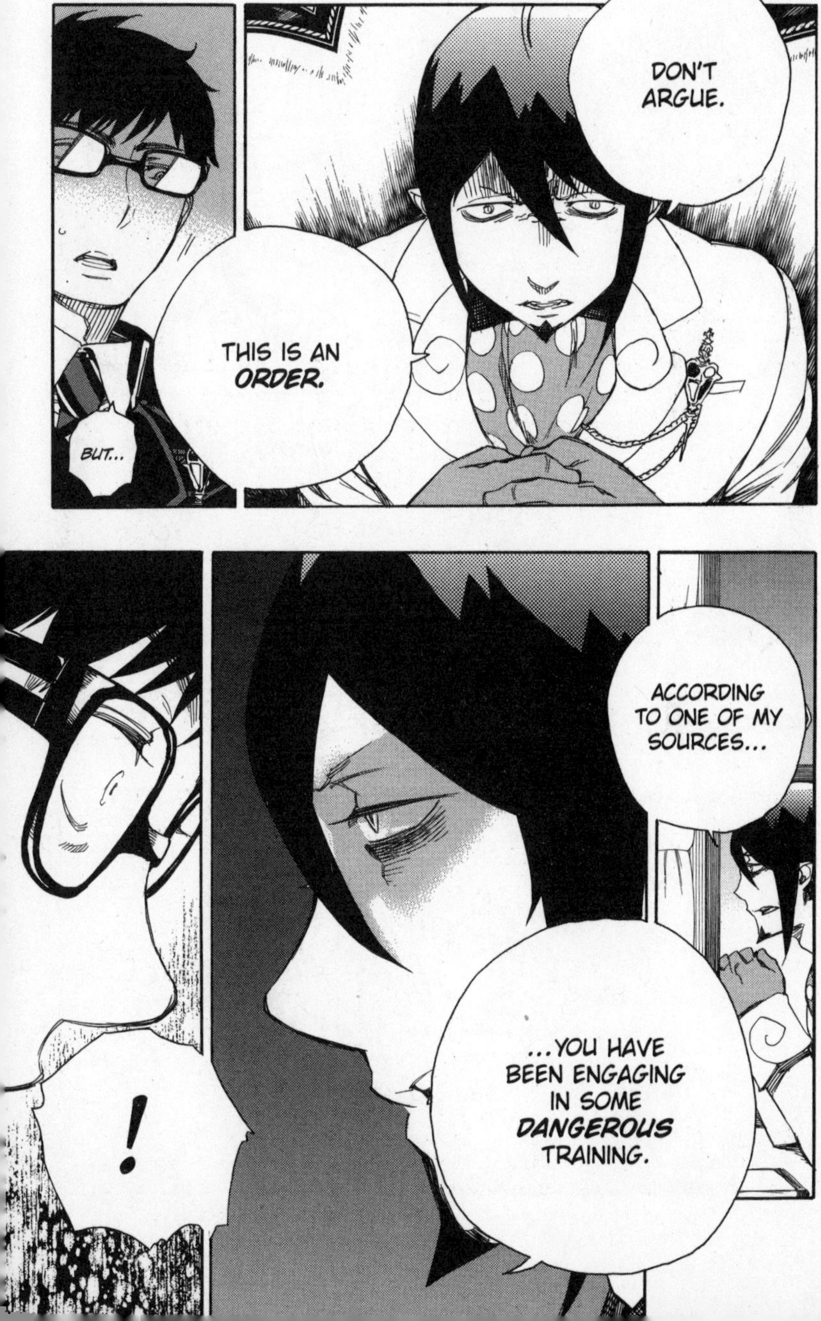
DON'T ARGUE.
THIS IS AN ORDER.
BUT...
ACCORDING TO ONE OF MY SOURCES...
...YOU HAVE BEEN ENGAGING IN SOME DANGEROUS TRAINING.
!

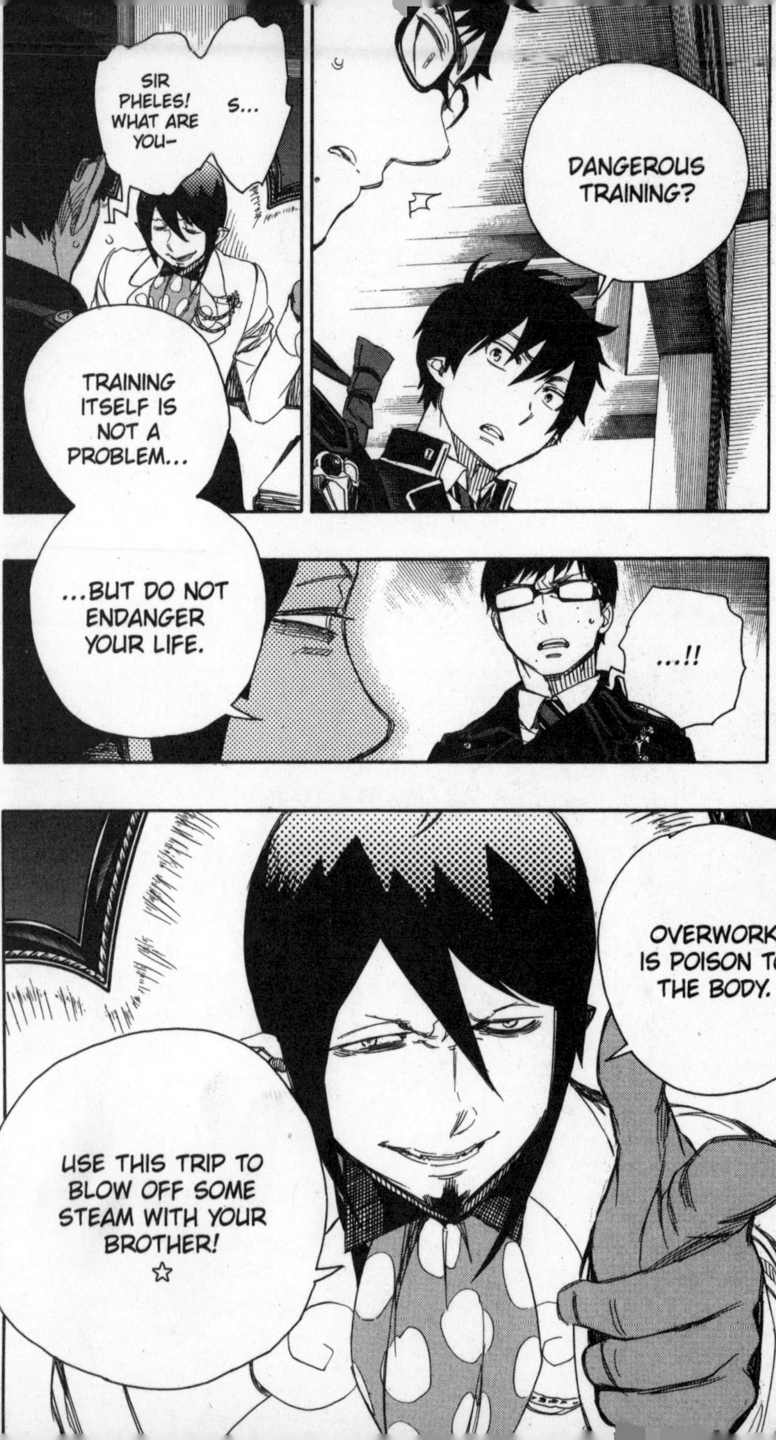
DANGEROUS TRAINING?
S...
SIR PHELES! WHAT ARE YOU-
TRAINING ITSELF IS NOT A PROBLEM...
...BUT DO NOT ENDANGER YOUR LIFE.
...!!
OVERWORK IS POISON TO THE BODY.
USE THIS TRIP TO BLOW OFF SOME STEAM WITH YOUR BROTHER! ☆

Chapter 74: Hachinohe Station in the Snow

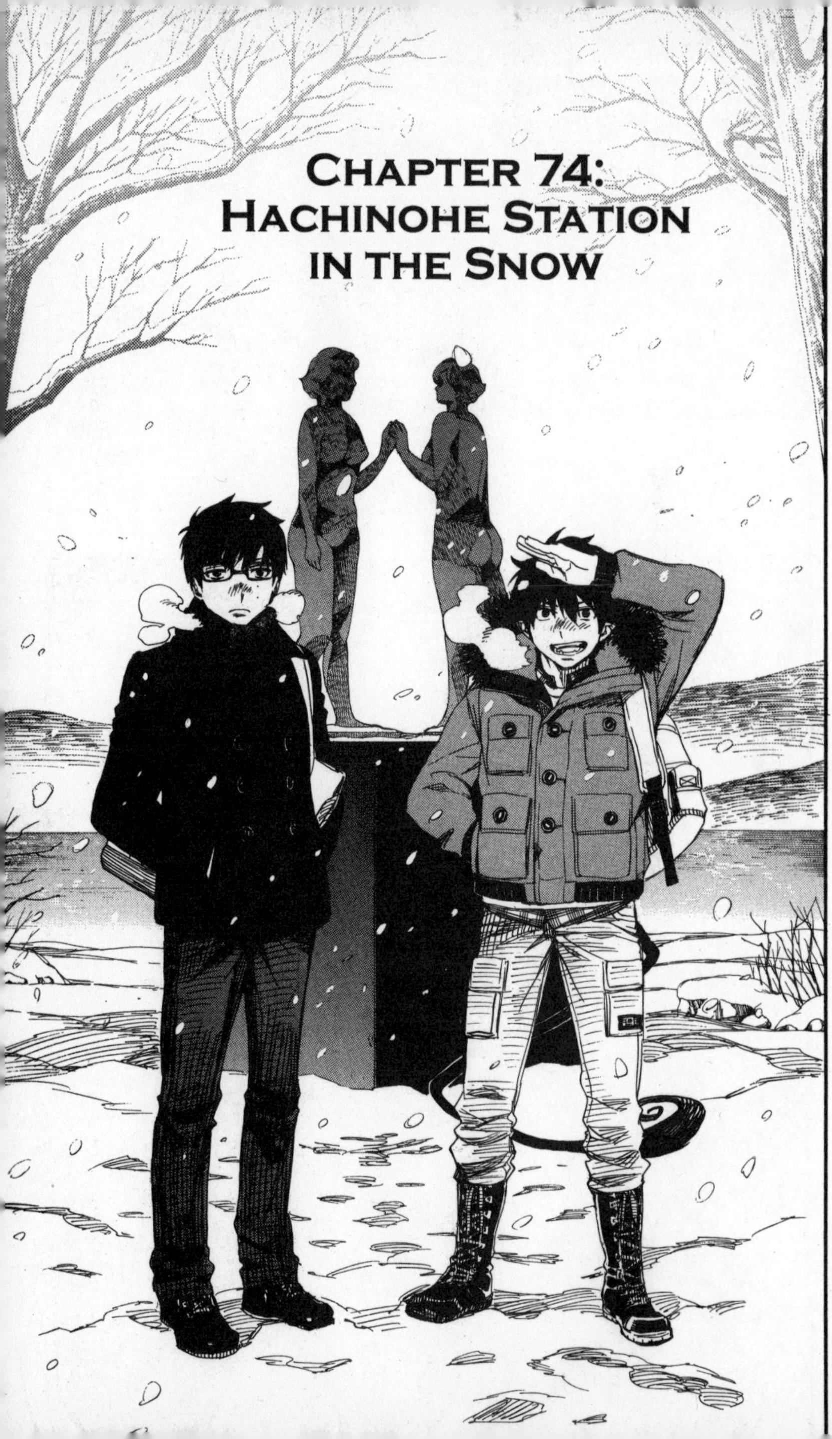

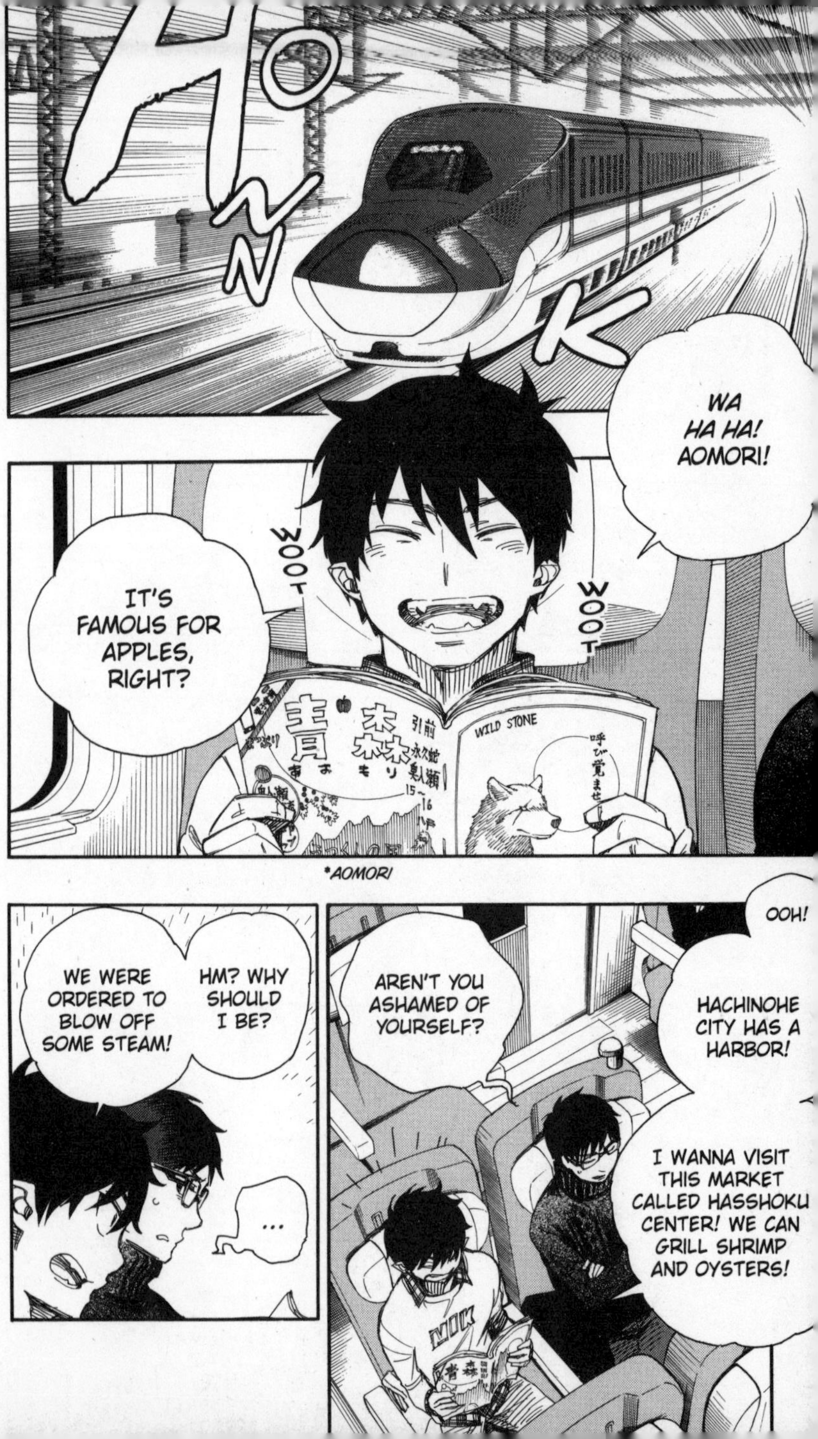
WA HA HA! AOMORI!
WOOT WOOT
IT'S FAMOUS FOR APPLES, RIGHT?
WOOT
WILD STONE
*AOMORI
OOH!
HACHINOHE CITY HAS A HARBOR!
I WANNA VISIT THIS MARKET CALLED HASSHOKU CENTER! WE CAN GRILL SHRIMP AND OYSTERS!
AREN'T YOU ASHAMED OF YOURSELF?
HM? WHY SHOULD I BE?
WE WERE ORDERED TO BLOW OFF SOME STEAM!
...

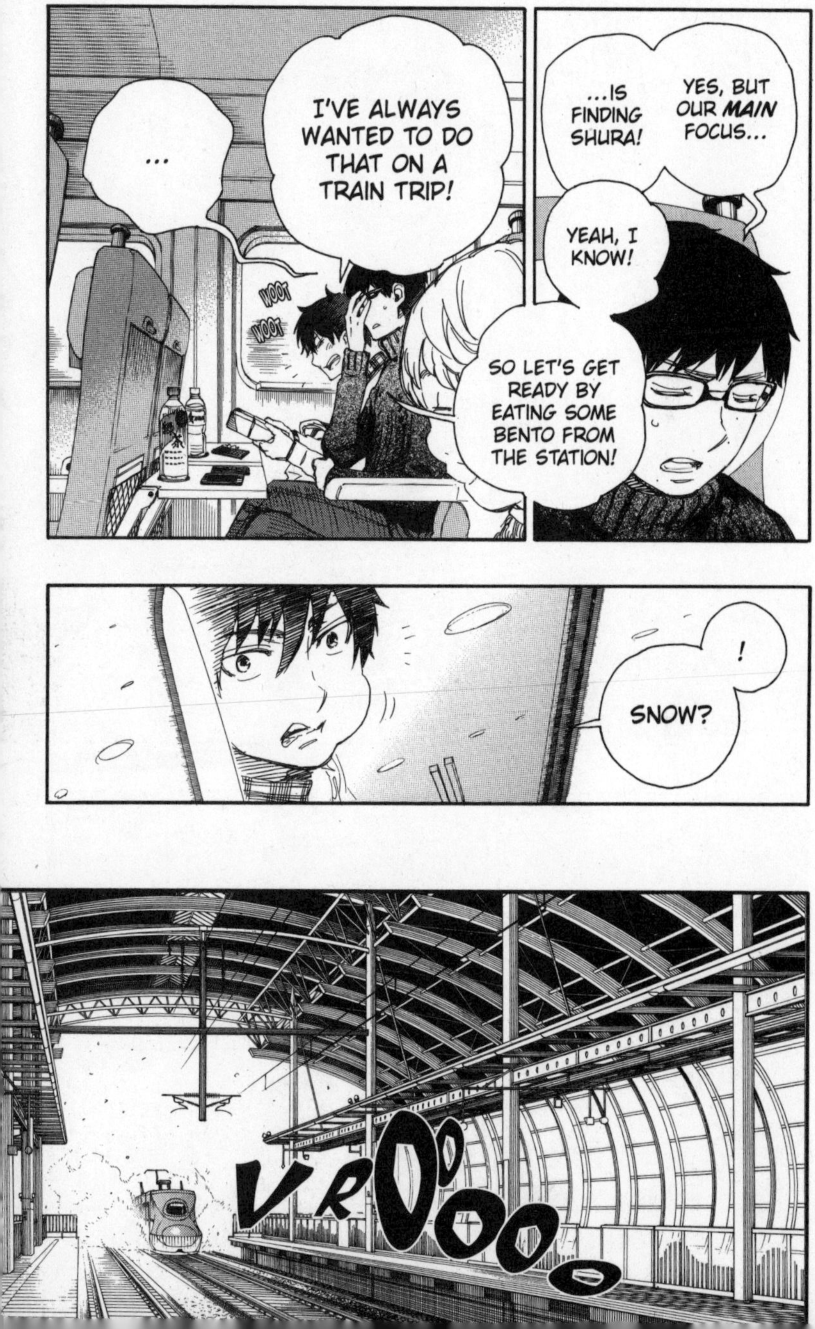
YES, BUT OUR *MAIN* FOCUS...
...IS FINDING SHURA!
YEAH, I KNOW!
SO LET'S GET READY BY EATING SOME BENTO FROM THE STATION!
I'VE ALWAYS WANTED TO DO THAT ON A TRAIN TRIP!
...
WOOT
WOOT
!
SNOW?
VROOOOOO

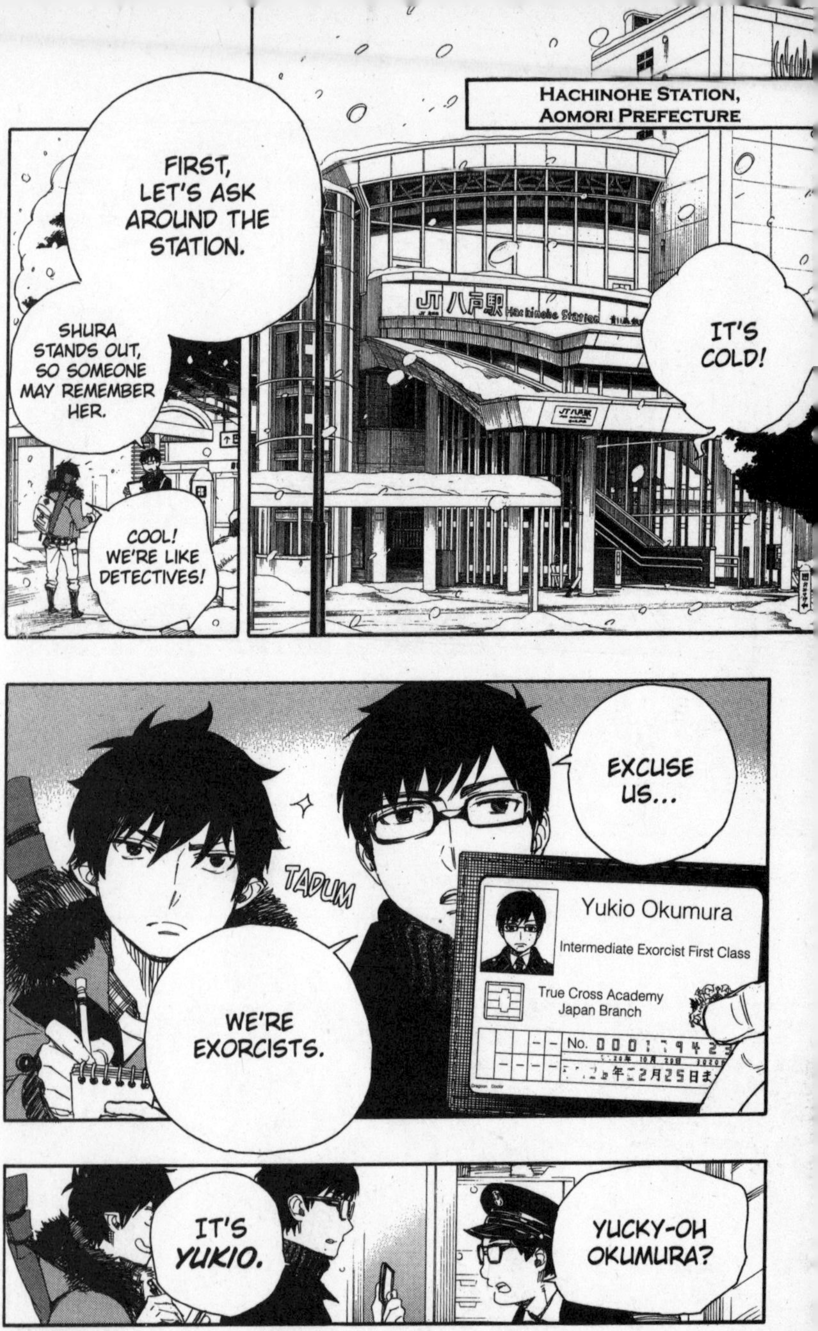

HACHINOHE STATION, AOMORI PREFECTURE
IT'S COLD!
Hachinohe Station
FIRST, LET'S ASK AROUND THE STATION.
SHURA STANDS OUT, SO SOMEONE MAY REMEMBER HER.
COOL! WE'RE LIKE DETECTIVES!
EXCUSE US...
TADUM
Yukio Okumura
Intermediate Exorcist First Class
True Cross Academy Japan Branch
WE'RE EXORCISTS.
YUCKY-OH OKUMURA?
IT'S YUKIO.

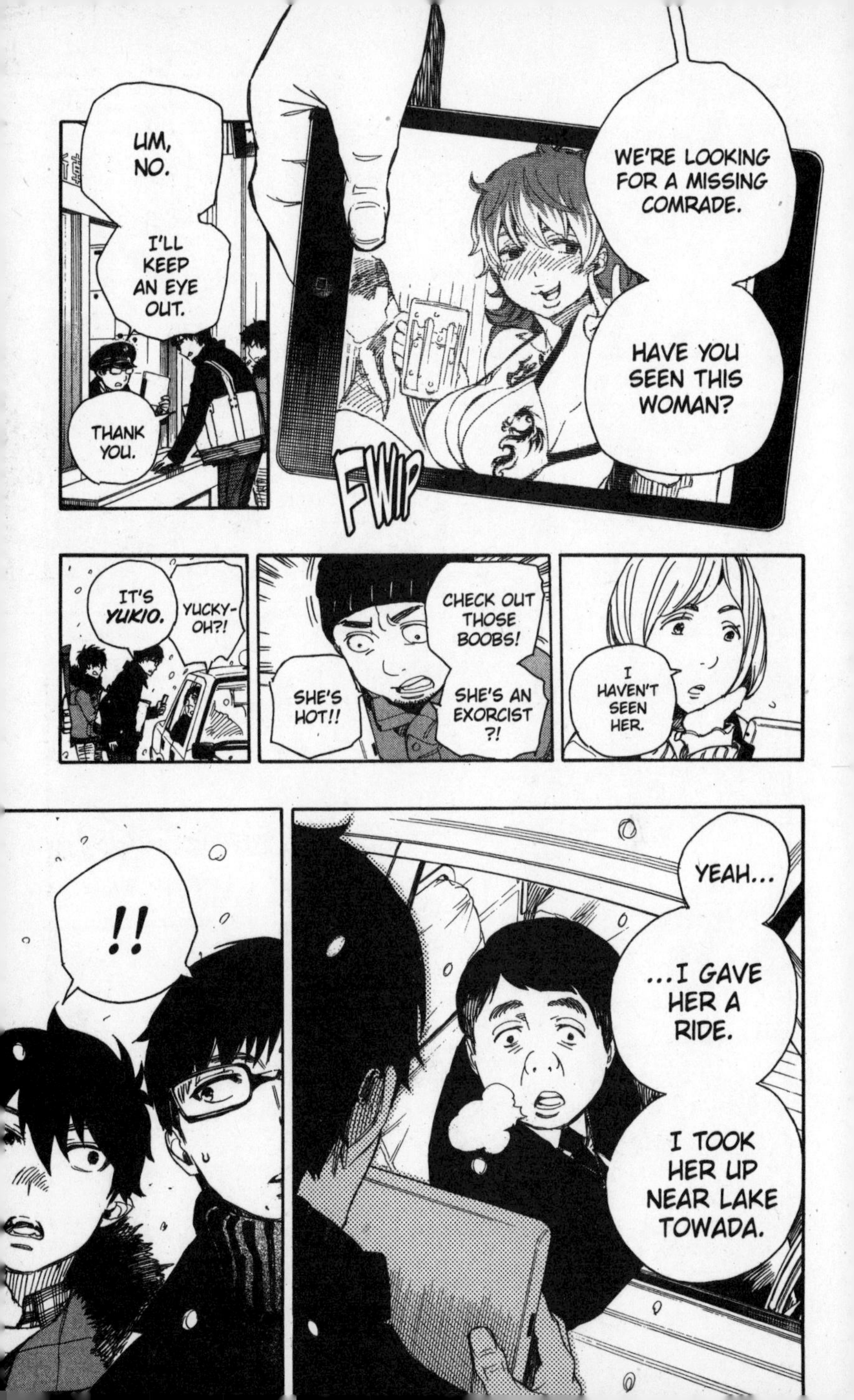
WE'RE LOOKING FOR A MISSING COMRADE.
HAVE YOU SEEN THIS WOMAN?
FWIP
UM, NO.
I'LL KEEP AN EYE OUT.
THANK YOU.
I HAVEN'T SEEN HER.
CHECK OUT THOSE BOOBS!
SHE'S AN EXORCIST?!
SHE'S HOT!!
YUCKY-OH?!
IT'S *YUKIO.*
YEAH...
...I GAVE HER A RIDE.
I TOOK HER UP NEAR LAKE TOWADA.
!!

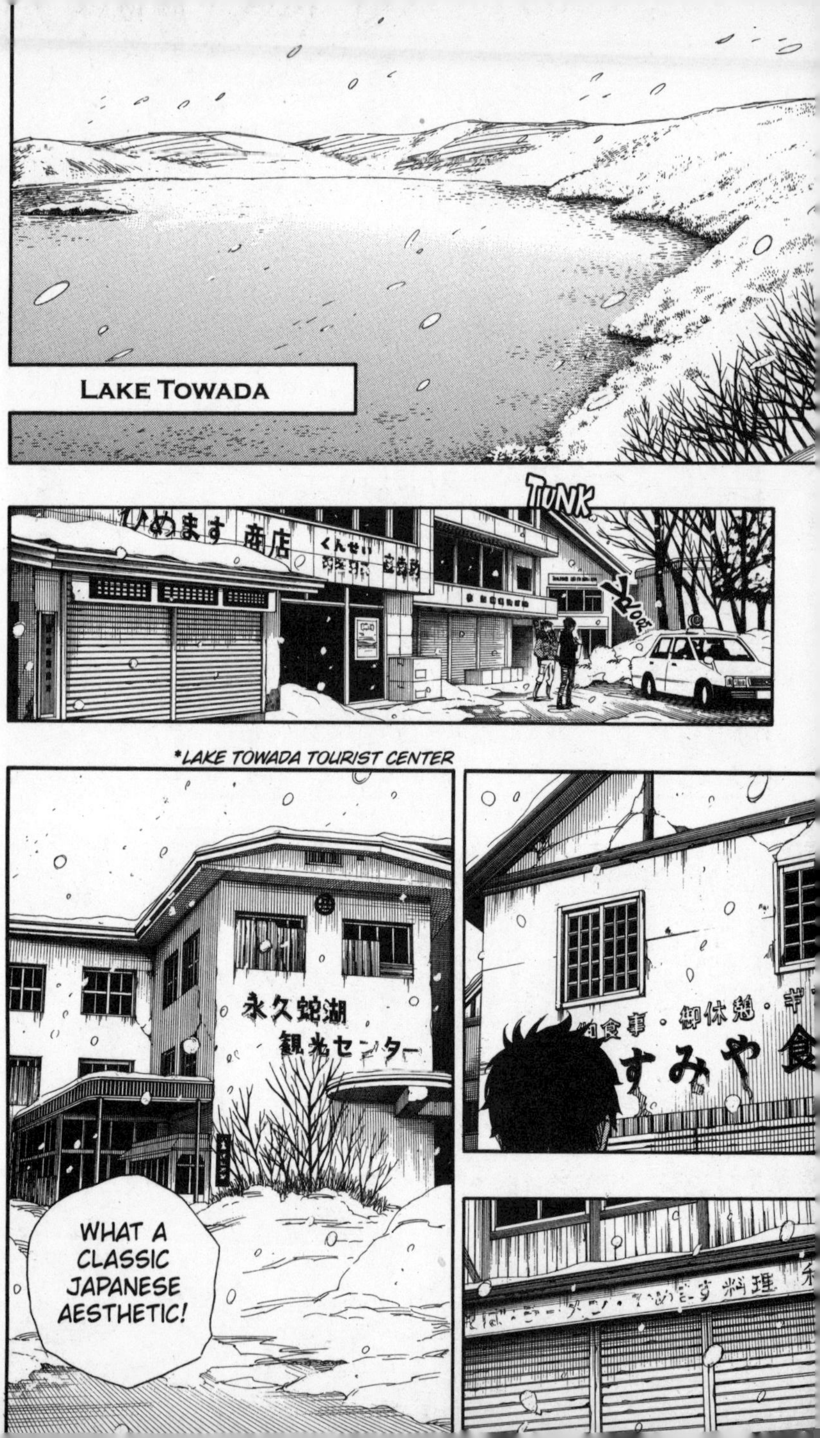
Lake Towada
TUNK
ひめます 商店
くんせい
*LAKE TOWADA TOURIST CENTER
食事・御休憩・
すみや食
料理
永久蛇湖
観光センター
WHAT A CLASSIC JAPANESE AESTHETIC!

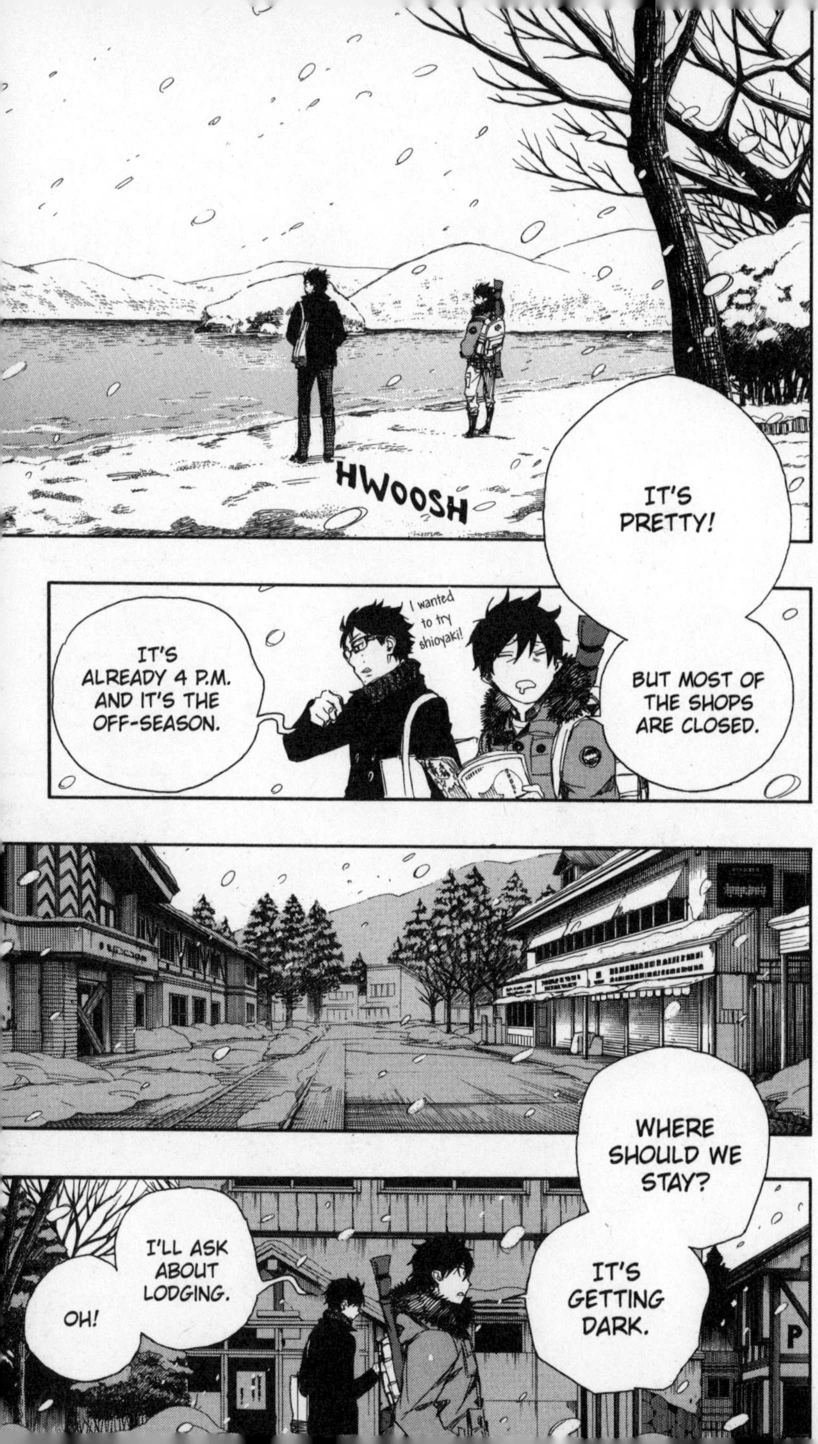
IT'S PRETTY!
HWOOSH
BUT MOST OF THE SHOPS ARE CLOSED.
I wanted to try shioyaki!
IT'S ALREADY 4 P.M. AND IT'S THE OFF-SEASON.
WHERE SHOULD WE STAY?
IT'S GETTING DARK.
I'LL ASK ABOUT LODGING.
OH!

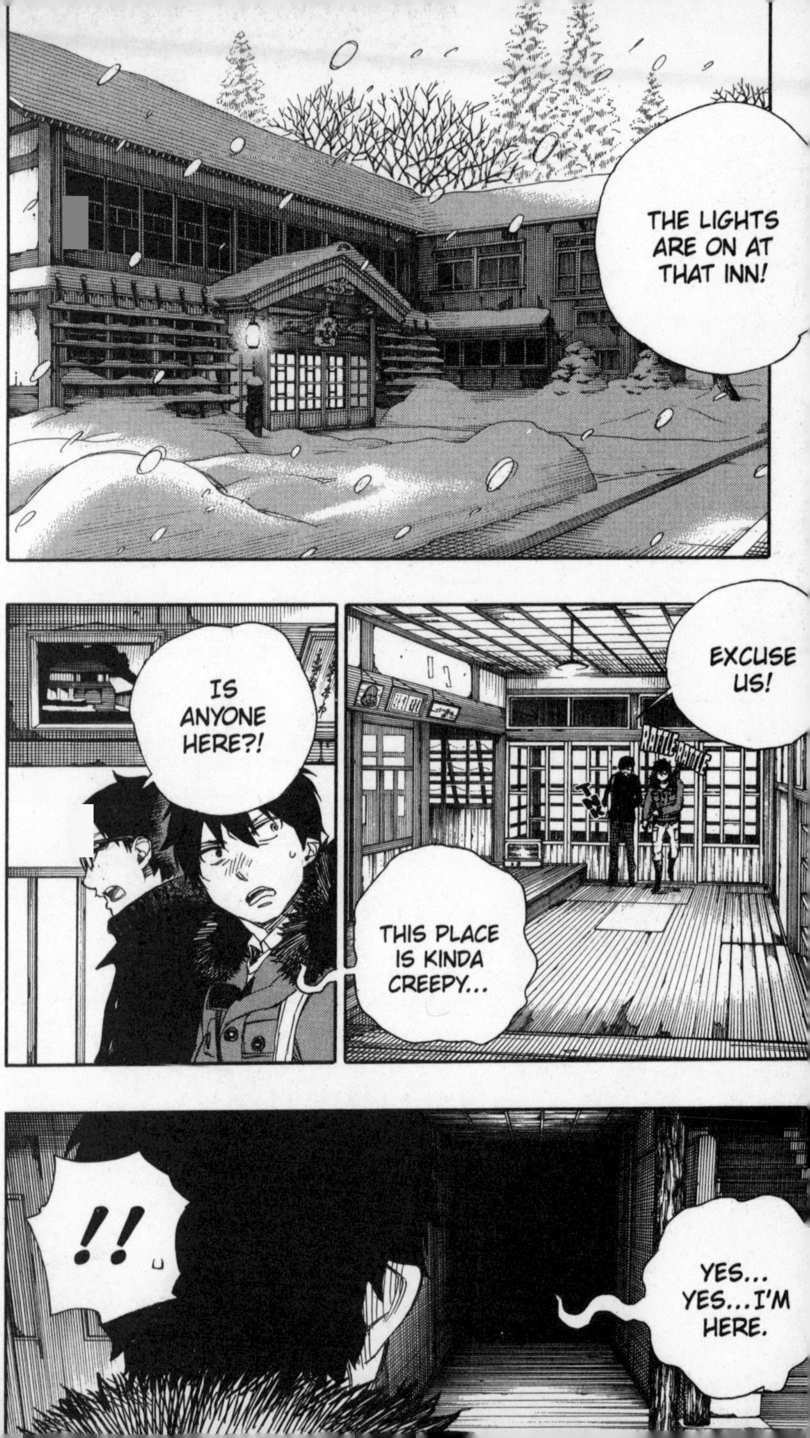
THE LIGHTS ARE ON AT THAT INN!
EXCUSE US!
RATTLE RATTLE
THIS PLACE IS KINDA CREEPY...
IS ANYONE HERE?!
YES... YES...I'M HERE.
!!

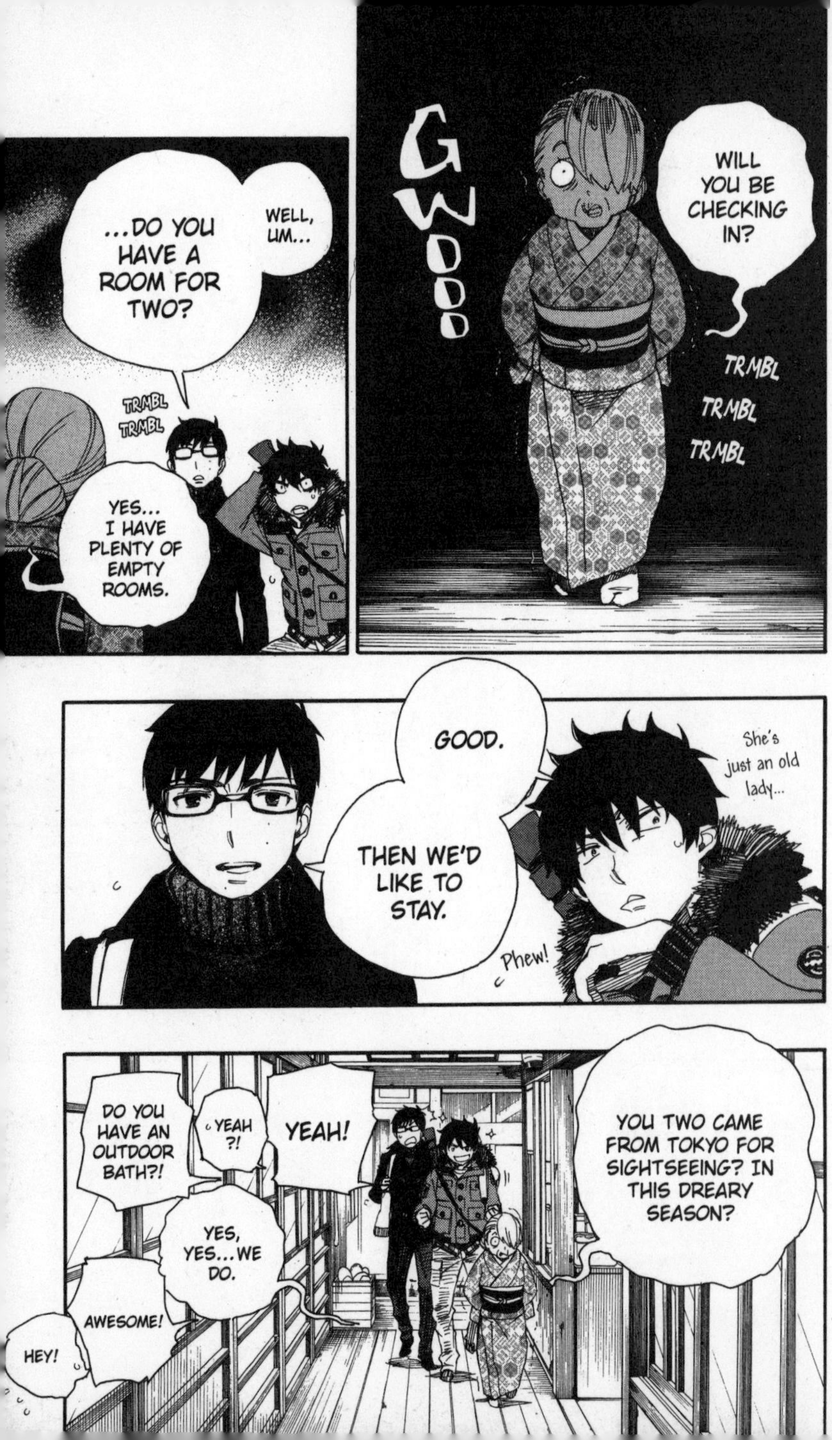
GWDDD
WILL YOU BE CHECKING IN?
TRMBL
TRMBL
TRMBL
WELL, UM...
...DO YOU HAVE A ROOM FOR TWO?
TRMBL
TRMBL
YES... I HAVE PLENTY OF EMPTY ROOMS.
She's just an old lady...
GOOD.
THEN WE'D LIKE TO STAY.
Phew!
YOU TWO CAME FROM TOKYO FOR SIGHTSEEING? IN THIS DREARY SEASON?
YEAH!
YEAH?!
DO YOU HAVE AN OUTDOOR BATH?!
YES, YES...WE DO.
AWESOME!
HEY!

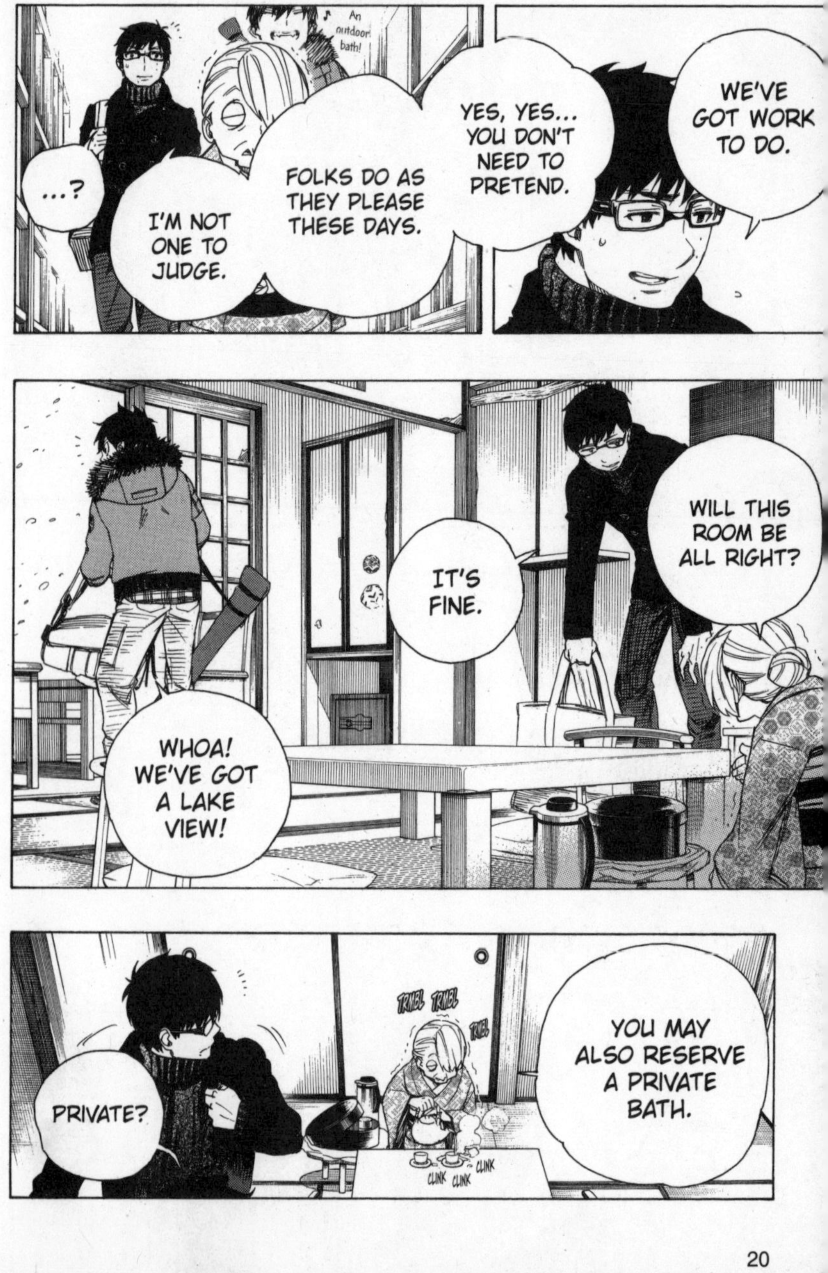
WE'VE GOT WORK TO DO.
YES, YES... YOU DON'T NEED TO PRETEND.
An outdoor bath!
FOLKS DO AS THEY PLEASE THESE DAYS.
I'M NOT ONE TO JUDGE.
...?
WILL THIS ROOM BE ALL RIGHT?
IT'S FINE.
WHOA! WE'VE GOT A LAKE VIEW!
YOU MAY ALSO RESERVE A PRIVATE BATH.
TRMBL TRMBL TRMBL
CLINK CLINK CLINK
PRIVATE?

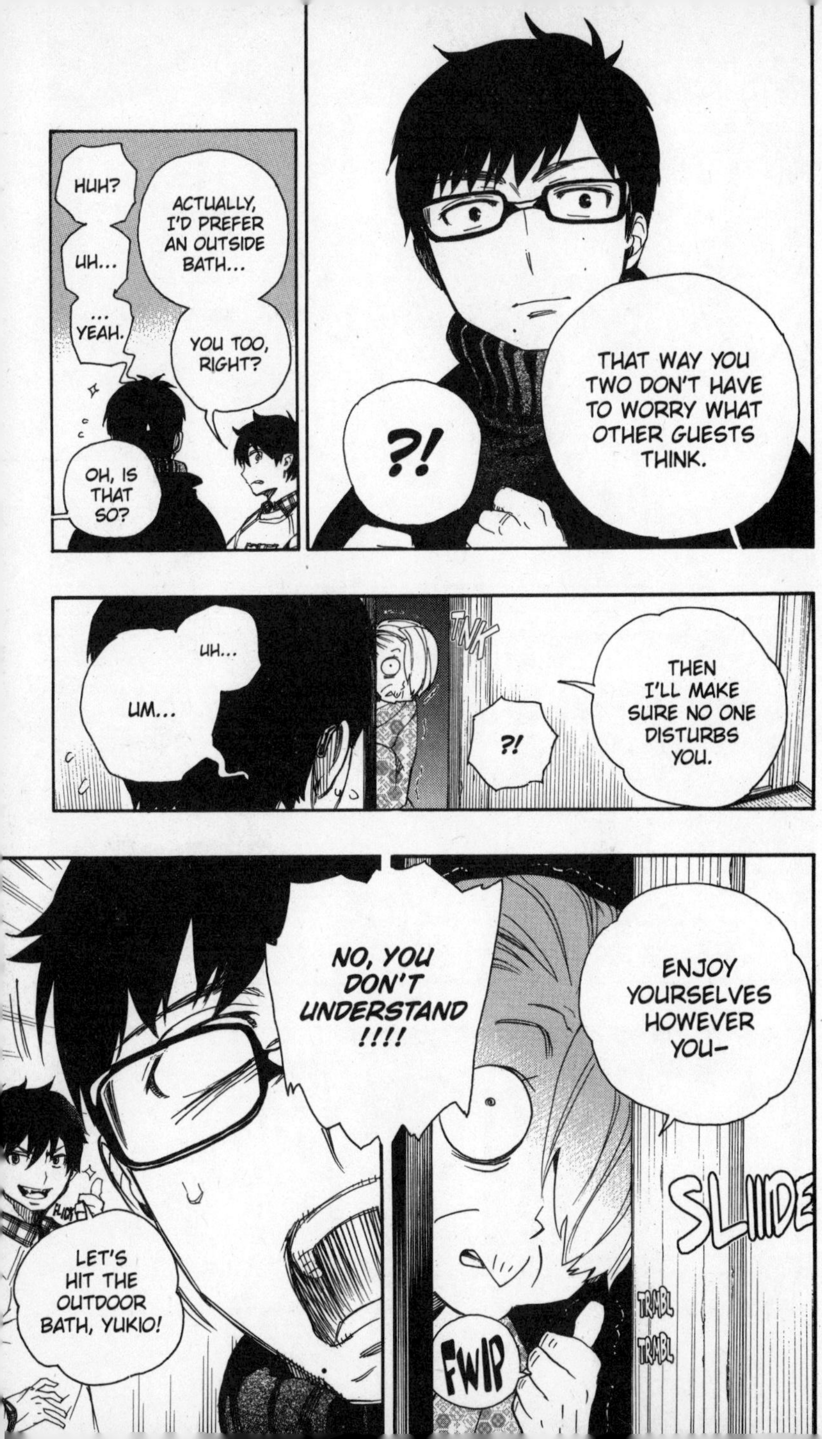

THAT WAY YOU TWO DON'T HAVE TO WORRY WHAT OTHER GUESTS THINK.
?!
ACTUALLY, I'D PREFER AN OUTSIDE BATH...
YOU TOO, RIGHT?
HUH?
UH...
...YEAH.
OH, IS THAT SO?
THEN I'LL MAKE SURE NO ONE DISTURBS YOU.
TNK
?!
UH...
UM...
ENJOY YOURSELVES HOWEVER YOU-
SLIIDE
NO, YOU DON'T UNDERSTAND!!!!
TRMBL
TRMBL
FWIP
FLICK
LET'S HIT THE OUTDOOR BATH, YUKIO!

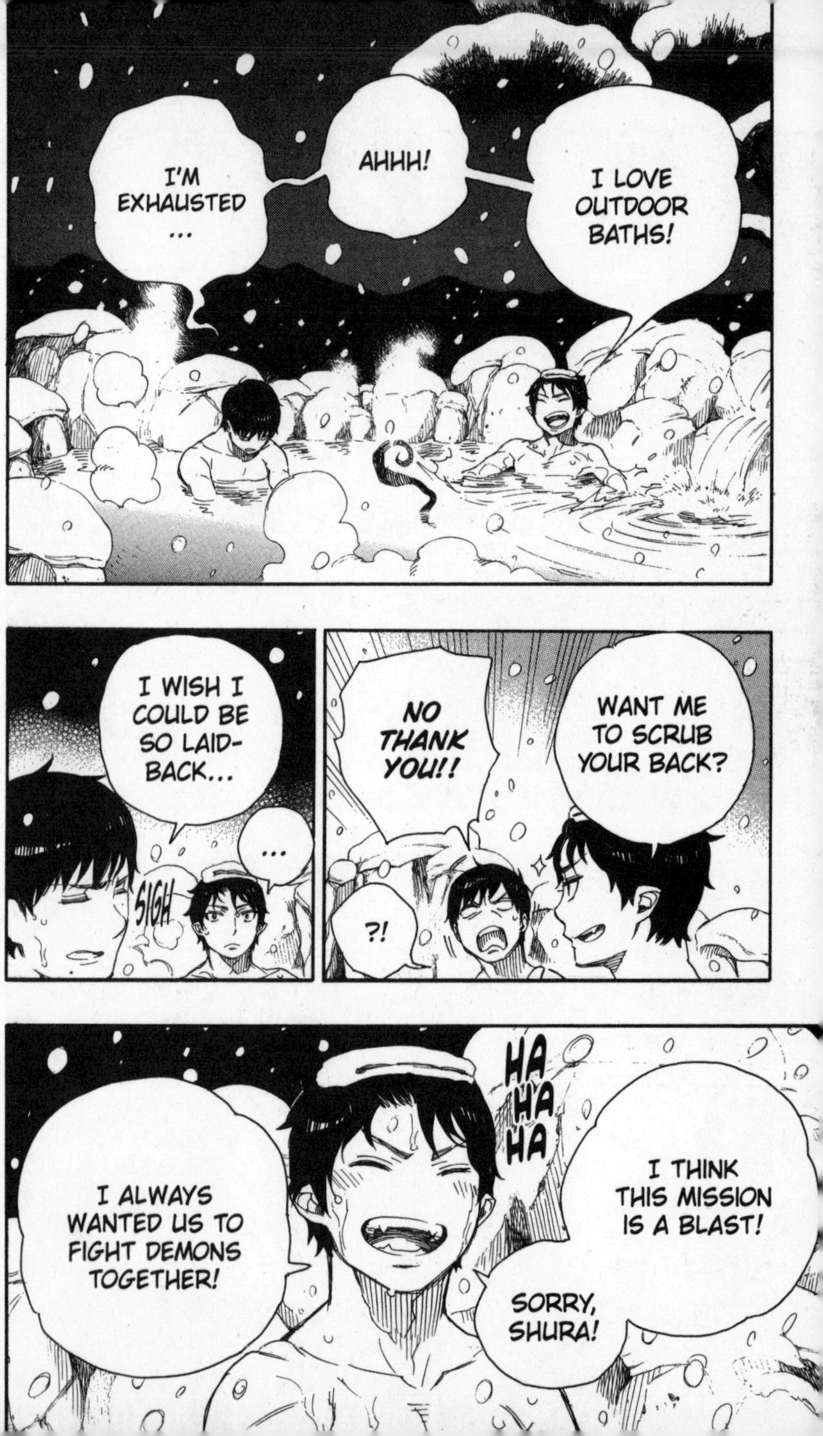
I LOVE OUTDOOR BATHS!
AHHH!
I'M EXHAUSTED ...
WANT ME TO SCRUB YOUR BACK?
NO THANK YOU!!
?!
I WISH I COULD BE SO LAID-BACK...
...
SIGH
HA HA HA
I THINK THIS MISSION IS A BLAST!
SORRY, SHURA!
I ALWAYS WANTED US TO FIGHT DEMONS TOGETHER!

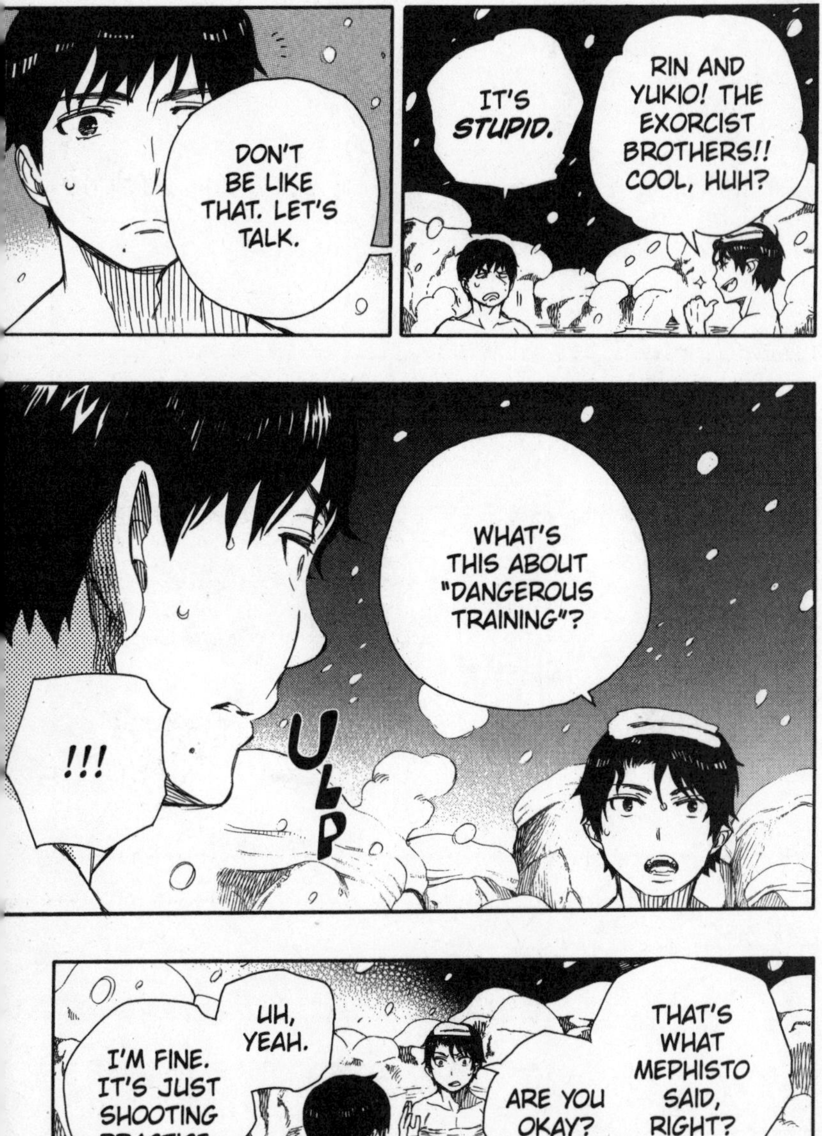
RIN AND YUKIO! THE EXORCIST BROTHERS!! COOL, HUH?
IT'S *STUPID.*
DON'T BE LIKE THAT. LET'S TALK.
WHAT'S THIS ABOUT "DANGEROUS TRAINING"?
ULP
!!!
THAT'S WHAT MEPHISTO SAID, RIGHT?
ARE YOU OKAY?
UH, YEAH.
I'M FINE. IT'S JUST SHOOTING PRACTICE.

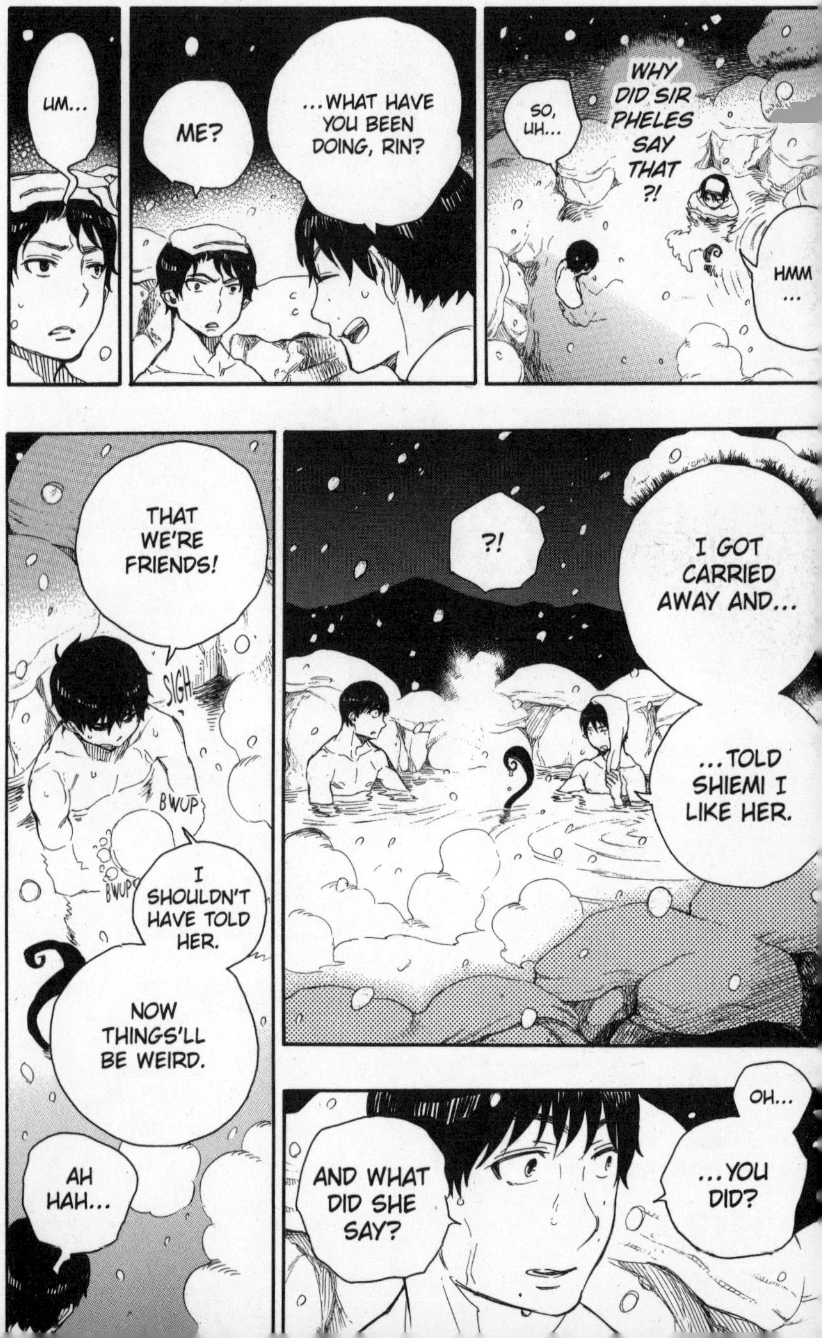
HMM...
WHY DID SIR PHELES SAY THAT?!
SO, UH...
...WHAT HAVE YOU BEEN DOING, RIN?
ME?
UM...
I GOT CARRIED AWAY AND...
...TOLD SHIEMI I LIKE HER.
?!
OH...
...YOU DID?
AND WHAT DID SHE SAY?
THAT WE'RE FRIENDS!
SIGH
BWUP
BWUP
I SHOULDN'T HAVE TOLD HER.
NOW THINGS'LL BE WEIRD.
AH HAH...

*YOU MUSTN'T PUT YOUR TOWEL INTO A PUBLIC BATH.

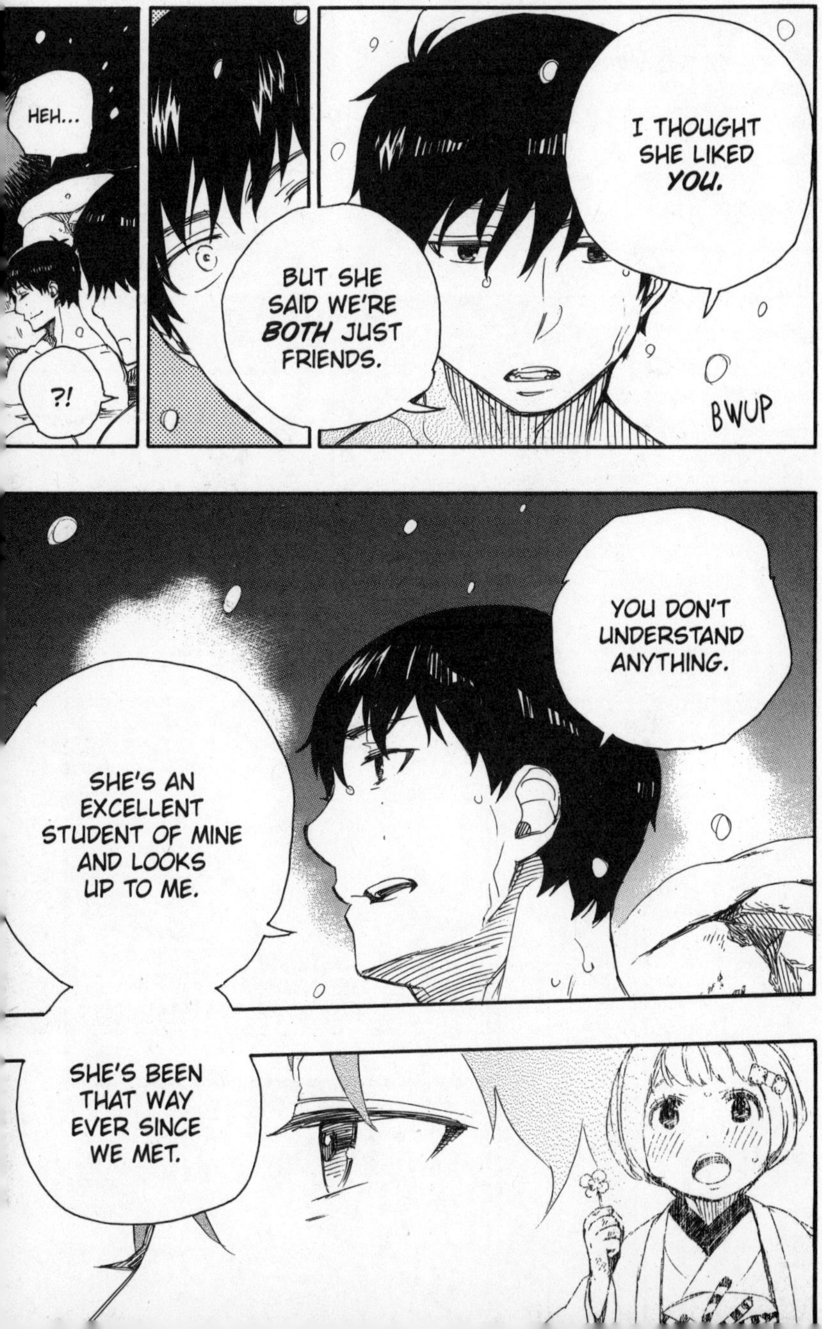
I THOUGHT SHE LIKED *YOU.*
BUT SHE SAID WE'RE *BOTH* JUST FRIENDS.
BWUP
HEH...
?!
YOU DON'T UNDERSTAND ANYTHING.
SHE'S AN EXCELLENT STUDENT OF MINE AND LOOKS UP TO ME.
SHE'S BEEN THAT WAY EVER SINCE WE MET.

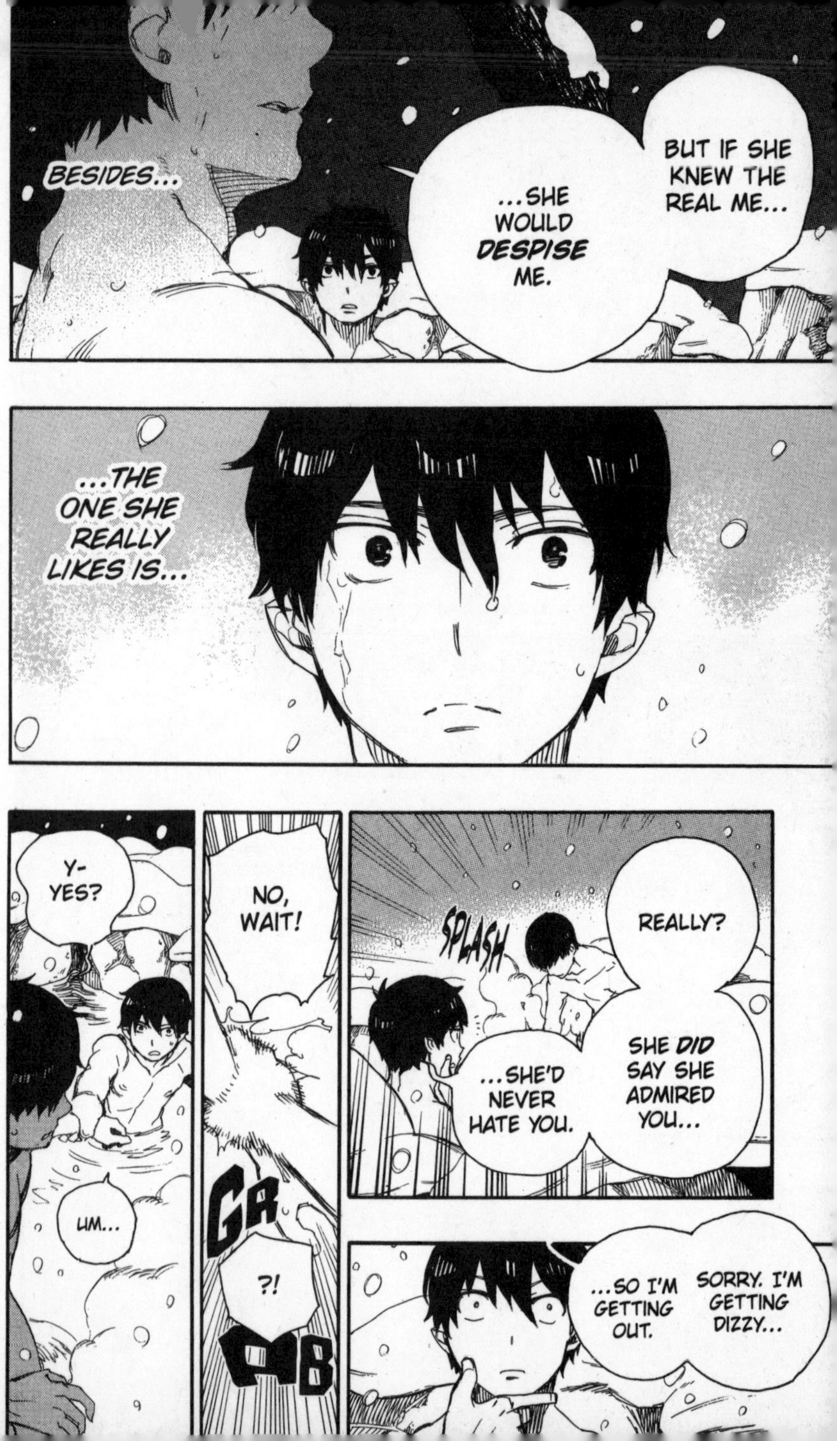
BUT IF SHE KNEW THE REAL ME...
...SHE WOULD DESPISE ME.
BESIDES...
...THE ONE SHE REALLY LIKES IS...
REALLY?
SHE DID SAY SHE ADMIRED YOU...
...SHE'D NEVER HATE YOU.
SPLASH
SORRY. I'M GETTING DIZZY...
...SO I'M GETTING OUT.
NO, WAIT!
GR
?!
AB
Y-YES?
UM...

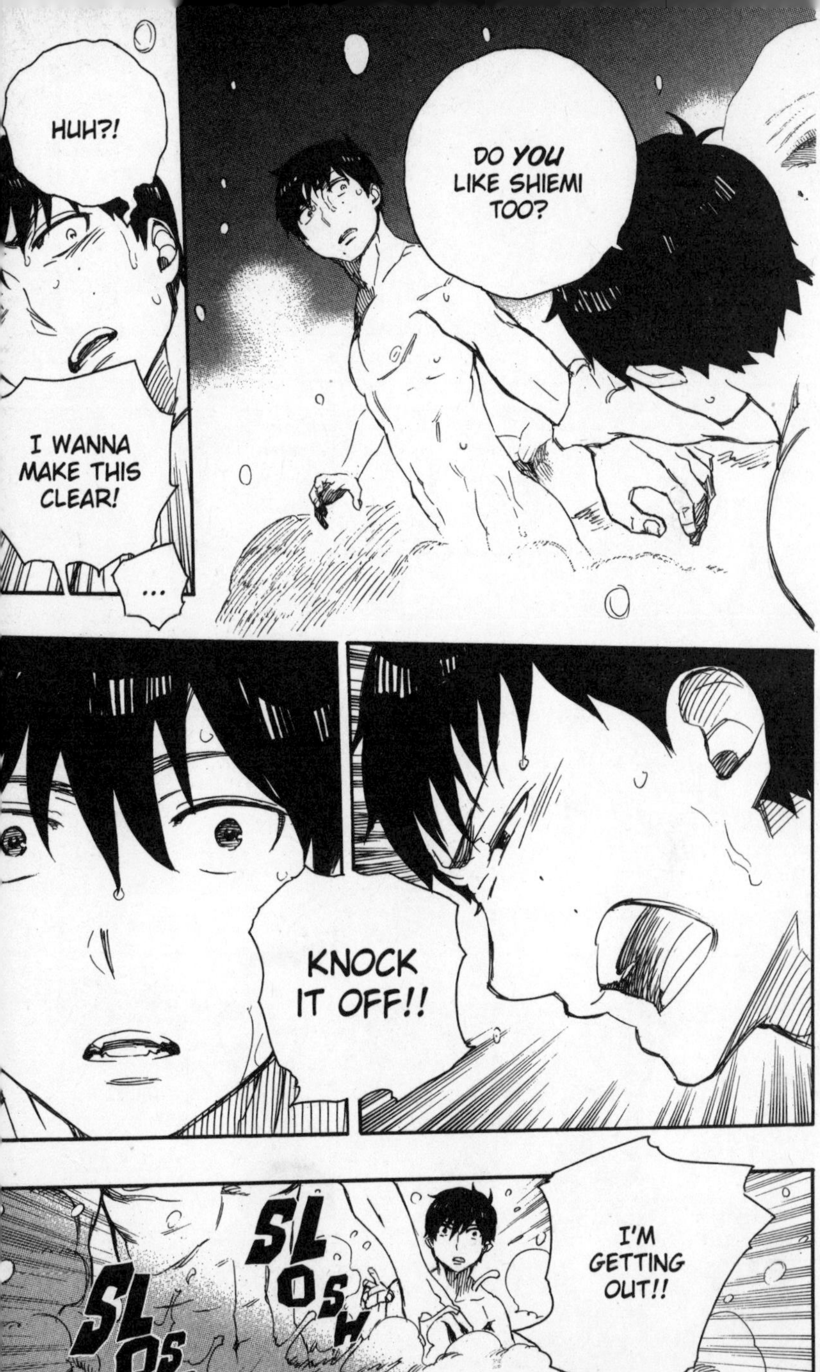
DO YOU LIKE SHIEMI TOO?
HUH?!
I WANNA MAKE THIS CLEAR!
...
KNOCK IT OFF!!
I'M GETTING OUT!!
SLOSH
SLOSH

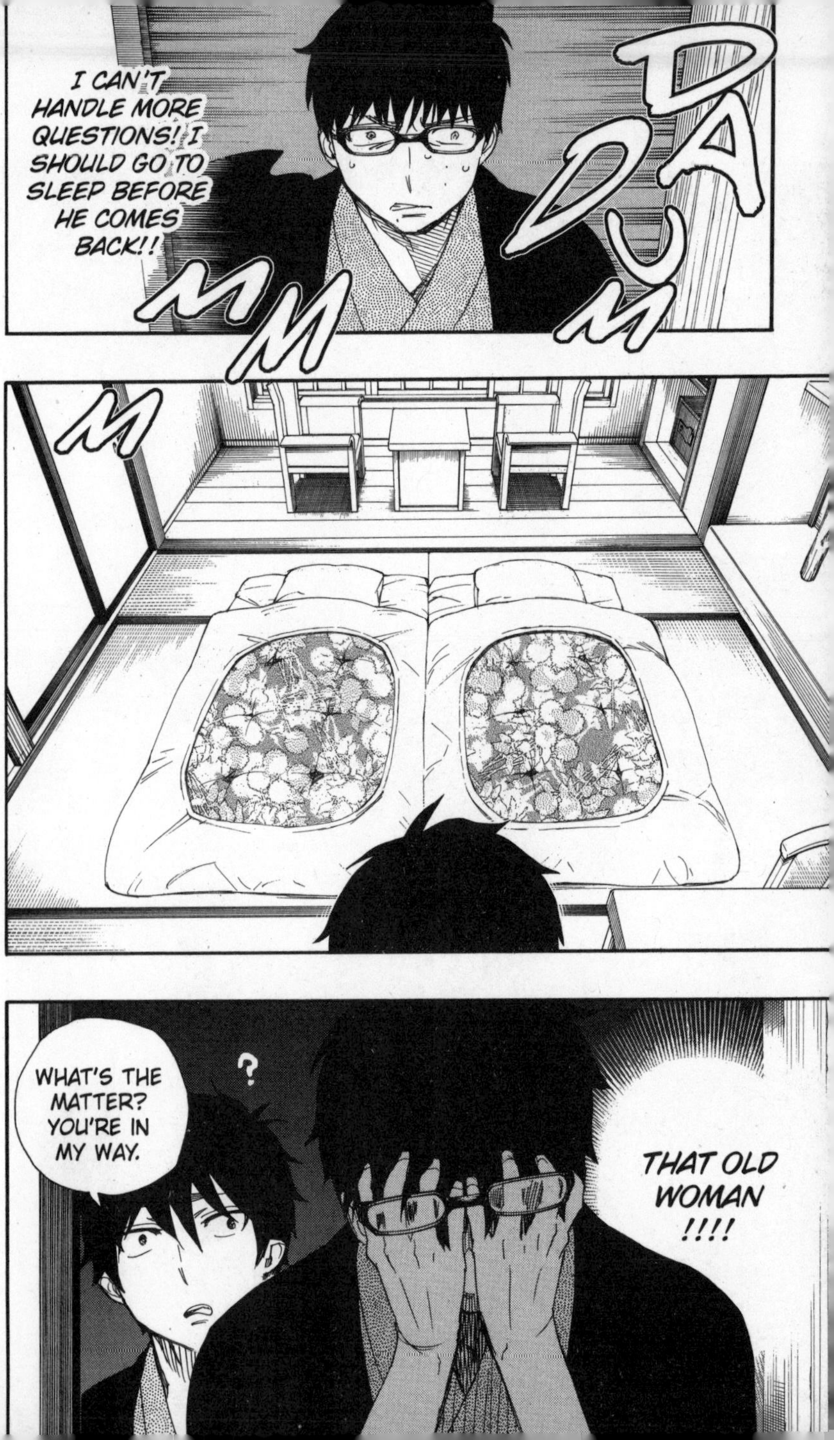

DADUMMMM
I CAN'T HANDLE MORE QUESTIONS! I SHOULD GO TO SLEEP BEFORE HE COMES BACK!!
THAT OLD WOMAN !!!!
WHAT'S THE MATTER? YOU'RE IN MY WAY.
?

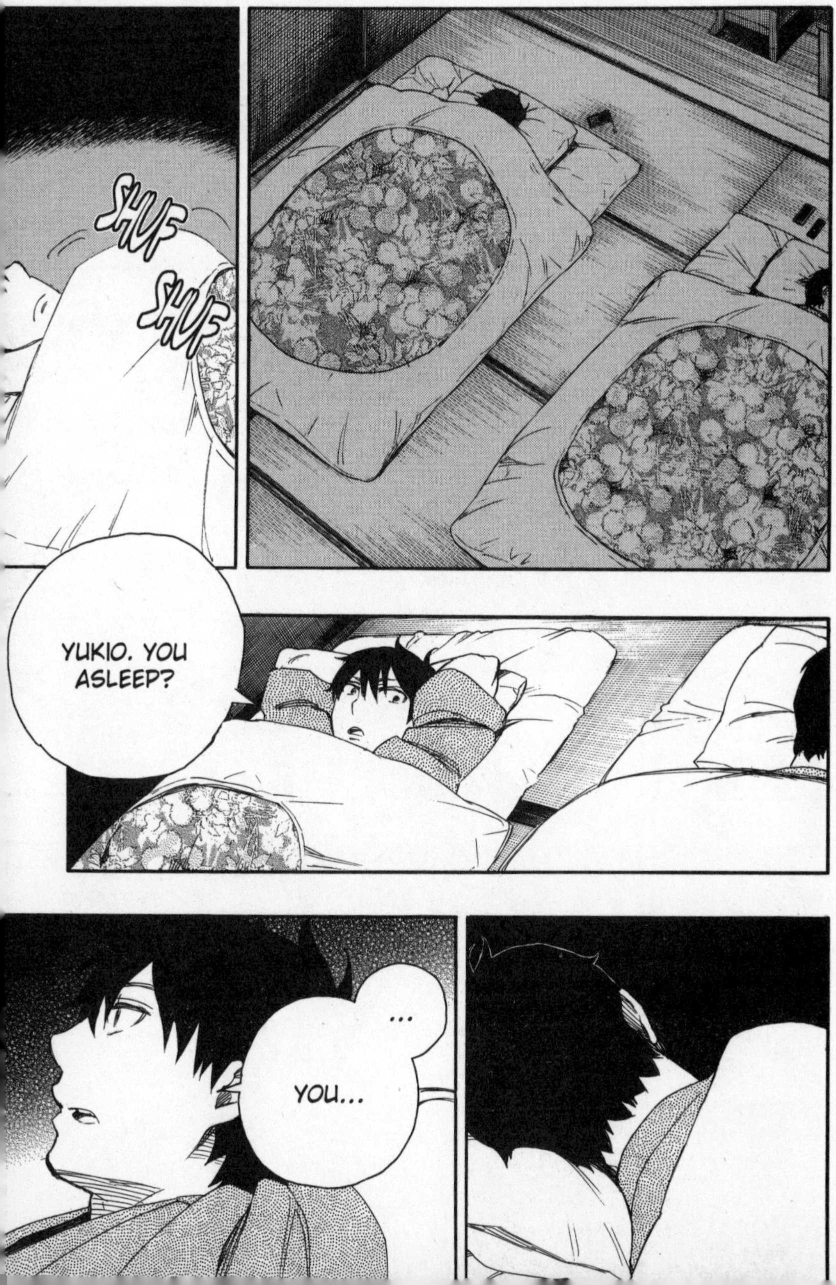
SHUF
SHUF
YUKIO. YOU ASLEEP?
...
YOU...

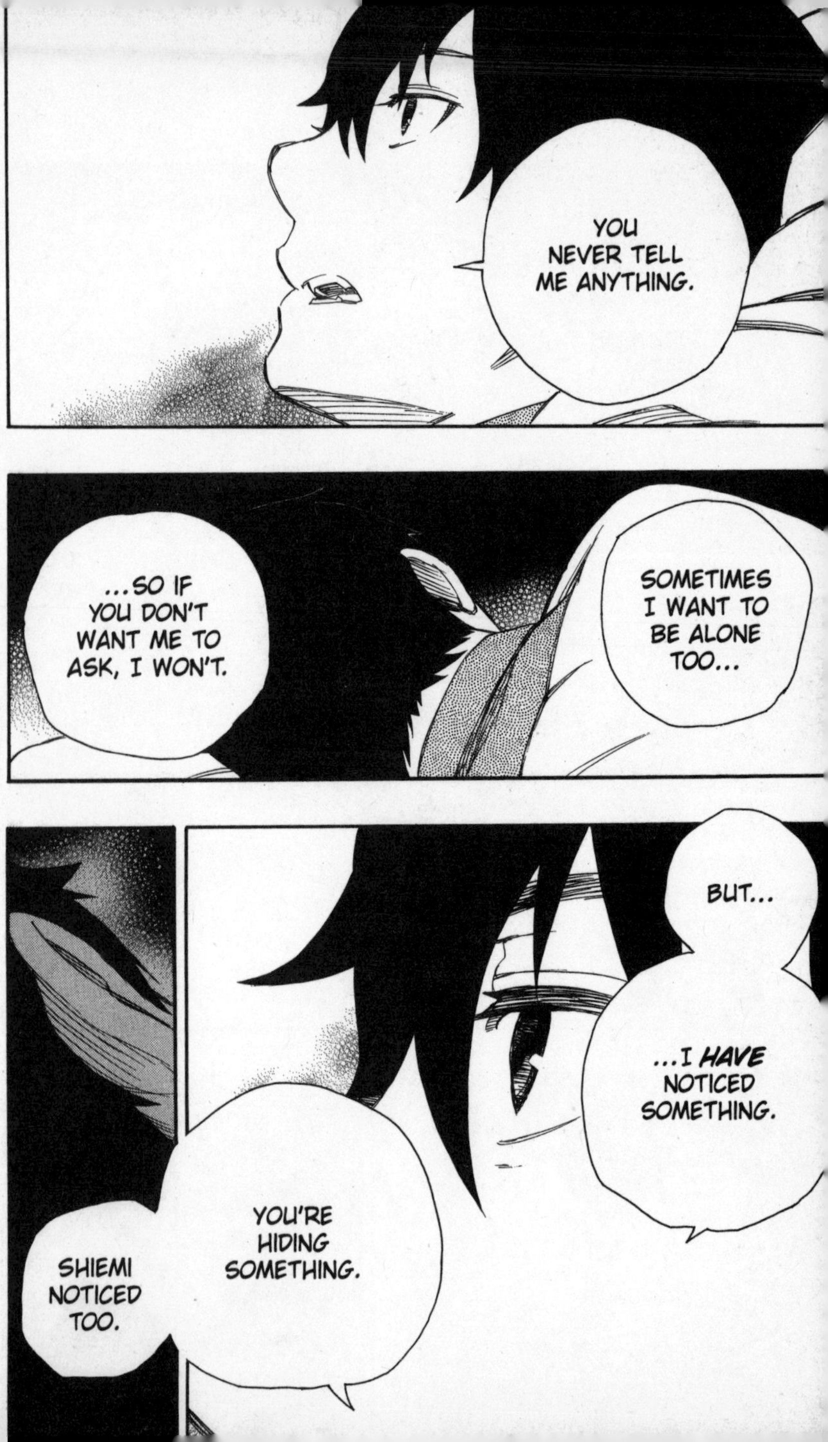
YOU NEVER TELL ME ANYTHING.
SOMETIMES I WANT TO BE ALONE TOO...
...SO IF YOU DON'T WANT ME TO ASK, I WON'T.
BUT...
...I *HAVE* NOTICED SOMETHING.
YOU'RE HIDING SOMETHING.
SHIEMI NOTICED TOO.

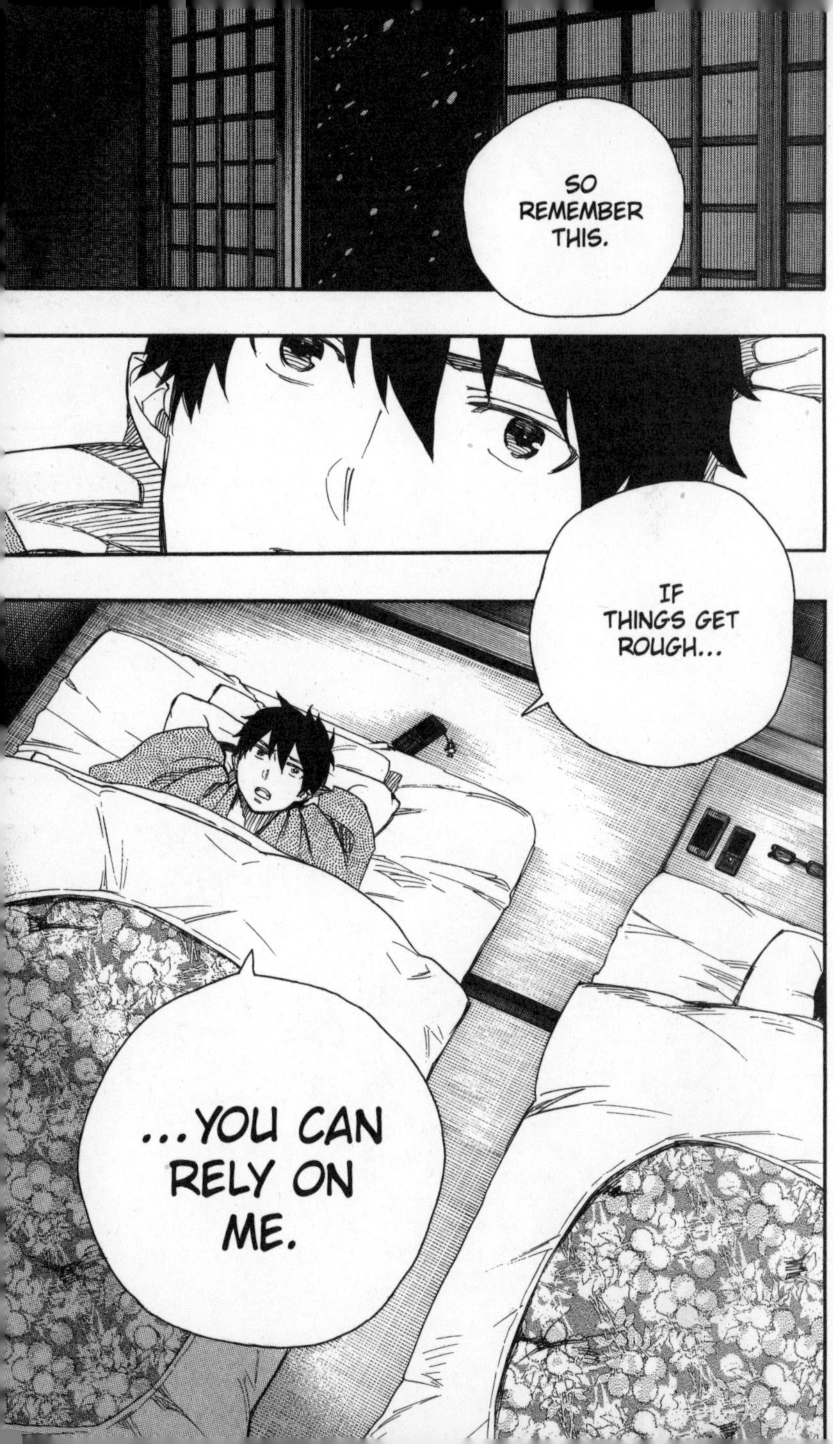
SO REMEMBER THIS.
IF THINGS GET ROUGH...
...YOU CAN RELY ON ME.

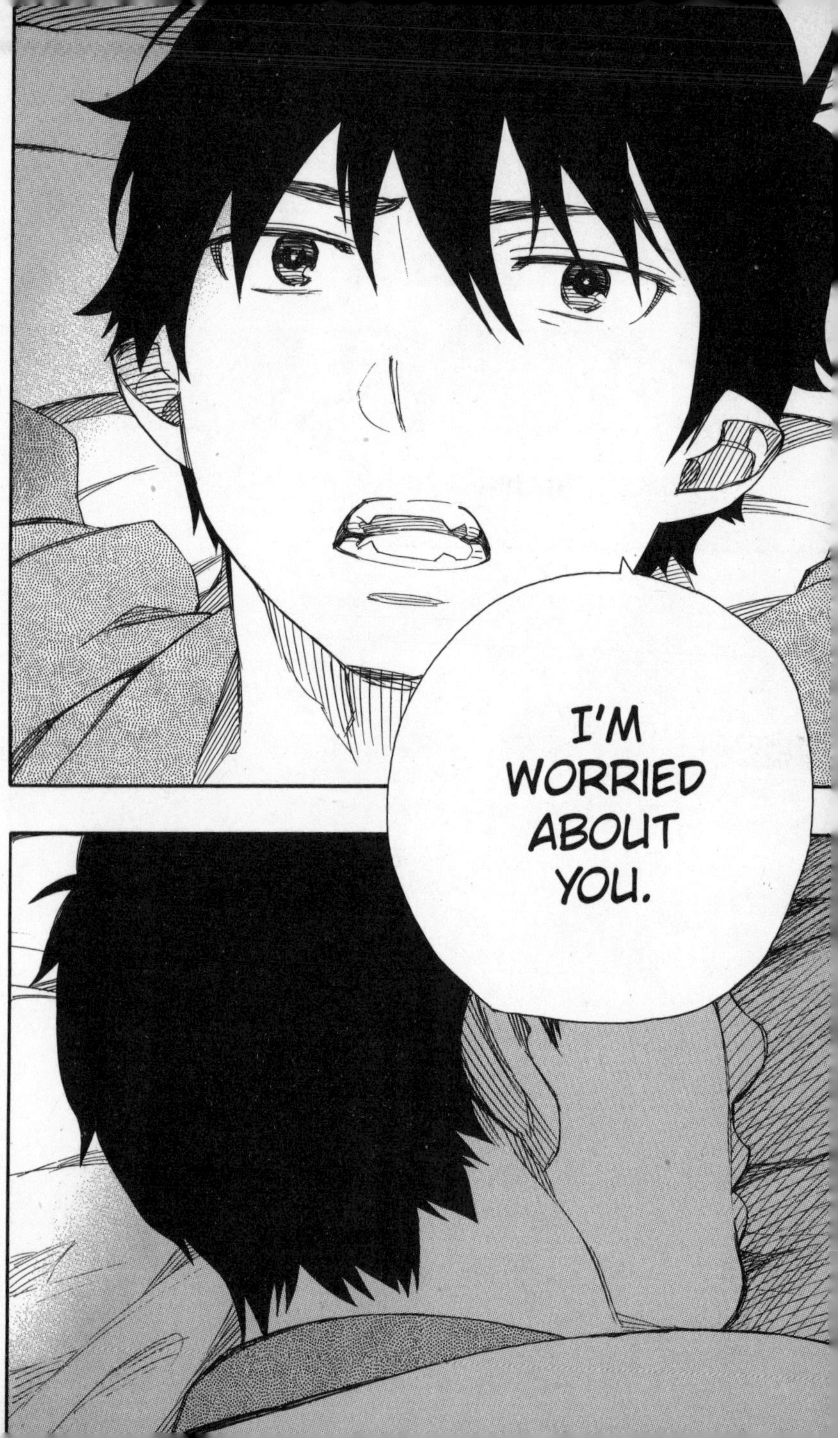
I'M WORRIED ABOUT YOU.

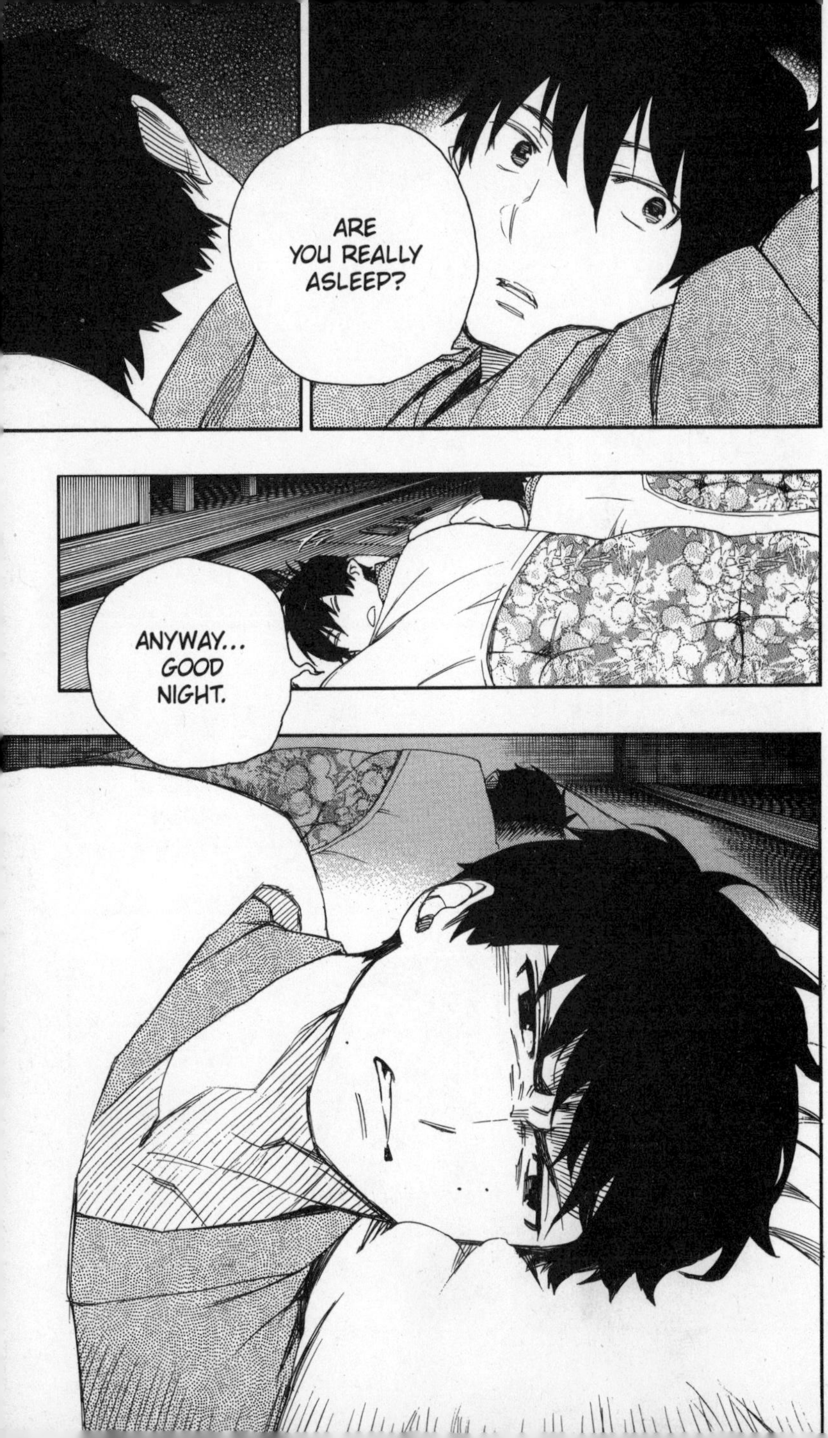
ARE YOU REALLY ASLEEP?
ANYWAY... GOOD NIGHT.

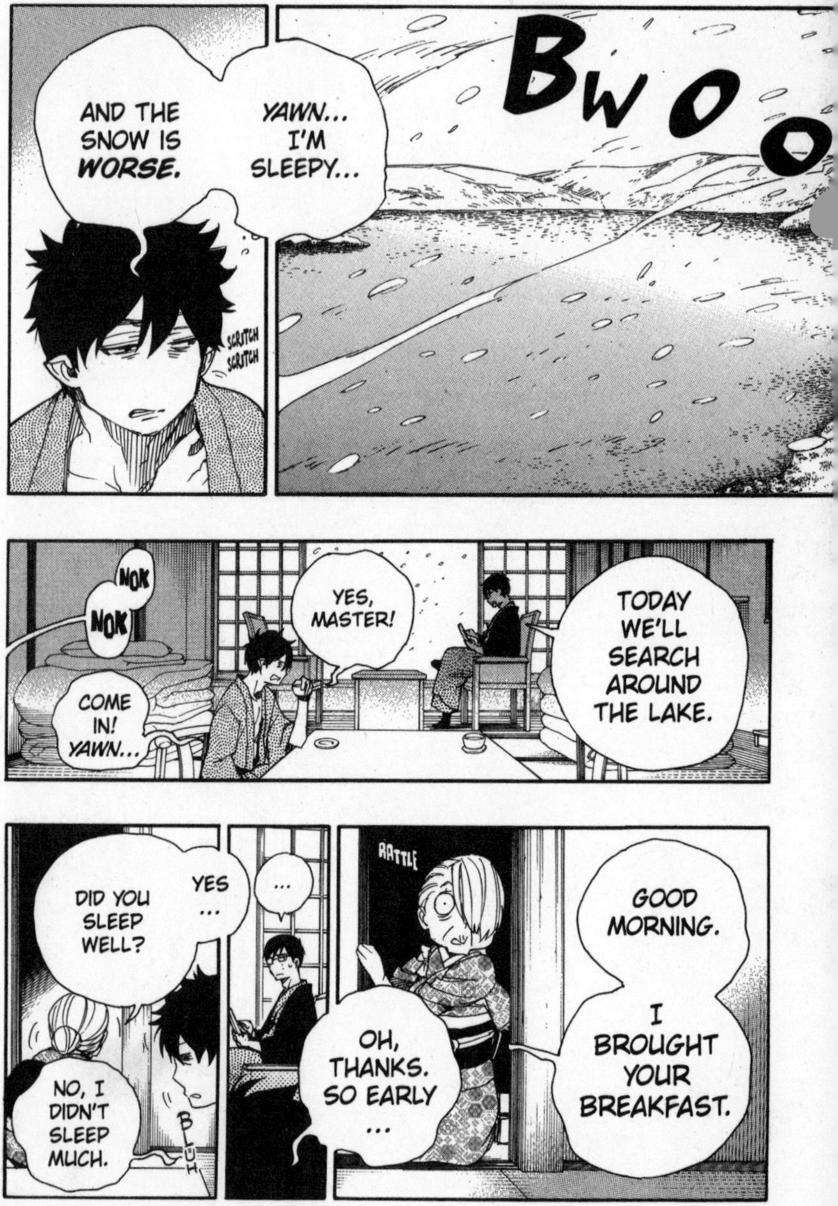
BWOO
YAWN... I'M SLEEPY...
AND THE SNOW IS WORSE.
SCRITCH SCRITCH
TODAY WE'LL SEARCH AROUND THE LAKE.
YES, MASTER!
NOK NOK
COME IN! YAWN...
RATTLE
GOOD MORNING.
I BROUGHT YOUR BREAKFAST.
OH, THANKS. SO EARLY...
...
YES...
DID YOU SLEEP WELL?
NO, I DIDN'T SLEEP MUCH.
BLUH

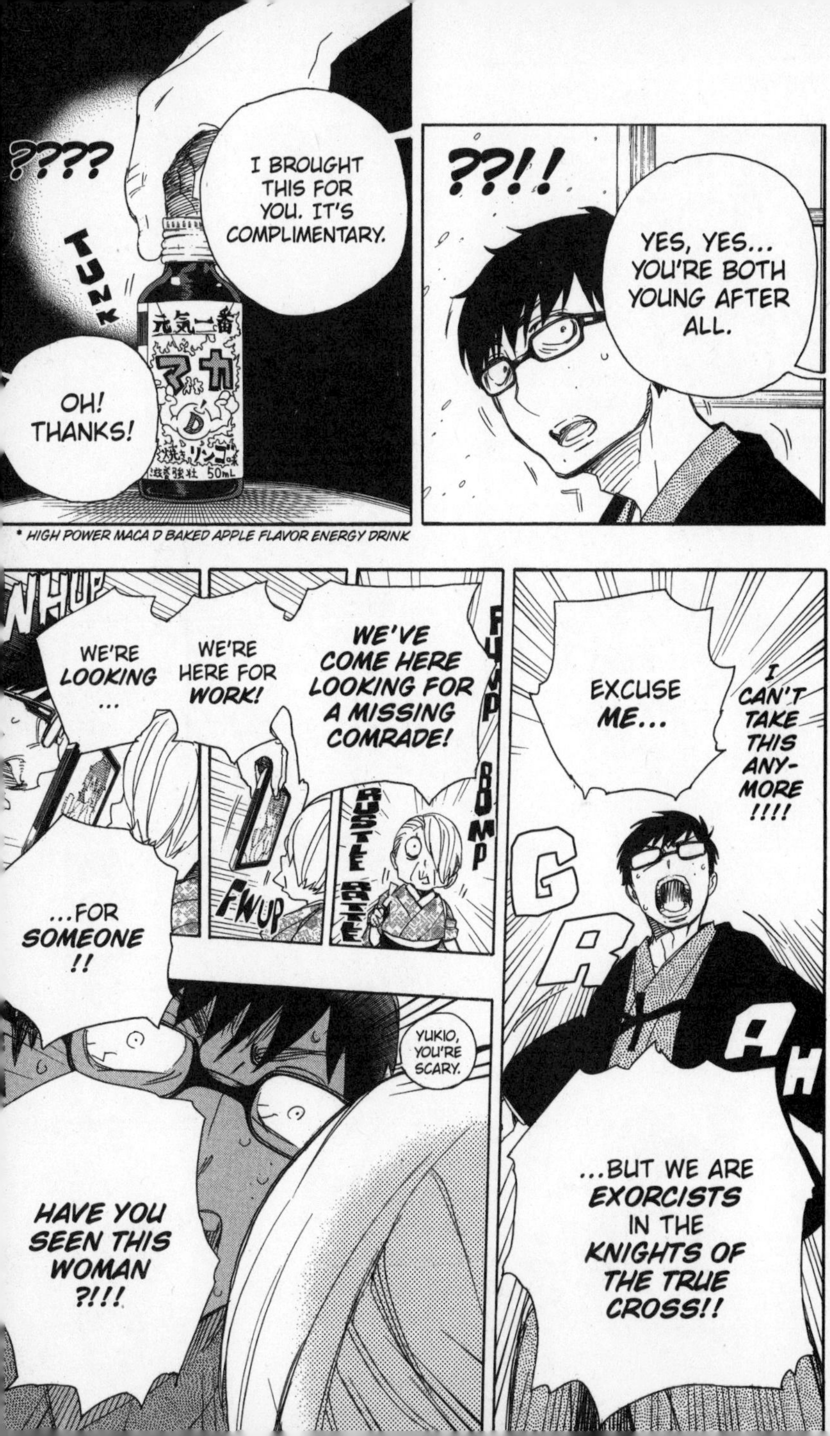
??!!
YES, YES... YOU'RE BOTH YOUNG AFTER ALL.
I BROUGHT THIS FOR YOU. IT'S COMPLIMENTARY.
????
TUNK
元気一番
マカ
D
50mL
OH! THANKS!
EXCUSE ME...
I CAN'T TAKE THIS ANYMORE!!!!
GRAAH
...BUT WE ARE EXORCISTS IN THE KNIGHTS OF THE TRUE CROSS!!
WE'VE COME HERE LOOKING FOR A MISSING COMRADE!
FUMP
BUMP
RUSTLE RATTLE
WE'RE HERE FOR WORK!
FWUP
WHUP
WE'RE LOOKING...
...FOR SOMEONE!!
YUKIO, YOU'RE SCARY.
HAVE YOU SEEN THIS WOMAN?!!!

* HIGH POWER MACA D BAKED APPLE FLAVOR ENERGY DRINK

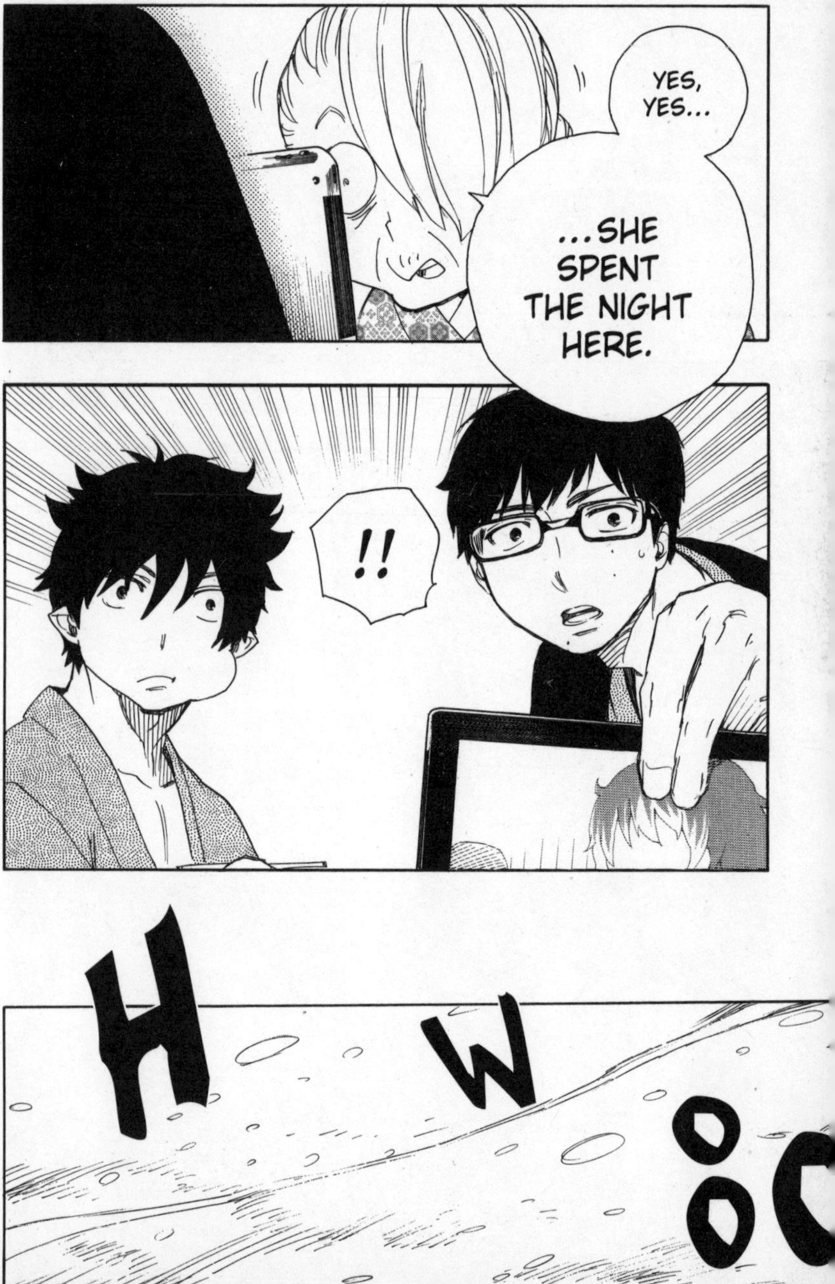
YES, YES...
...SHE SPENT THE NIGHT HERE.
!!
HWOO

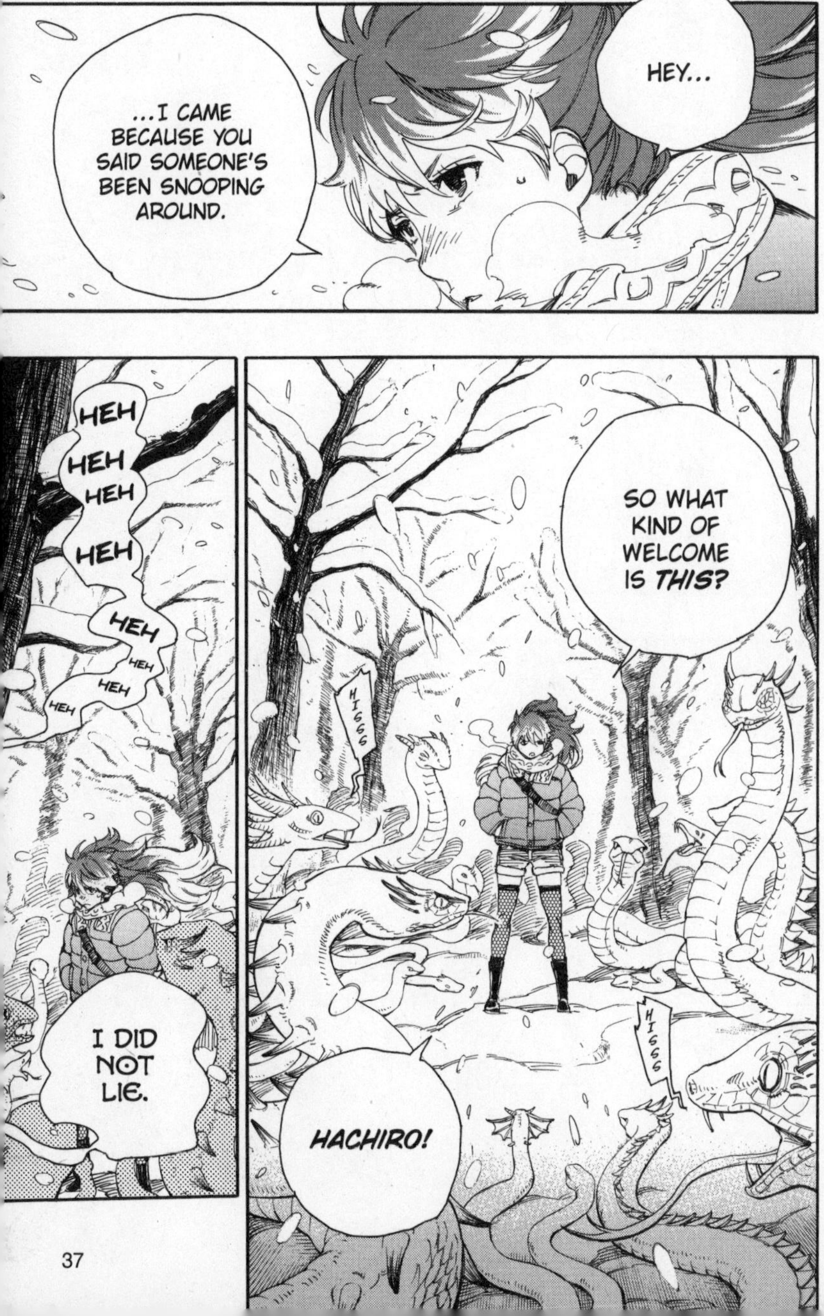
HEY...
...I CAME BECAUSE YOU SAID SOMEONE'S BEEN SNOOPING AROUND.
SO WHAT KIND OF WELCOME IS *THIS?*
HISSS
HISSS
HACHIRO!
HEH HEH HEH HEH HEH HEH HEH HEH
I DID NOT LIE.

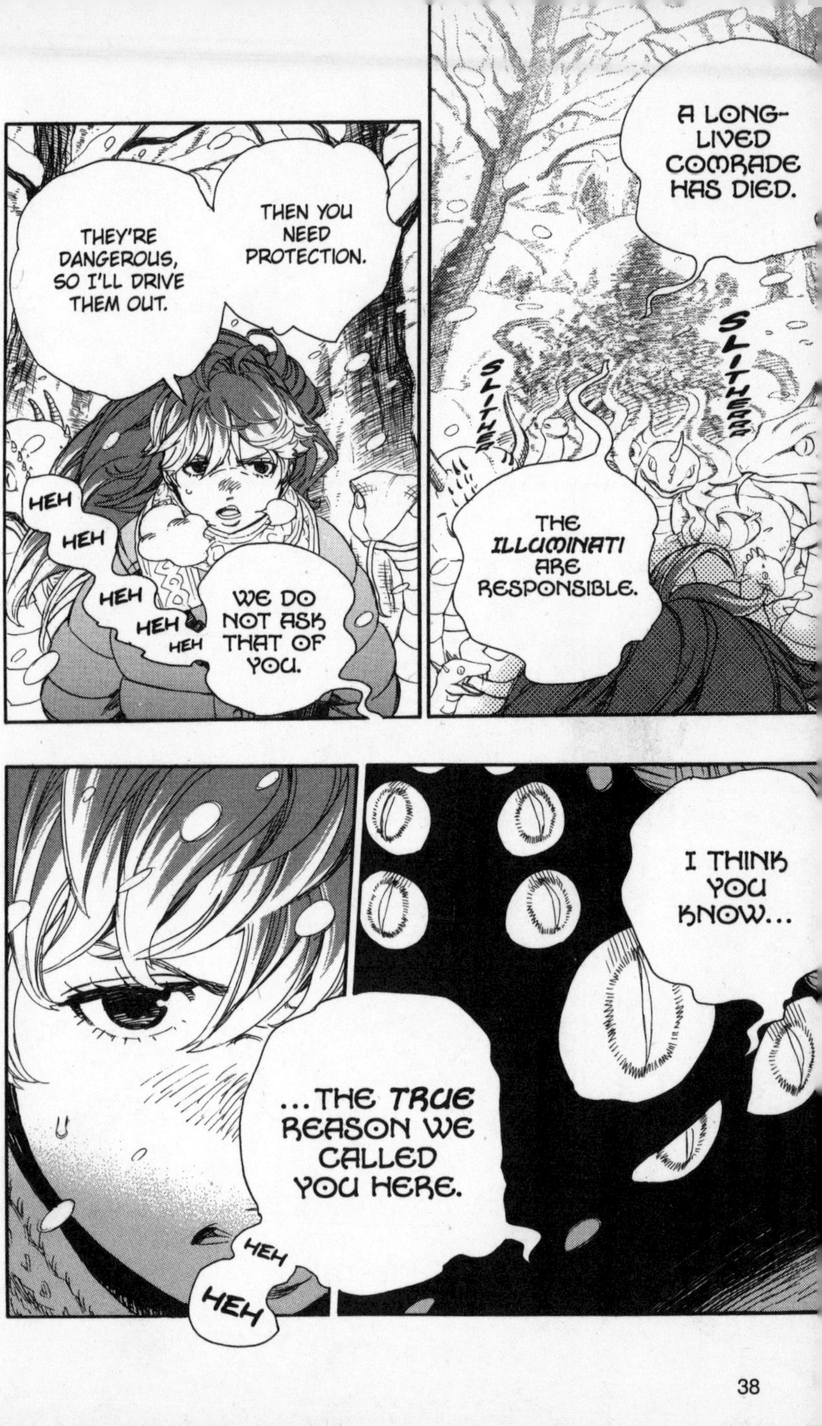
A LONG-LIVED COMRADE HAS DIED.
SLITHERRR
SLITHER
THE *ILLUMINATI* ARE RESPONSIBLE.
THEN YOU NEED PROTECTION.
THEY'RE DANGEROUS, SO I'LL DRIVE THEM OUT.
HEH HEH HEH HEH HEH
WE DO NOT ASK THAT OF YOU.
I THINK YOU KNOW...
...THE *TRUE* REASON WE CALLED YOU HERE.
HEH HEH

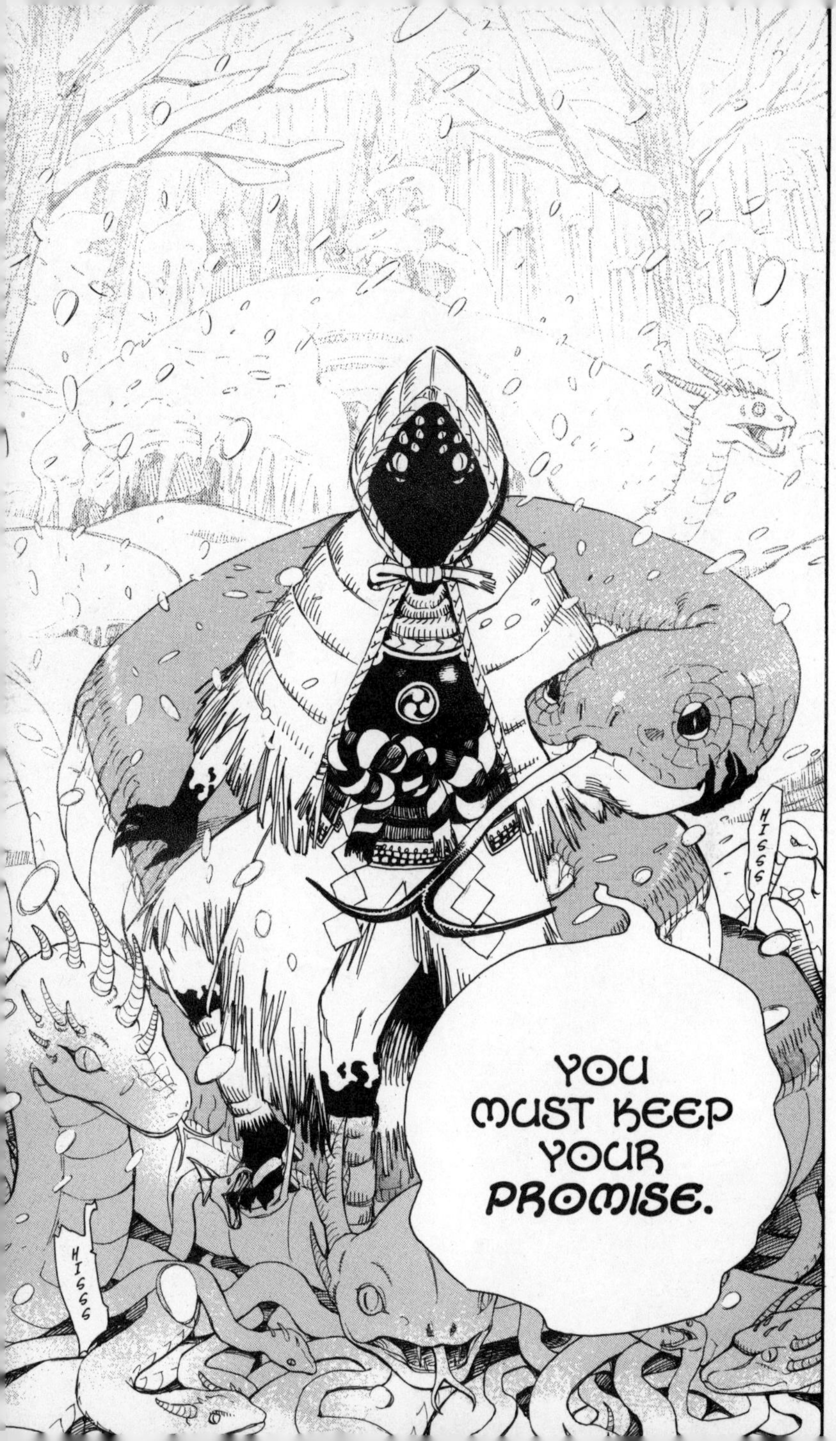
HISSS
YOU MUST KEEP YOUR PROMISE.
HISSS

Blue Exorcist Chapter 74: Hachinohe Station in the Snow

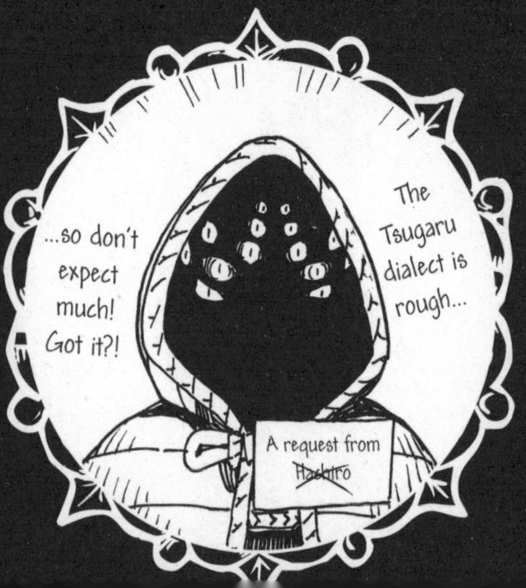
The Tsugaru dialect is rough...
...so don't expect much! Got it?!
A request from ~~Hachiro~~

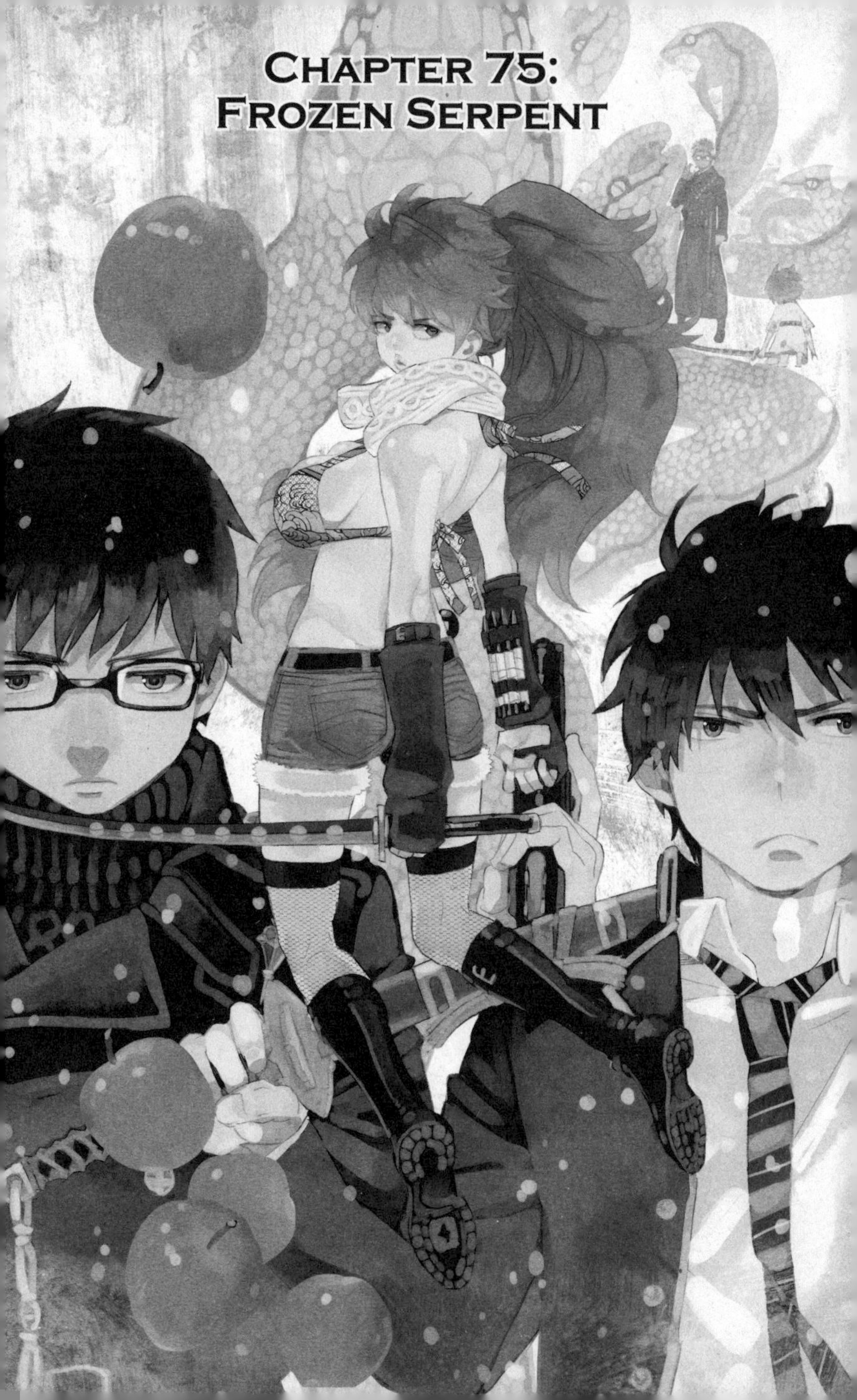
Chapter 75:
Frozen Serpent

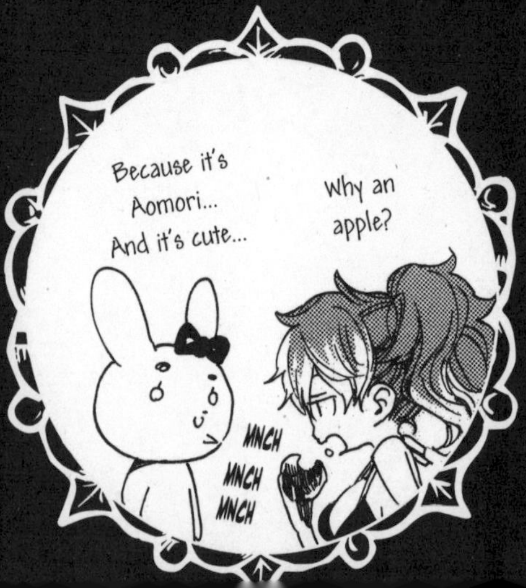
Why an apple?
Because it's Aomori... And it's cute...
MNCH
MNCH
MNCH

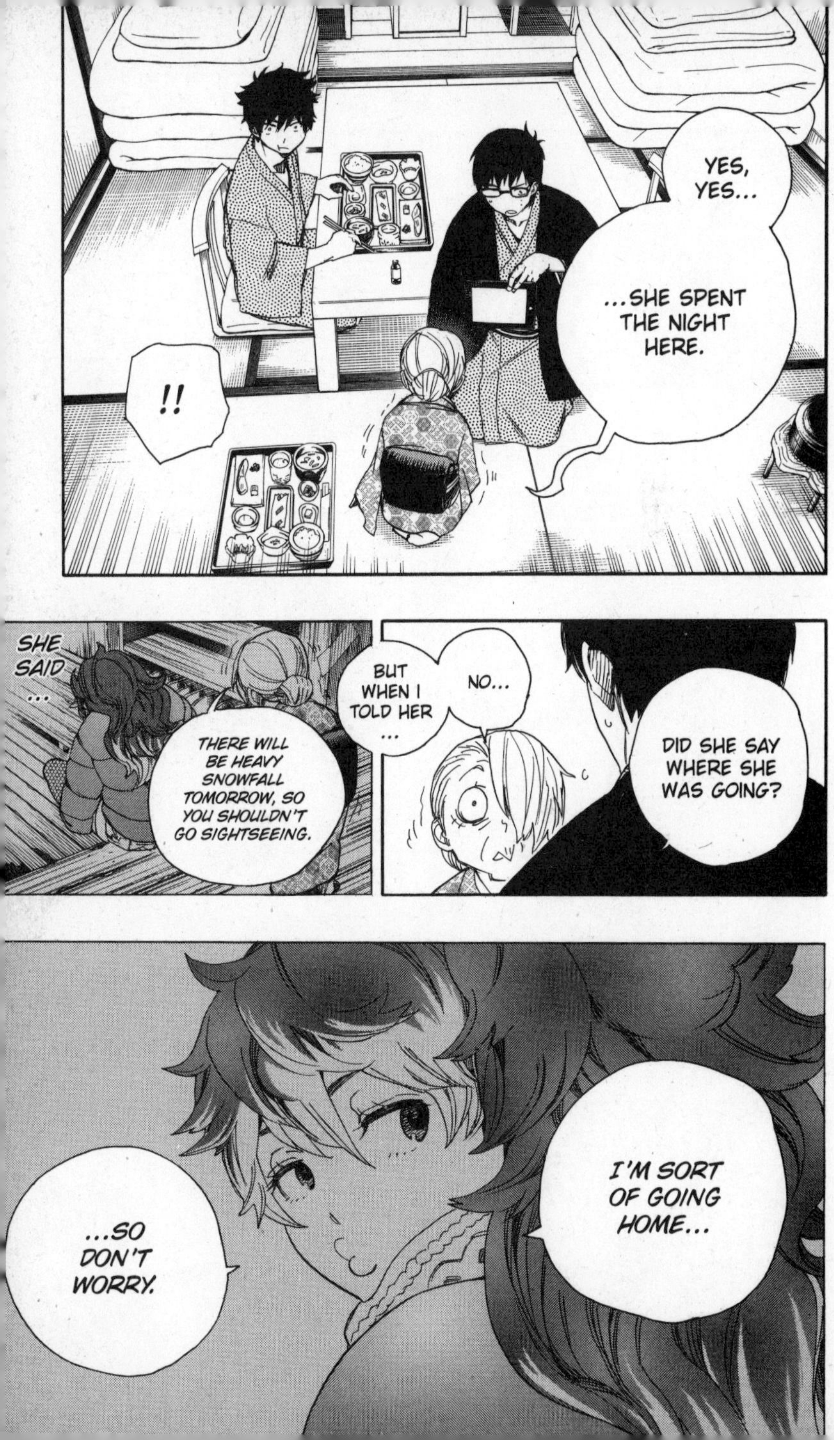
YES, YES...
...SHE SPENT THE NIGHT HERE.
!!
DID SHE SAY WHERE SHE WAS GOING?
NO...
BUT WHEN I TOLD HER ...
THERE WILL BE HEAVY SNOWFALL TOMORROW, SO YOU SHOULDN'T GO SIGHTSEEING.
SHE SAID ...
I'M SORT OF GOING HOME...
...SO DON'T WORRY.

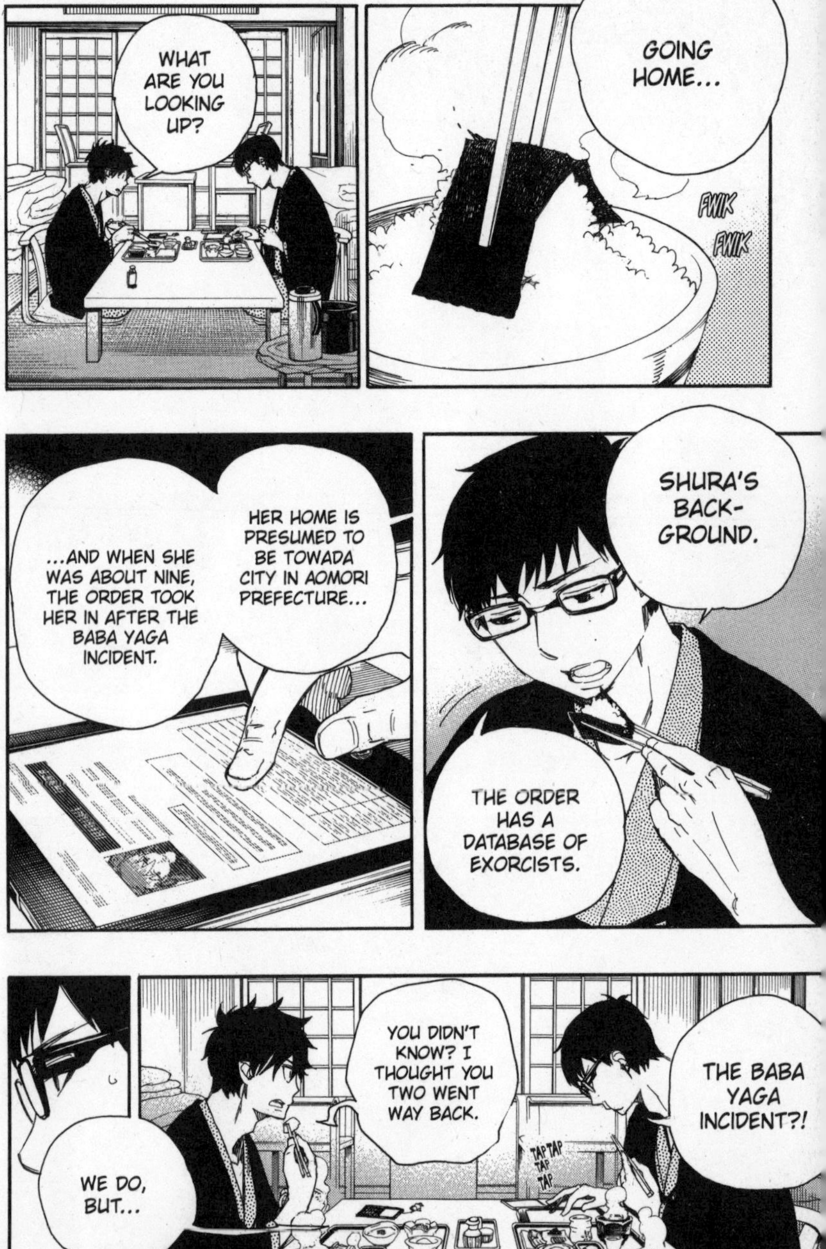
GOING HOME...
FWIK
FWIK
WHAT ARE YOU LOOKING UP?
SHURA'S BACK-GROUND.
THE ORDER HAS A DATABASE OF EXORCISTS.
HER HOME IS PRESUMED TO BE TOWADA CITY IN AOMORI PREFECTURE...
...AND WHEN SHE WAS ABOUT NINE, THE ORDER TOOK HER IN AFTER THE BABA YAGA INCIDENT.
THE BABA YAGA INCIDENT?!
TAP TAP
TAP
TAP
YOU DIDN'T KNOW? I THOUGHT YOU TWO WENT WAY BACK.
WE DO, BUT...

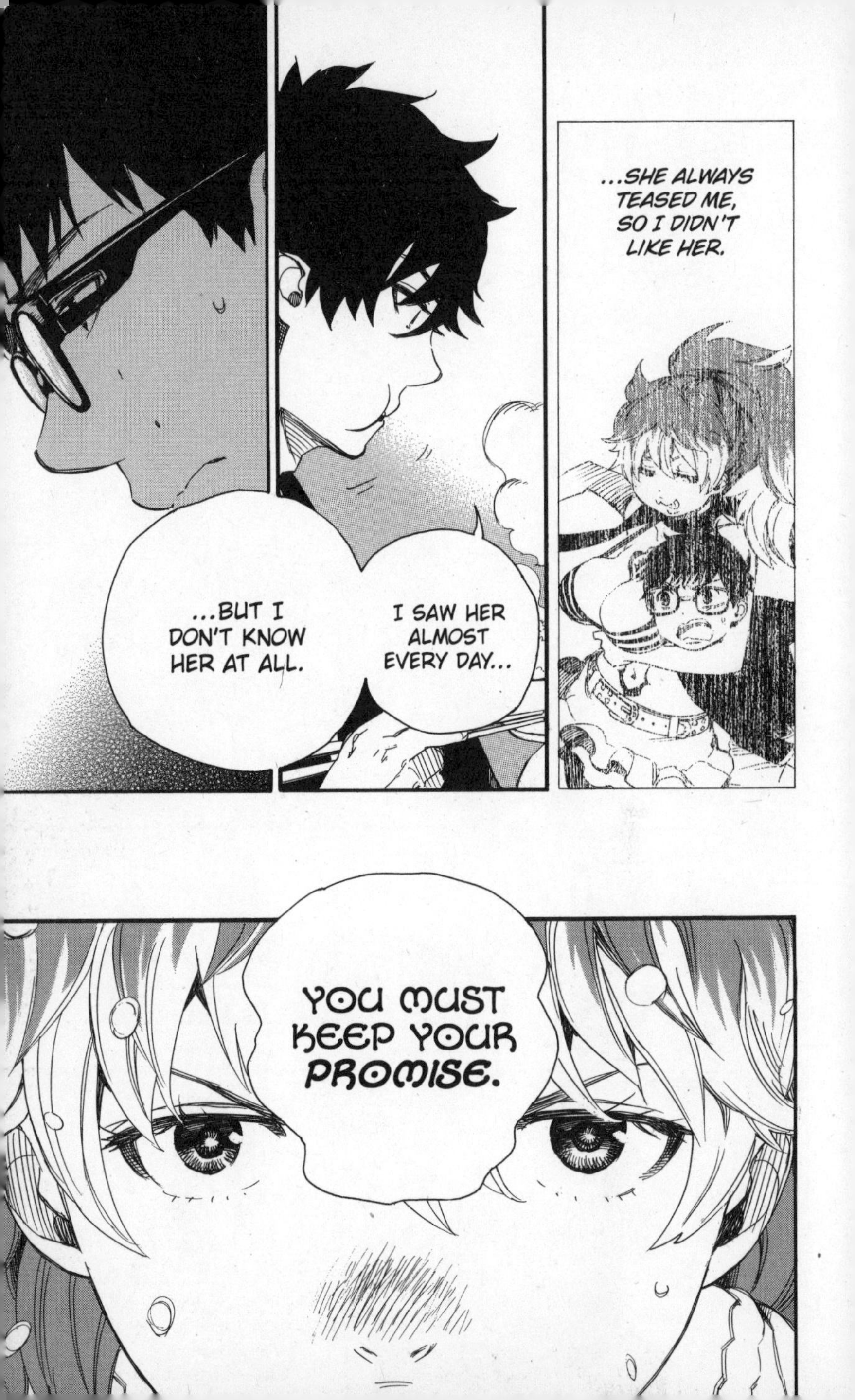
...SHE ALWAYS TEASED ME, SO I DIDN'T LIKE HER.
I SAW HER ALMOST EVERY DAY...
...BUT I DON'T KNOW HER AT ALL.
YOU MUST KEEP YOUR PROMISE.

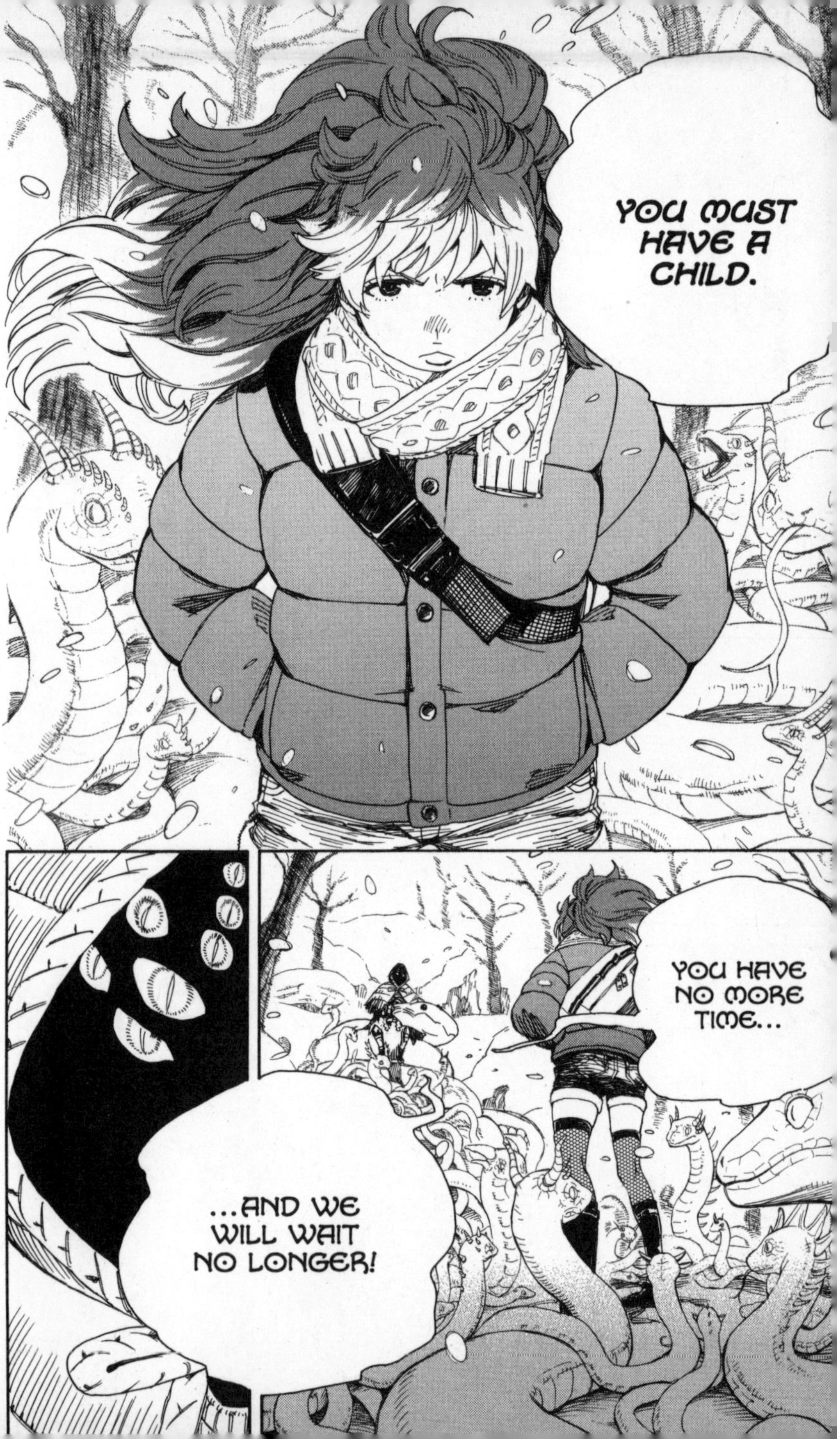
YOU MUST HAVE A CHILD.
YOU HAVE NO MORE TIME...
...AND WE WILL WAIT NO LONGER!

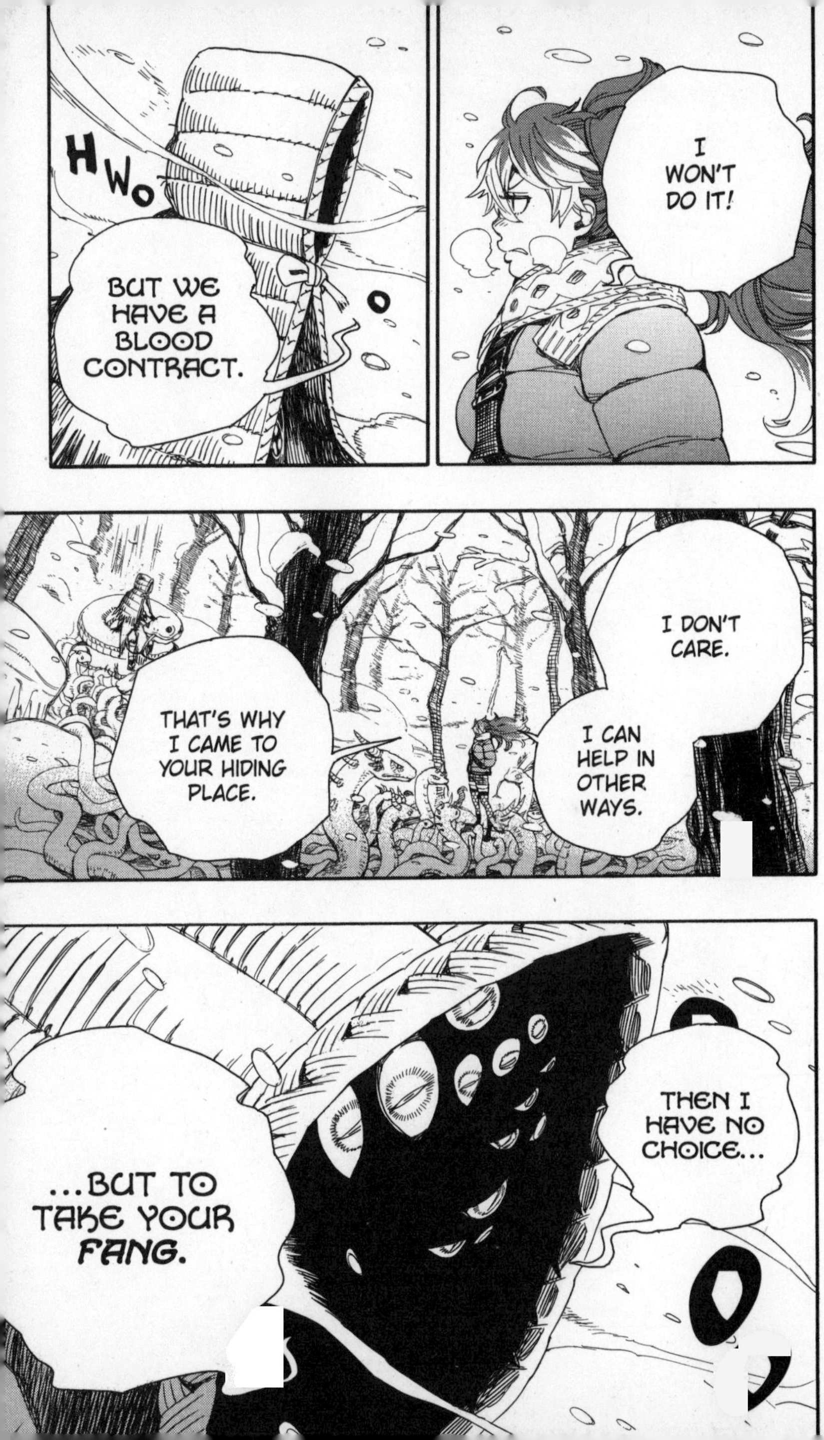
I WON'T DO IT!
HWO
BUT WE HAVE A BLOOD CONTRACT.
I DON'T CARE.
I CAN HELP IN OTHER WAYS.
THAT'S WHY I CAME TO YOUR HIDING PLACE.
THEN I HAVE NO CHOICE...
...BUT TO TAKE YOUR FANG.

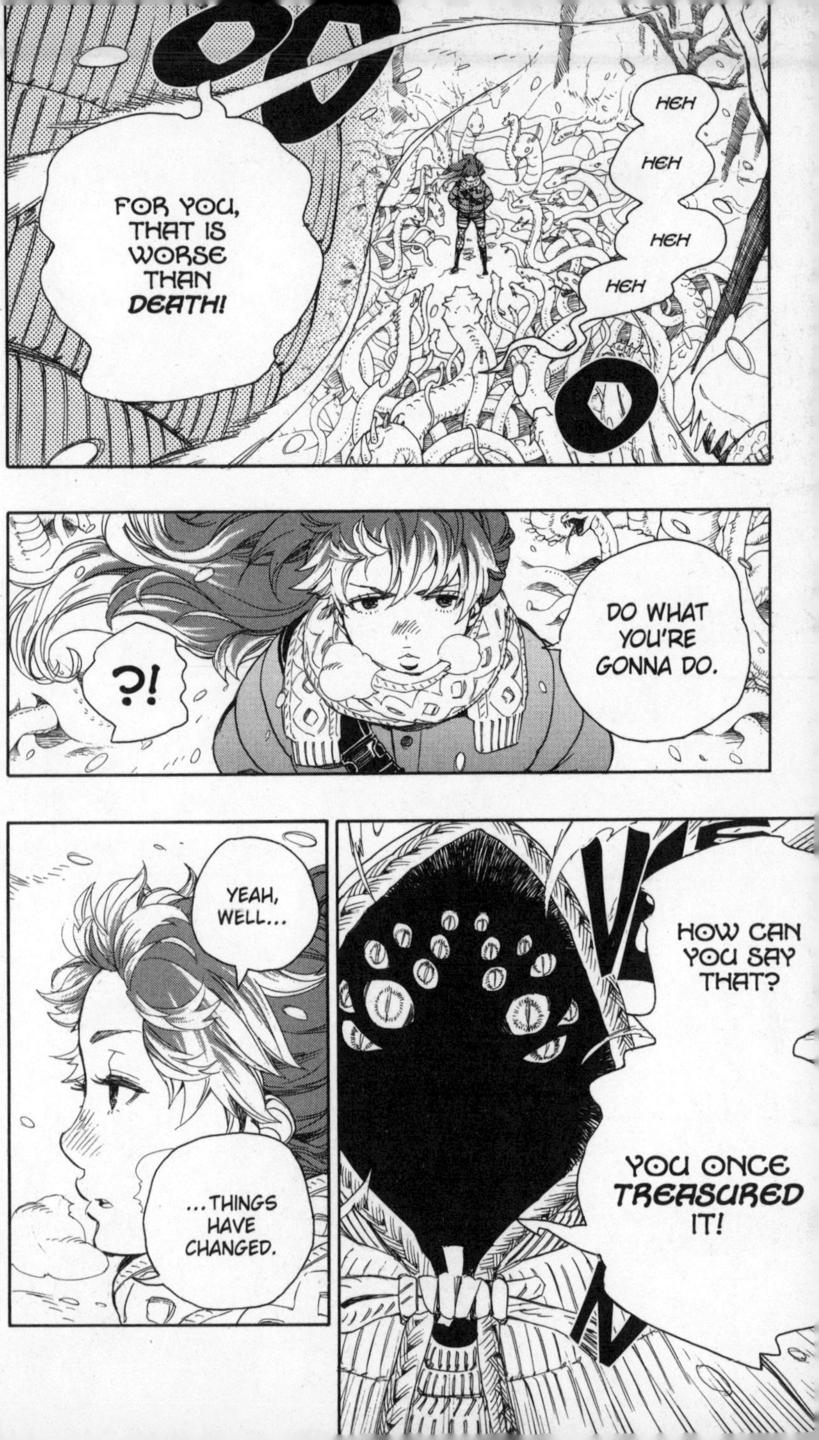
HEH
HEH
HEH
HEH
FOR YOU, THAT IS WORSE THAN *DEATH!*
DO WHAT YOU'RE GONNA DO.
?!
HOW CAN YOU SAY THAT?
YOU ONCE *TREASURED* IT!
YEAH, WELL...
...THINGS HAVE CHANGED.

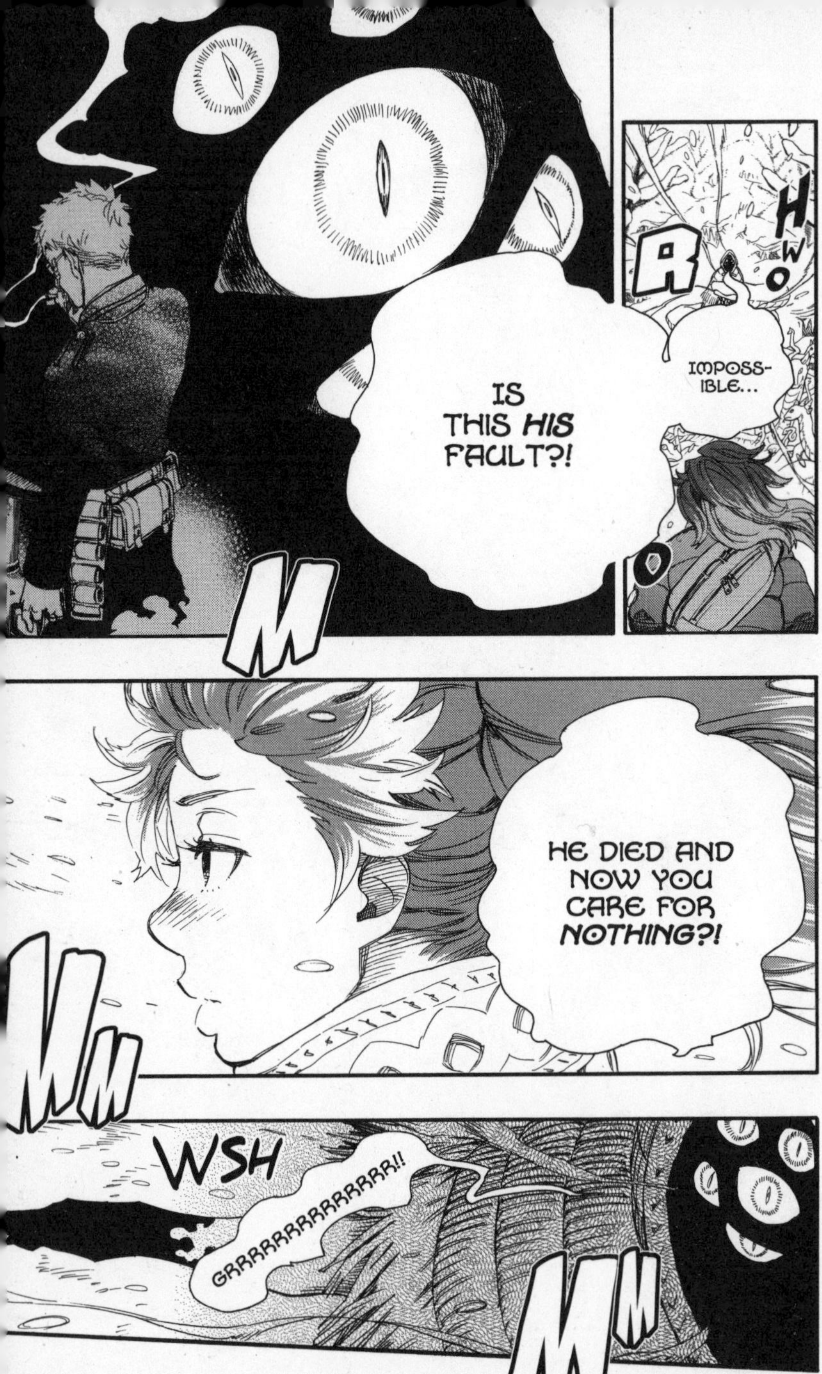
IMPOSS-IBLE...
IS THIS *HIS* FAULT?!
M
HE DIED AND NOW YOU CARE FOR *NOTHING?!*
MM
GRRRRRRRRRRRRRR!!
WSH
MM

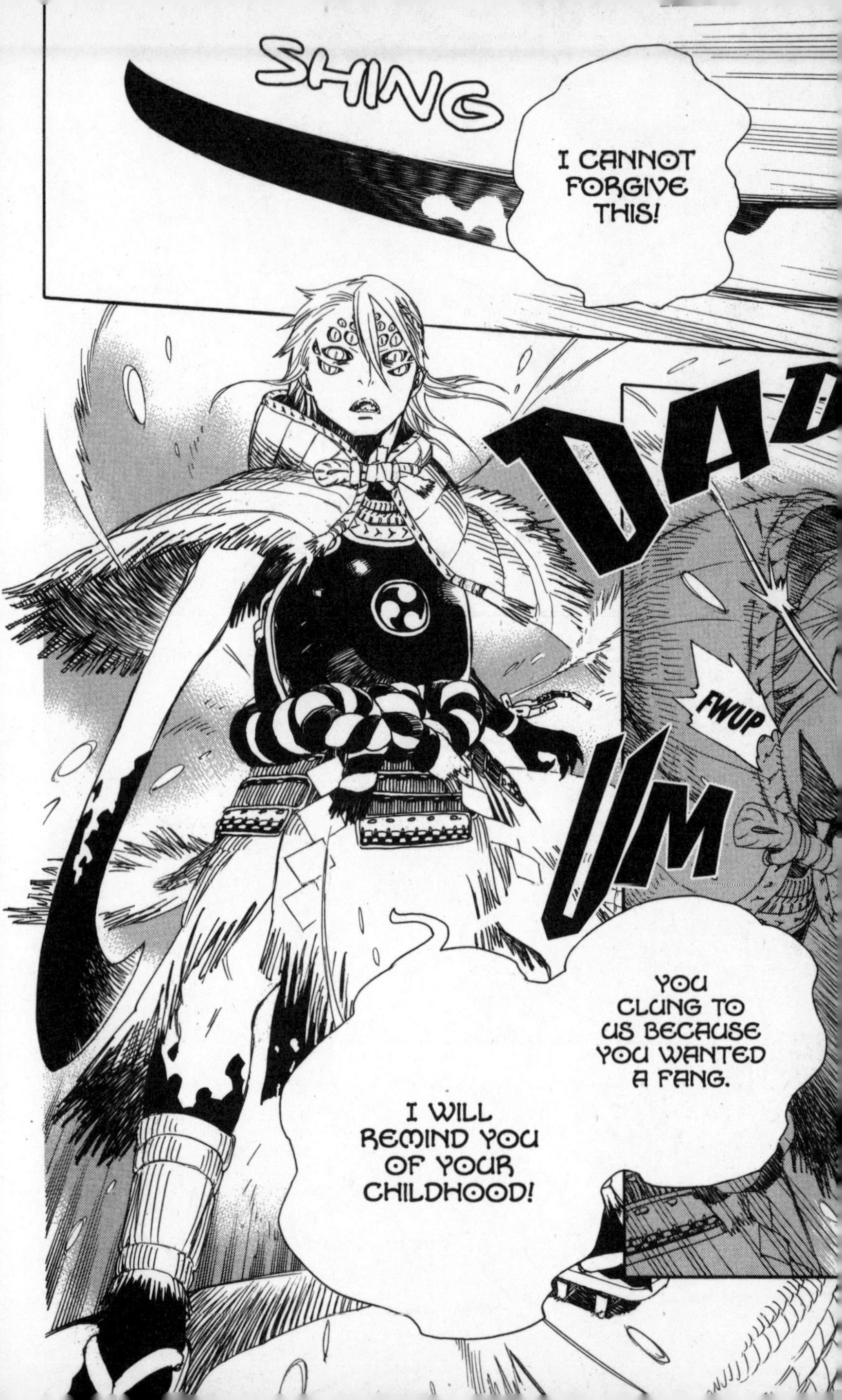
I CANNOT FORGIVE THIS!
SHING
DAD
FWUP
UM
YOU CLUNG TO US BECAUSE YOU WANTED A FANG.
I WILL REMIND YOU OF YOUR CHILDHOOD!

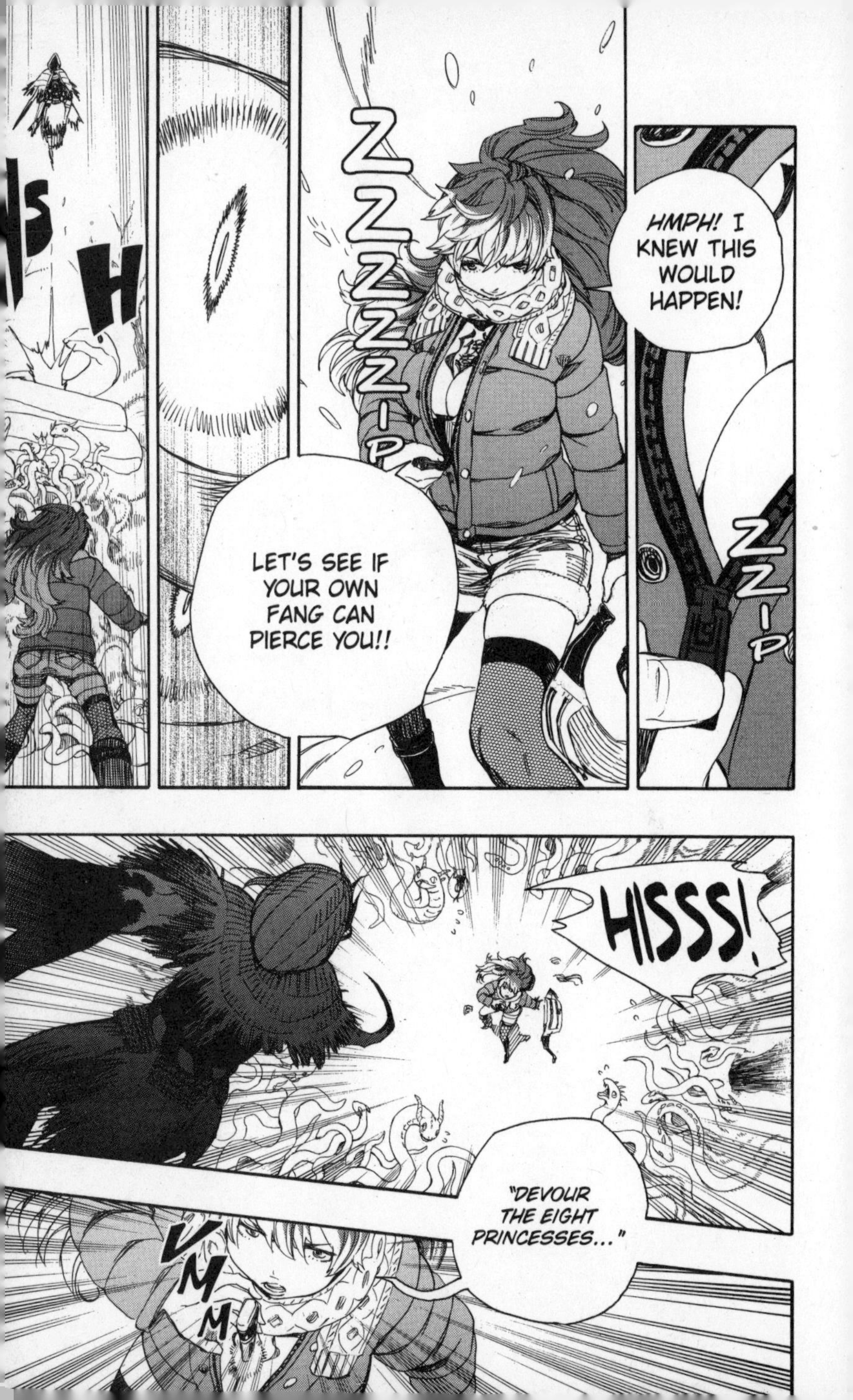
HMPH! I KNEW THIS WOULD HAPPEN!
ZZIP
ZZZZZIP
LET'S SEE IF YOUR OWN FANG CAN PIERCE YOU!!
HISSS!
"DEVOUR THE EIGHT PRINCESSES..."
VMM

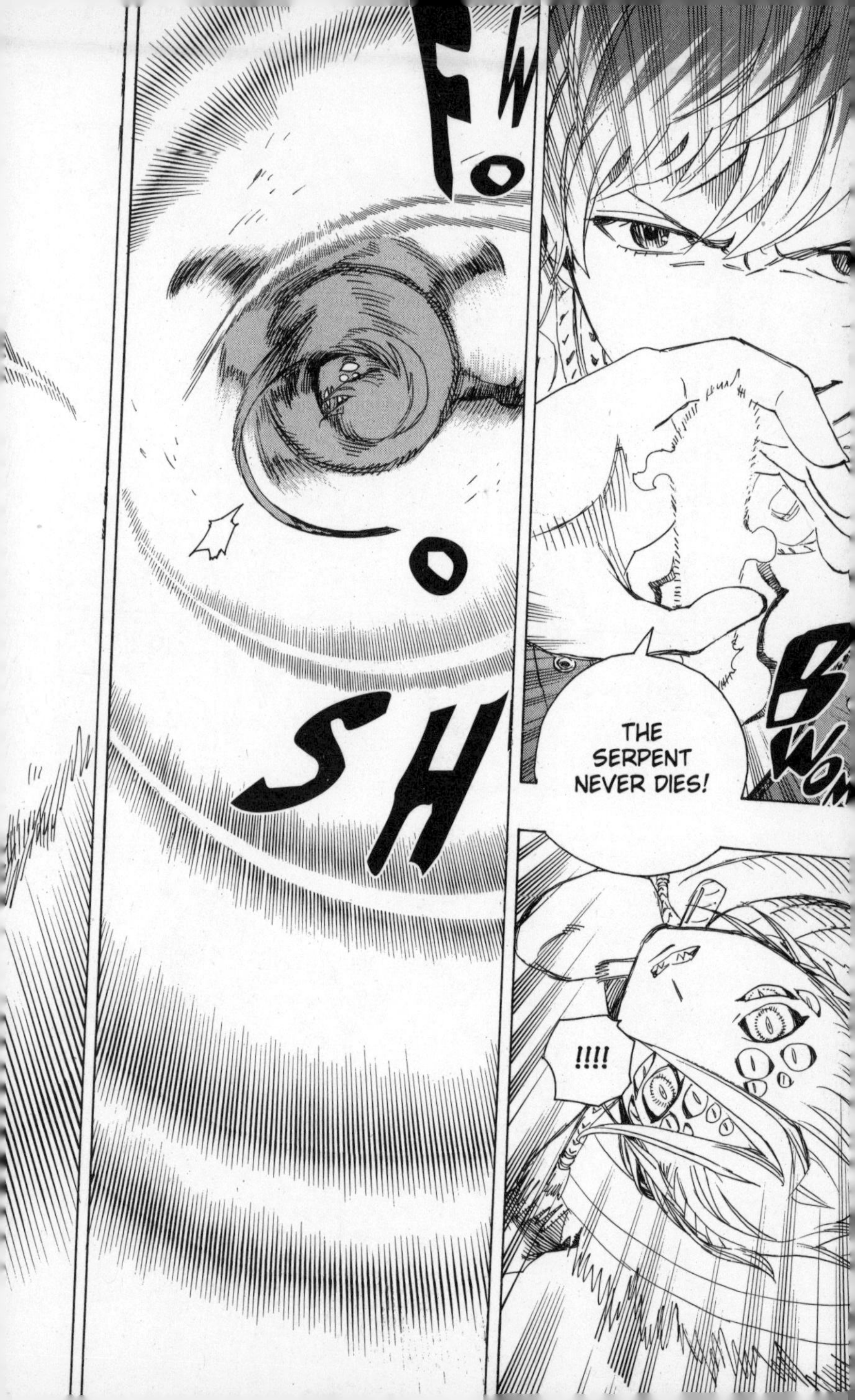
THE SERPENT NEVER DIES!
BWOM
!!!!
FWOOSH

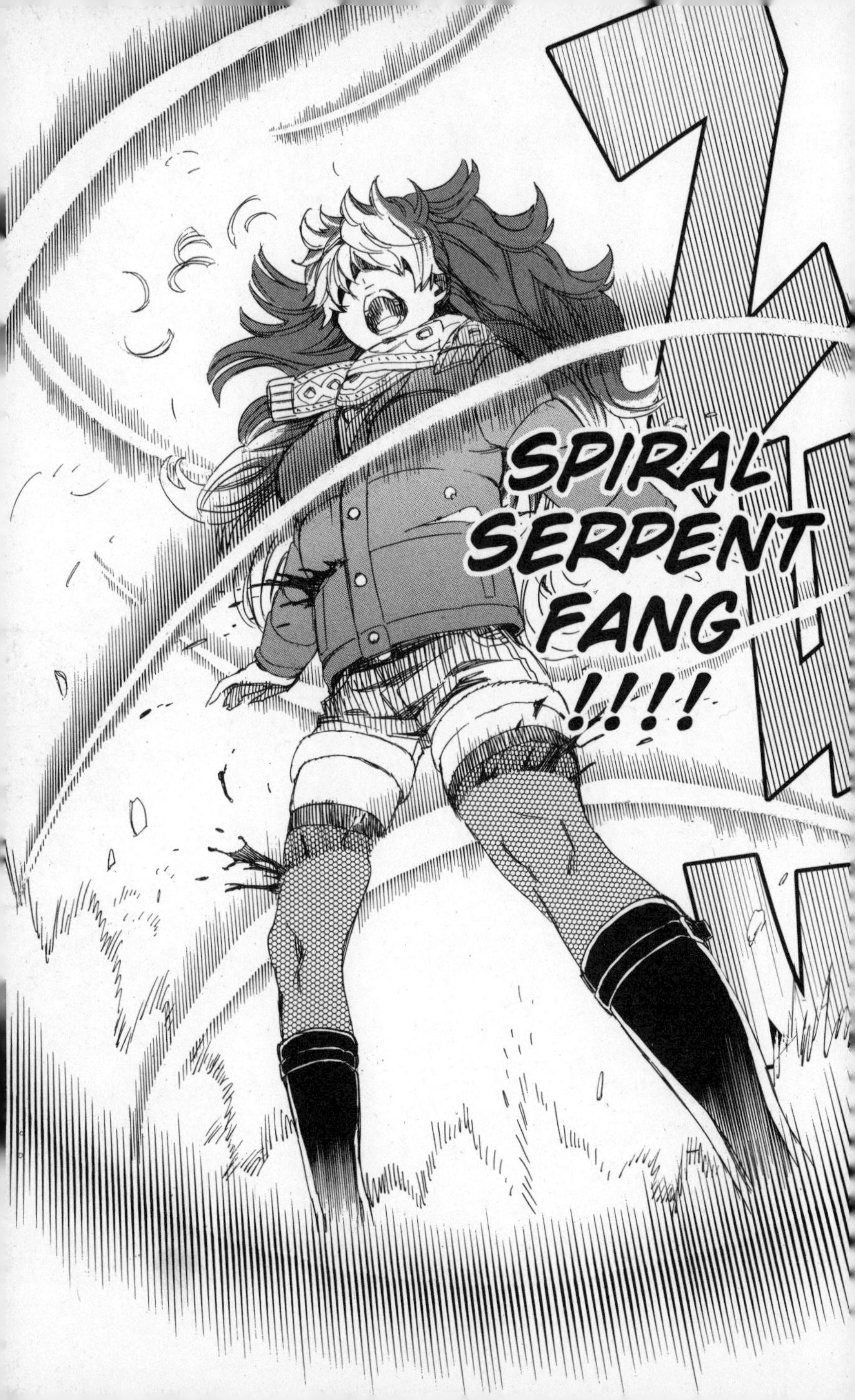
SPIRAL SERPENT FANG!!!!

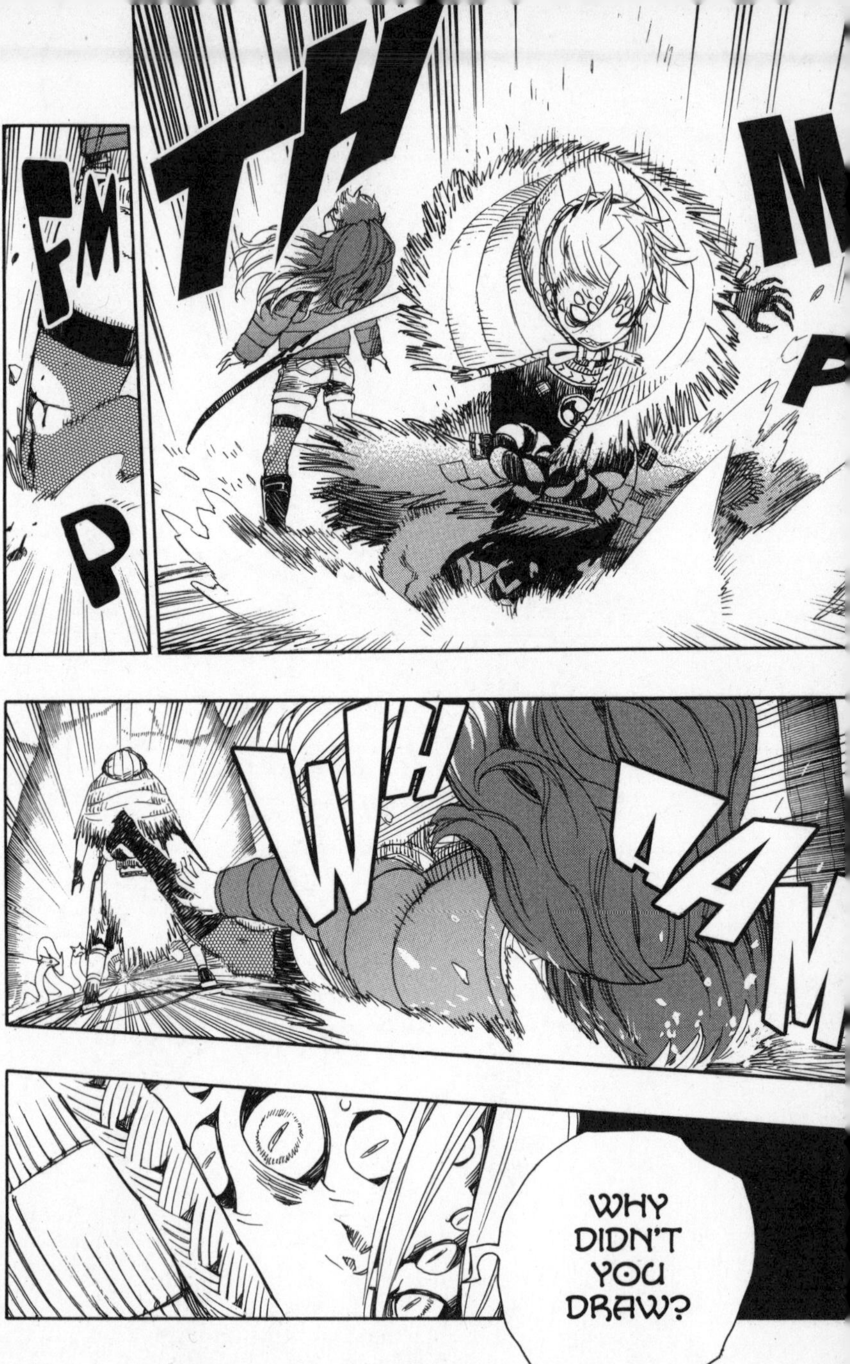

MP
TTH
FMP
WH
AAM
WHY DIDN'T YOU DRAW?

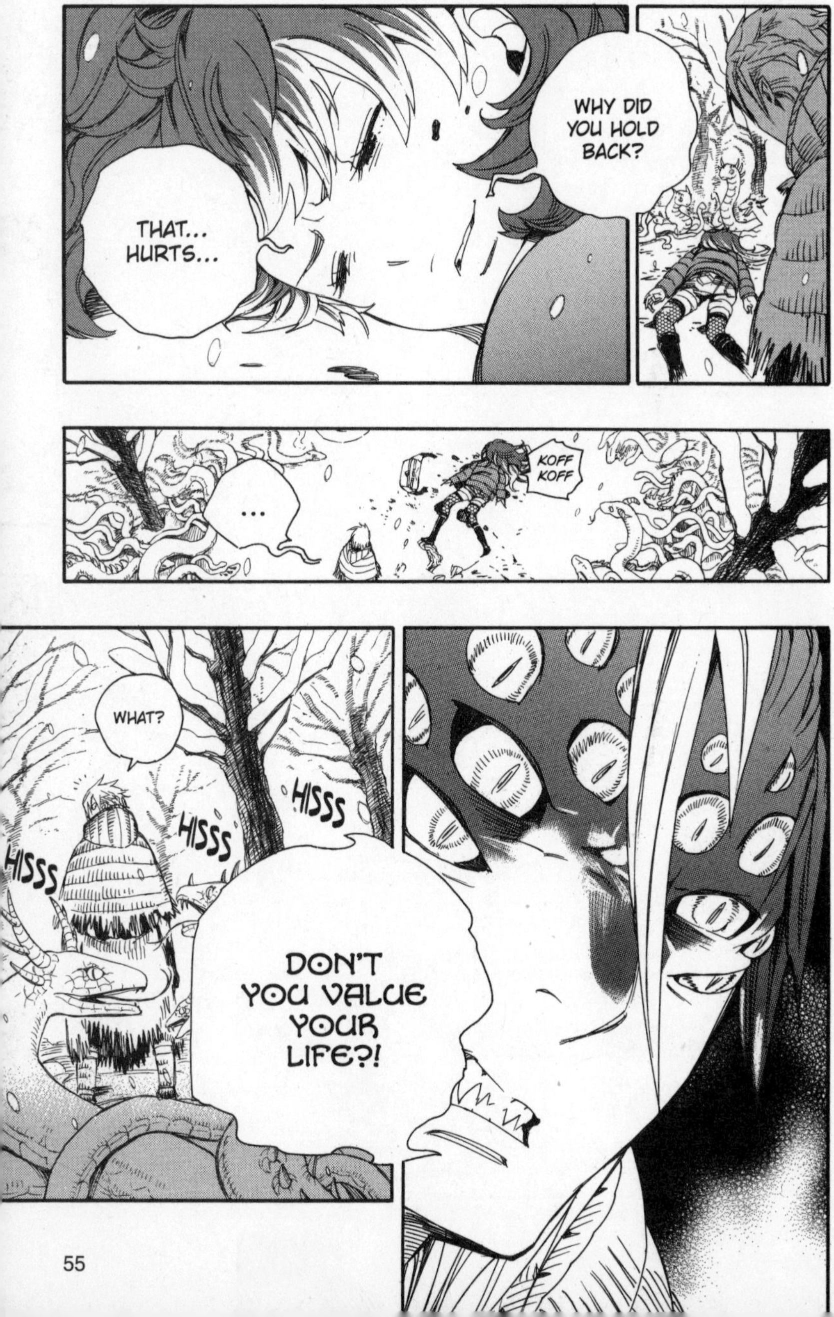
WHY DID YOU HOLD BACK?
THAT... HURTS...
KOFF KOFF
...
WHAT?
HISSS
HISSS
HISSS
DON'T YOU VALUE YOUR LIFE?!

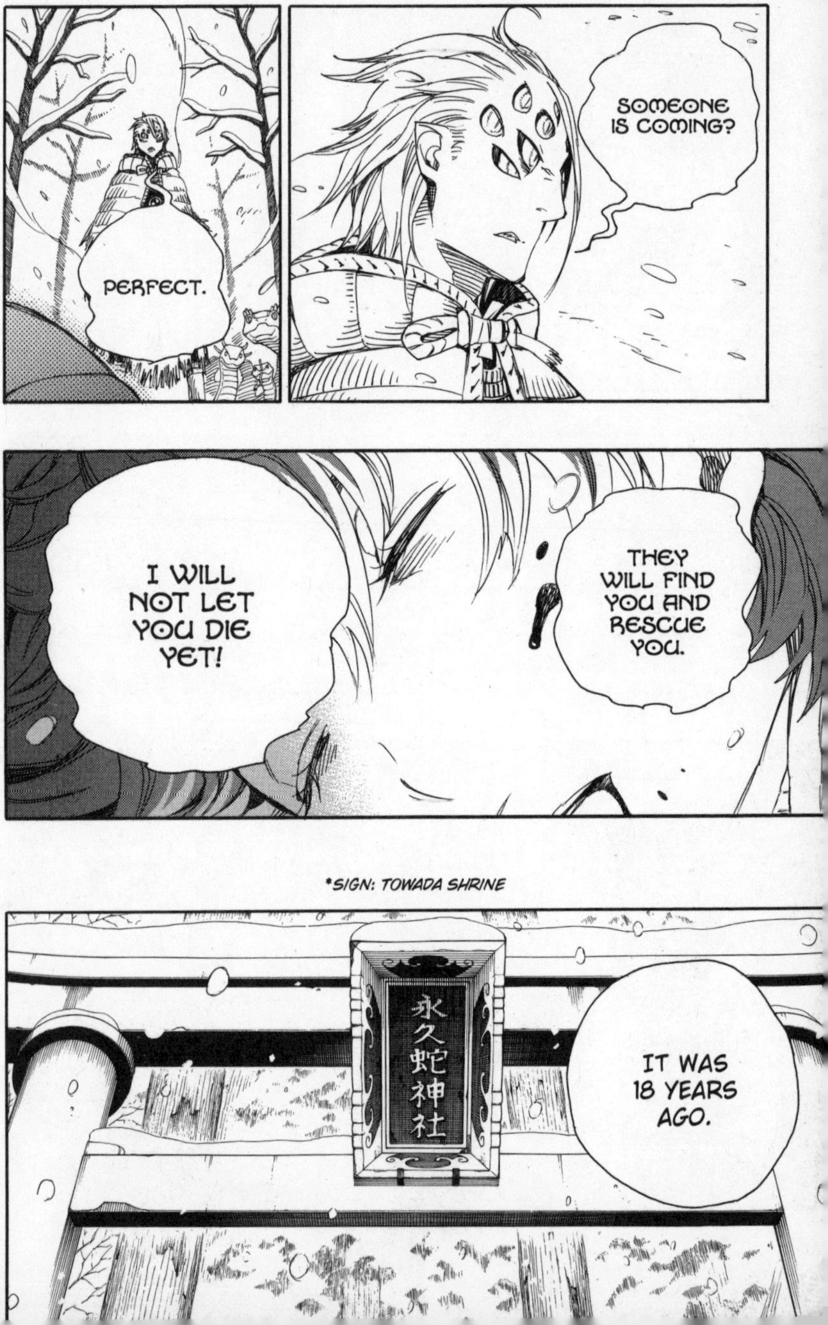
SOMEONE IS COMING?
PERFECT.
THEY WILL FIND YOU AND RESCUE YOU.
I WILL NOT LET YOU DIE YET!
*SIGN: TOWADA SHRINE
永久蛇神社
IT WAS 18 YEARS AGO.

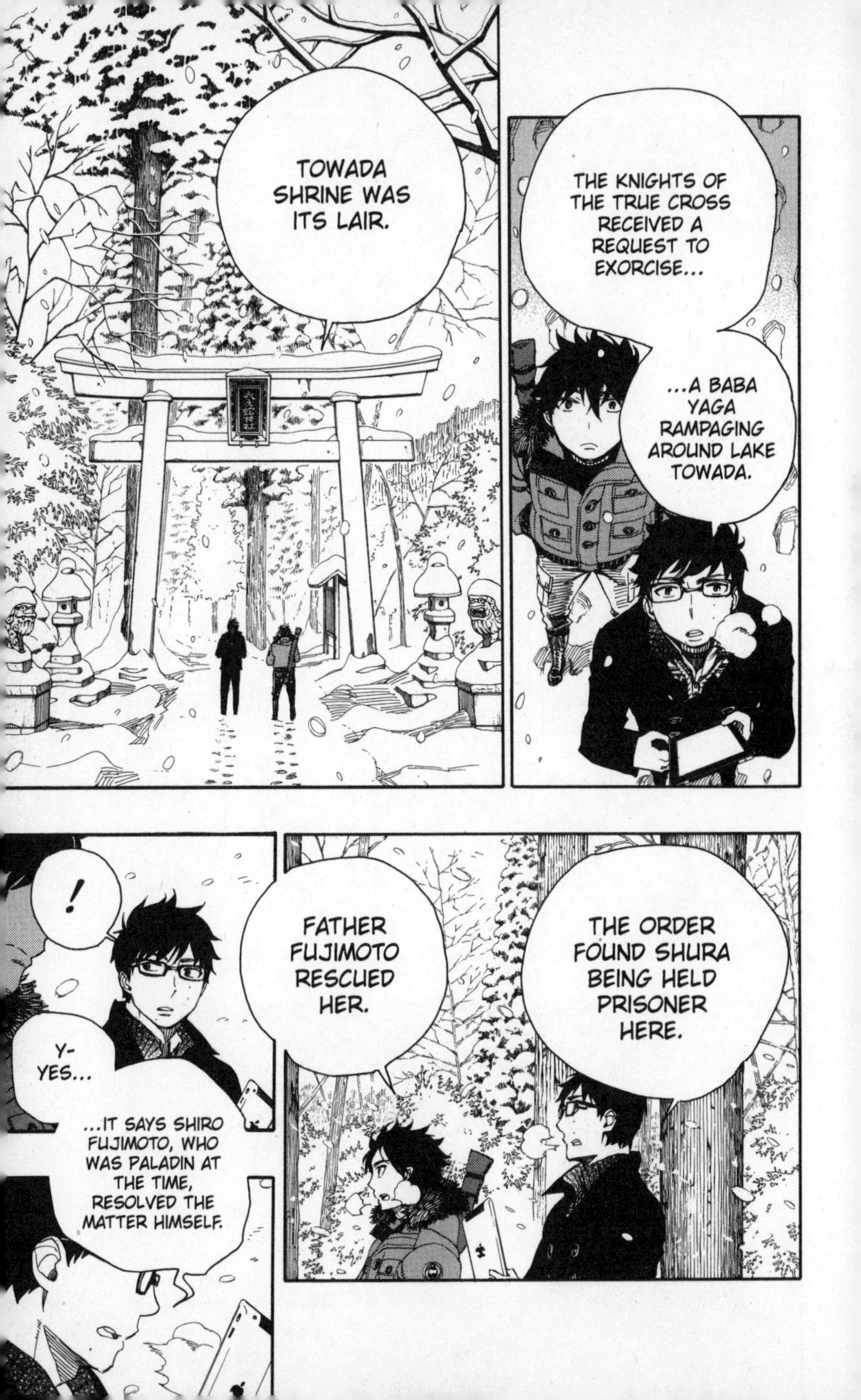
THE KNIGHTS OF THE TRUE CROSS RECEIVED A REQUEST TO EXORCISE...
...A BABA YAGA RAMPAGING AROUND LAKE TOWADA.
TOWADA SHRINE WAS ITS LAIR.
THE ORDER FOUND SHURA BEING HELD PRISONER HERE.
FATHER FUJIMOTO RESCUED HER.
!
Y-YES...
...IT SAYS SHIRO FUJIMOTO, WHO WAS PALADIN AT THE TIME, RESOLVED THE MATTER HIMSELF.

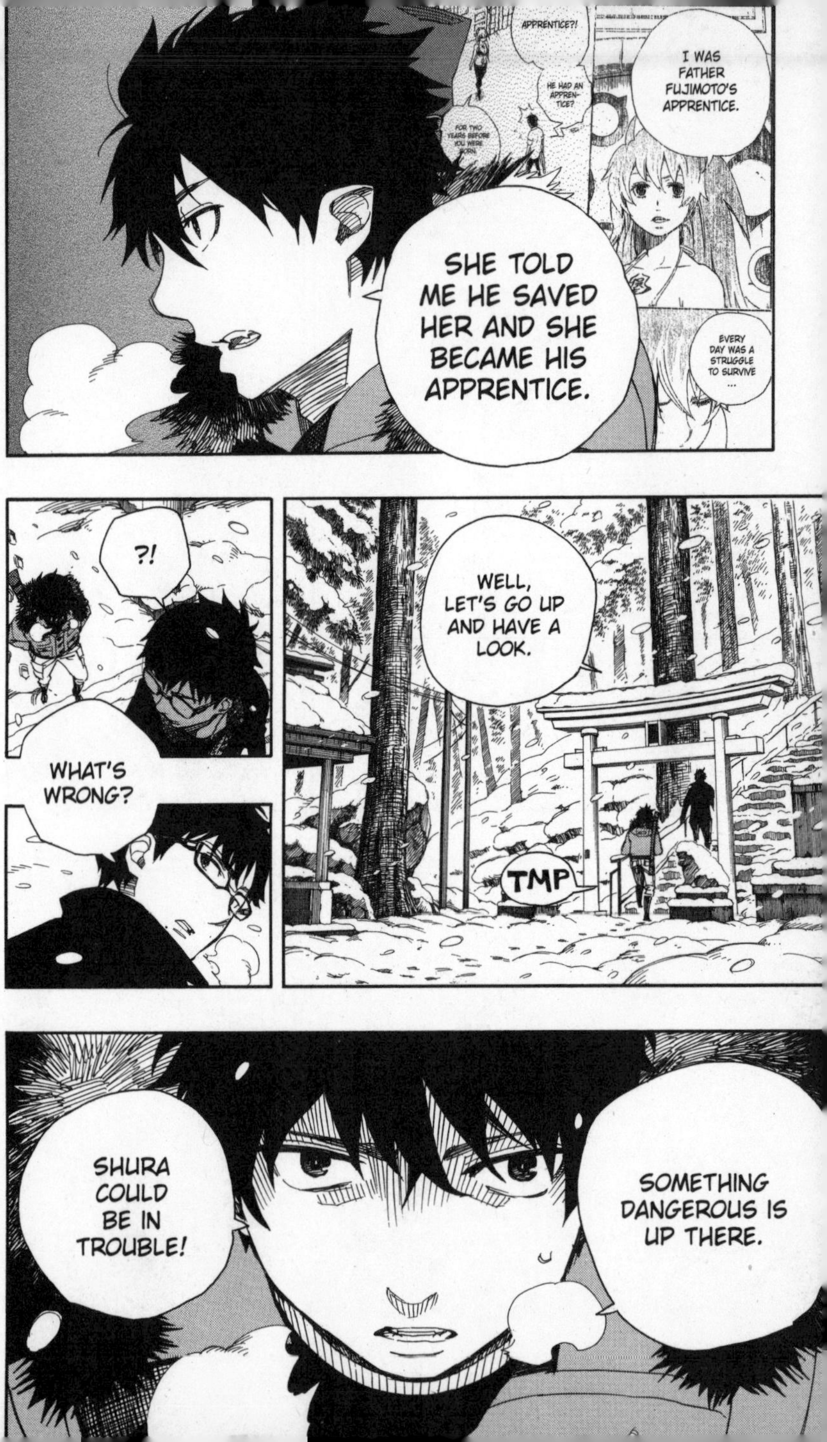
I WAS FATHER FUJIMOTO'S APPRENTICE.
EVERY DAY WAS A STRUGGLE TO SURVIVE ...
APPRENTICE?!
HE HAD AN APPRENTICE?
FOR TWO YEARS BEFORE YOU WERE BORN.
SHE TOLD ME HE SAVED HER AND SHE BECAME HIS APPRENTICE.
WELL, LET'S GO UP AND HAVE A LOOK.
TMP
?!
WHAT'S WRONG?
SOMETHING DANGEROUS IS UP THERE.
SHURA COULD BE IN TROUBLE!

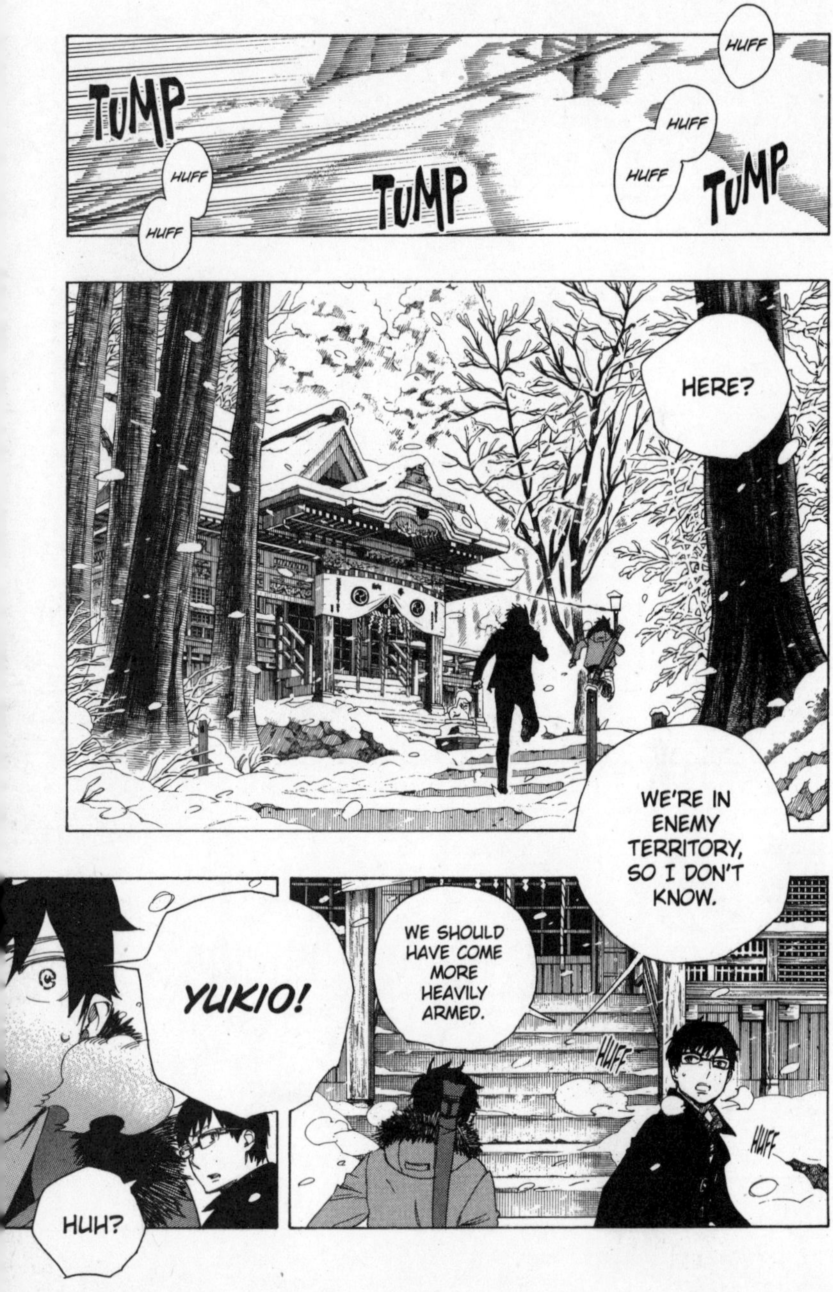
HUFF
HUFF
HUFF
TUMP
TUMP
TUMP
HUFF
HUFF
HERE?
WE'RE IN ENEMY TERRITORY, SO I DON'T KNOW.
WE SHOULD HAVE COME MORE HEAVILY ARMED.
HUFF
HUFF
YUKIO!
HUH?

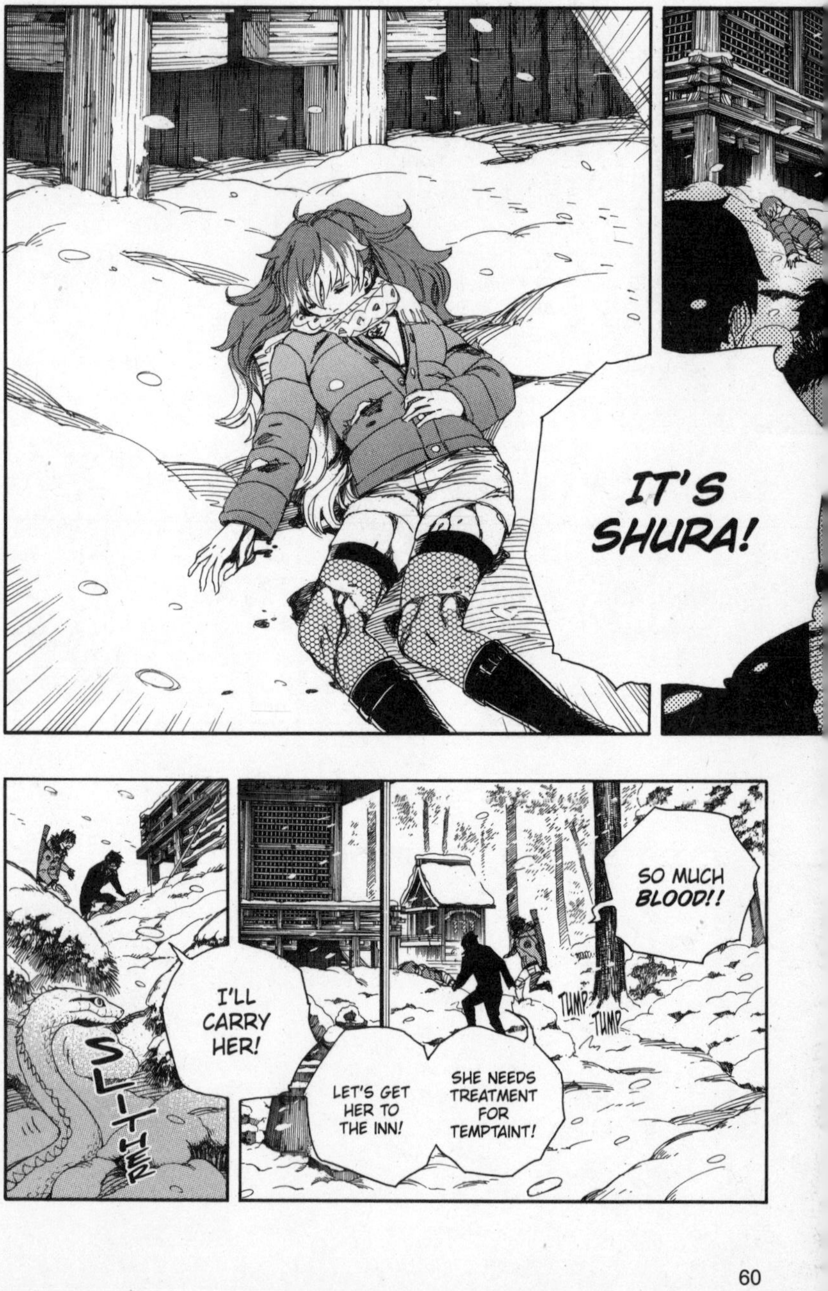
IT'S SHURA!
SO MUCH BLOOD!!
TUMP
TUMP
SHE NEEDS TREATMENT FOR TEMPTAINT!
LET'S GET HER TO THE INN!
I'LL CARRY HER!
SLITHER

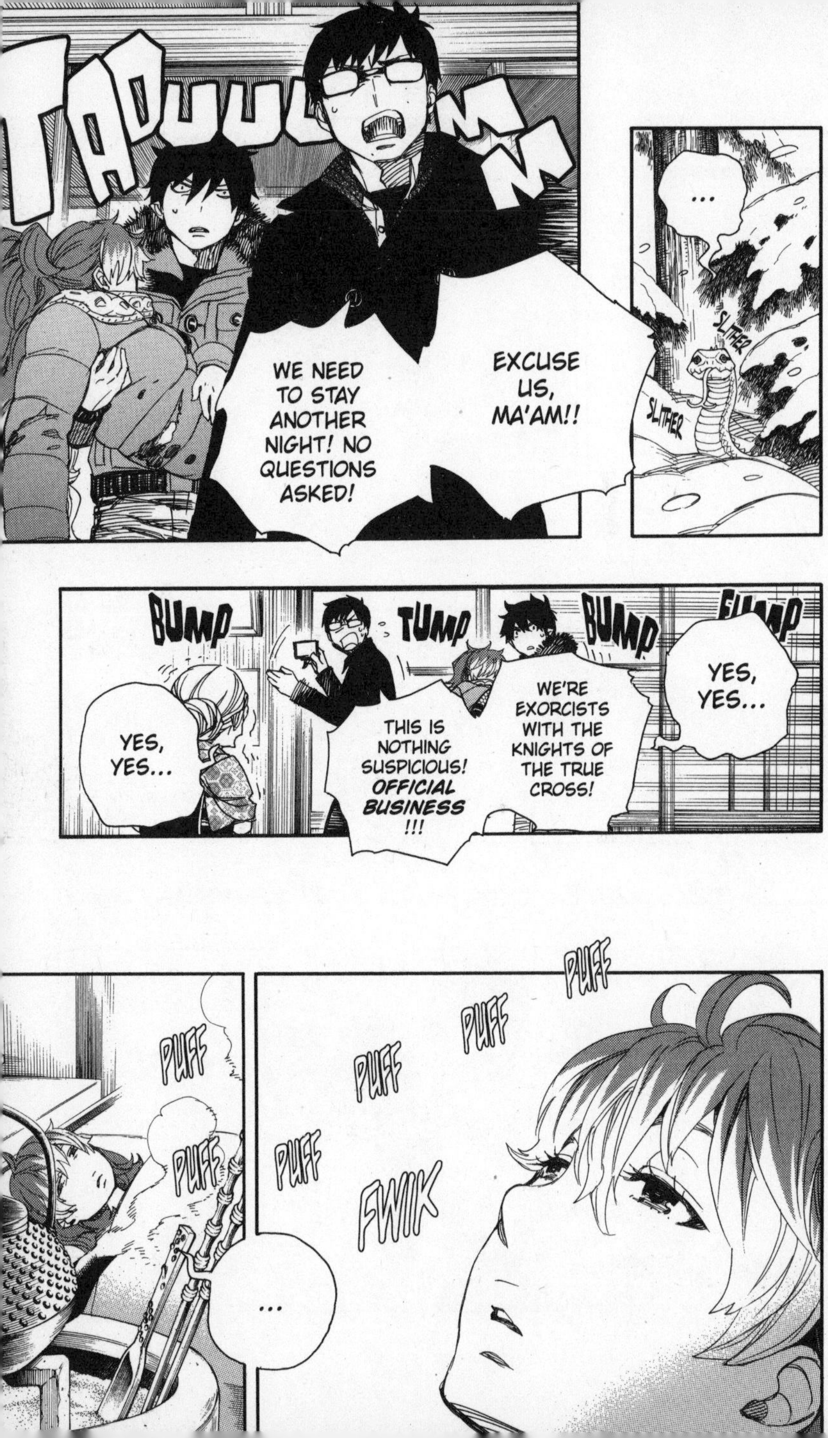
...
SLITHER
SLITHER
TADUUUMMM
EXCUSE US, MA'AM!!
WE NEED TO STAY ANOTHER NIGHT! NO QUESTIONS ASKED!
YES, YES...
BUMP
WE'RE EXORCISTS WITH THE KNIGHTS OF THE TRUE CROSS!
TUMP
THIS IS NOTHING SUSPICIOUS! OFFICIAL BUSINESS!!!
BUMP
YES, YES...
PUFF
PUFF
PUFF
PUFF
FWIK
PUFF
PUFF
...

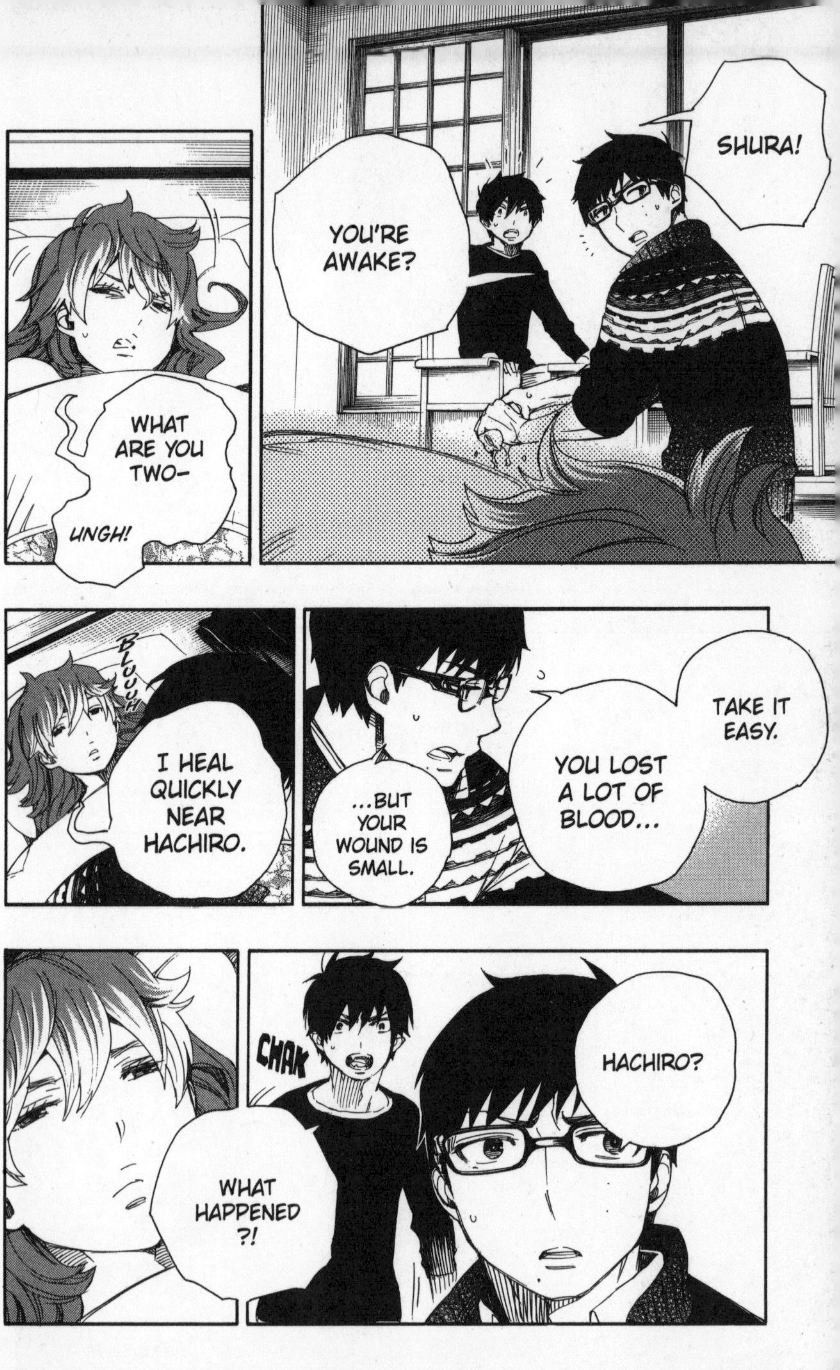
SHURA!
YOU'RE AWAKE?
WHAT ARE YOU TWO-
UNGH!
TAKE IT EASY.
YOU LOST A LOT OF BLOOD...
...BUT YOUR WOUND IS SMALL.
BLUUUH
I HEAL QUICKLY NEAR HACHIRO.
HACHIRO?
CHAK
WHAT HAPPENED ?!

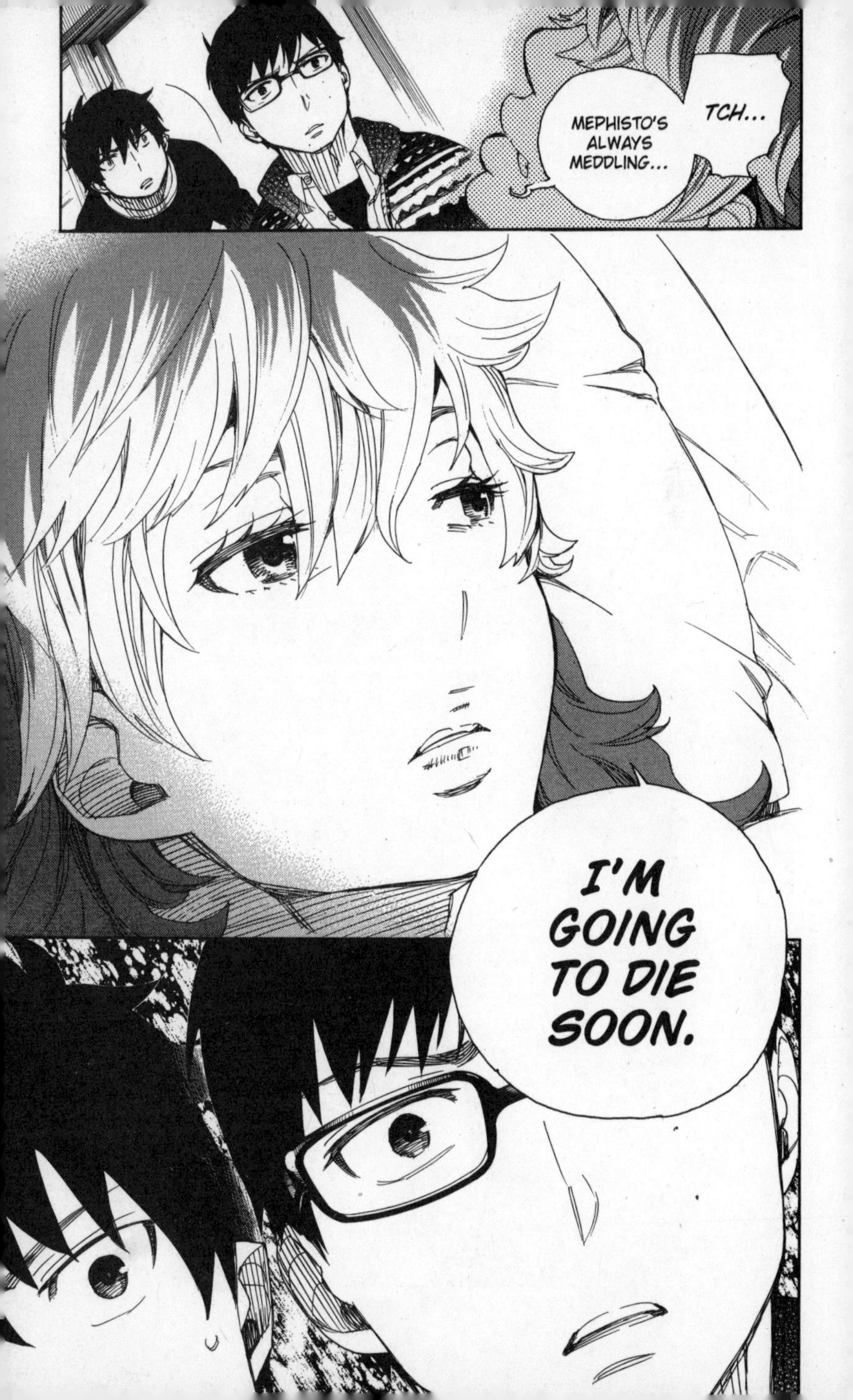
TCH...
MEPHISTO'S ALWAYS MEDDLING...
I'M GOING TO DIE SOON.

Blue Exorcist Chapter 75: Frozen Serpent

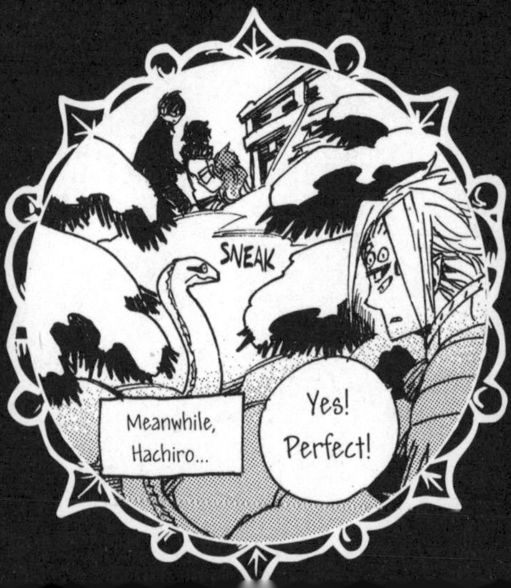
SNEAK
Yes! Perfect!
Meanwhile, Hachiro...

Chapter 76: Goodbye to You

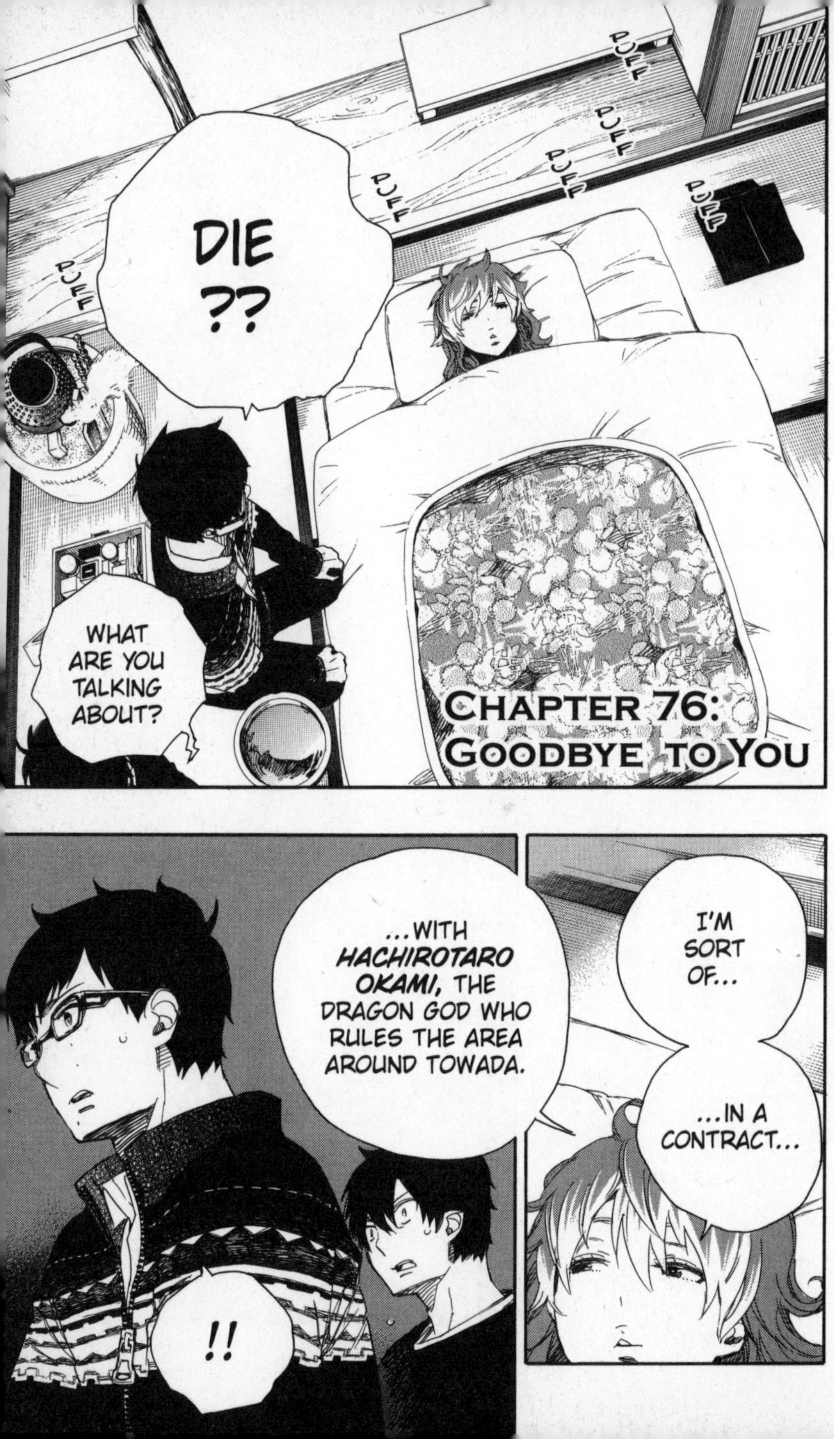
PUFF
PUFF
PUFF
PUFF
PUFF
PUFF
PUFF
DIE ??
WHAT ARE YOU TALKING ABOUT?
I'M SORT OF...
...IN A CONTRACT...
...WITH HACHIROTARO OKAMI, THE DRAGON GOD WHO RULES THE AREA AROUND TOWADA.
!!

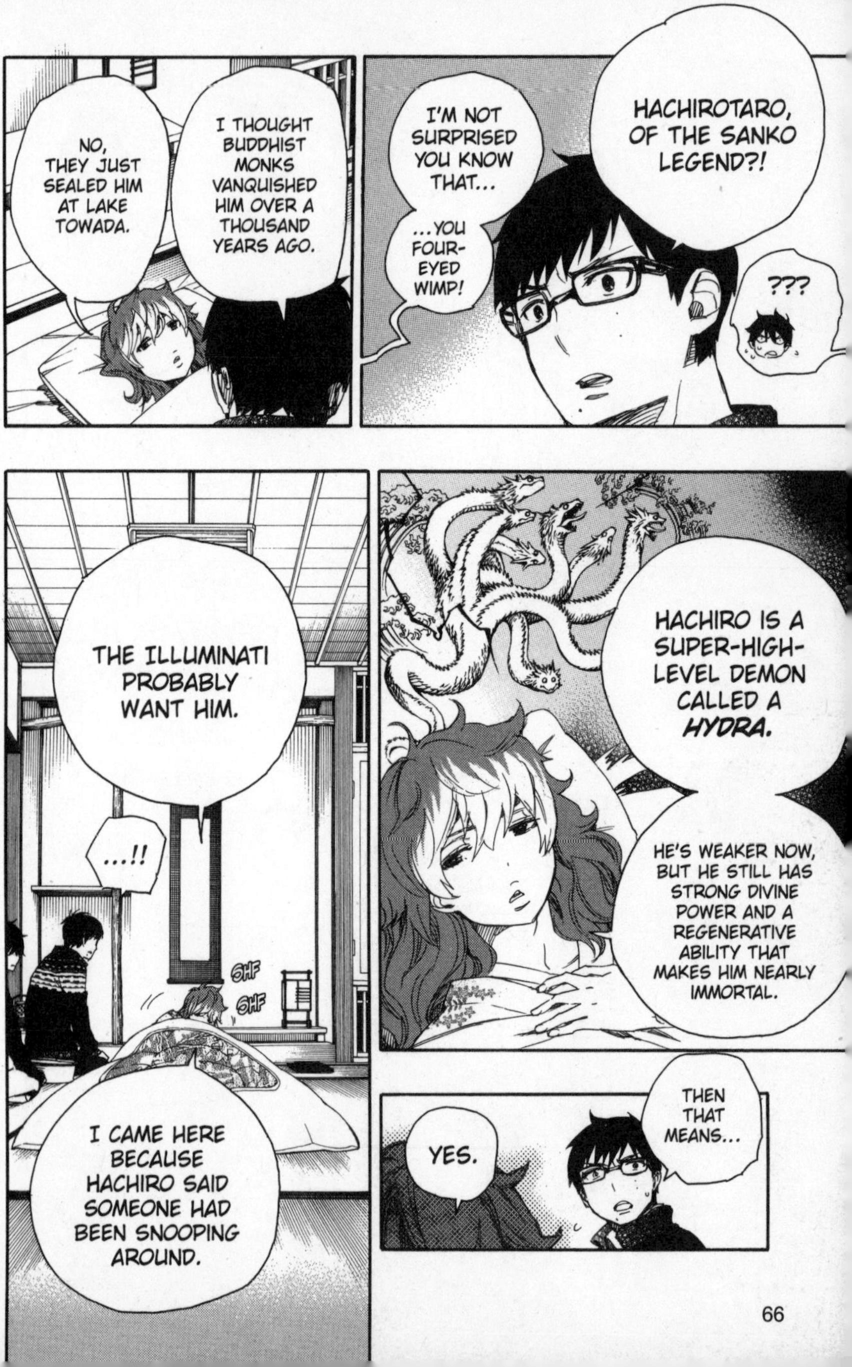
HACHIROTARO, OF THE SANKO LEGEND?!
I'M NOT SURPRISED YOU KNOW THAT...
...YOU FOUR-EYED WIMP!
???
I THOUGHT BUDDHIST MONKS VANQUISHED HIM OVER A THOUSAND YEARS AGO.
NO, THEY JUST SEALED HIM AT LAKE TOWADA.
HACHIRO IS A SUPER-HIGH-LEVEL DEMON CALLED A *HYDRA.*
HE'S WEAKER NOW, BUT HE STILL HAS STRONG DIVINE POWER AND A REGENERATIVE ABILITY THAT MAKES HIM NEARLY IMMORTAL.
THEN THAT MEANS...
YES.
THE ILLUMINATI PROBABLY WANT HIM.
...!!
SHF
SHF
I CAME HERE BECAUSE HACHIRO SAID SOMEONE HAD BEEN SNOOPING AROUND.

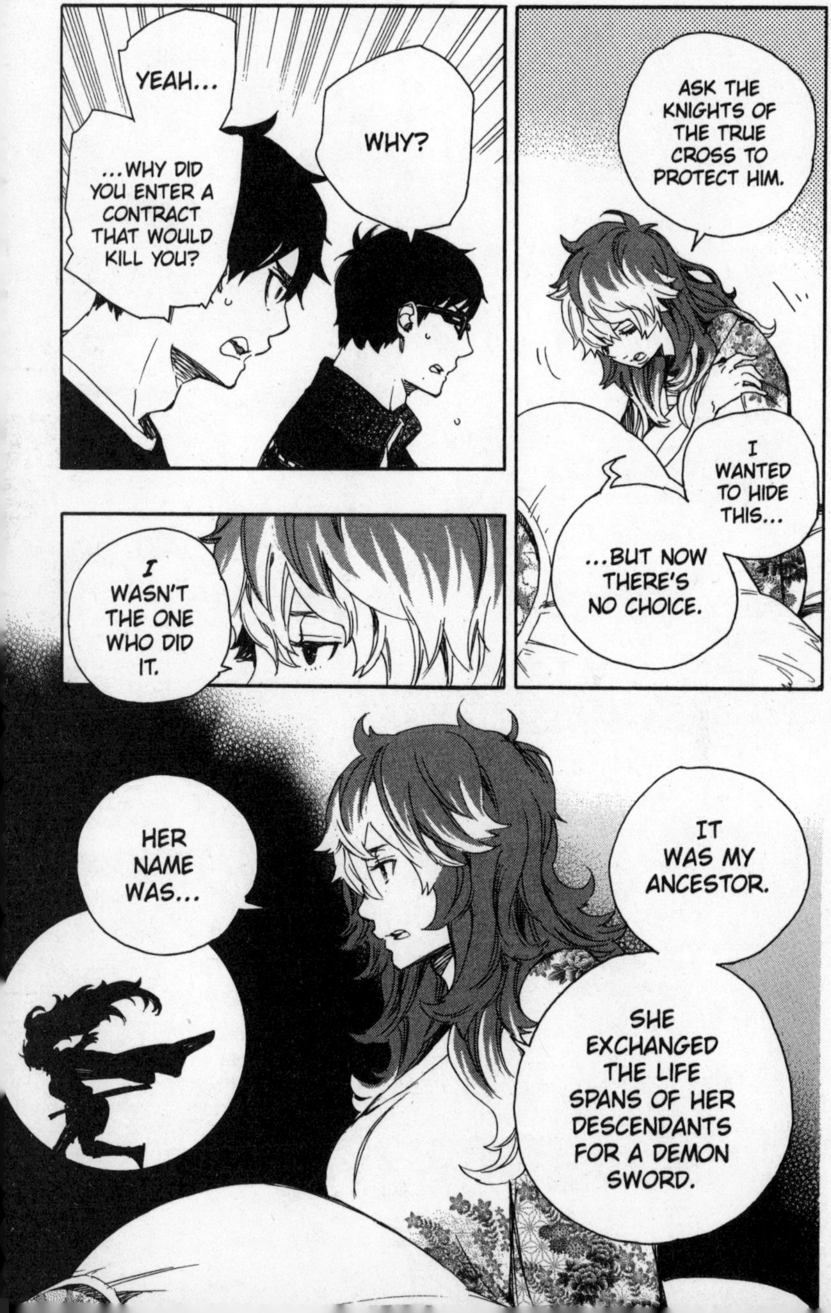
ASK THE KNIGHTS OF THE TRUE CROSS TO PROTECT HIM.
I WANTED TO HIDE THIS...
...BUT NOW THERE'S NO CHOICE.
YEAH...
...WHY DID YOU ENTER A CONTRACT THAT WOULD KILL YOU?
WHY?
I WASN'T THE ONE WHO DID IT.
IT WAS MY ANCESTOR.
SHE EXCHANGED THE LIFE SPANS OF HER DESCENDANTS FOR A DEMON SWORD.
HER NAME WAS...

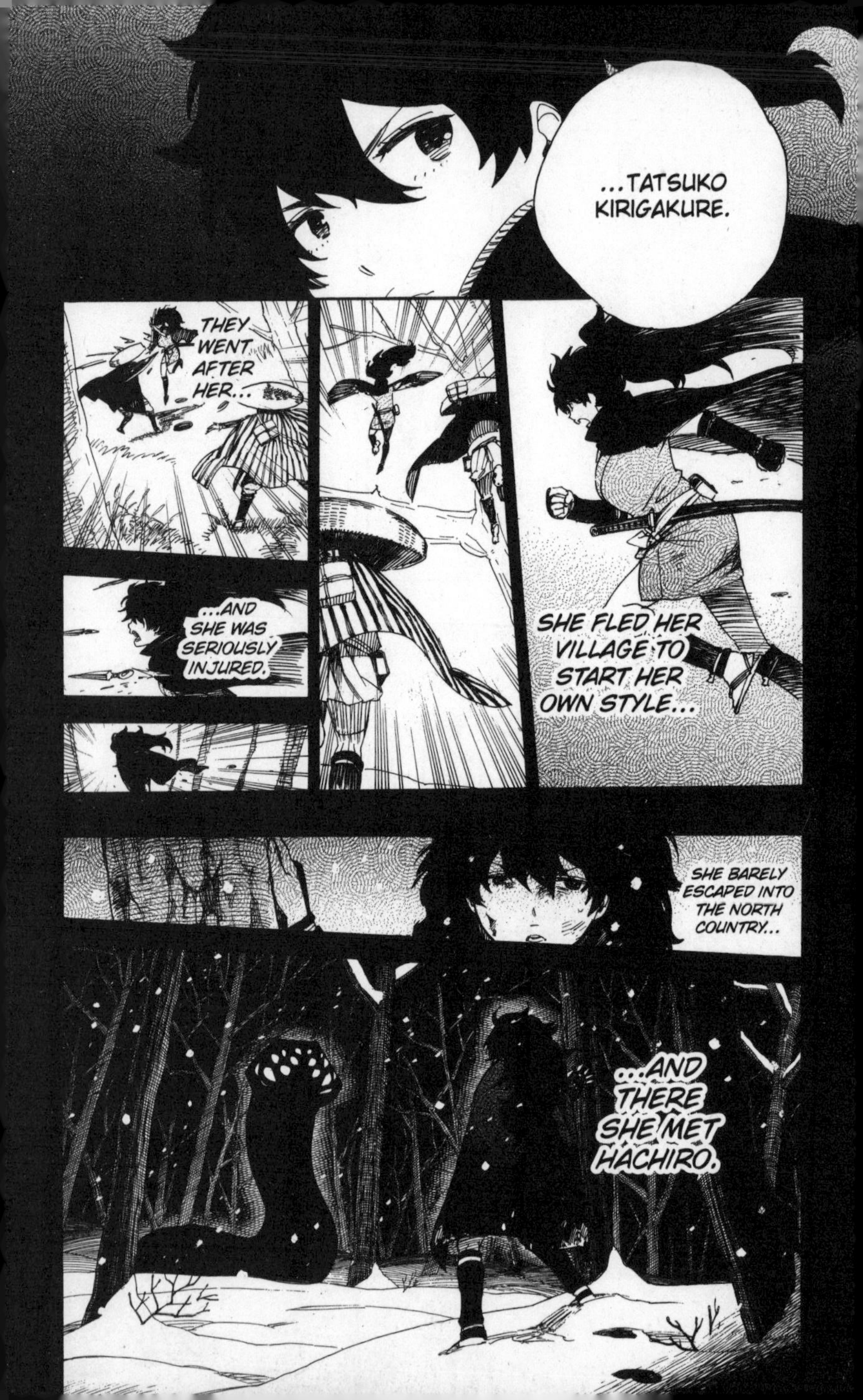
...TATSUKO KIRIGAKURE.
SHE FLED HER VILLAGE TO START HER OWN STYLE...
THEY WENT AFTER HER...
...AND SHE WAS SERIOUSLY INJURED.
SHE BARELY ESCAPED INTO THE NORTH COUNTRY...
...AND THERE SHE MET HACHIRO.

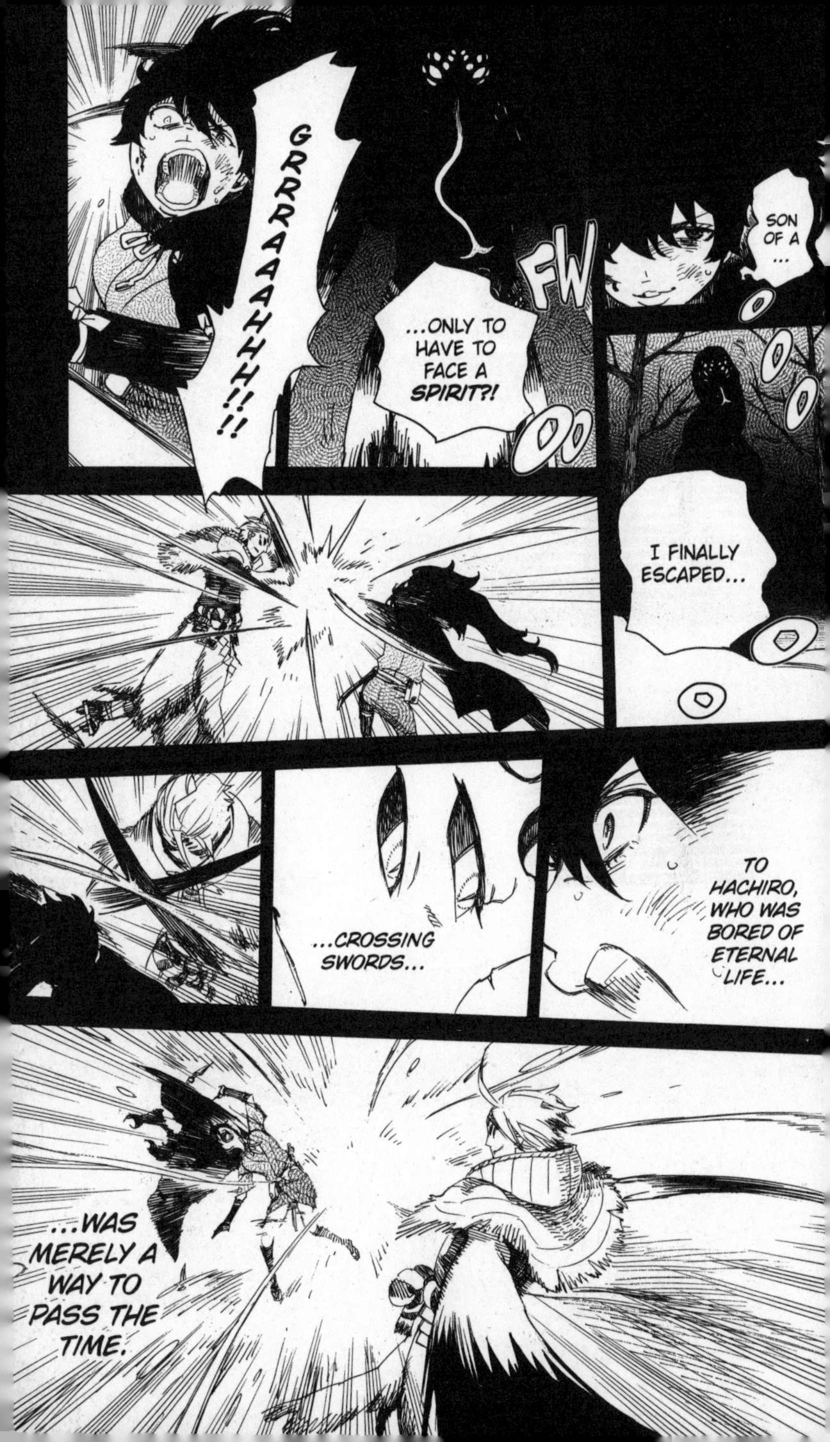
SON OF A ...
I FINALLY ESCAPED...
...ONLY TO HAVE TO FACE A SPIRIT?!
FW
GRRRAAAAHHHH!!!!
TO HACHIRO, WHO WAS BORED OF ETERNAL LIFE...
...CROSSING SWORDS...
...WAS MERELY A WAY TO PASS THE TIME.

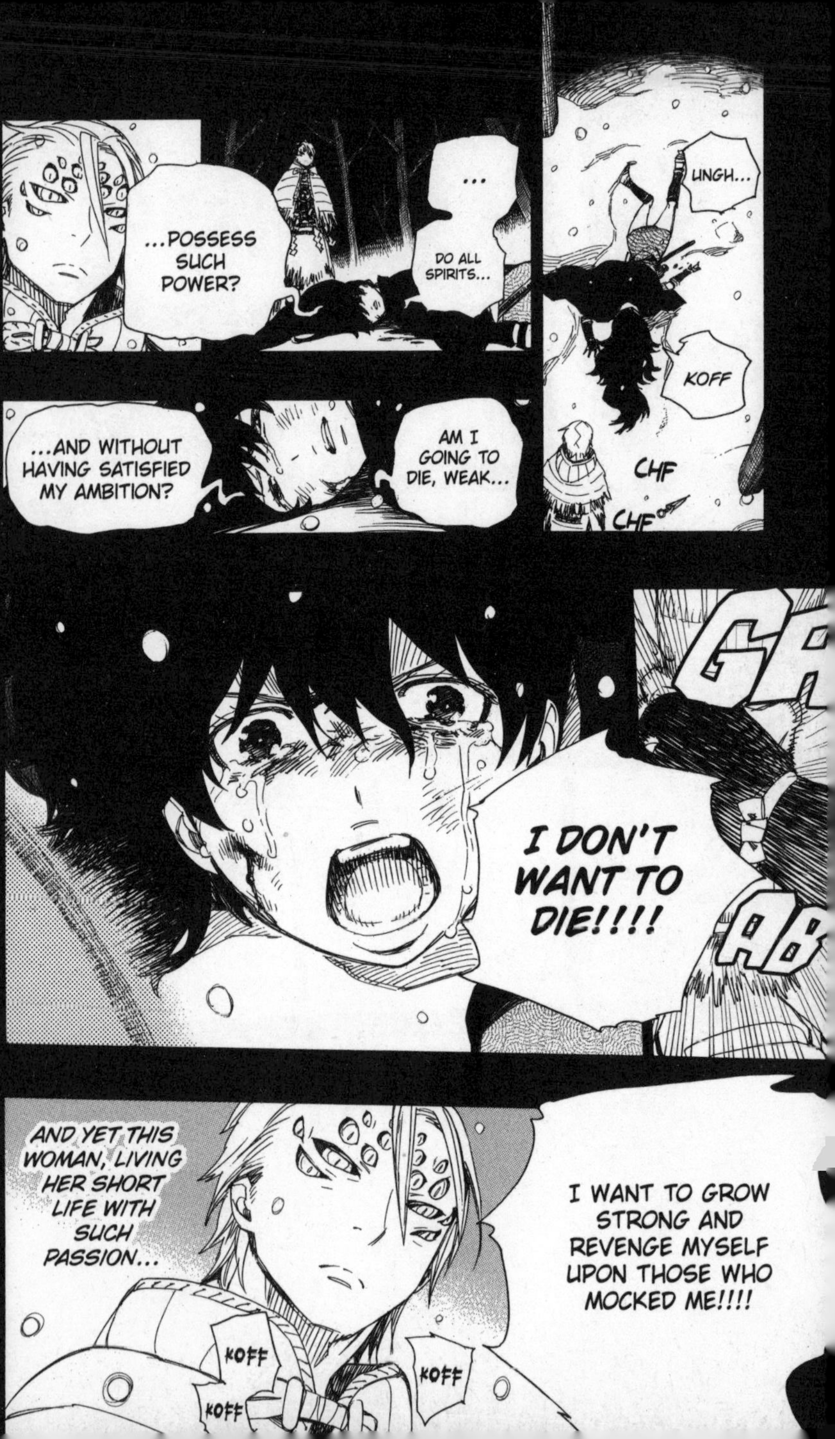
UNGH...
KOFF
CHF
CHF
...
DO ALL SPIRITS...
...POSSESS SUCH POWER?
AM I GOING TO DIE, WEAK...
...AND WITHOUT HAVING SATISFIED MY AMBITION?
I DON'T WANT TO DIE!!!!
I WANT TO GROW STRONG AND REVENGE MYSELF UPON THOSE WHO MOCKED ME!!!!
AND YET THIS WOMAN, LIVING HER SHORT LIFE WITH SUCH PASSION...
KOFF
KOFF
KOFF

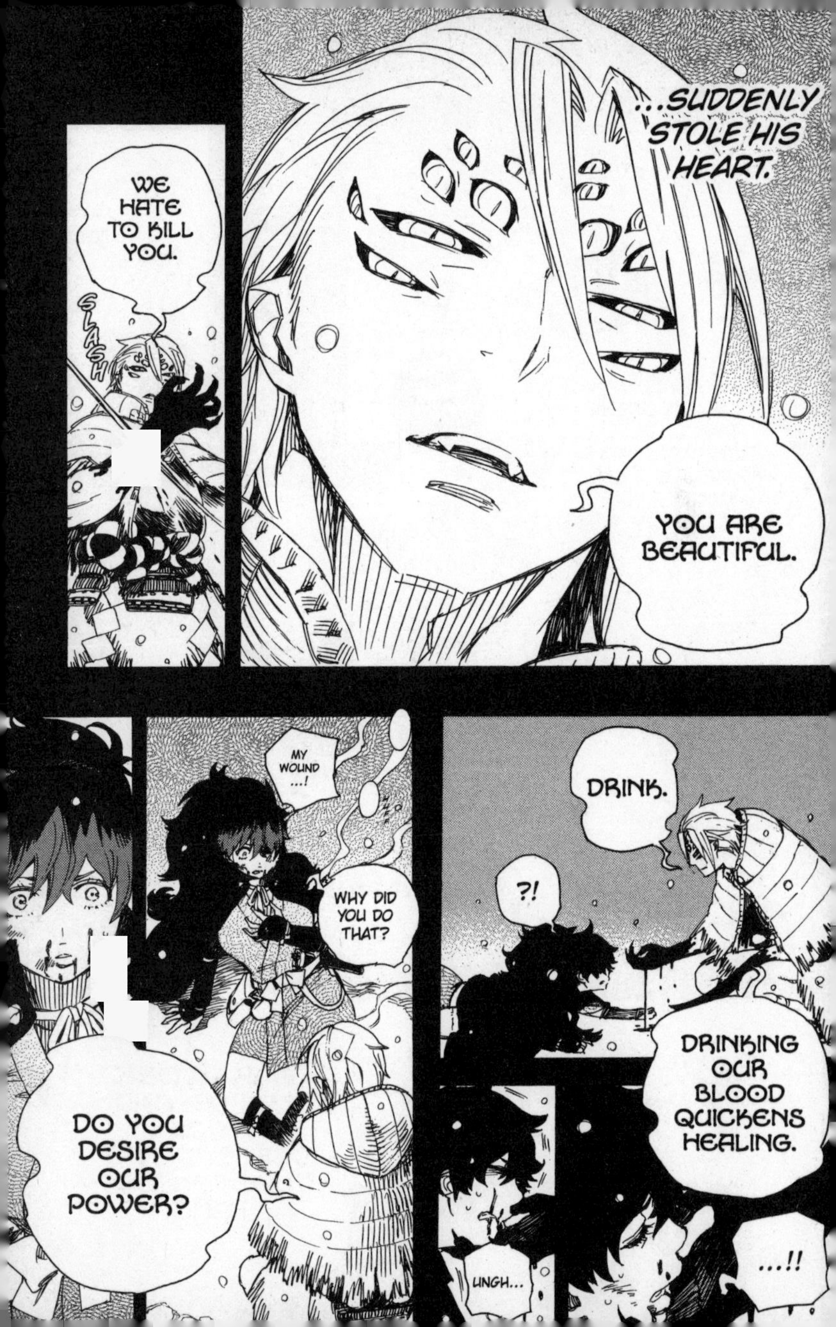
...SUDDENLY STOLE HIS HEART.
YOU ARE BEAUTIFUL.
WE HATE TO KILL YOU.
SLASH
DRINK.
?!
DRINKING OUR BLOOD QUICKENS HEALING.
...!!
UNGH...
MY WOUND ...!
WHY DID YOU DO THAT?
DO YOU DESIRE OUR POWER?

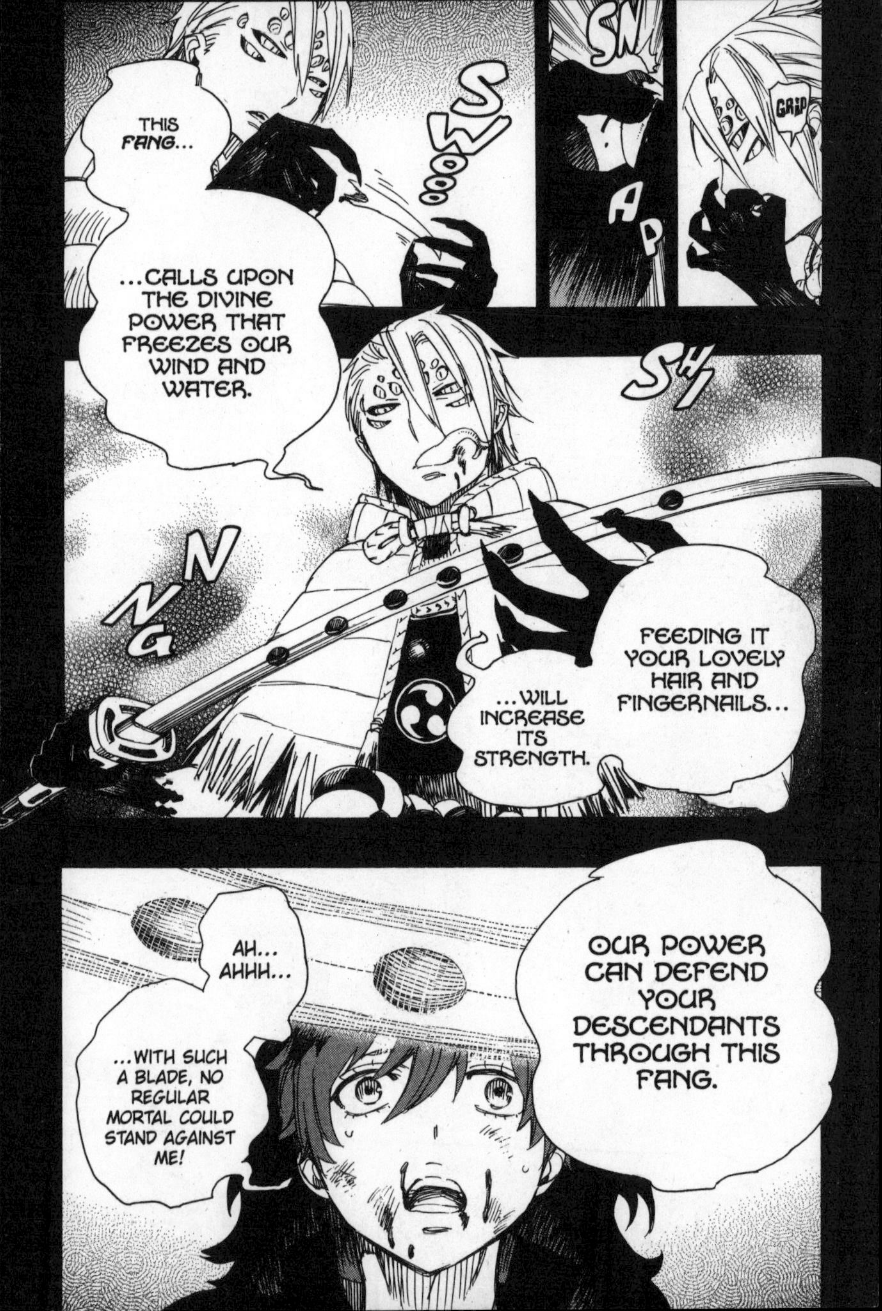
SNAP
GRIP
THIS FANG...
SWOOO
...CALLS UPON THE DIVINE POWER THAT FREEZES OUR WIND AND WATER.
SHI
FEEDING IT YOUR LOVELY HAIR AND FINGERNAILS...
...WILL INCREASE ITS STRENGTH.
NNG
OUR POWER CAN DEFEND YOUR DESCENDANTS THROUGH THIS FANG.
AH... AHHH...
...WITH SUCH A BLADE, NO REGULAR MORTAL COULD STAND AGAINST ME!

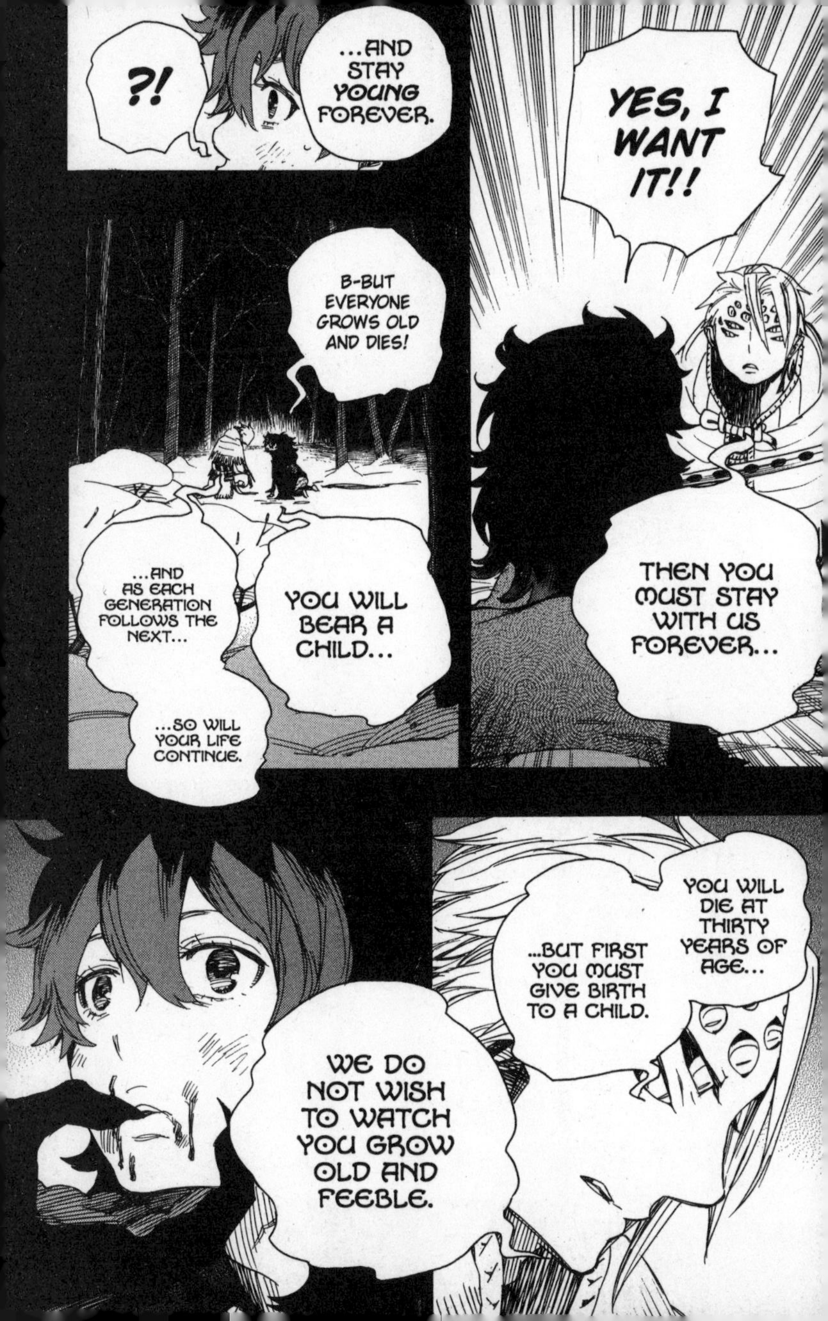
YES, I WANT IT!!
THEN YOU MUST STAY WITH US FOREVER...
...AND STAY YOUNG FOREVER.
?!
B-BUT EVERYONE GROWS OLD AND DIES!
YOU WILL BEAR A CHILD...
...AND AS EACH GENERATION FOLLOWS THE NEXT...
...SO WILL YOUR LIFE CONTINUE.
YOU WILL DIE AT THIRTY YEARS OF AGE...
...BUT FIRST YOU MUST GIVE BIRTH TO A CHILD.
WE DO NOT WISH TO WATCH YOU GROW OLD AND FEEBLE.

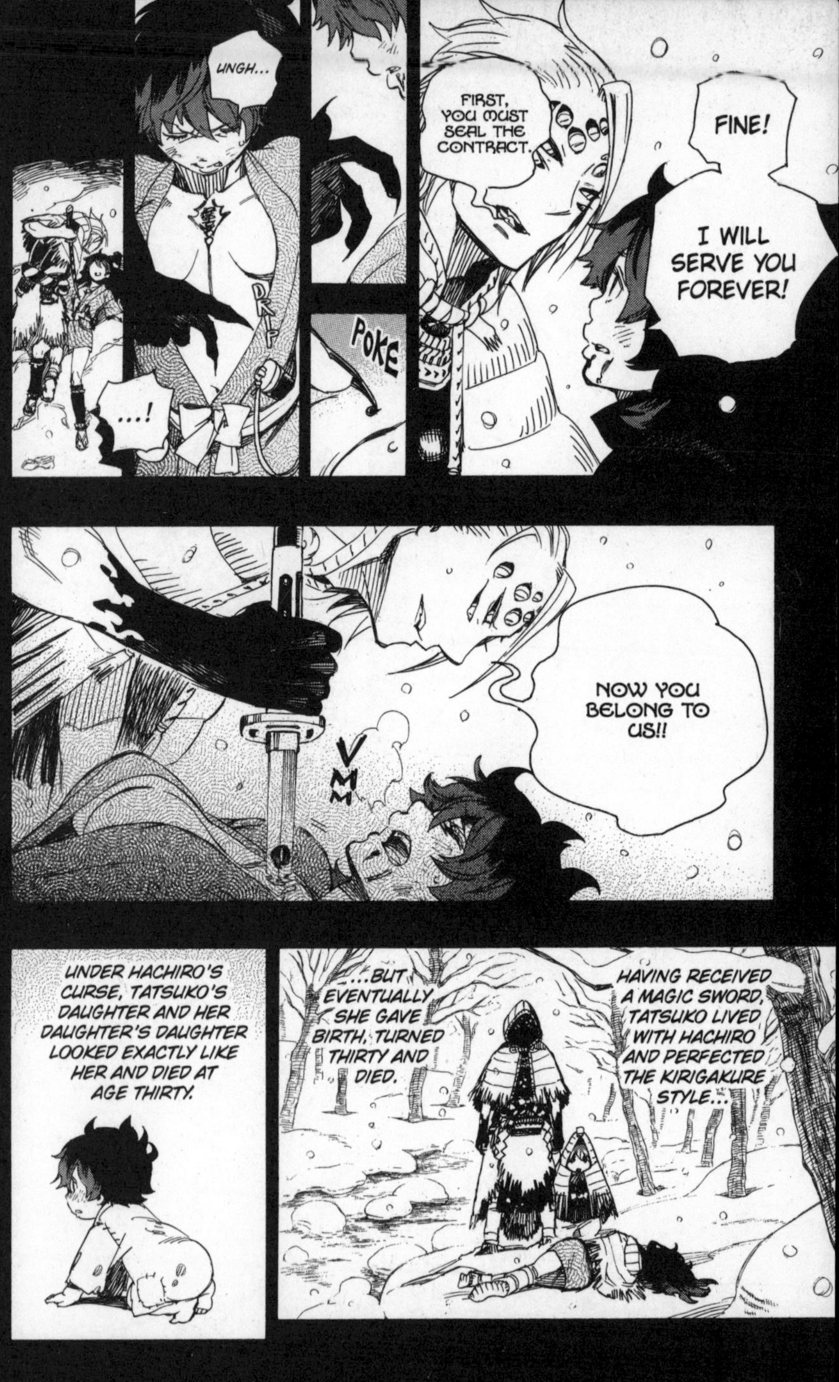
FINE!
I WILL SERVE YOU FOREVER!
FIRST, YOU MUST SEAL THE CONTRACT.
POKE
UNGH...
DRIP
...!
NOW YOU BELONG TO US!!
VMM
HAVING RECEIVED A MAGIC SWORD, TATSUKO LIVED WITH HACHIRO AND PERFECTED THE KIRIGAKURE STYLE...
...BUT EVENTUALLY SHE GAVE BIRTH, TURNED THIRTY AND DIED.
UNDER HACHIRO'S CURSE, TATSUKO'S DAUGHTER AND HER DAUGHTER'S DAUGHTER LOOKED EXACTLY LIKE HER AND DIED AT AGE THIRTY.

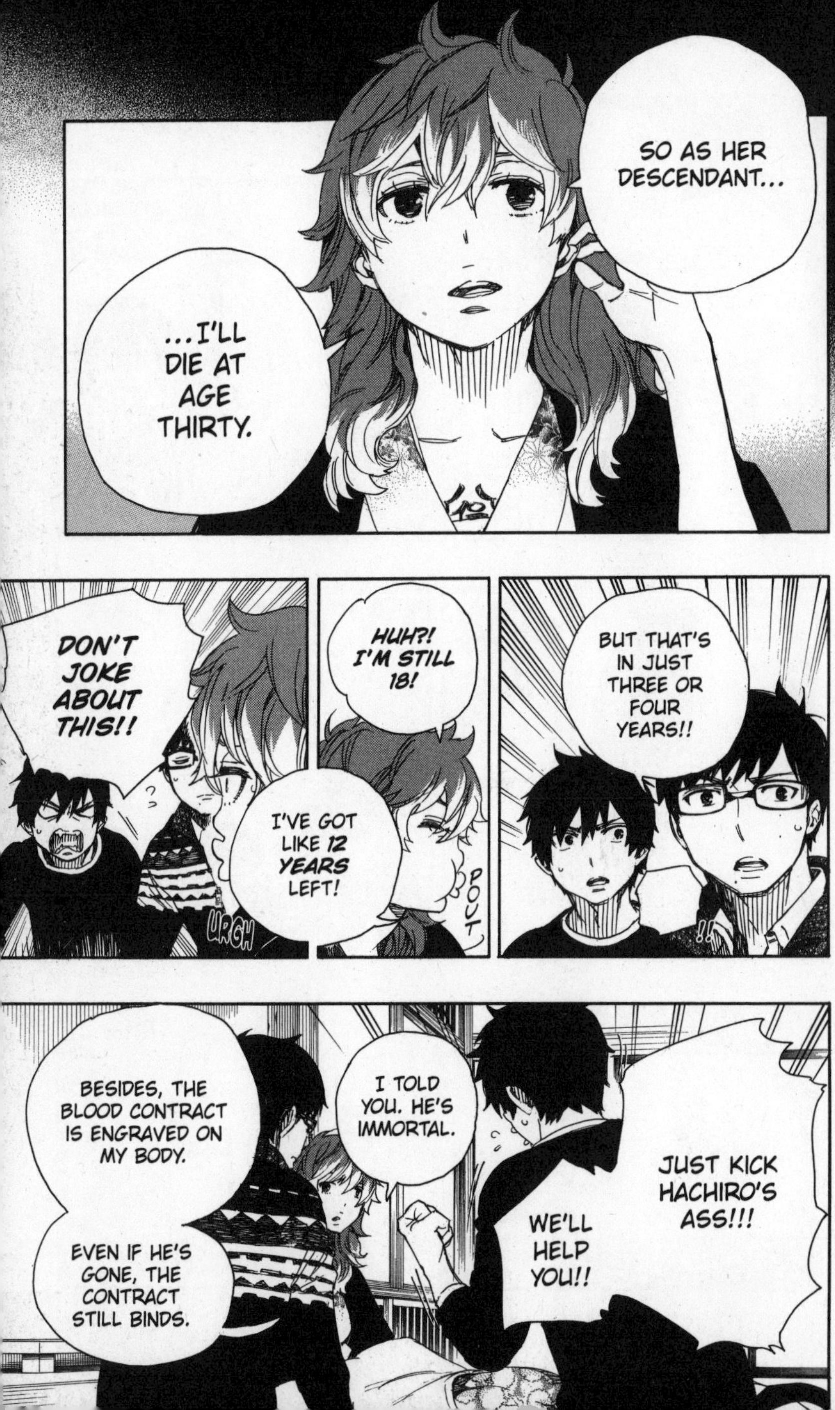
SO AS HER DESCENDANT...
...I'LL DIE AT AGE THIRTY.
BUT THAT'S IN JUST THREE OR FOUR YEARS!!
!!
HUH?! I'M STILL 18!
I'VE GOT LIKE **12 YEARS** LEFT!
POUT
DON'T JOKE ABOUT THIS!!
URGH
JUST KICK HACHIRO'S ASS!!!
WE'LL HELP YOU!!
I TOLD YOU. HE'S IMMORTAL.
BESIDES, THE BLOOD CONTRACT IS ENGRAVED ON MY BODY.
EVEN IF HE'S GONE, THE CONTRACT STILL BINDS.

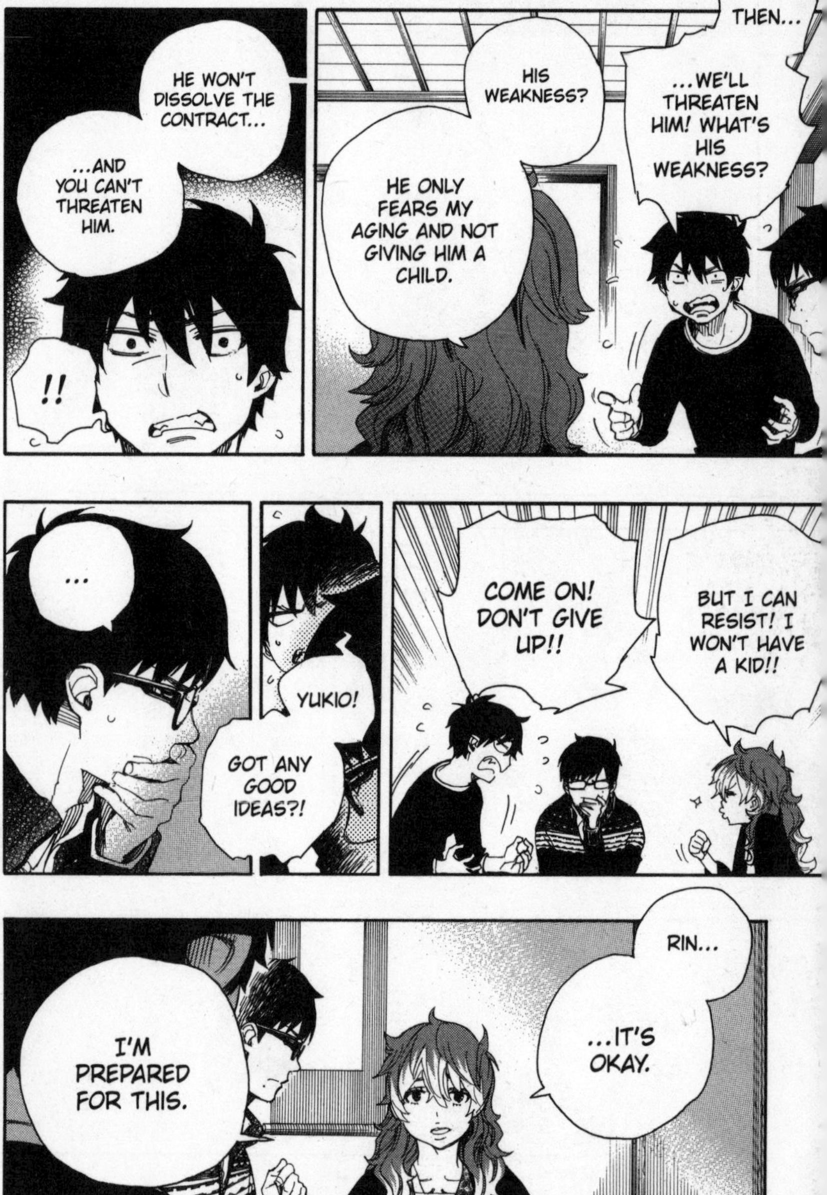
THEN...
...WE'LL THREATEN HIM! WHAT'S HIS WEAKNESS?
HIS WEAKNESS?
HE ONLY FEARS MY AGING AND NOT GIVING HIM A CHILD.
HE WON'T DISSOLVE THE CONTRACT...
...AND YOU CAN'T THREATEN HIM.
!!
BUT I CAN RESIST! I WON'T HAVE A KID!!
COME ON! DON'T GIVE UP!!
YUKIO!
GOT ANY GOOD IDEAS?!
...
RIN...
...IT'S OKAY.
I'M PREPARED FOR THIS.

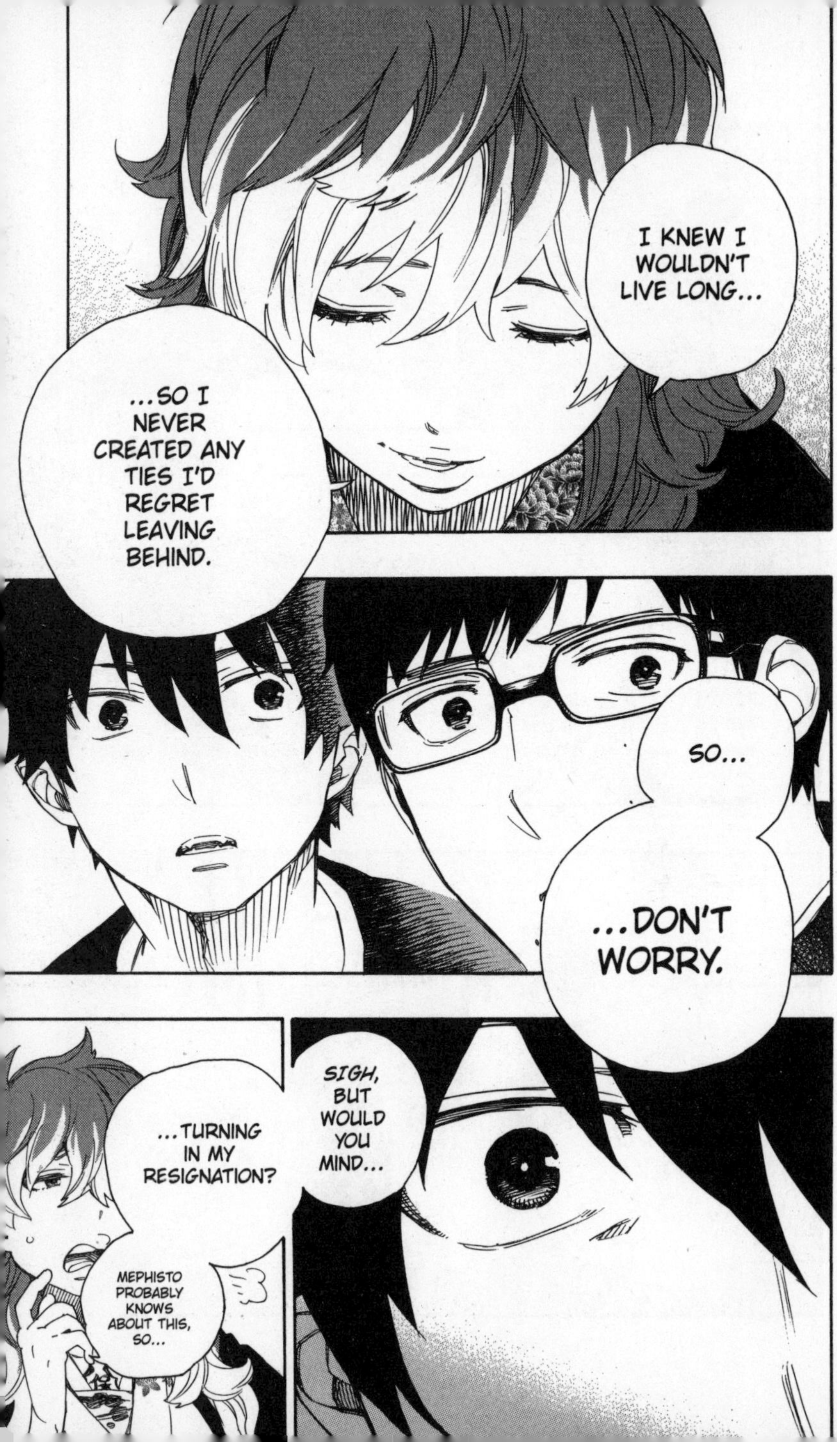
I KNEW I WOULDN'T LIVE LONG...
...SO I NEVER CREATED ANY TIES I'D REGRET LEAVING BEHIND.
SO...
...DON'T WORRY.
SIGH, BUT WOULD YOU MIND...
...TURNING IN MY RESIGNATION?
MEPHISTO PROBABLY KNOWS ABOUT THIS, SO...

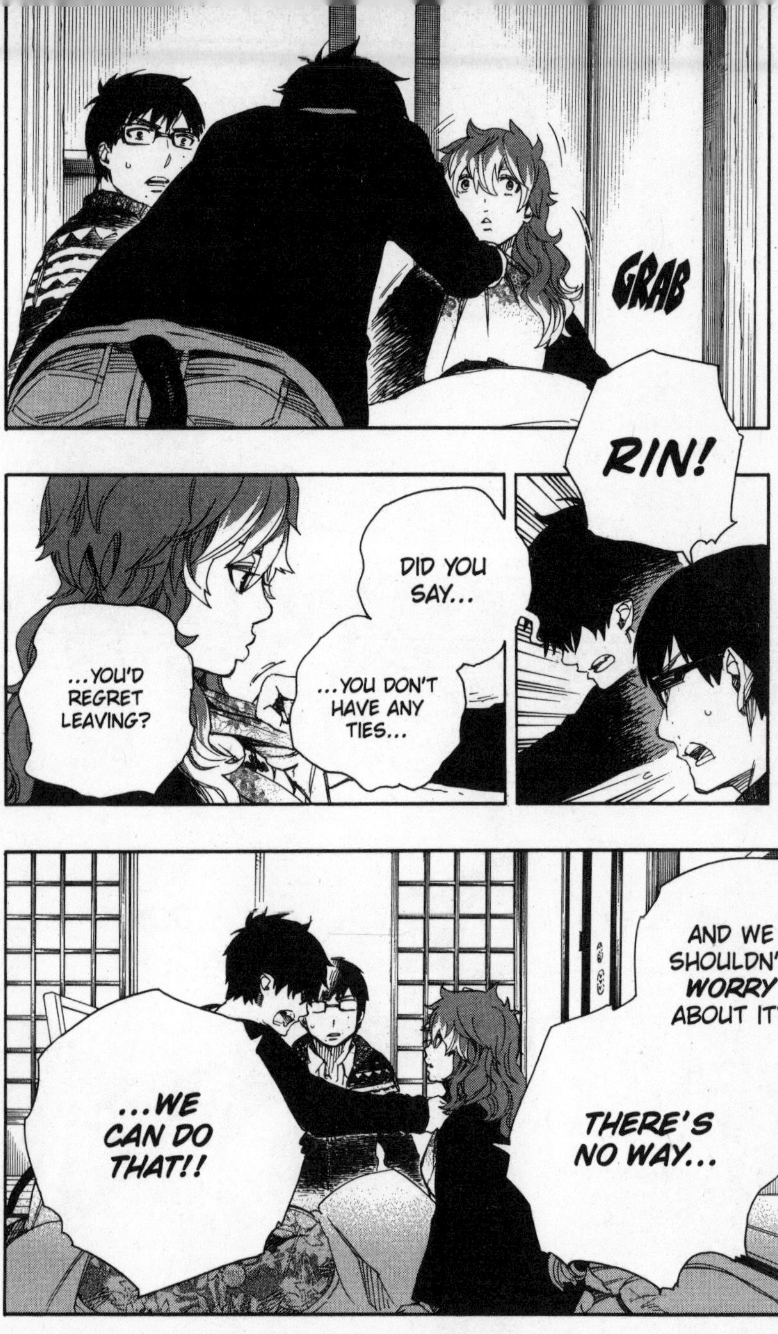
GRAB
RIN!
DID YOU SAY...
...YOU DON'T HAVE ANY TIES...
...YOU'D REGRET LEAVING?
AND WE SHOULDN'T WORRY ABOUT IT?
THERE'S NO WAY...
...WE CAN DO THAT!!

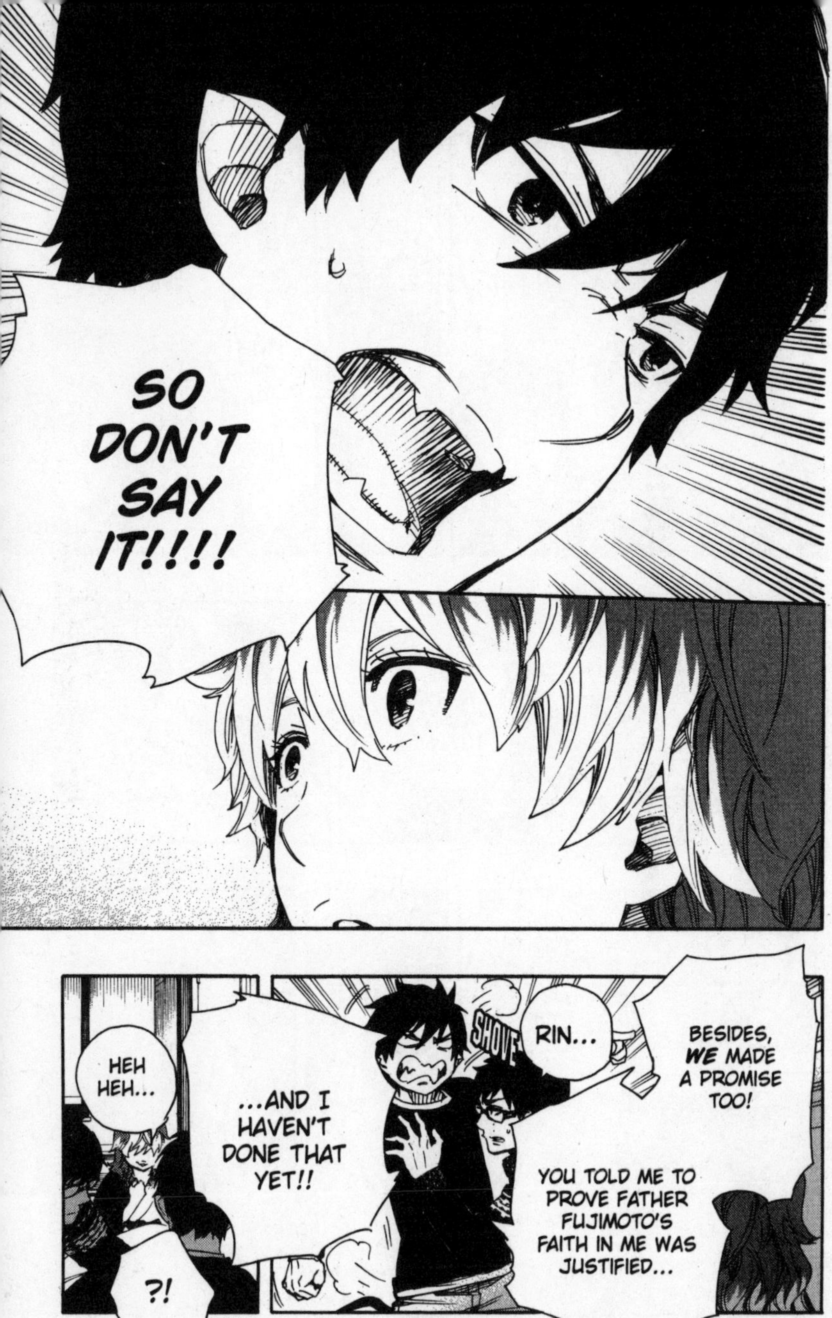
SO DON'T SAY IT!!!!
BESIDES, WE MADE A PROMISE TOO!
RIN...
SHOVE
YOU TOLD ME TO PROVE FATHER FUJIMOTO'S FAITH IN ME WAS JUSTIFIED...
...AND I HAVEN'T DONE THAT YET!!
HEH HEH...
?!

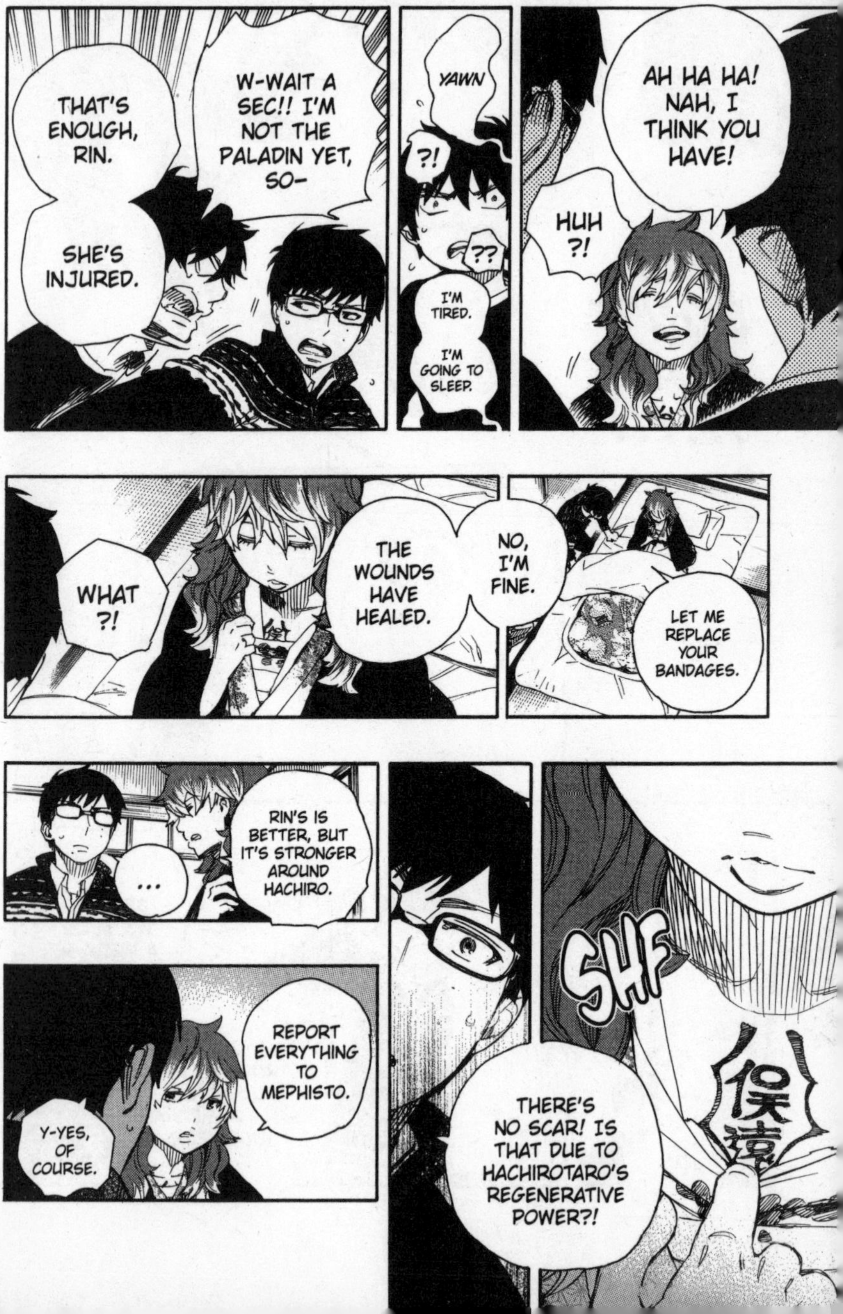
AH HA HA! NAH, I THINK YOU HAVE!
HUH ?!
YAWN
?!
??
I'M TIRED.
I'M GOING TO SLEEP.
W-WAIT A SEC!! I'M NOT THE PALADIN YET, SO-
THAT'S ENOUGH, RIN.
SHE'S INJURED.
LET ME REPLACE YOUR BANDAGES.
NO, I'M FINE.
THE WOUNDS HAVE HEALED.
WHAT ?!
SHF
THERE'S NO SCAR! IS THAT DUE TO HACHIROTARO'S REGENERATIVE POWER?!
RIN'S IS BETTER, BUT IT'S STRONGER AROUND HACHIRO.
...
REPORT EVERYTHING TO MEPHISTO.
Y-YES, OF COURSE.

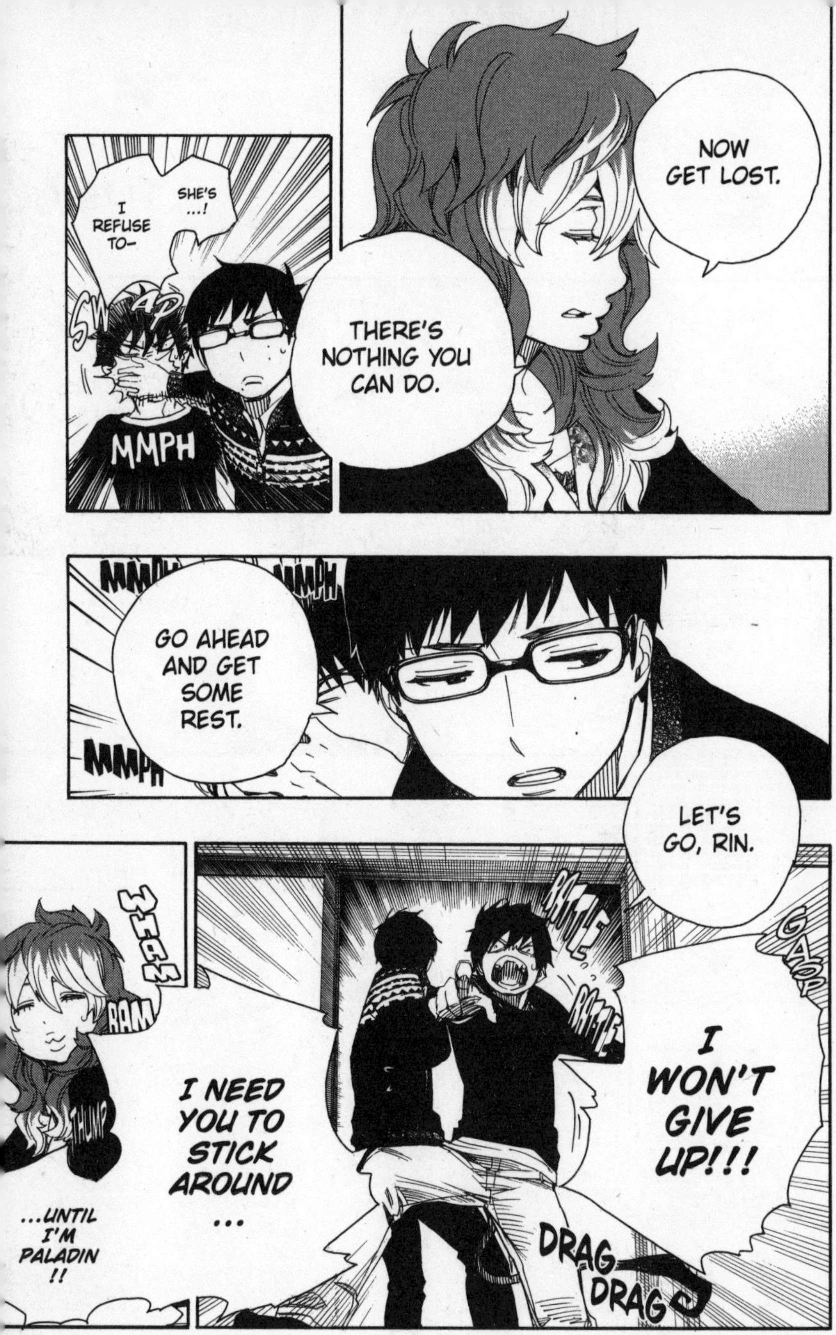
NOW GET LOST.
THERE'S NOTHING YOU CAN DO.
SHE'S ...!
I REFUSE TO—
SWAP
MMPH
MMPH
MMPH
GO AHEAD AND GET SOME REST.
MMPH
LET'S GO, RIN.
GASP
I WON'T GIVE UP!!!
RATTLE
RATTLE
DRAG
DRAG
I NEED YOU TO STICK AROUND ...
WHAM
BAM
THUMP
...UNTIL I'M PALADIN !!

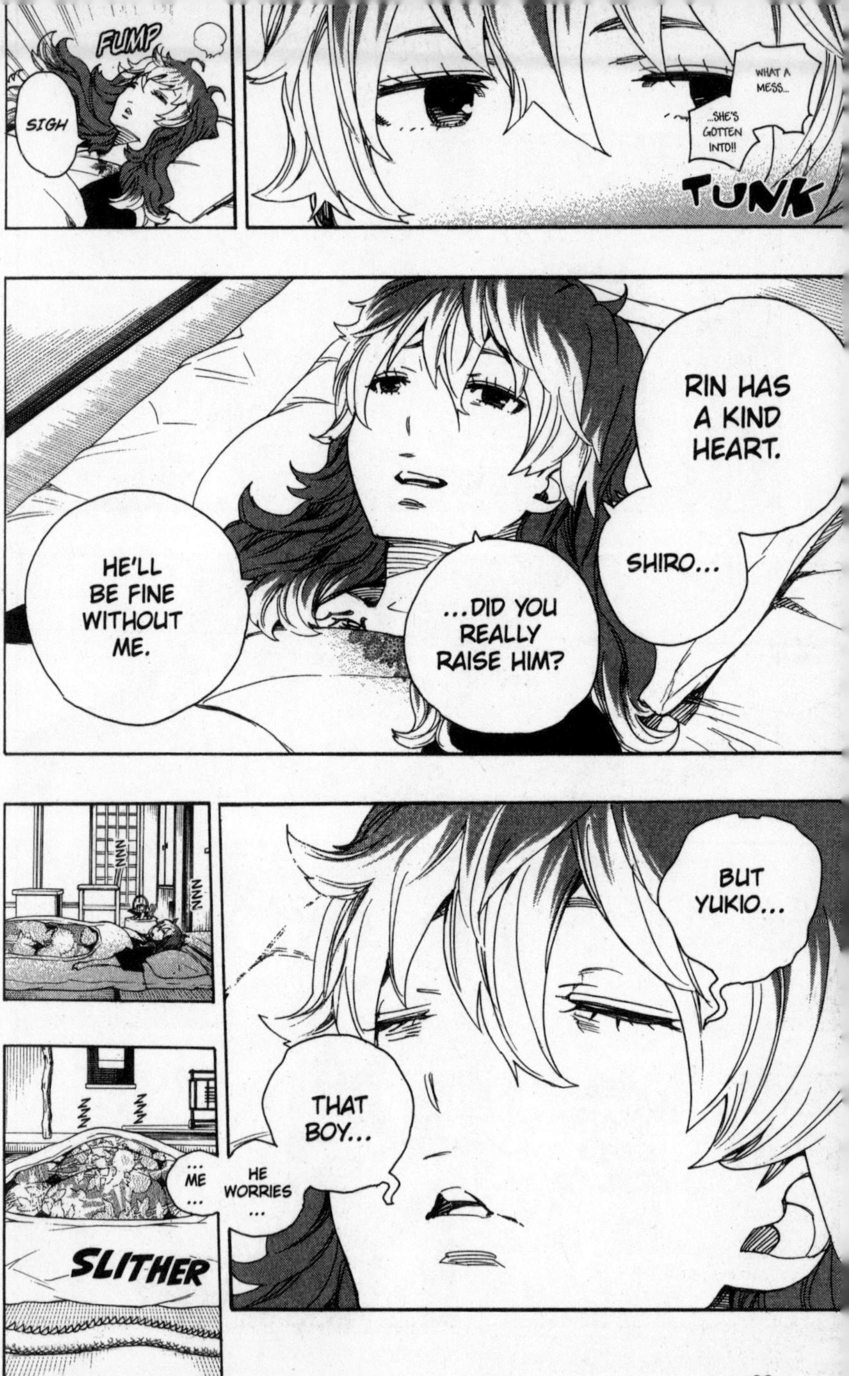
WHAT A MESS...
...SHE'S GOTTEN INTO!!
TUNK
FUMP
SIGH
RIN HAS A KIND HEART.
SHIRO...
...DID YOU REALLY RAISE HIM?
HE'LL BE FINE WITHOUT ME.
BUT YUKIO...
THAT BOY...
HE WORRIES ...
... ME ...
ZZZ
ZZZ
ZZZ
ZZZ
SLITHER

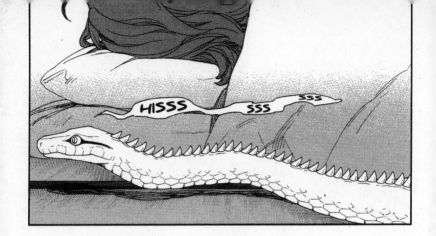

HISSS SSS SSS

ARRRGH! SHURA'S GONNA DIE!

WHAT CAN WE DO?!

YES.

ALL RIGHT, THANK YOU.

I CONTACTED SIR PHELES.

BIP

BIP

REINFORCEMENTS WILL ARRIVE LATER TONIGHT.

DID HE SAY ANYTHING ABOUT SHURA?

HE SAID, "AW, YOU GUYS'LL HANDLE IT! ☆"

I HATE THAT GUY!!!!

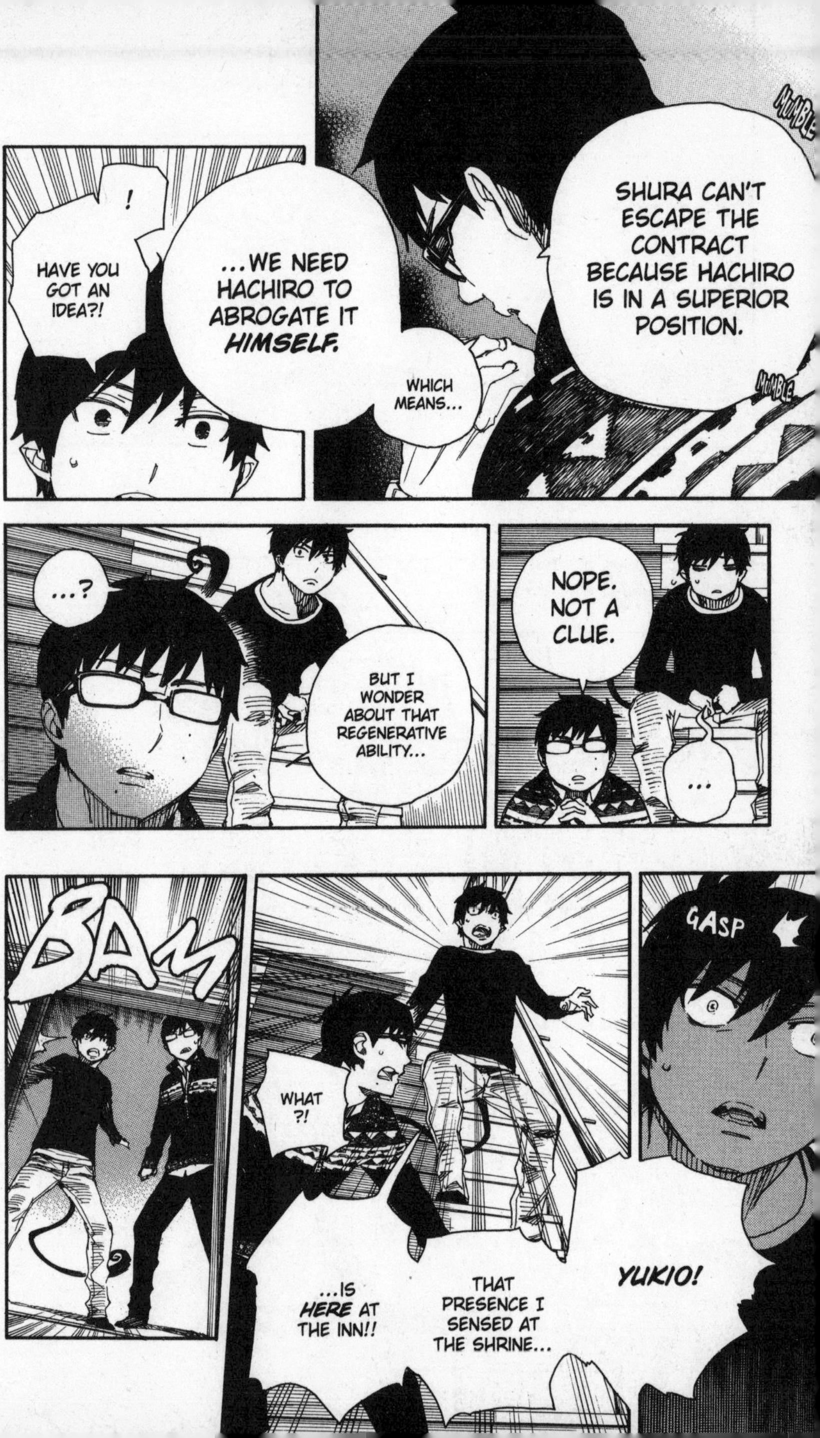
MUMBLE
SHURA CAN'T ESCAPE THE CONTRACT BECAUSE HACHIRO IS IN A SUPERIOR POSITION.
MUMBLE
WHICH MEANS...
...WE NEED HACHIRO TO ABROGATE IT *HIMSELF.*
!
HAVE YOU GOT AN IDEA?!
NOPE. NOT A CLUE.
...
...?
BUT I WONDER ABOUT THAT REGENERATIVE ABILITY...
GASP
YUKIO!
THAT PRESENCE I SENSED AT THE SHRINE...
...IS *HERE* AT THE INN!!
WHAT ?!
BAM

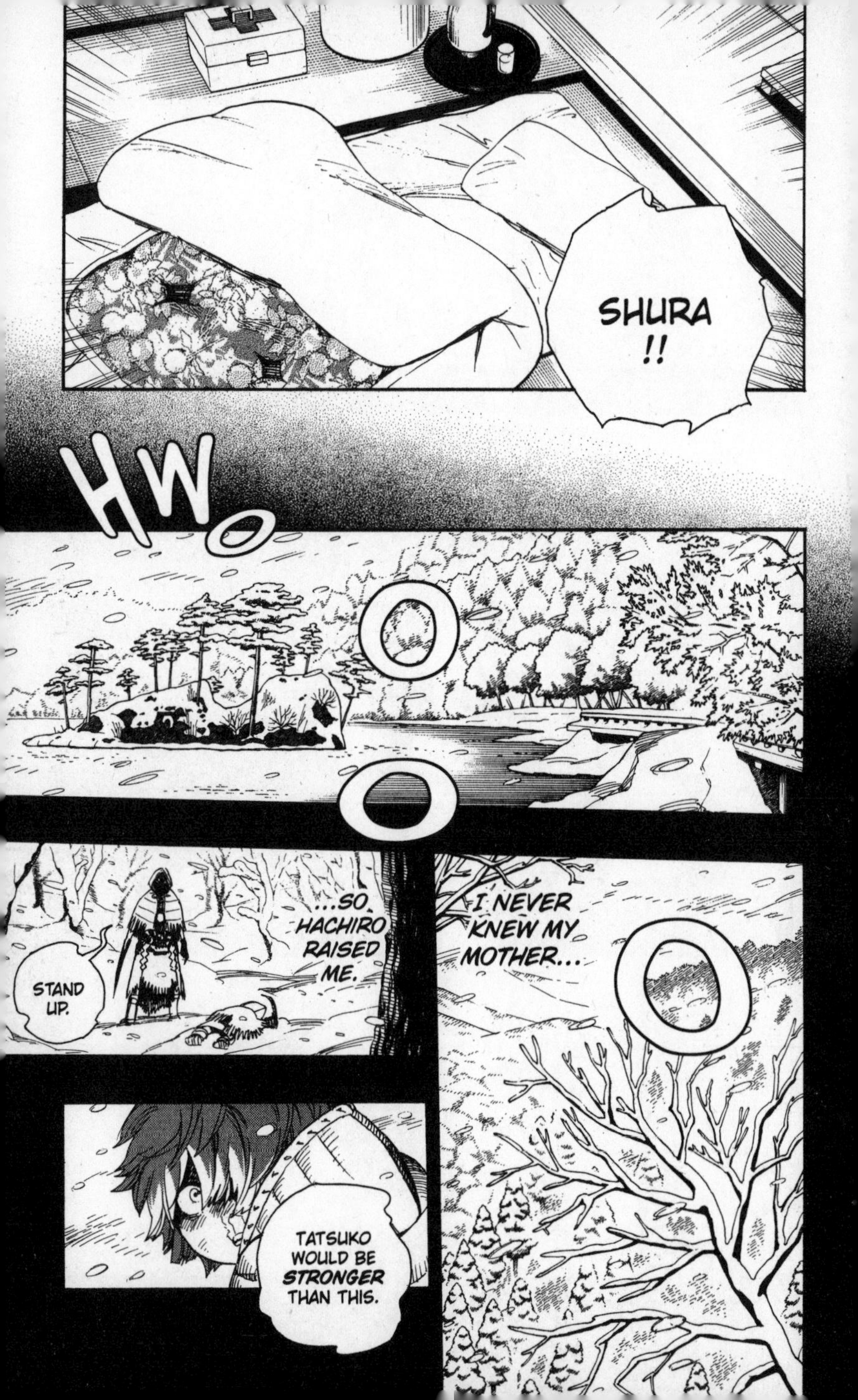
SHURA !!
HWOOOO
I NEVER KNEW MY MOTHER...
...SO HACHIRO RAISED ME.
STAND UP.
TATSUKO WOULD BE STRONGER THAN THIS.

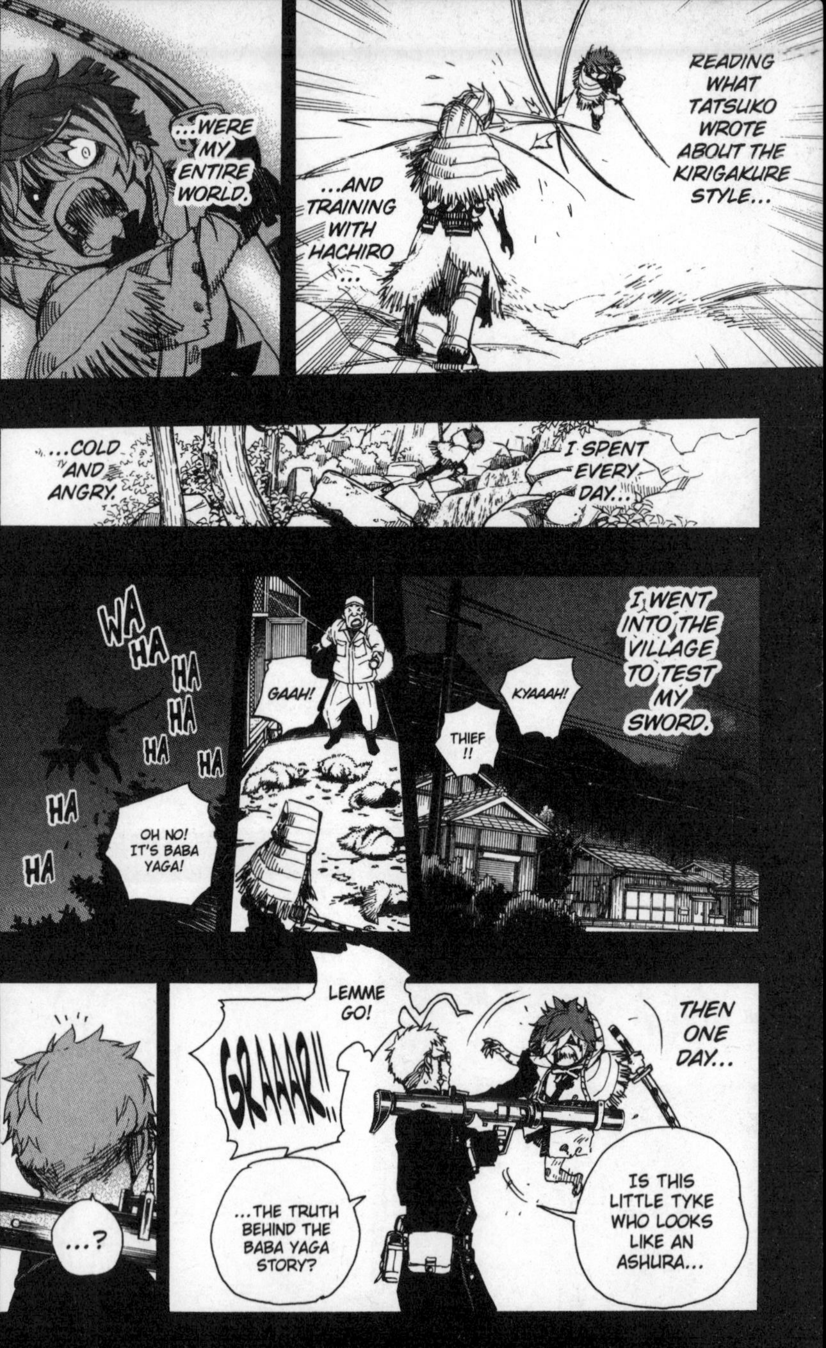
READING WHAT TATSUKO WROTE ABOUT THE KIRIGAKURE STYLE...
...AND TRAINING WITH HACHIRO...
...WERE MY ENTIRE WORLD.
I SPENT EVERY DAY...
...COLD AND ANGRY.
I WENT INTO THE VILLAGE TO TEST MY SWORD.
KYAAAH!
THIEF!!
GAAH!
WA HA HA HA HA HA HA HA
OH NO! IT'S BABA YAGA!
THEN ONE DAY...
LEMME GO!
GRAAAR!!
IS THIS LITTLE TYKE WHO LOOKS LIKE AN ASHURA...
...THE TRUTH BEHIND THE BABA YAGA STORY?
...?

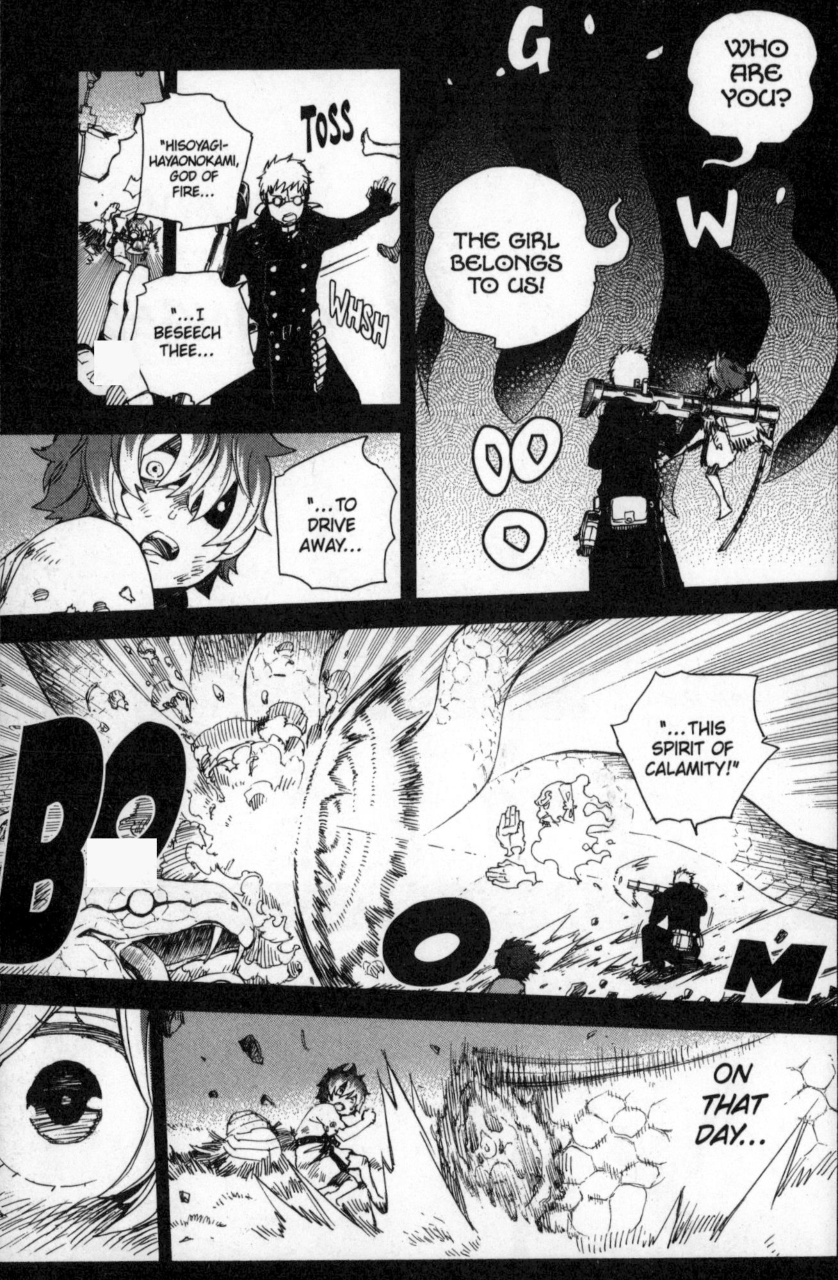
G
WHO ARE YOU?
W
THE GIRL BELONGS TO US!
OOO
"HISOYAGI-HAYAONOKAMI, GOD OF FIRE...
TOSS
"...I BESEECH THEE...
WHSH
"...TO DRIVE AWAY...
"...THIS SPIRIT OF CALAMITY!"
BOOM
ON THAT DAY...

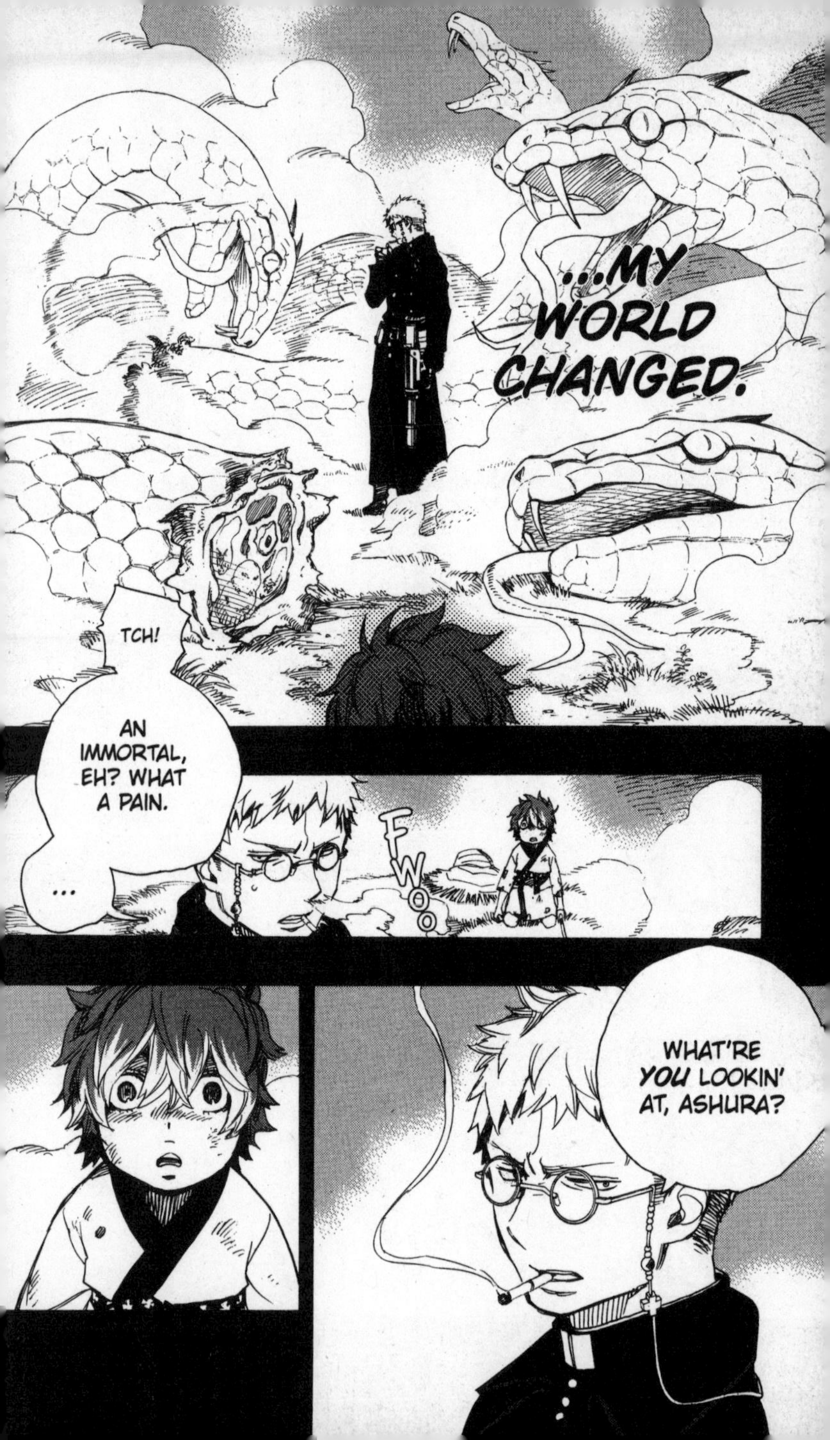
...MY WORLD CHANGED.
TCH!
AN IMMORTAL, EH? WHAT A PAIN.
FWOO
...
WHAT'RE *YOU* LOOKIN' AT, ASHURA?

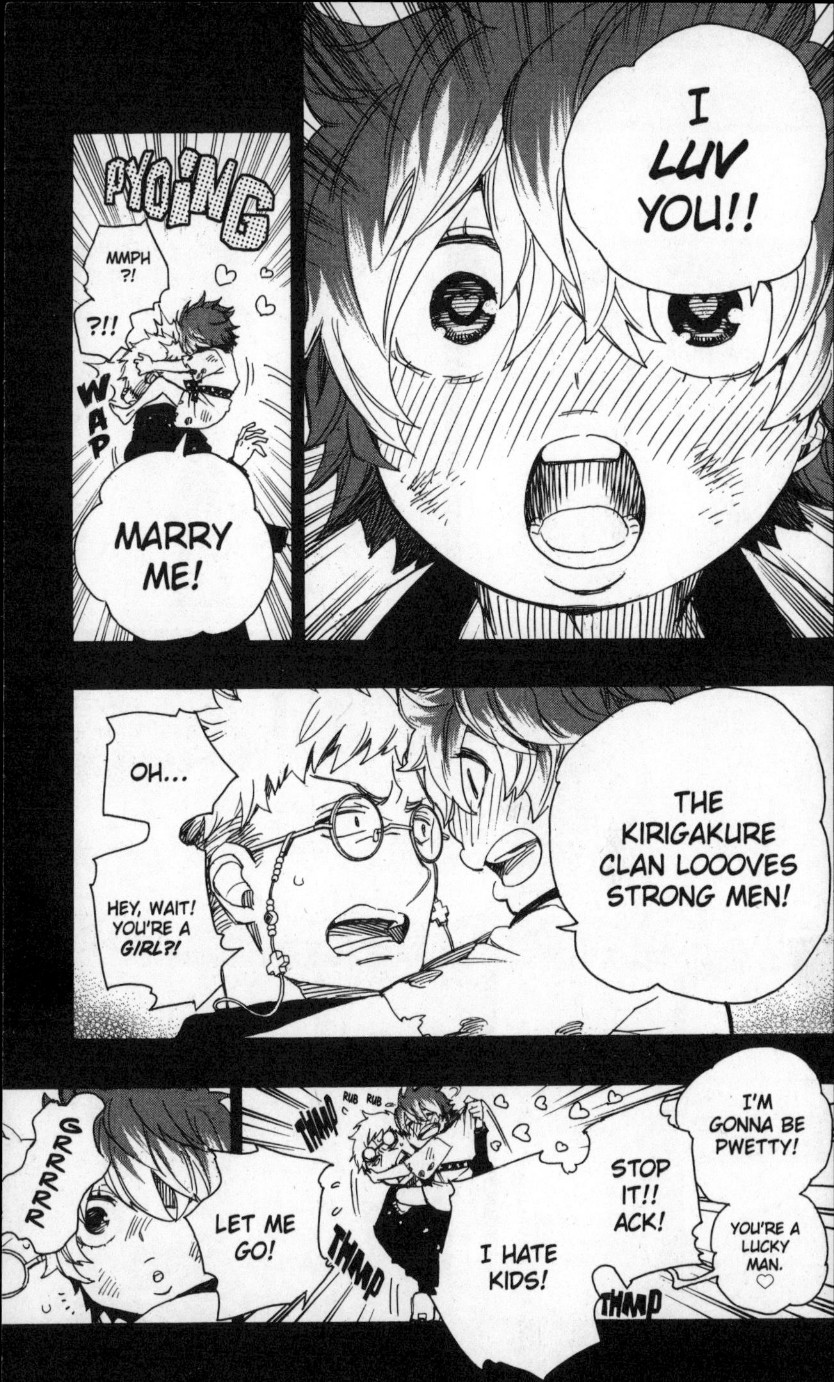
I LUV YOU!!
PYOING
MMPH ?!
?!!
WAP
MARRY ME!
THE KIRIGAKURE CLAN LOOOVES STRONG MEN!
OH...
HEY, WAIT! YOU'RE A GIRL?!
I'M GONNA BE PWETTY!
YOU'RE A LUCKY MAN. ♡
STOP IT!! ACK!
RUB RUB
THMP
THMP
I HATE KIDS!
THMP
LET ME GO!
GRRRRR

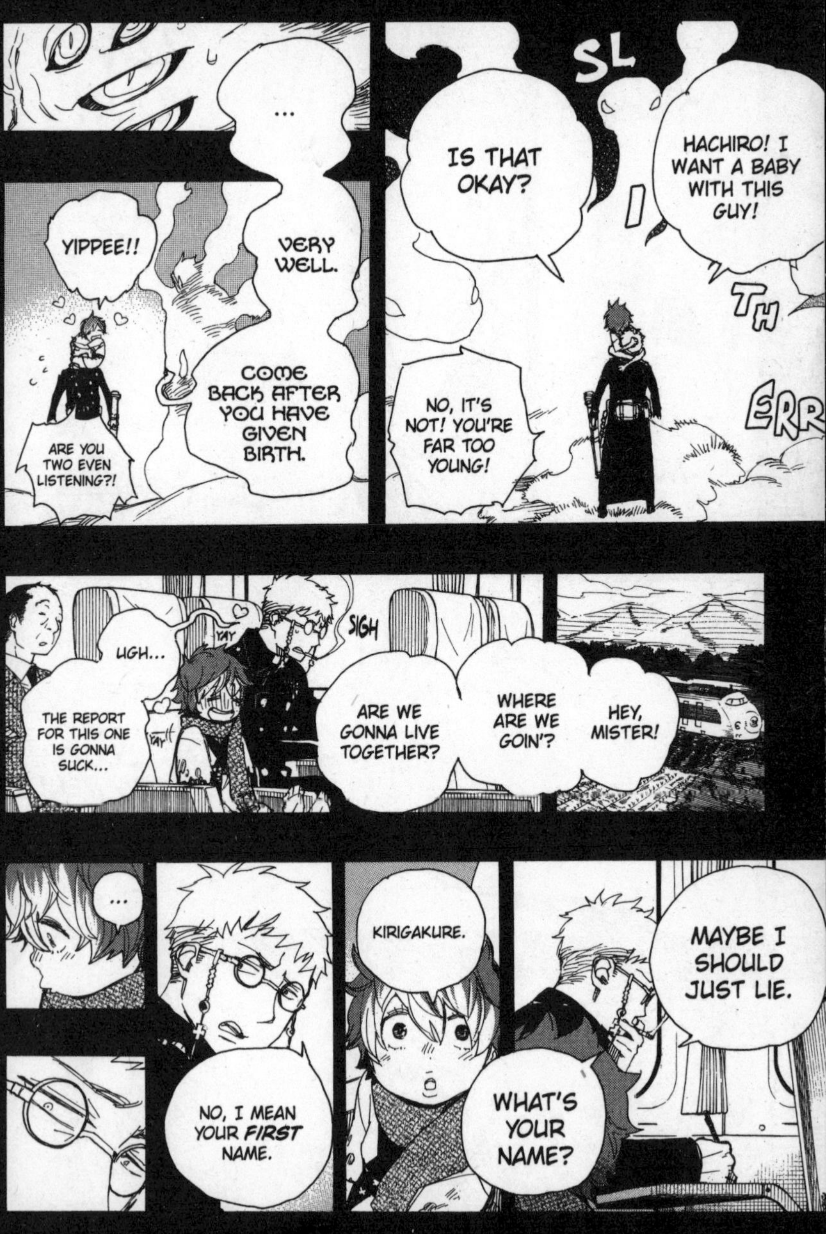
HACHIRO! I WANT A BABY WITH THIS GUY!
SL
I
TH
ERR
IS THAT OKAY?
NO, IT'S NOT! YOU'RE FAR TOO YOUNG!
...
VERY WELL.
COME BACK AFTER YOU HAVE GIVEN BIRTH.
YIPPEE!!
ARE YOU TWO EVEN LISTENING?!
HEY, MISTER!
WHERE ARE WE GOIN'?
ARE WE GONNA LIVE TOGETHER?
SIGH
YAY
UGH...
THE REPORT FOR THIS ONE IS GONNA SUCK...
YAY
MAYBE I SHOULD JUST LIE.
WHAT'S YOUR NAME?
KIRIGAKURE.
NO, I MEAN YOUR *FIRST* NAME.
...

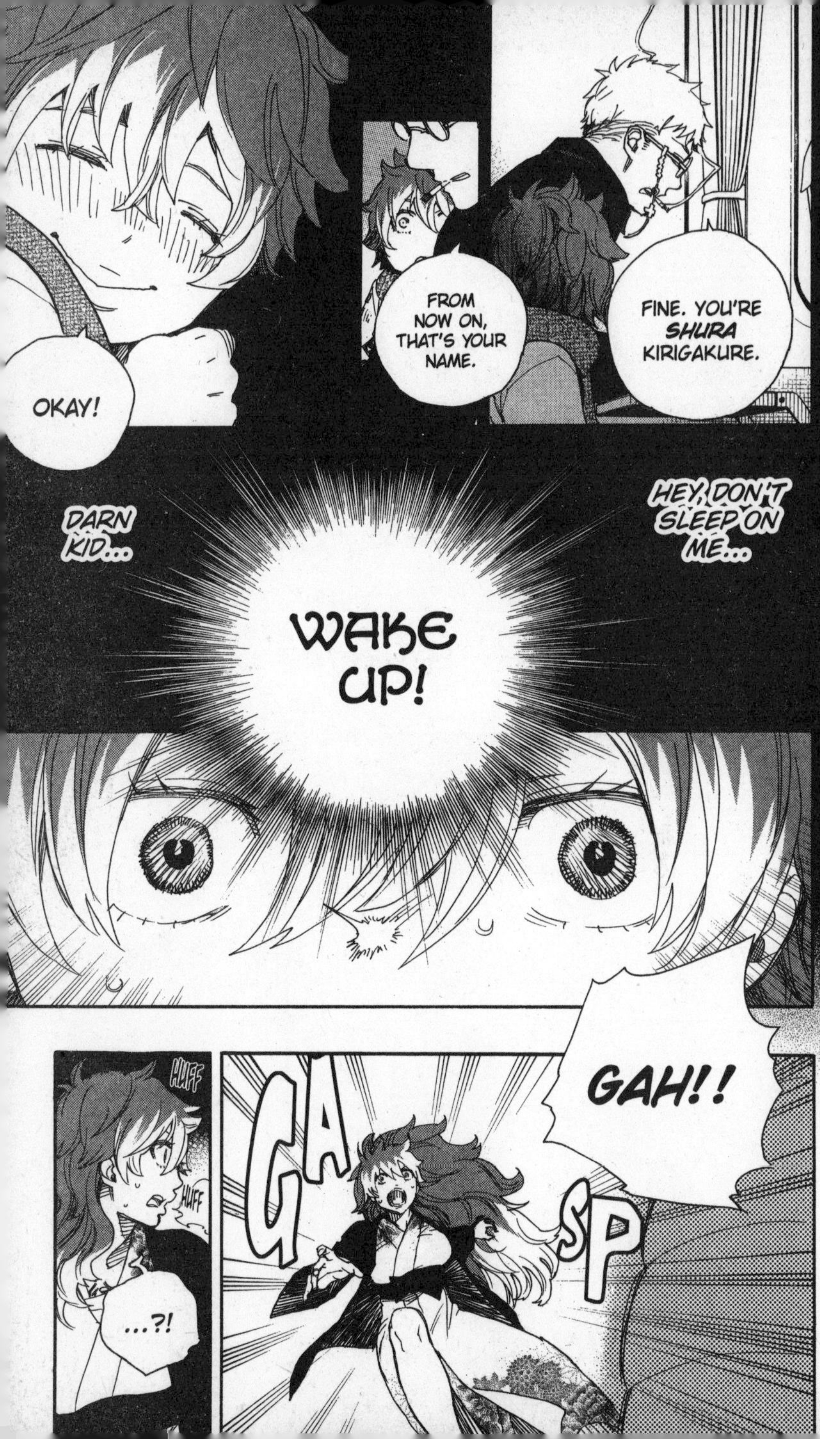
FINE. YOU'RE SHURA KIRIGAKURE.
FROM NOW ON, THAT'S YOUR NAME.
OKAY!
HEY, DON'T SLEEP ON ME...
DARN KID...
WAKE UP!
GAH!!
GASP
HUFF
HUFF
...?!

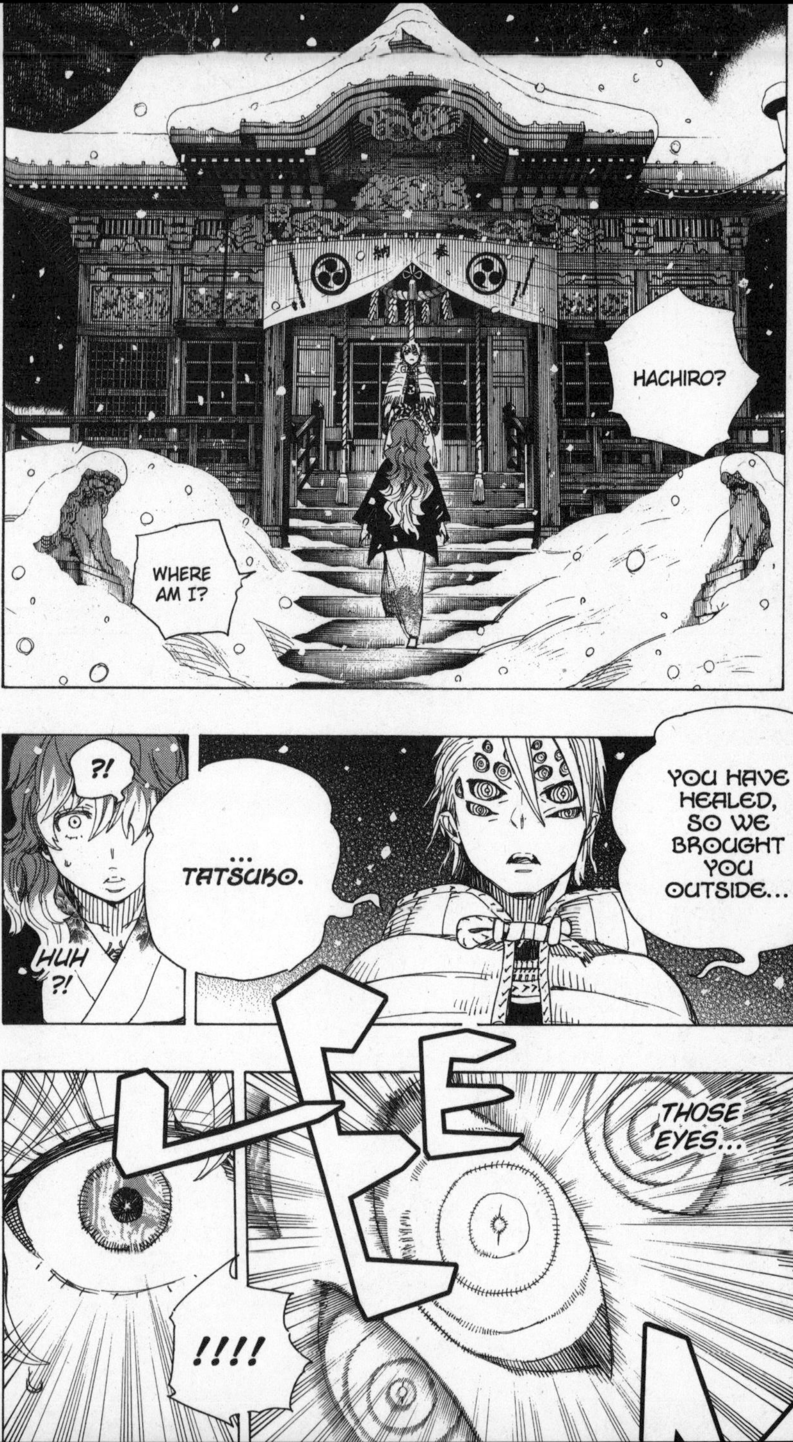
HACHIRO?
WHERE AM I?
YOU HAVE HEALED, SO WE BROUGHT YOU OUTSIDE...
... TATSUKO.
?!
HUH ?!
THOSE EYES...
!!!!

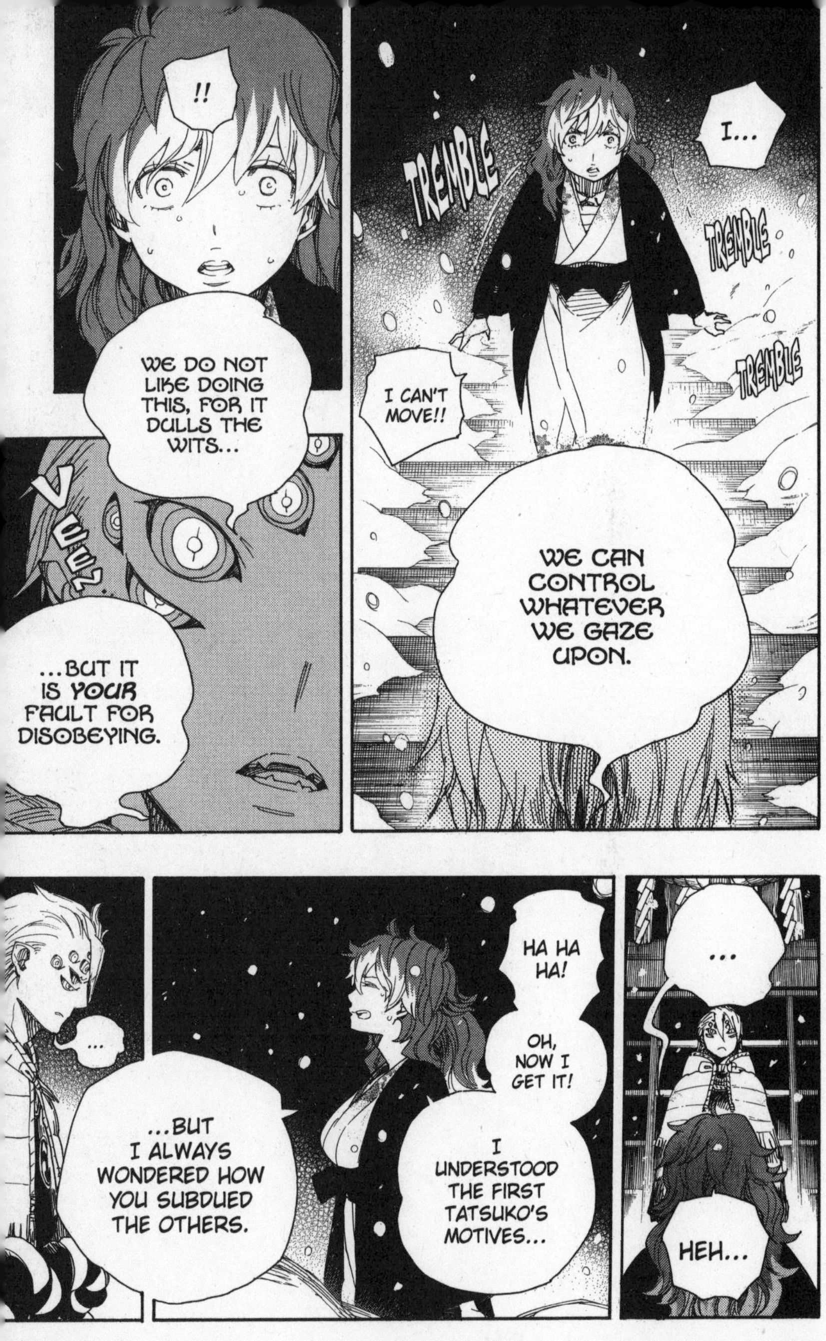
I...
TREMBLE
TREMBLE
TREMBLE
I CAN'T MOVE!!
WE CAN CONTROL WHATEVER WE GAZE UPON.
!!
WE DO NOT LIKE DOING THIS, FOR IT DULLS THE WITS...
VEEN
...BUT IT IS *YOUR* FAULT FOR DISOBEYING.
...
HEH...
HA HA HA!
OH, NOW I GET IT!
I UNDERSTOOD THE FIRST TATSUKO'S MOTIVES...
...BUT I ALWAYS WONDERED HOW YOU SUBDUED THE OTHERS.
...

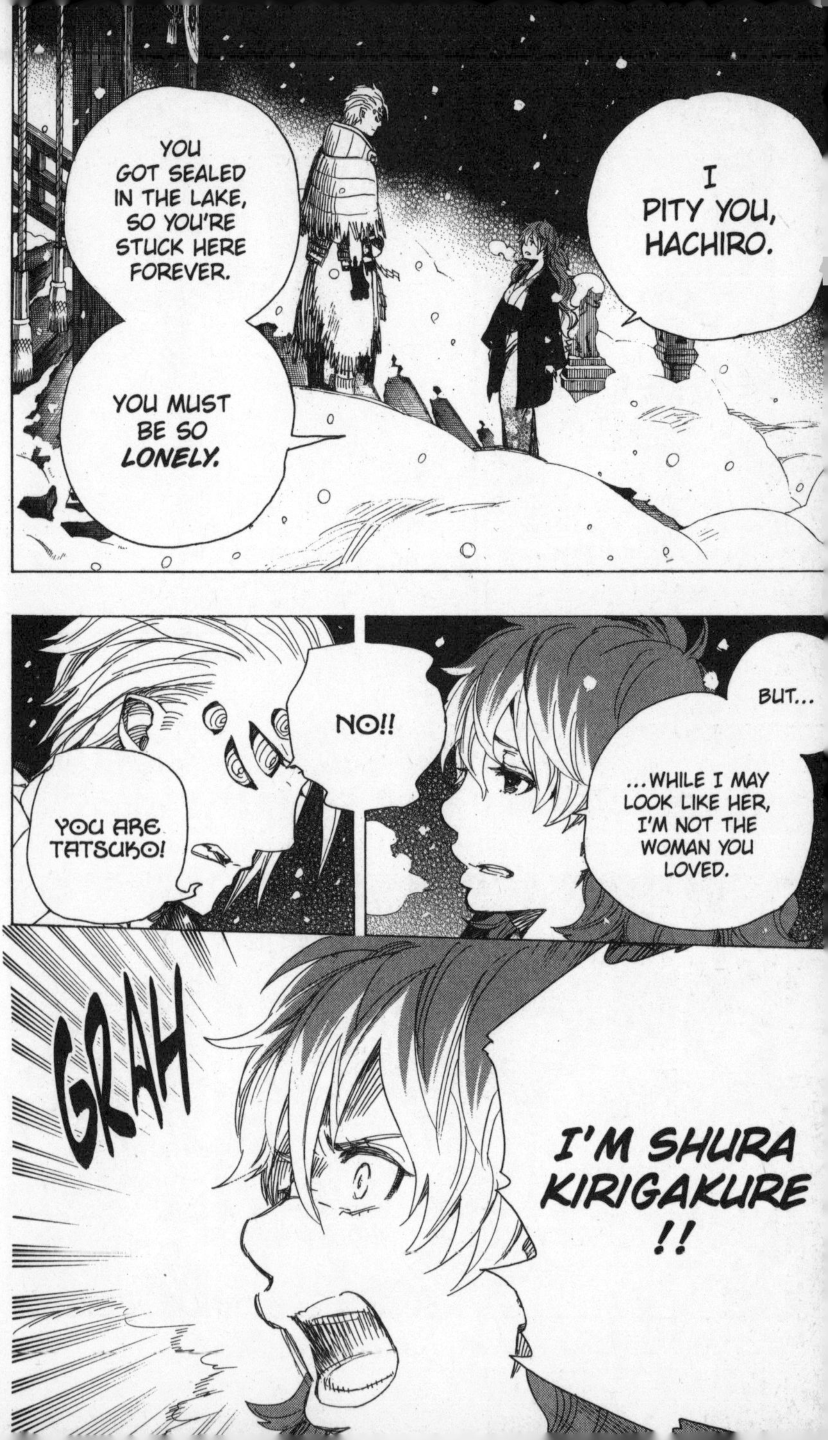
I PITY YOU, HACHIRO.
YOU GOT SEALED IN THE LAKE, SO YOU'RE STUCK HERE FOREVER.
YOU MUST BE SO LONELY.
BUT...
...WHILE I MAY LOOK LIKE HER, I'M NOT THE WOMAN YOU LOVED.
NO!!
YOU ARE TATSUKO!
I'M SHURA KIRIGAKURE !!
GRAH

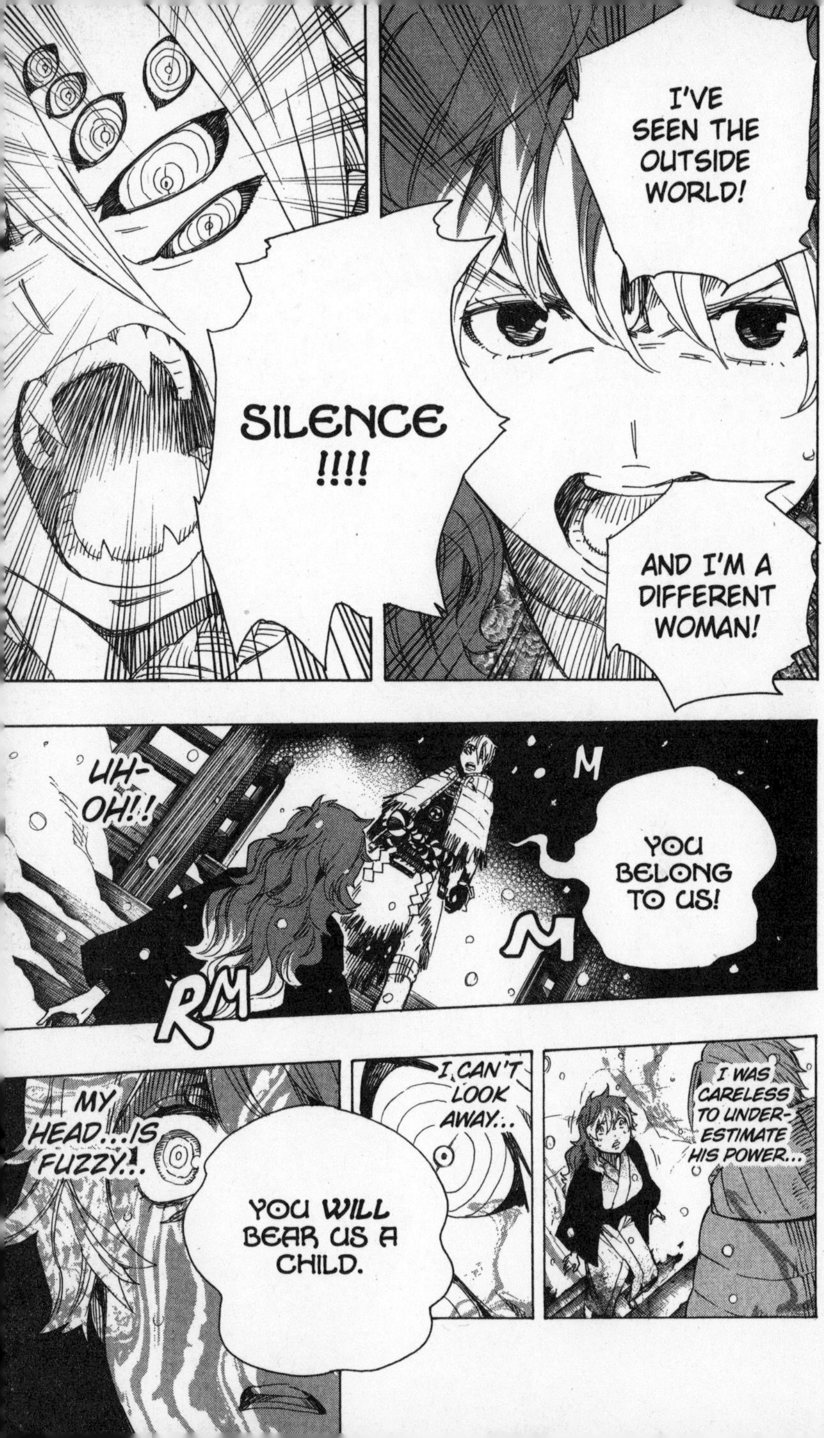
I'VE SEEN THE OUTSIDE WORLD!
AND I'M A DIFFERENT WOMAN!
SILENCE !!!!
M
YOU BELONG TO US!
M
UH-OH!!
RM
I WAS CARELESS TO UNDER-ESTIMATE HIS POWER...
I CAN'T LOOK AWAY...
MY HEAD...IS FUZZY...
YOU WILL BEAR US A CHILD.

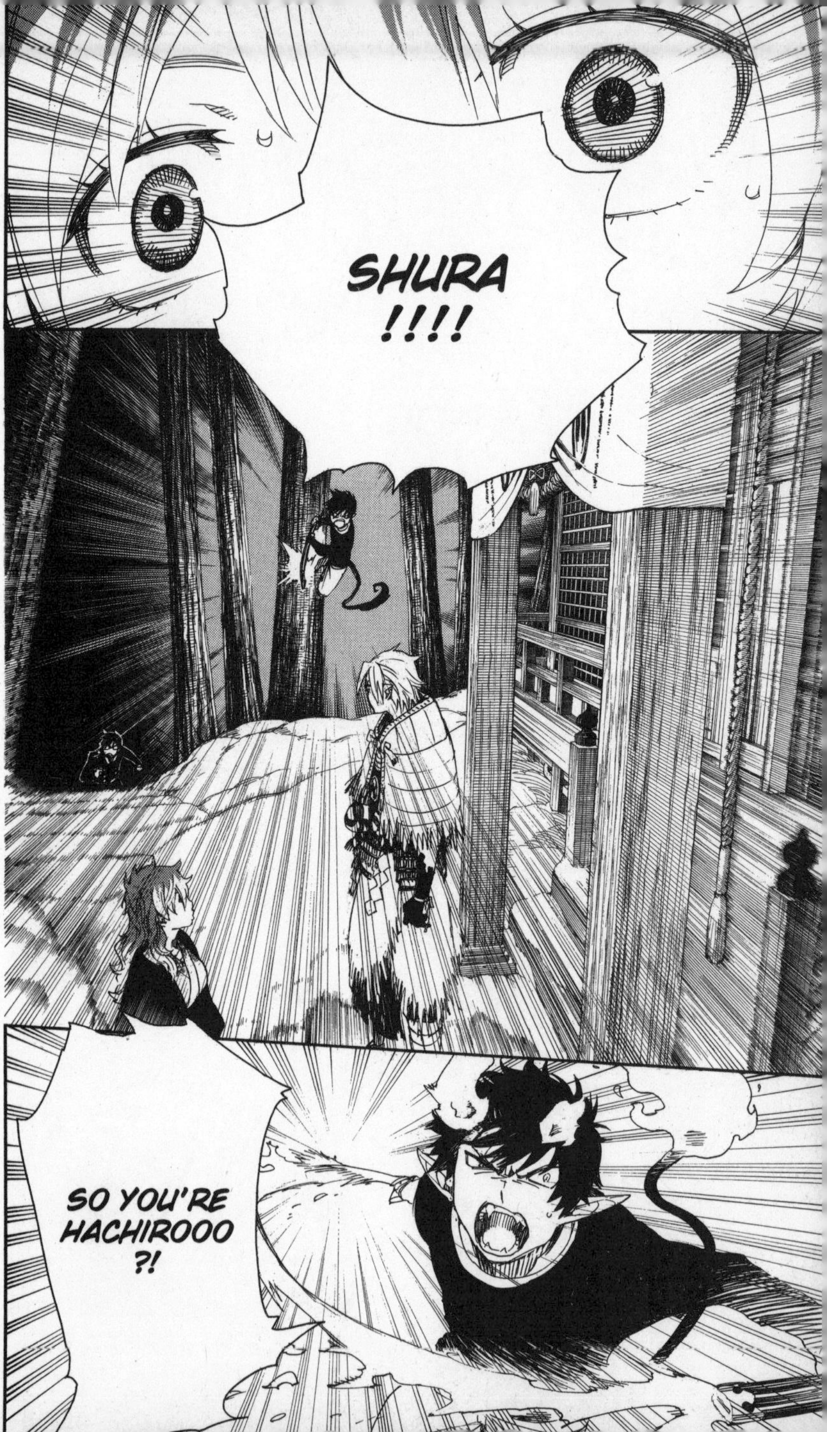
SHURA !!!!
SO YOU'RE HACHIROOO ?!

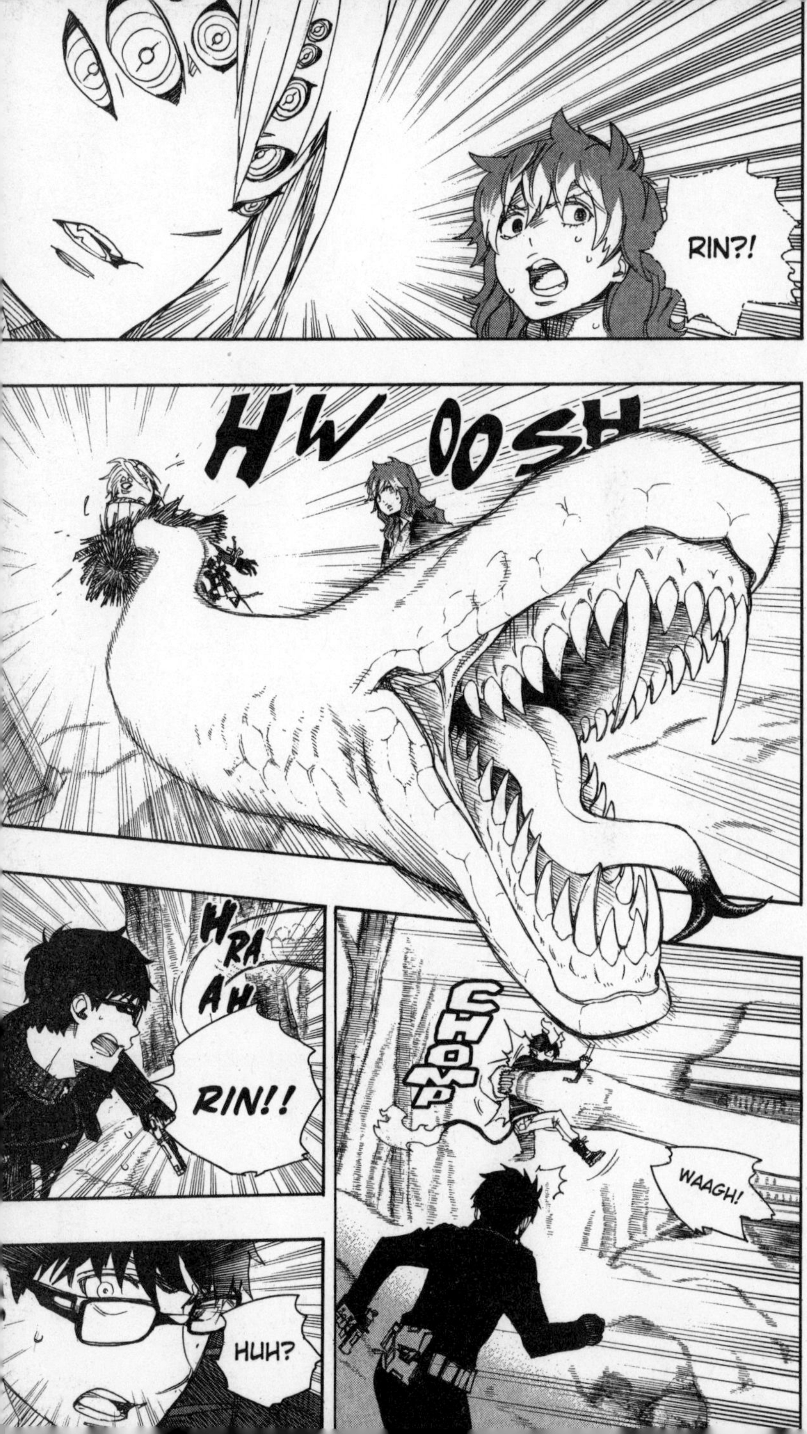
RIN?!
HWOOSH
CHOMP
WAAGH!
HRAAH
RIN!!
HUH?

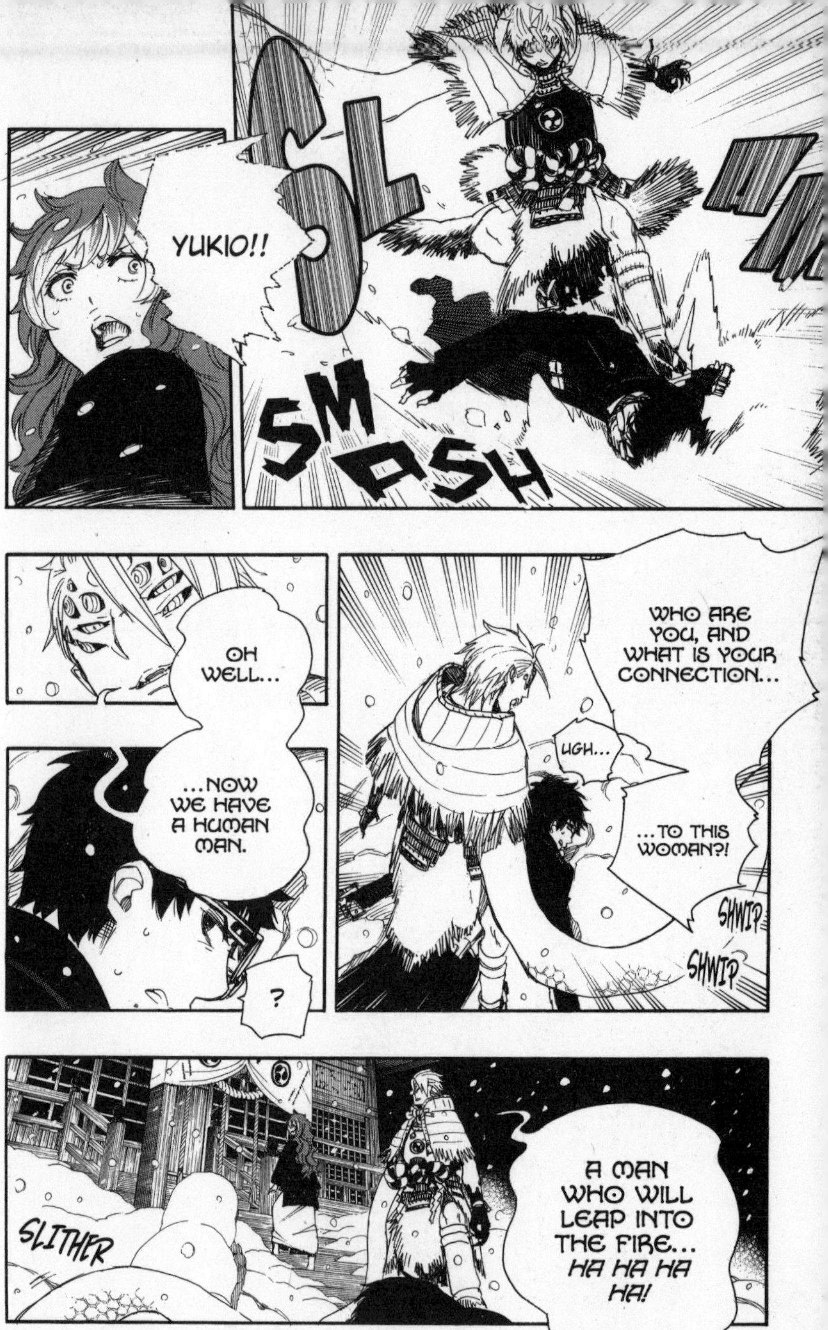

SL
AM
SMASH
YUKIO!!
WHO ARE YOU, AND WHAT IS YOUR CONNECTION...
UGH...
...TO THIS WOMAN?!
SHWIP
SHWIP
OH WELL...
...NOW WE HAVE A HUMAN MAN.
?
A MAN WHO WILL LEAP INTO THE FIRE... *HA HA HA HA!*
SLITHER

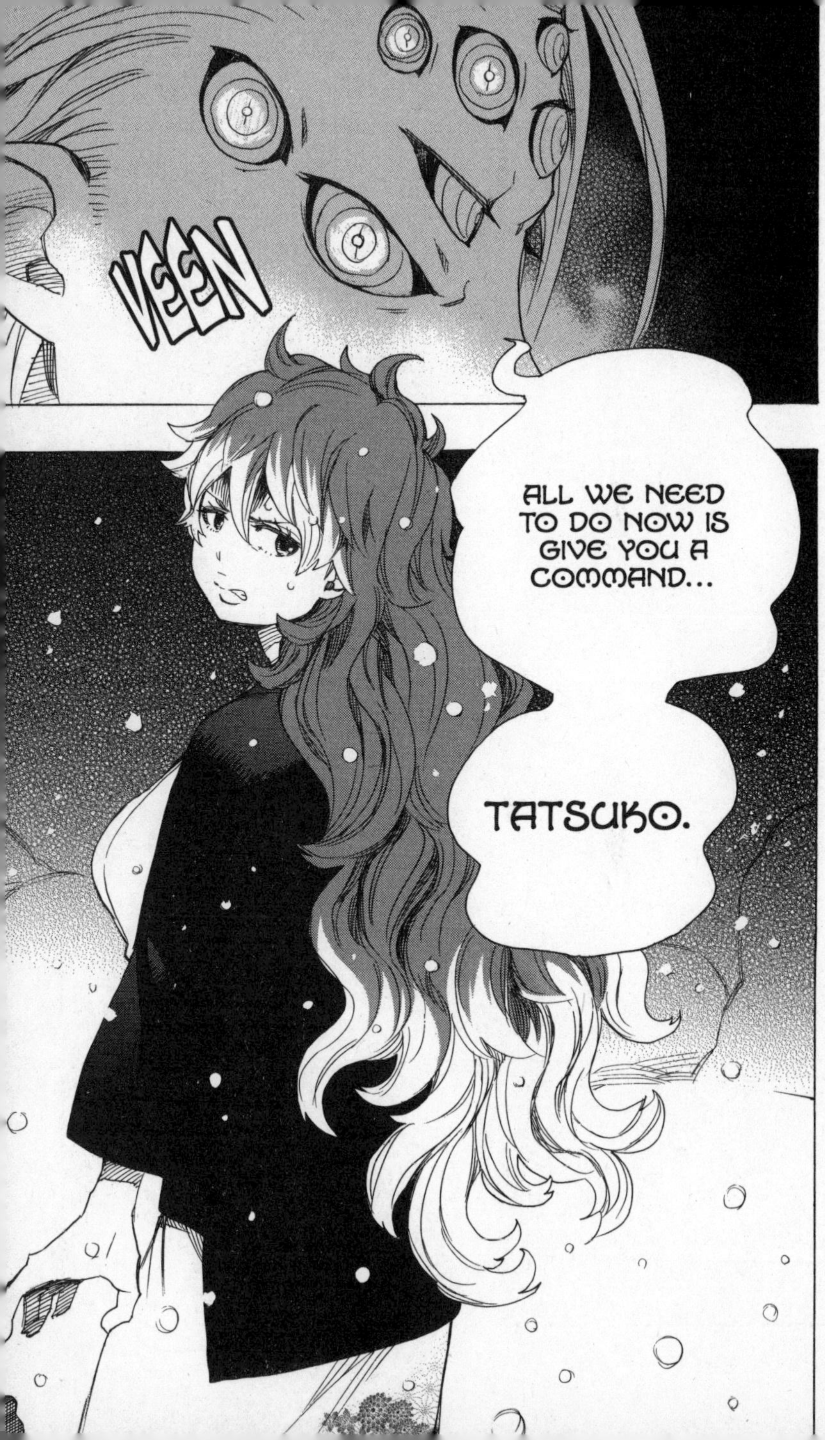
VEEN
ALL WE NEED TO DO NOW IS GIVE YOU A COMMAND...
TATSUKO.

BLUE EXORCIST CHAPTER 76: GOODBYE TO YOU

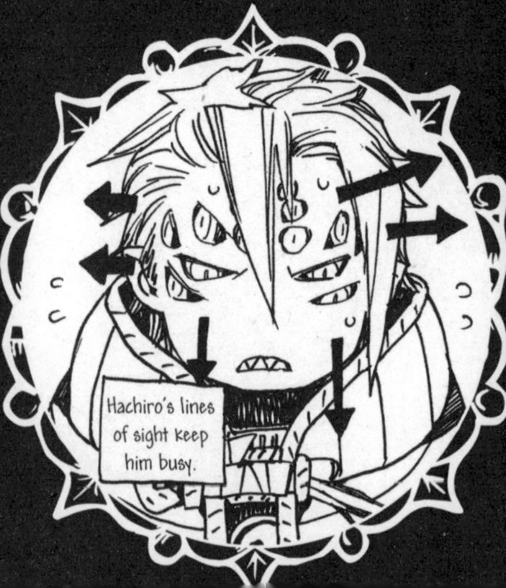
Hachiro's lines of sight keep him busy.

Chapter 77: It's All Right If I Don't Go Back

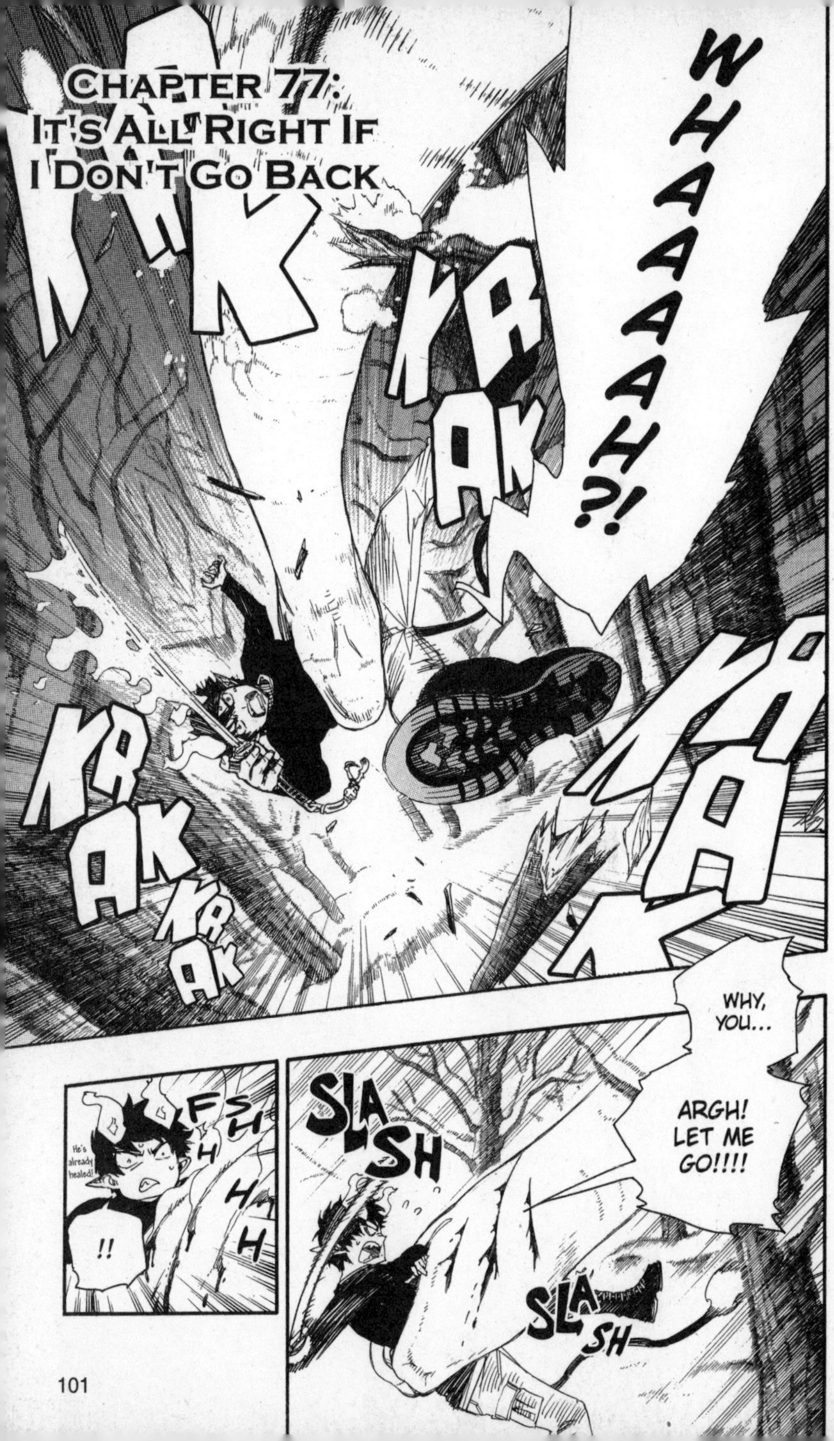
KRAAK
WHAAAAAH?!
KRAAK
KRAAK
KRAAK
KRAAK
WHY, YOU...
ARGH! LET ME GO!!!!
SLASH
SLASH
FSHHHHH
He's already healed!
!!

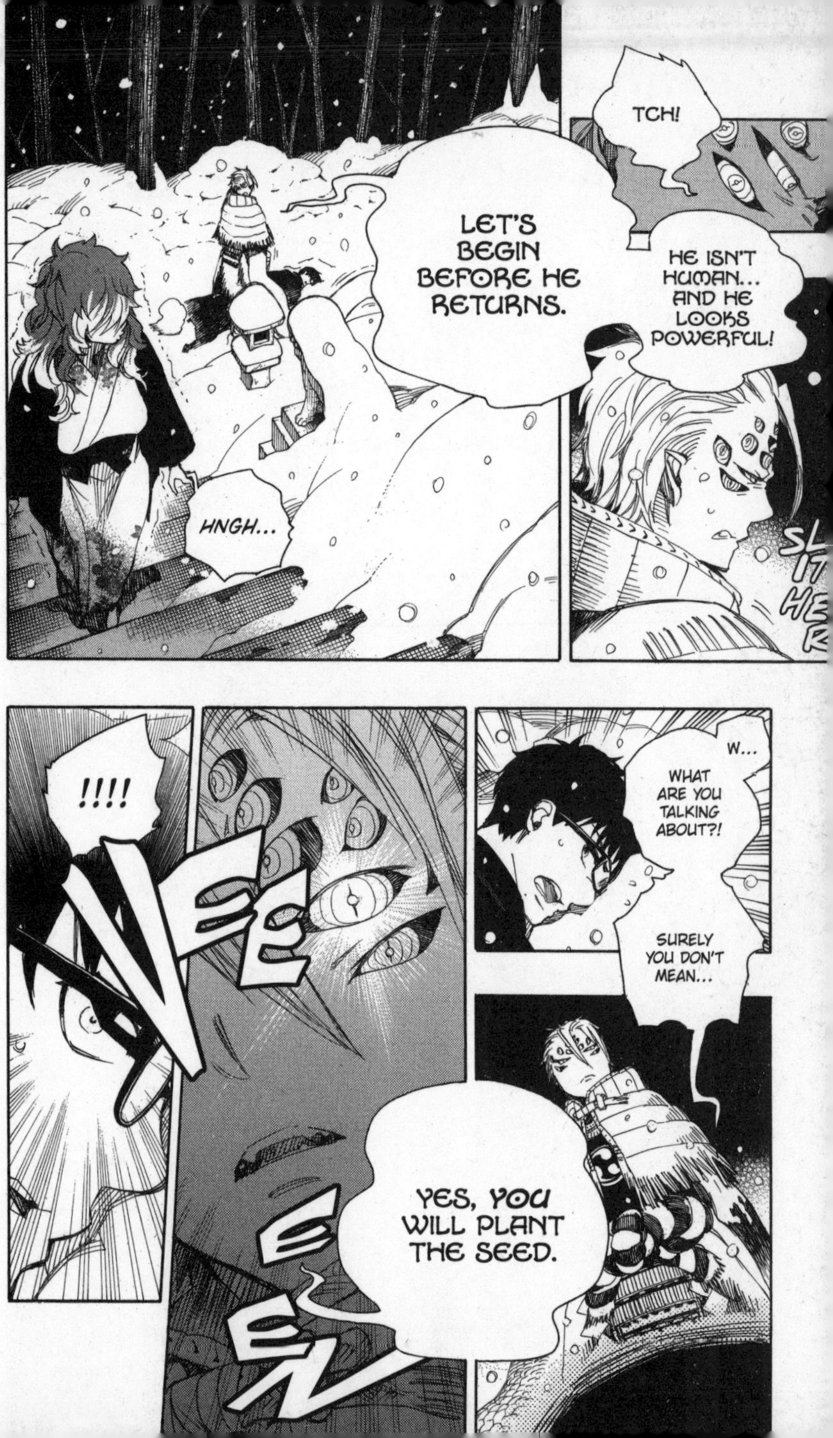
TCH!
HE ISN'T HUMAN... AND HE LOOKS POWERFUL!
LET'S BEGIN BEFORE HE RETURNS.
HNGH...
W...
WHAT ARE YOU TALKING ABOUT?!
SURELY YOU DON'T MEAN...
YES, YOU WILL PLANT THE SEED.
!!!!

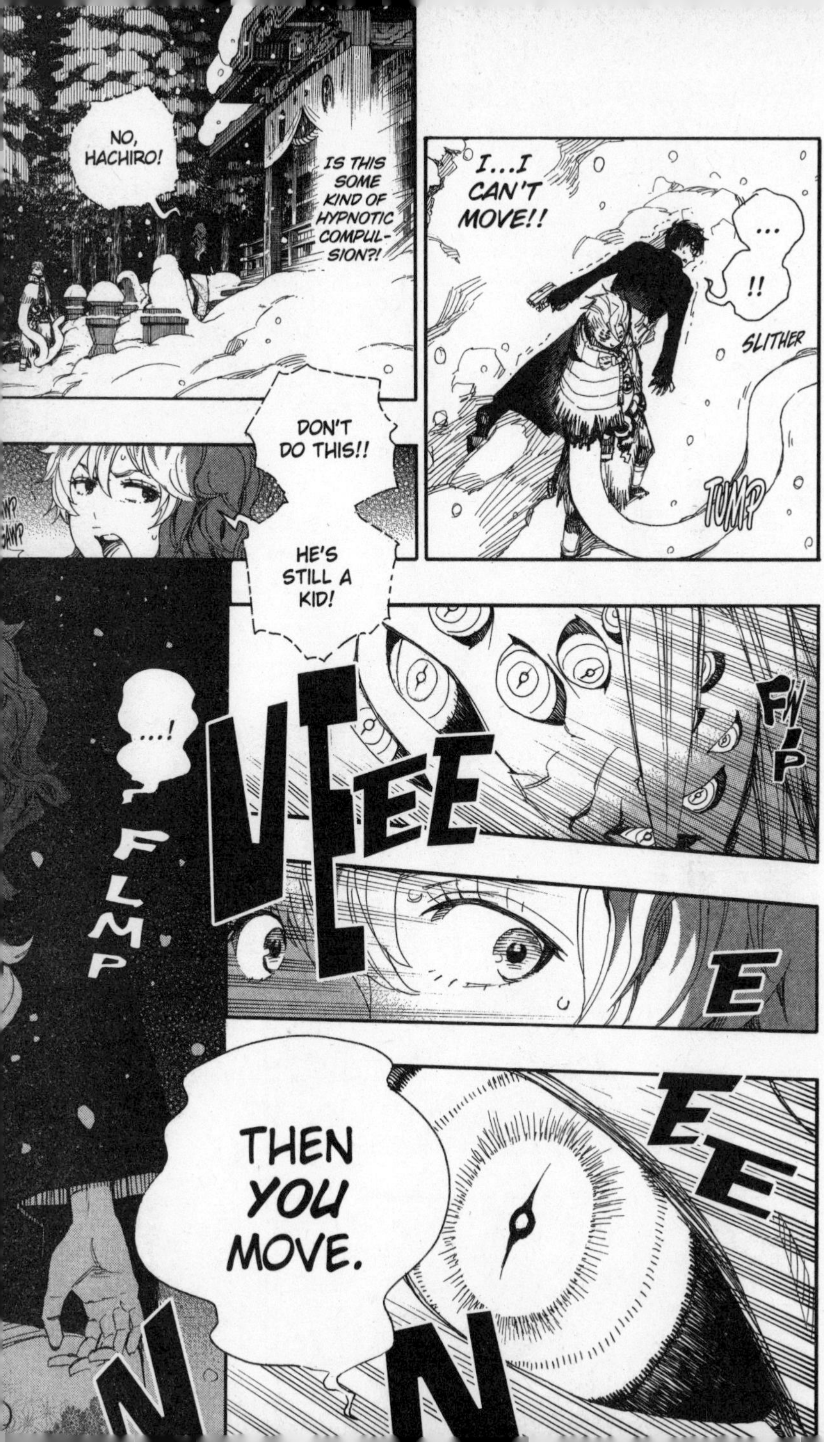
I...I CAN'T MOVE!!
...
!!
SLITHER
TUMP
NO, HACHIRO!
IS THIS SOME KIND OF HYPNOTIC COMPULSION?!
DON'T DO THIS!!
HE'S STILL A KID!
FWIP
VEEE
E
EE
...!
FLMP
THEN YOU MOVE.
MN

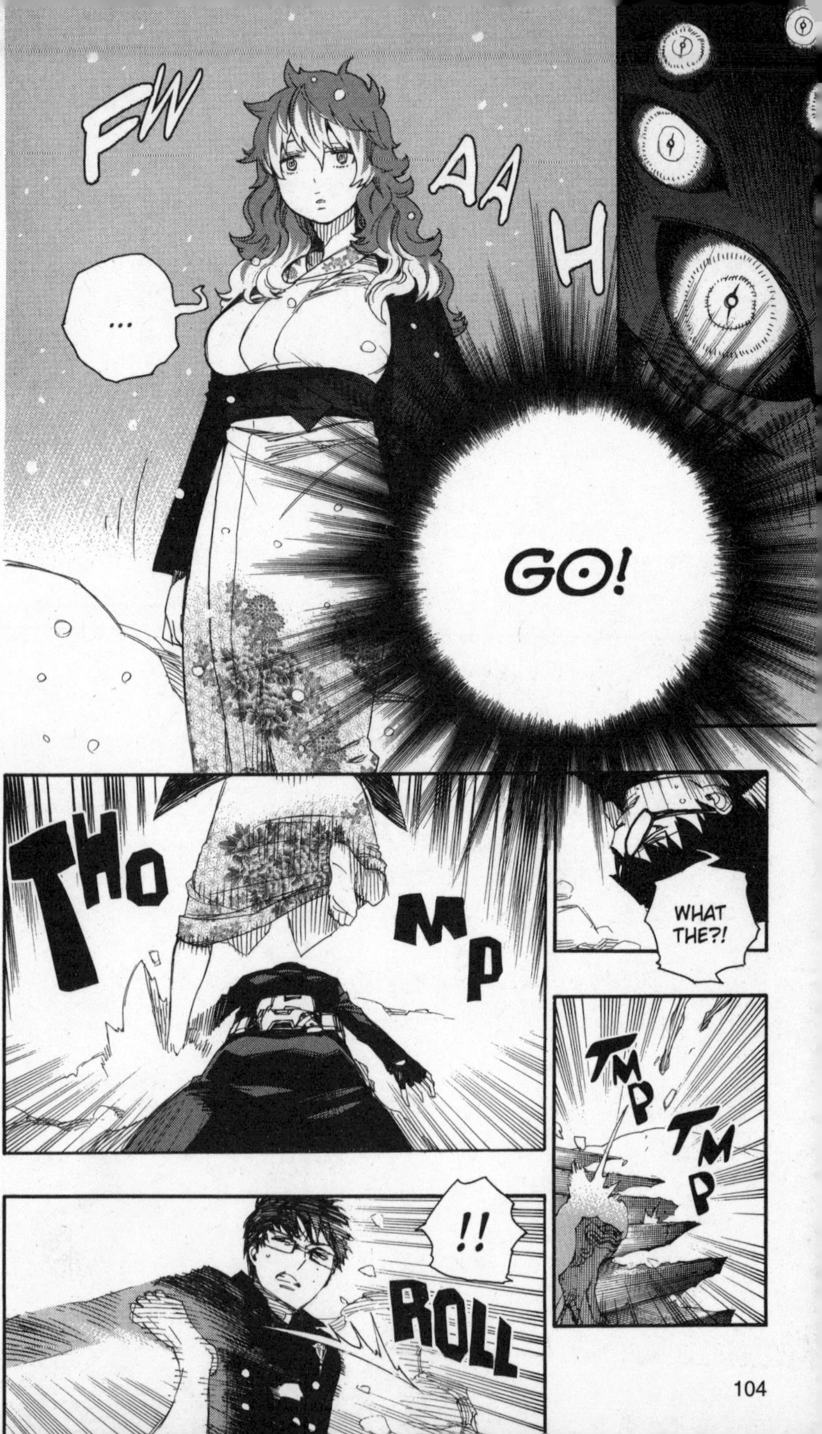
FWAAH
...
GO!
WHAT THE?!
TMP TMP
THOMP
!!
ROLL

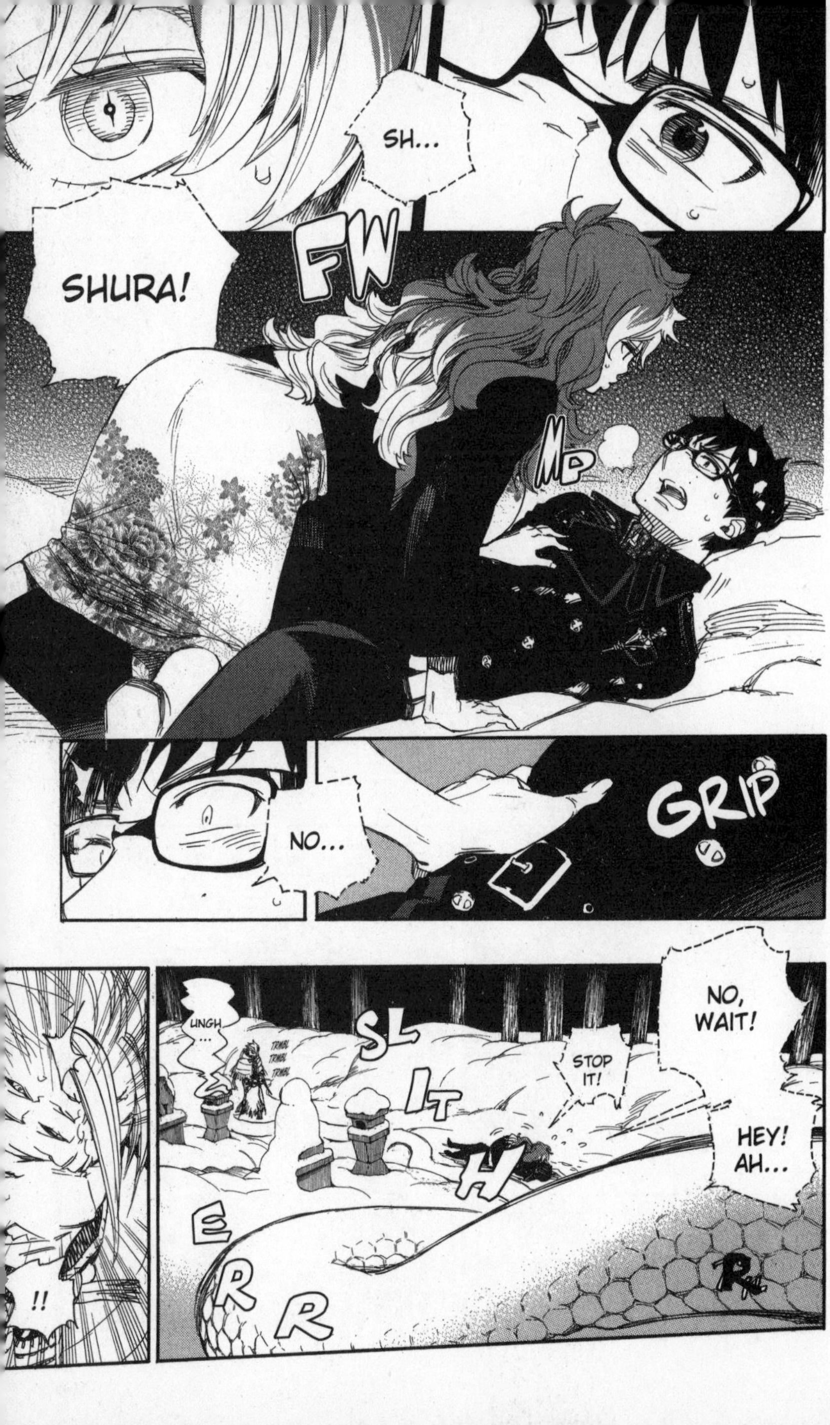
SH...
SHURA!
FW
MP
GRIP
NO...
NO, WAIT!
HEY! AH...
STOP IT!
SLITH
UNGH...
TRMBL TRMBL TRMBL
ERR
R
!!

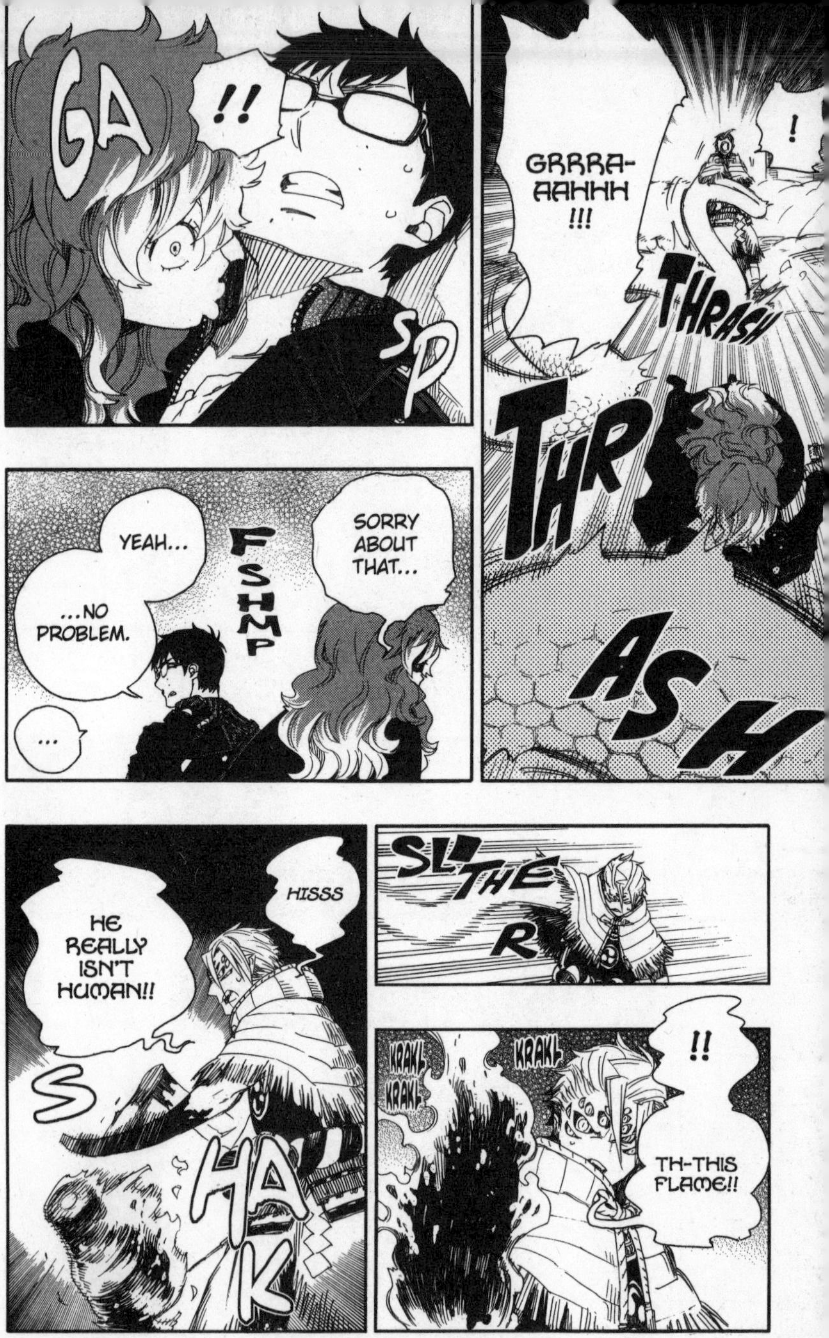
!
GRRRA-AAHHH!!!
THRASH
THR
ASH
GA
!!
SP
SORRY ABOUT THAT...
FSHMP
YEAH...
...NO PROBLEM.
...
SLITHER
!!
KRAKL
KRAKL KRAKL
TH-THIS FLAME!!
HISSS
HE REALLY ISN'T HUMAN!!
SHAK

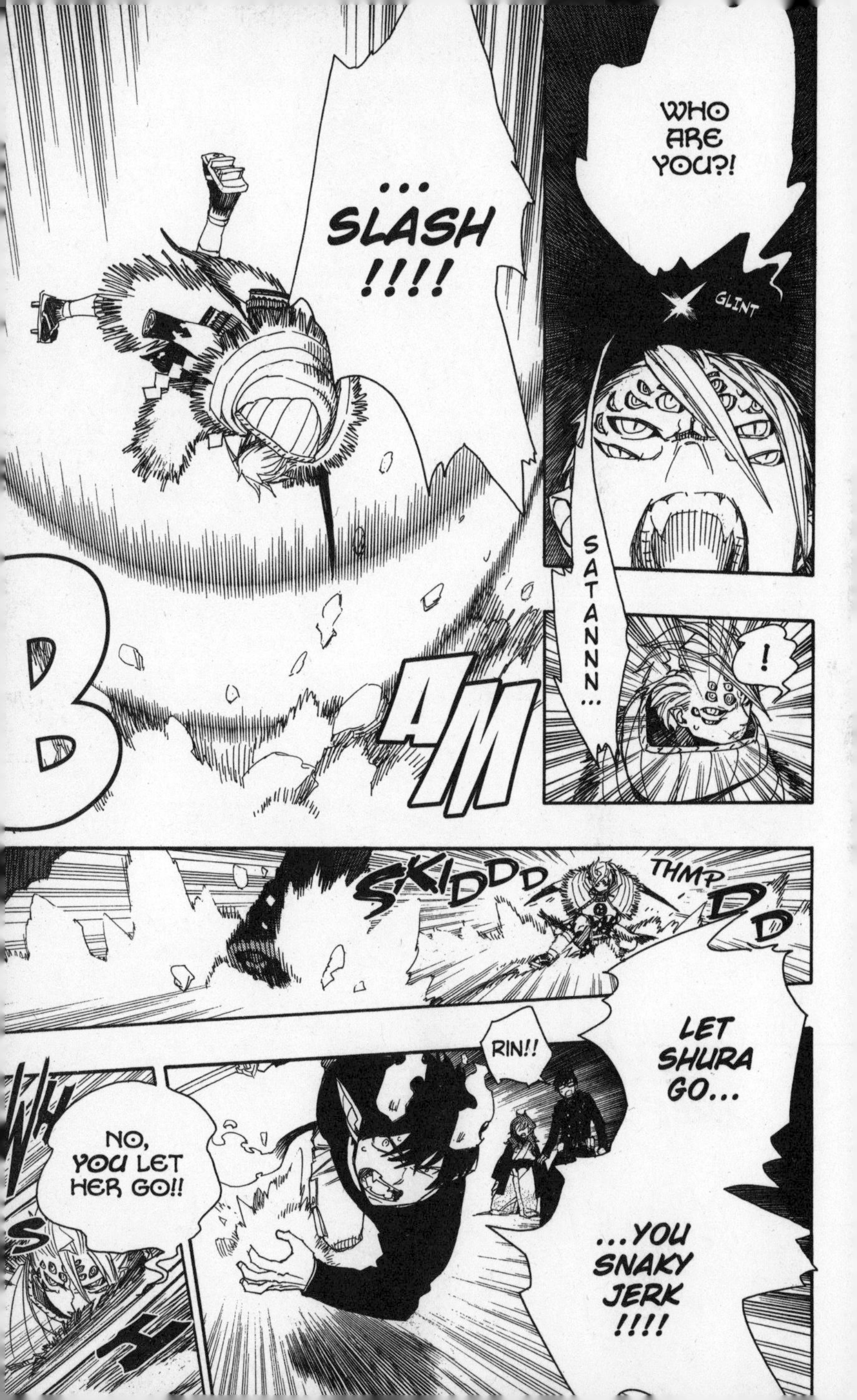
WHO ARE YOU?!
GLINT
SATANNN...
!
...SLASH!!!!
BAM
SKIDDDD
THMP
DD
LET SHURA GO...
RIN!!
...YOU SNAKY JERK!!!!
NO, YOU LET HER GO!!
WHSH

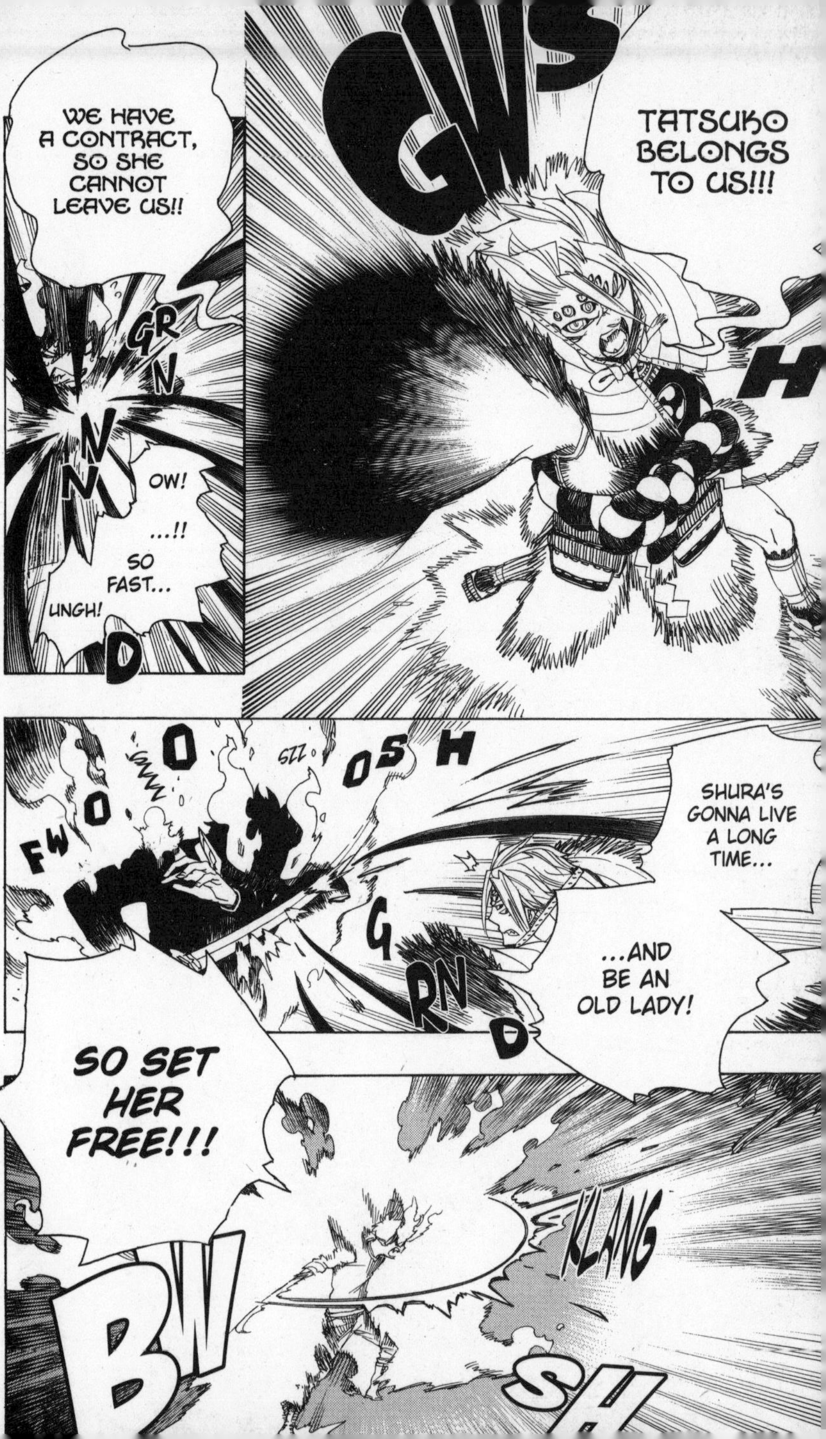
GWS
TATSUKO BELONGS TO US!!!
WE HAVE A CONTRACT, SO SHE CANNOT LEAVE US!!
GR N
OW!
...!!
SO FAST...
UNGH!
SHURA'S GONNA LIVE A LONG TIME...
...AND BE AN OLD LADY!
G RN D
OSH
SZZ
FW O O
SO SET HER FREE!!!
KLANG
SH
BW

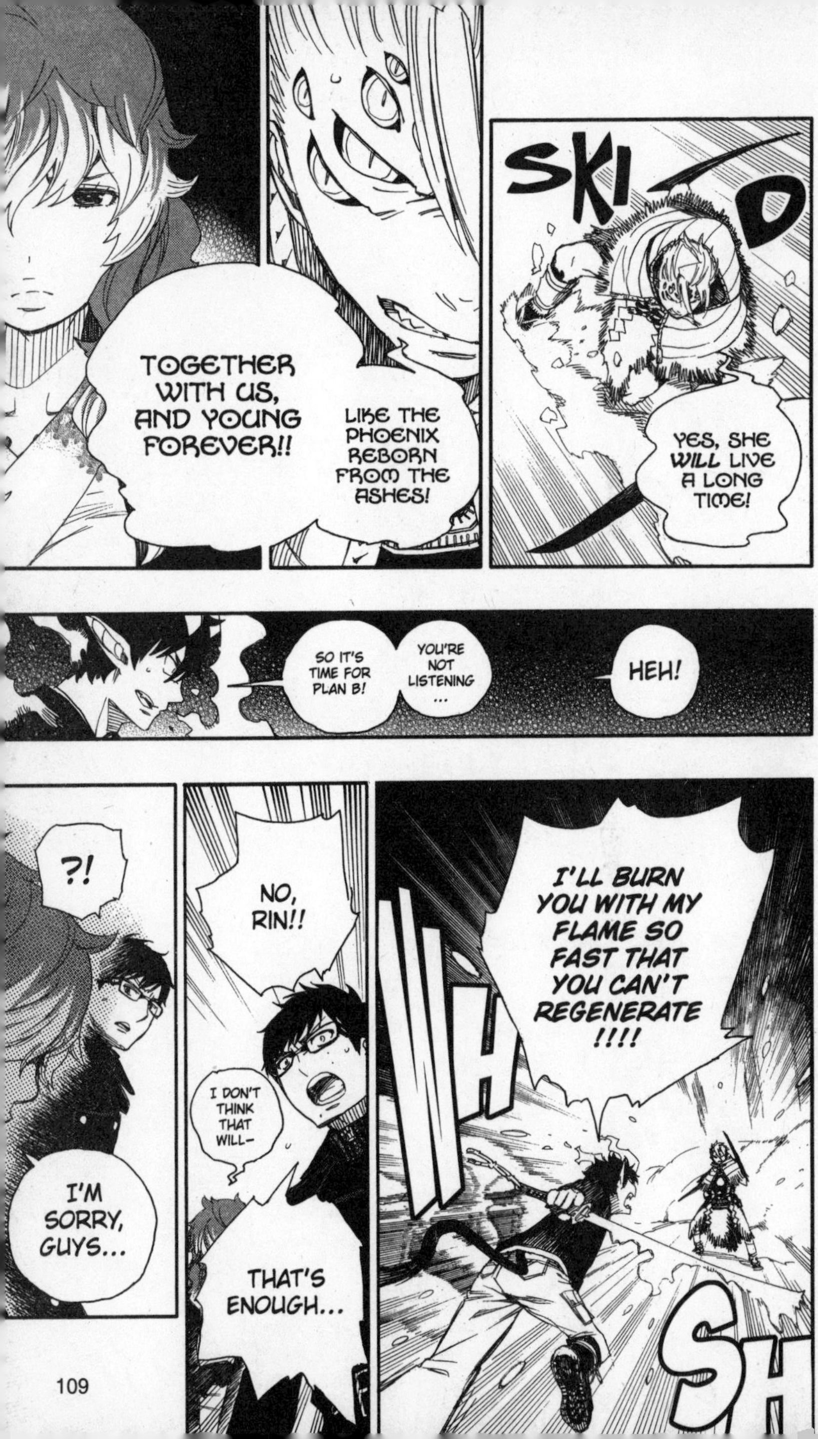
SKID
YES, SHE WILL LIVE A LONG TIME!
LIKE THE PHOENIX REBORN FROM THE ASHES!
TOGETHER WITH US, AND YOUNG FOREVER!!
HEH!
YOU'RE NOT LISTENING...
SO IT'S TIME FOR PLAN B!
I'LL BURN YOU WITH MY FLAME SO FAST THAT YOU CAN'T REGENERATE!!!!
WH
SH
NO, RIN!!
I DON'T THINK THAT WILL–
THAT'S ENOUGH...
?!
I'M SORRY, GUYS...

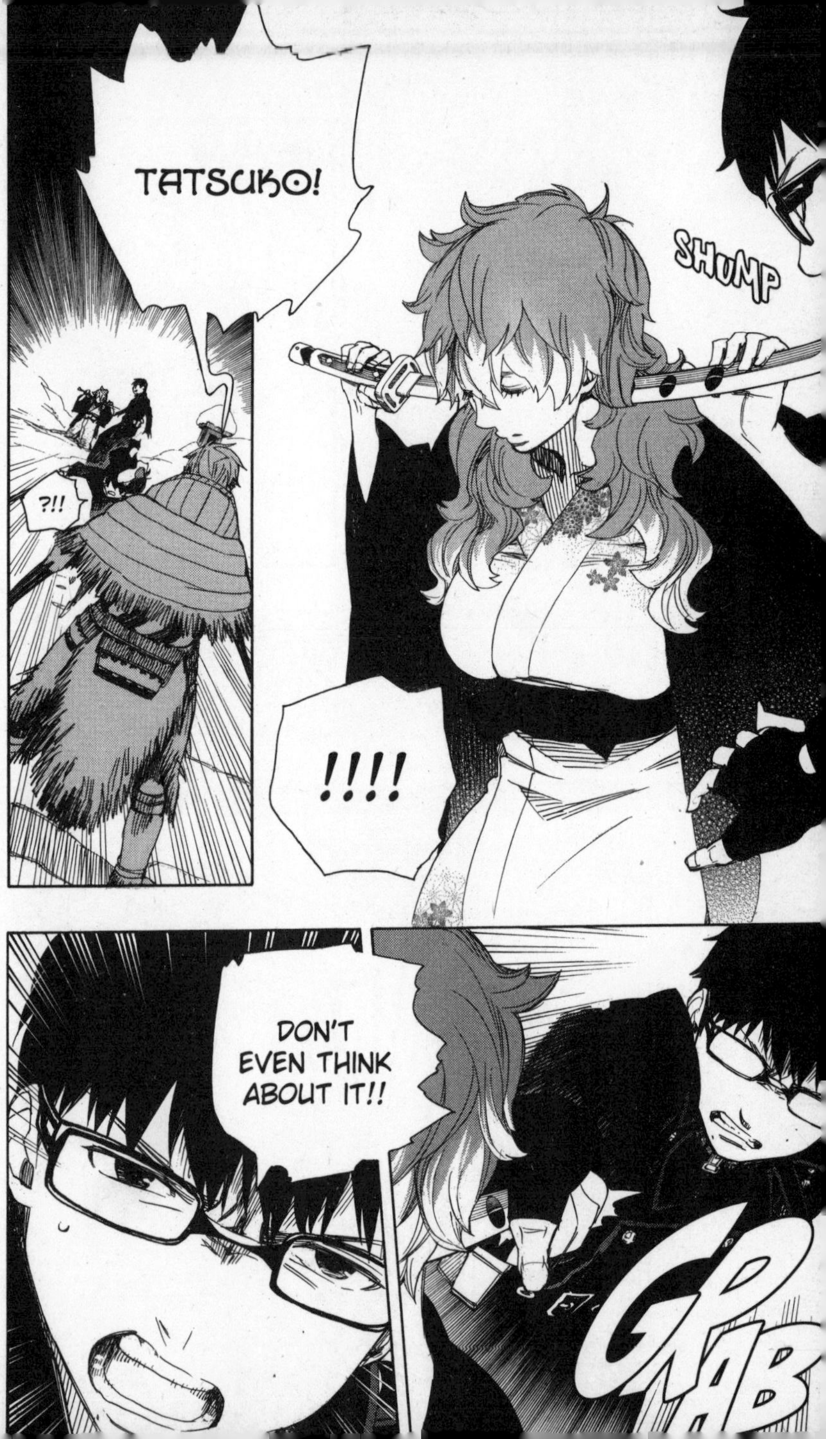
SHUMP
!!!!
TATSUKO!
?!!
GRAB
DON'T EVEN THINK ABOUT IT!!

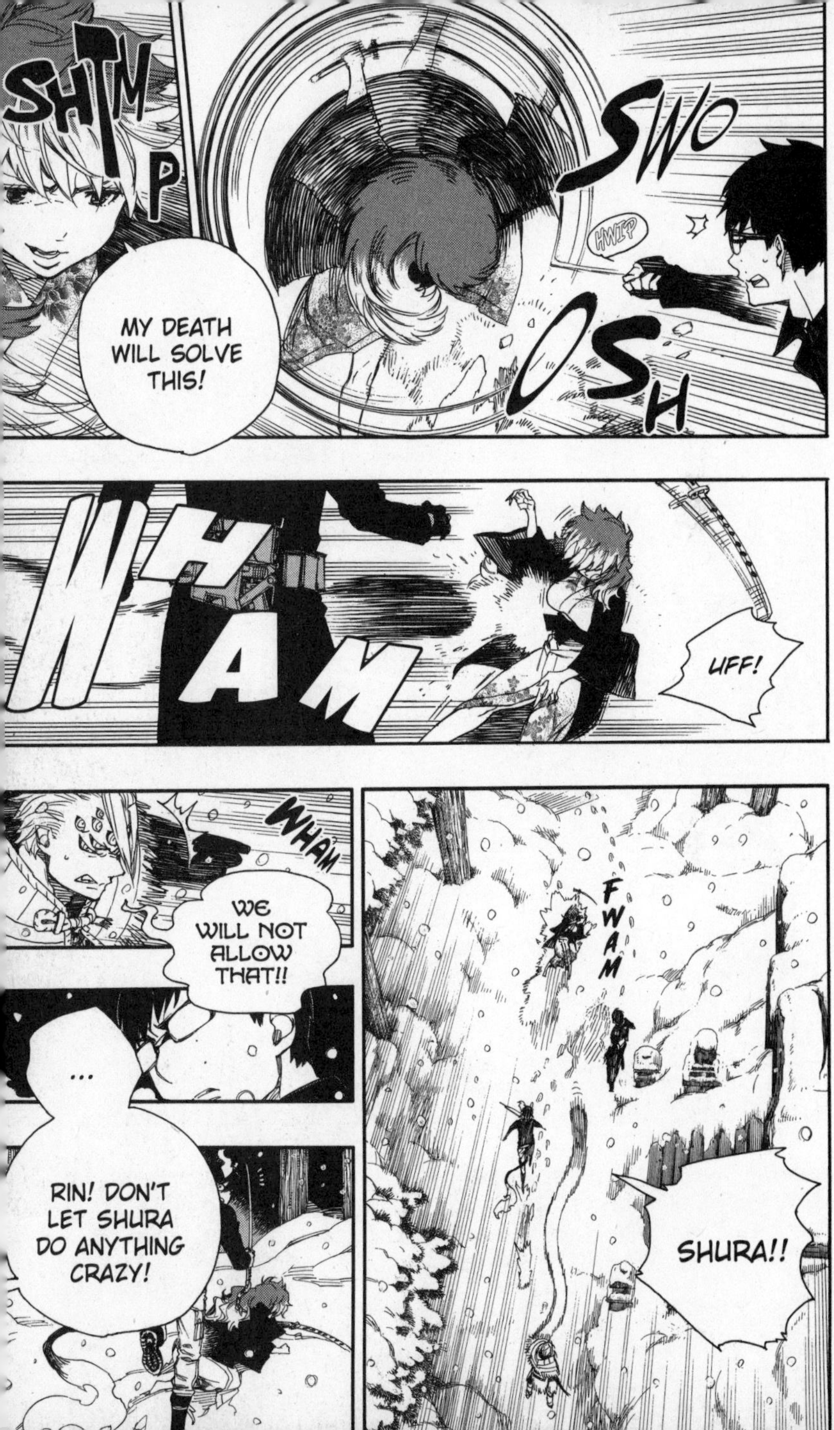
SWOOSH
HWIP
SHTMP
MY DEATH WILL SOLVE THIS!
UFF!
WHAM
FWAM
SHURA!!
WHAM
WE WILL NOT ALLOW THAT!!
...
RIN! DON'T LET SHURA DO ANYTHING CRAZY!

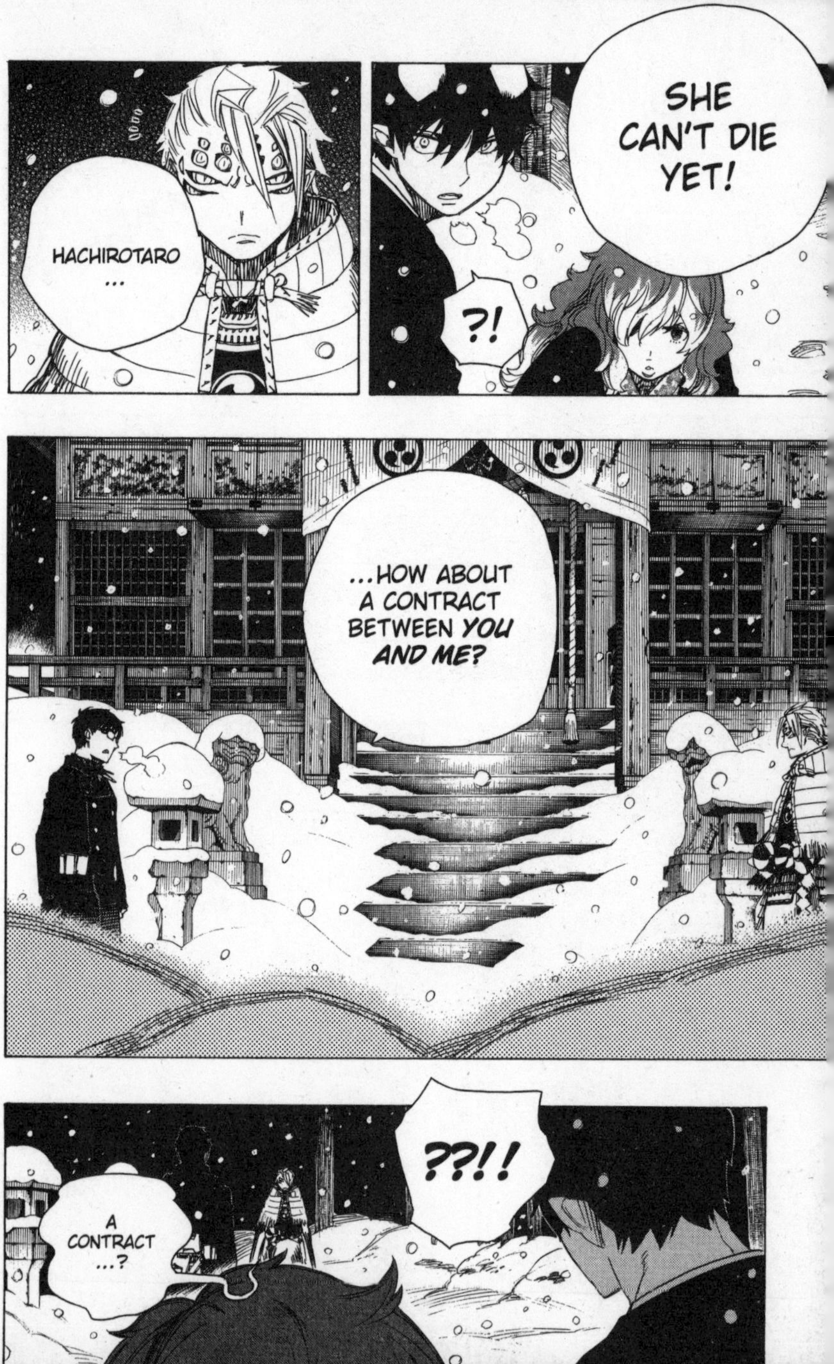
SHE CAN'T DIE YET!
?!
HACHIROTARO ...
...HOW ABOUT A CONTRACT BETWEEN *YOU AND ME?*
??!!
A CONTRACT ...?

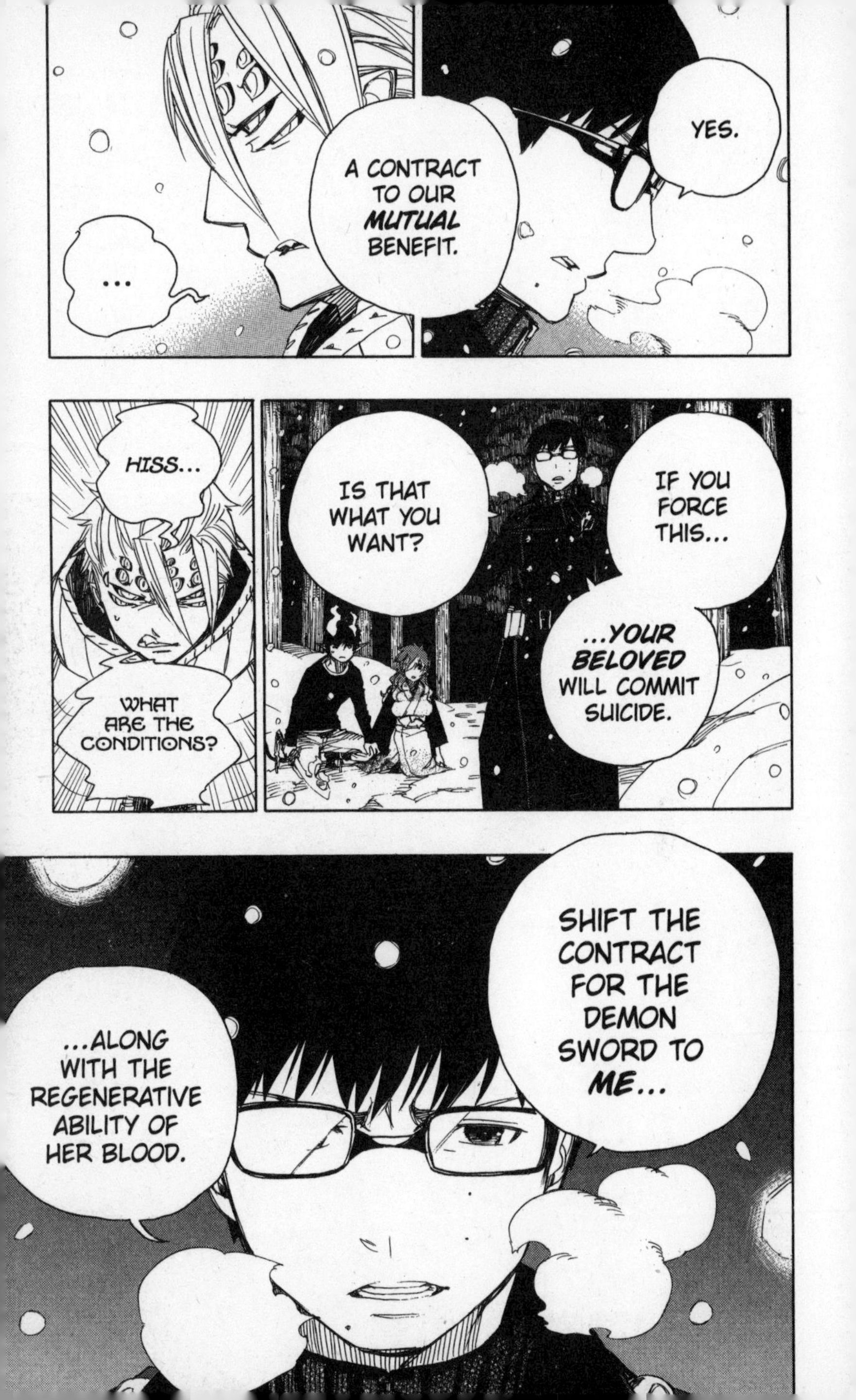
YES.
A CONTRACT TO OUR MUTUAL BENEFIT.
...
IF YOU FORCE THIS...
...YOUR BELOVED WILL COMMIT SUICIDE.
IS THAT WHAT YOU WANT?
HISS...
WHAT ARE THE CONDITIONS?
SHIFT THE CONTRACT FOR THE DEMON SWORD TO ME...
...ALONG WITH THE REGENERATIVE ABILITY OF HER BLOOD.

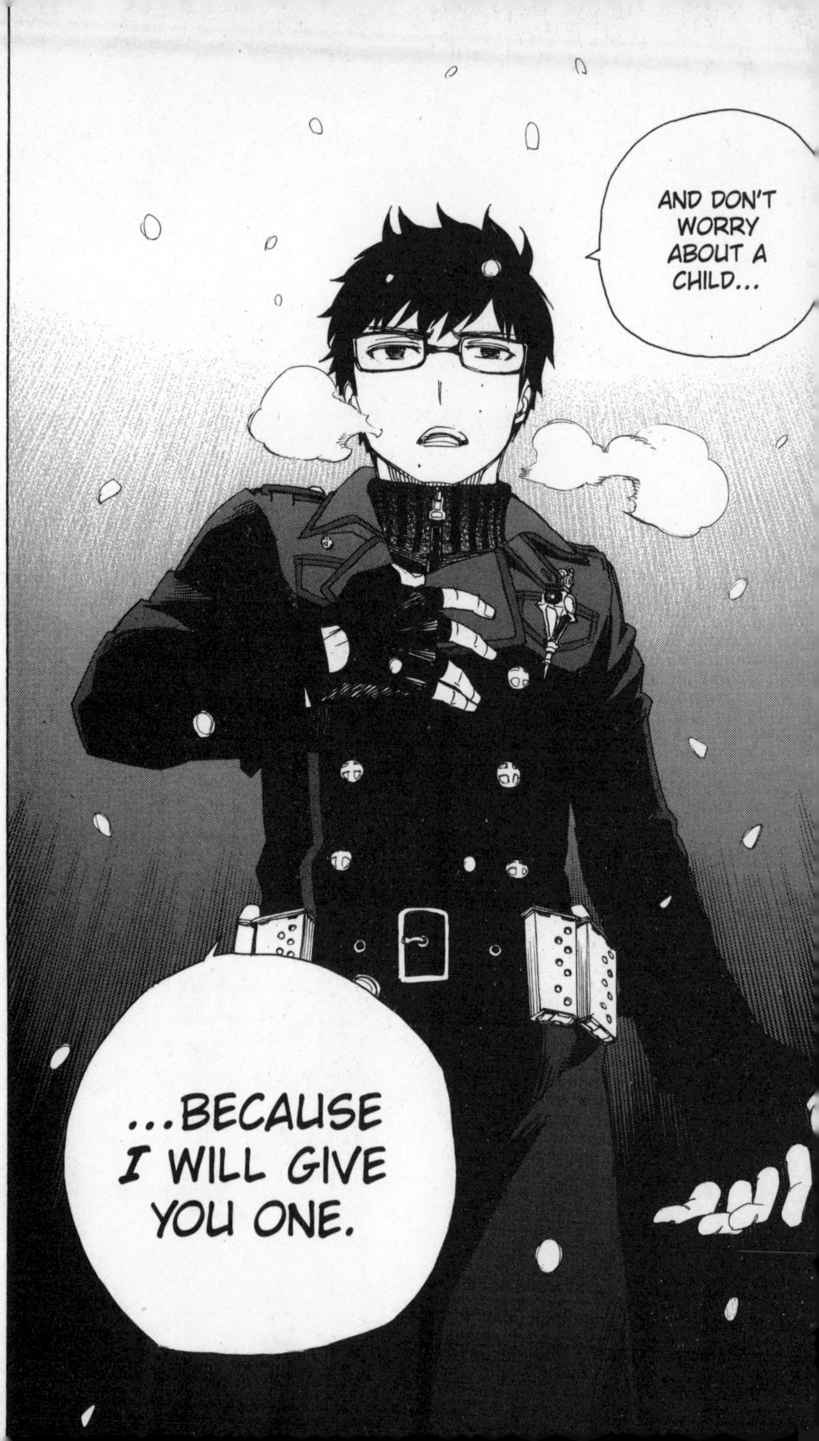
AND DON'T WORRY ABOUT A CHILD...
...BECAUSE I WILL GIVE YOU ONE.

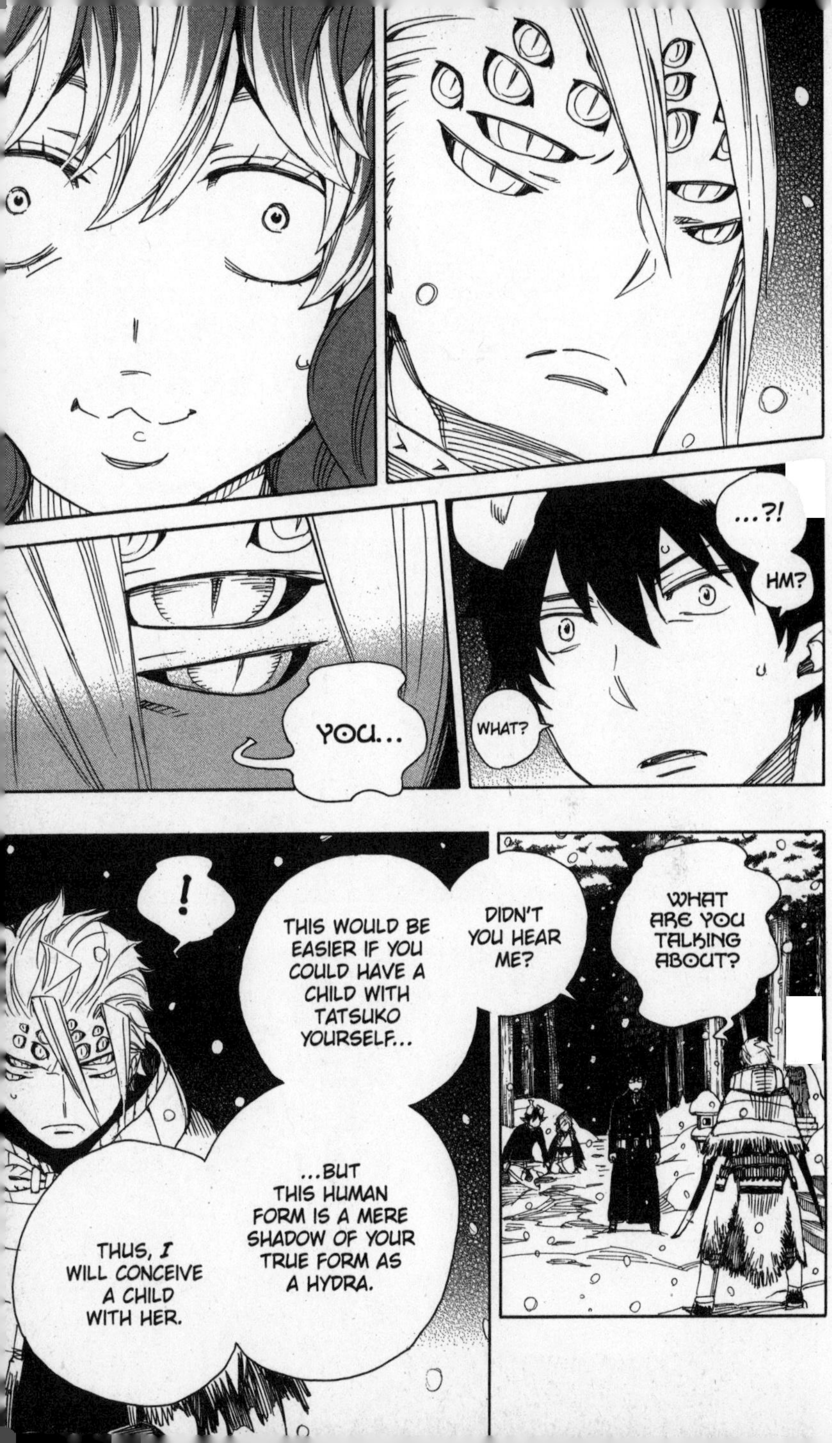
...?!
HM?
WHAT?
YOU...
WHAT ARE YOU TALKING ABOUT?
DIDN'T YOU HEAR ME?
!
THIS WOULD BE EASIER IF YOU COULD HAVE A CHILD WITH TATSUKO YOURSELF...
...BUT THIS HUMAN FORM IS A MERE SHADOW OF YOUR TRUE FORM AS A HYDRA.
THUS, I WILL CONCEIVE A CHILD WITH HER.

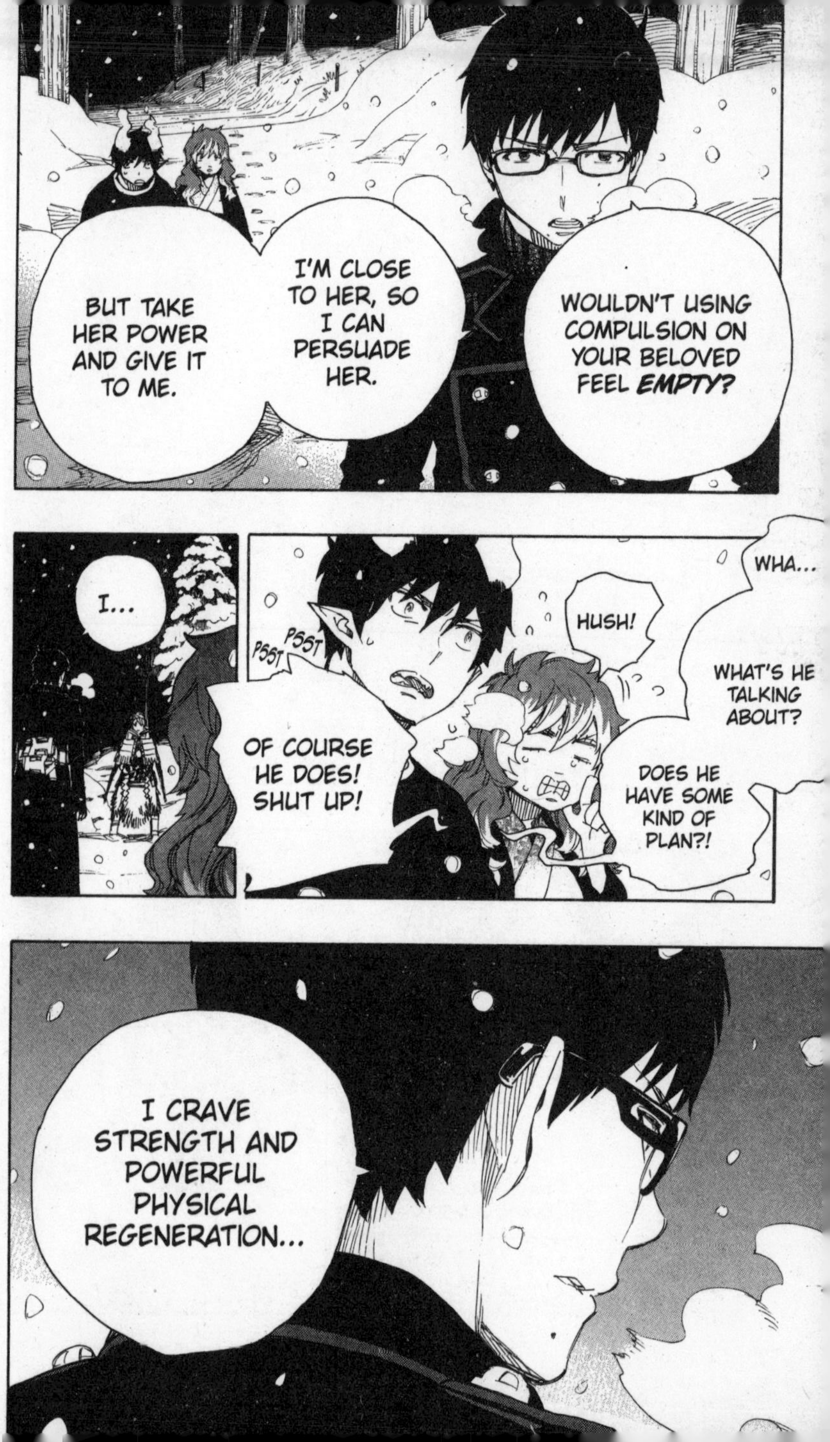
WOULDN'T USING COMPULSION ON YOUR BELOVED FEEL *EMPTY?*
I'M CLOSE TO HER, SO I CAN PERSUADE HER.
BUT TAKE HER POWER AND GIVE IT TO ME.
WHA...
WHAT'S HE TALKING ABOUT?
DOES HE HAVE SOME KIND OF PLAN?!
HUSH!
PSST PSST
OF COURSE HE DOES! SHUT UP!
I...
I CRAVE STRENGTH AND POWERFUL PHYSICAL REGENERATION...

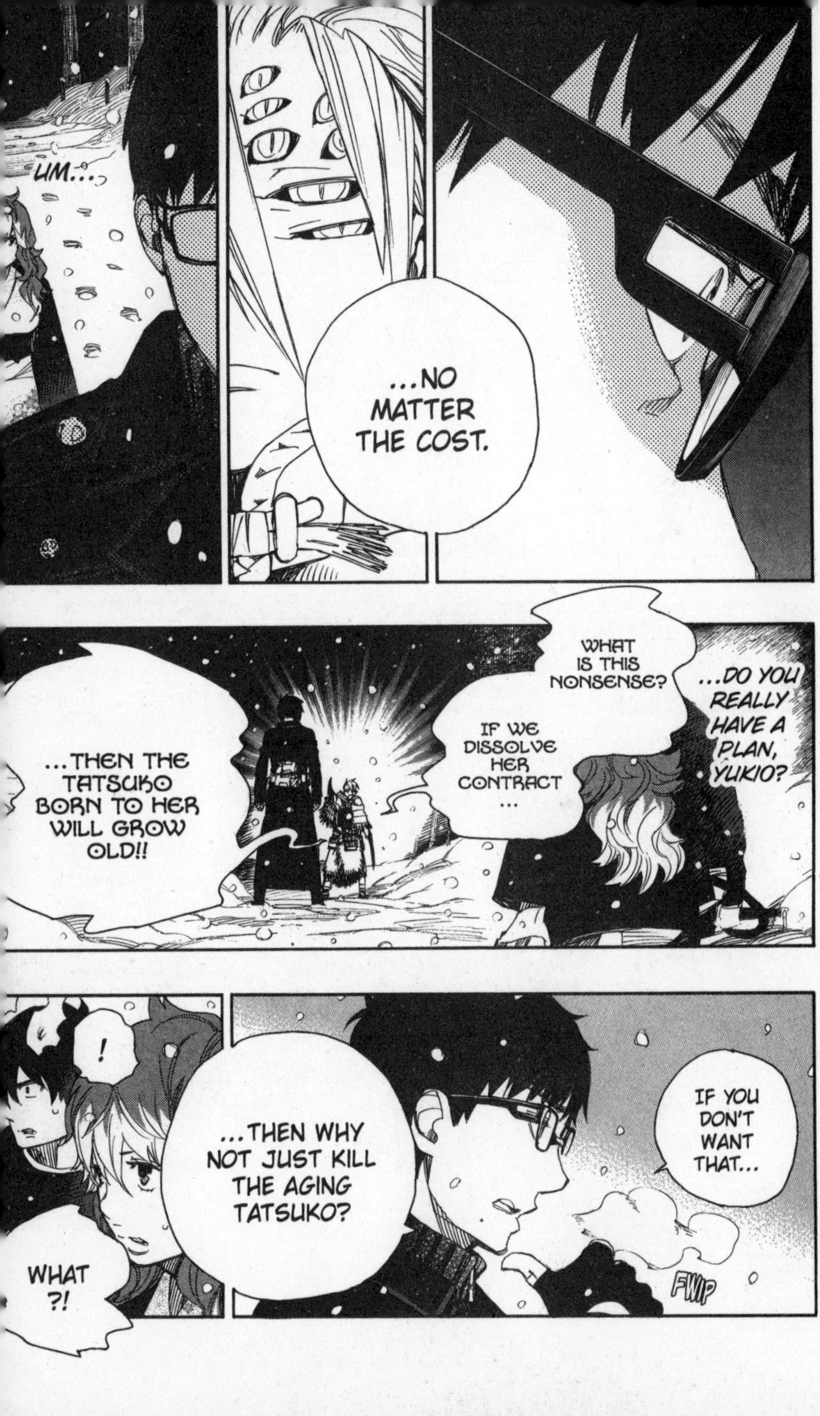
...NO MATTER THE COST.
UM...
...DO YOU REALLY HAVE A PLAN, YUKIO?
WHAT IS THIS NONSENSE?
IF WE DISSOLVE HER CONTRACT...
...THEN THE TATSUKO BORN TO HER WILL GROW OLD!!
IF YOU DON'T WANT THAT...
FWIP
...THEN WHY NOT JUST KILL THE AGING TATSUKO?
!
WHAT?!

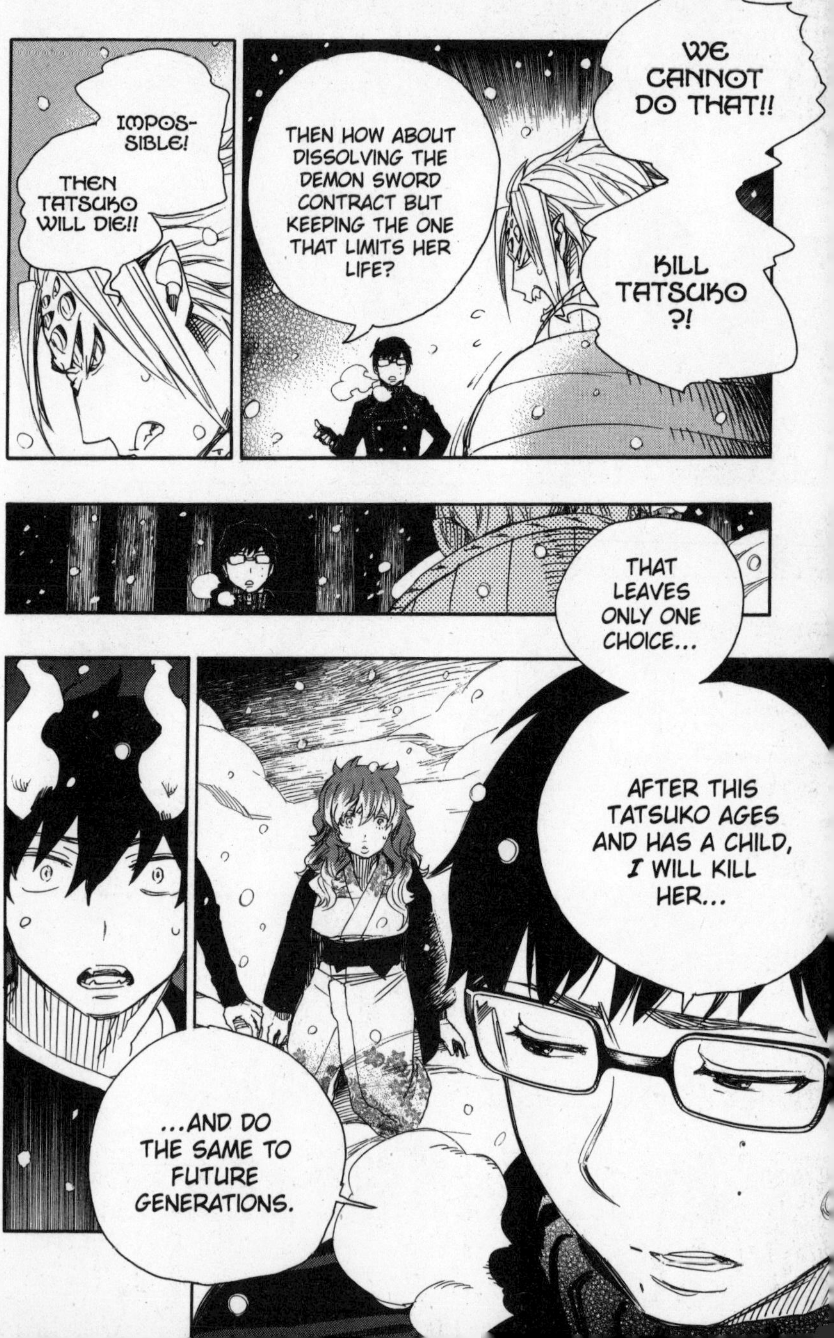
WE CANNOT DO THAT!!
KILL TATSUKO?!
THEN HOW ABOUT DISSOLVING THE DEMON SWORD CONTRACT BUT KEEPING THE ONE THAT LIMITS HER LIFE?
IMPOSSIBLE!
THEN TATSUKO WILL DIE!!
THAT LEAVES ONLY ONE CHOICE...
AFTER THIS TATSUKO AGES AND HAS A CHILD, I WILL KILL HER...
...AND DO THE SAME TO FUTURE GENERATIONS.

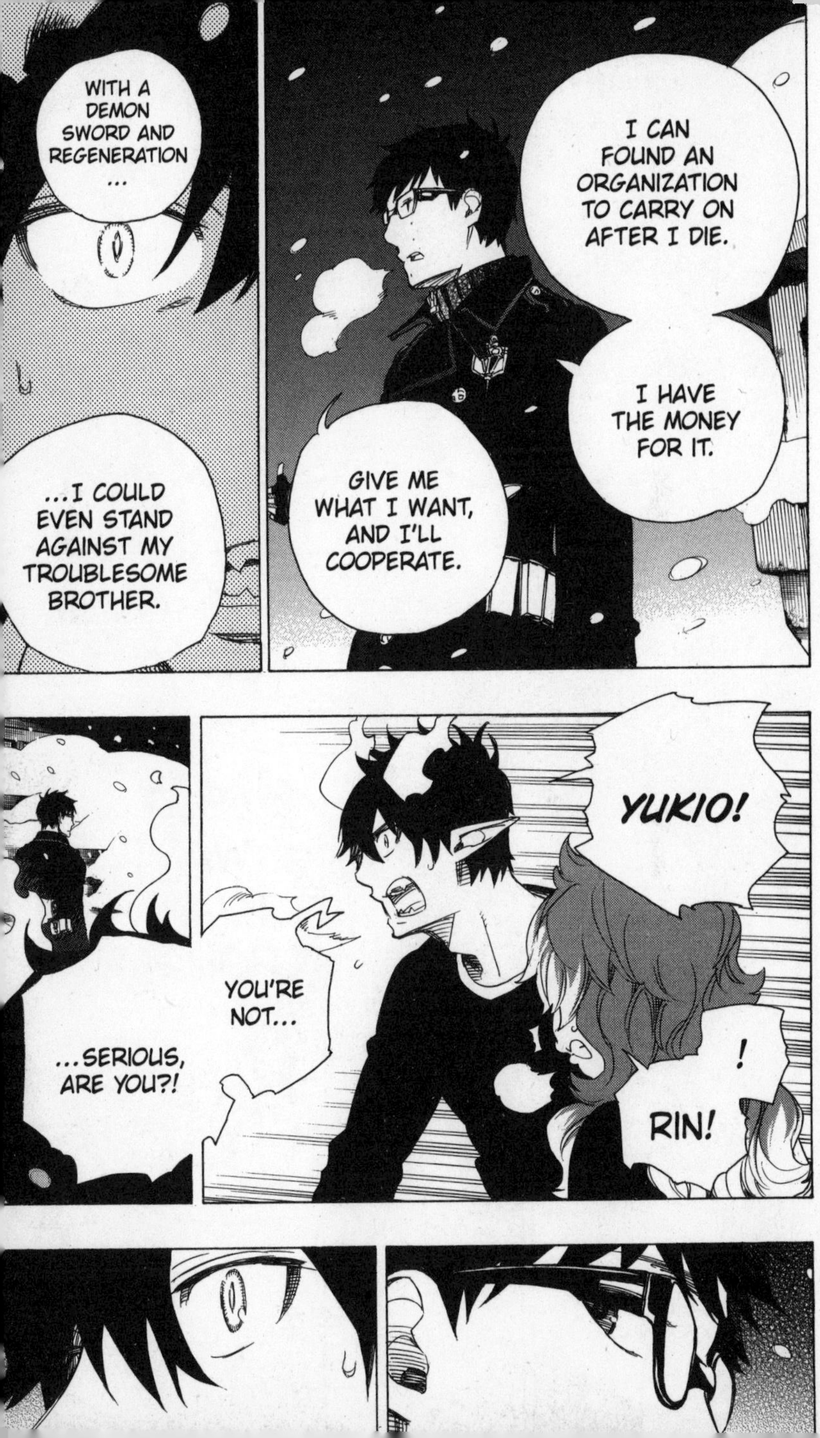
I CAN FOUND AN ORGANIZATION TO CARRY ON AFTER I DIE.
I HAVE THE MONEY FOR IT.
GIVE ME WHAT I WANT, AND I'LL COOPERATE.
WITH A DEMON SWORD AND REGENERATION ...
...I COULD EVEN STAND AGAINST MY TROUBLESOME BROTHER.
YUKIO!
!
RIN!
YOU'RE NOT...
...SERIOUS, ARE YOU?!

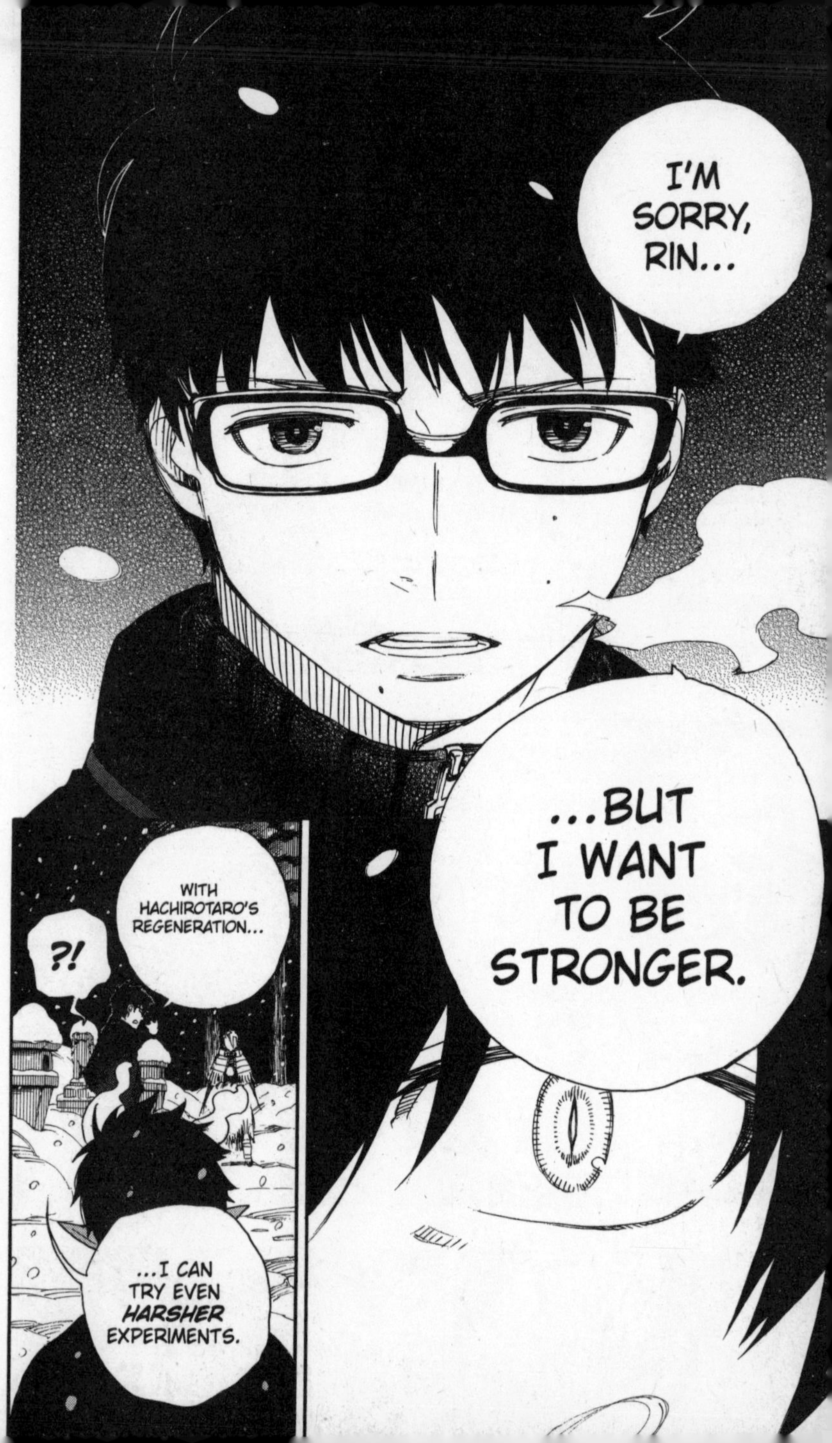
I'M SORRY, RIN...
...BUT I WANT TO BE STRONGER.
WITH HACHIROTARO'S REGENERATION...
?!
...I CAN TRY EVEN *HARSHER* EXPERIMENTS.

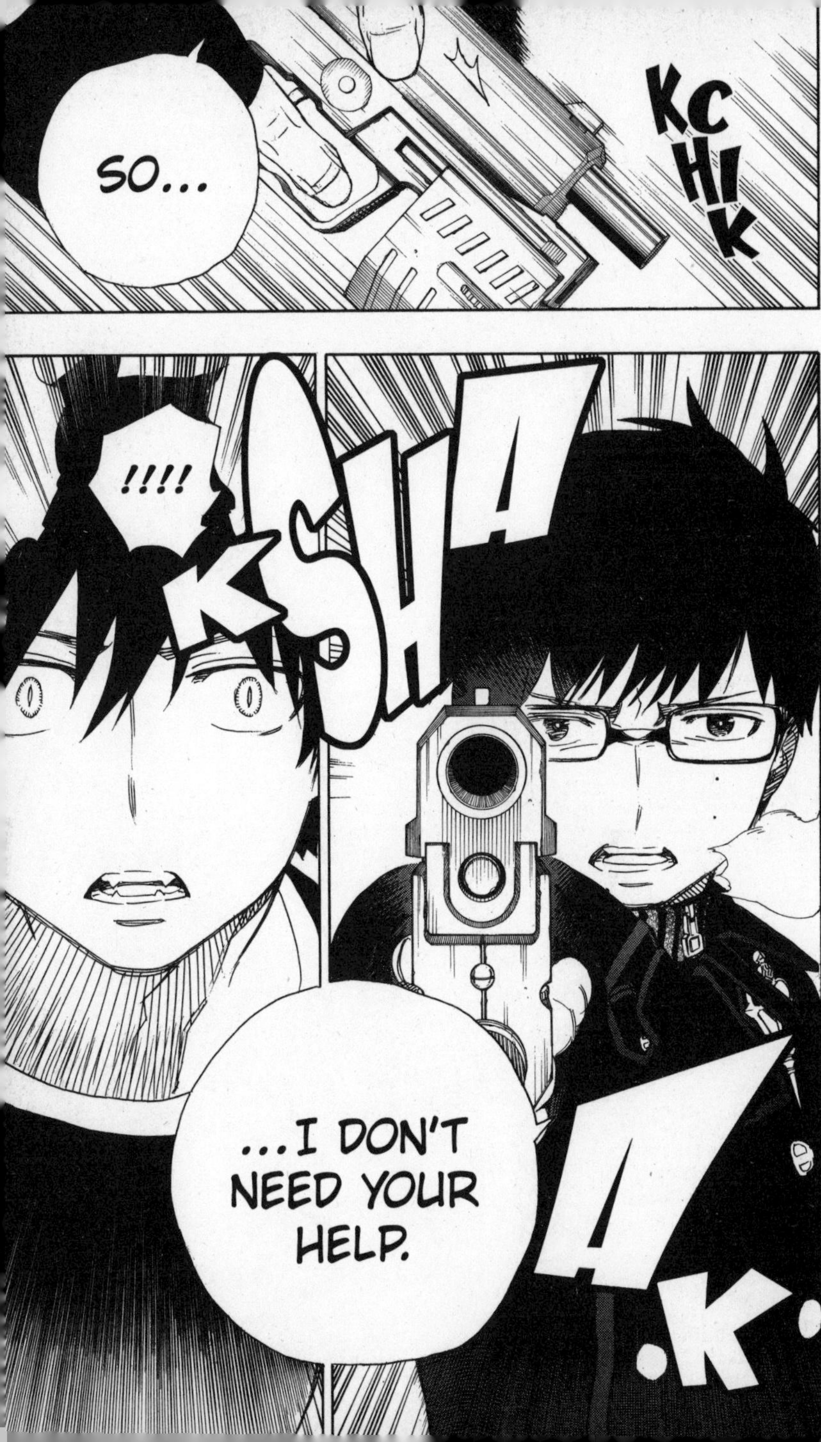
KCHIK
SO...
KSHA
...I DON'T NEED YOUR HELP.
A.K.
!!!!

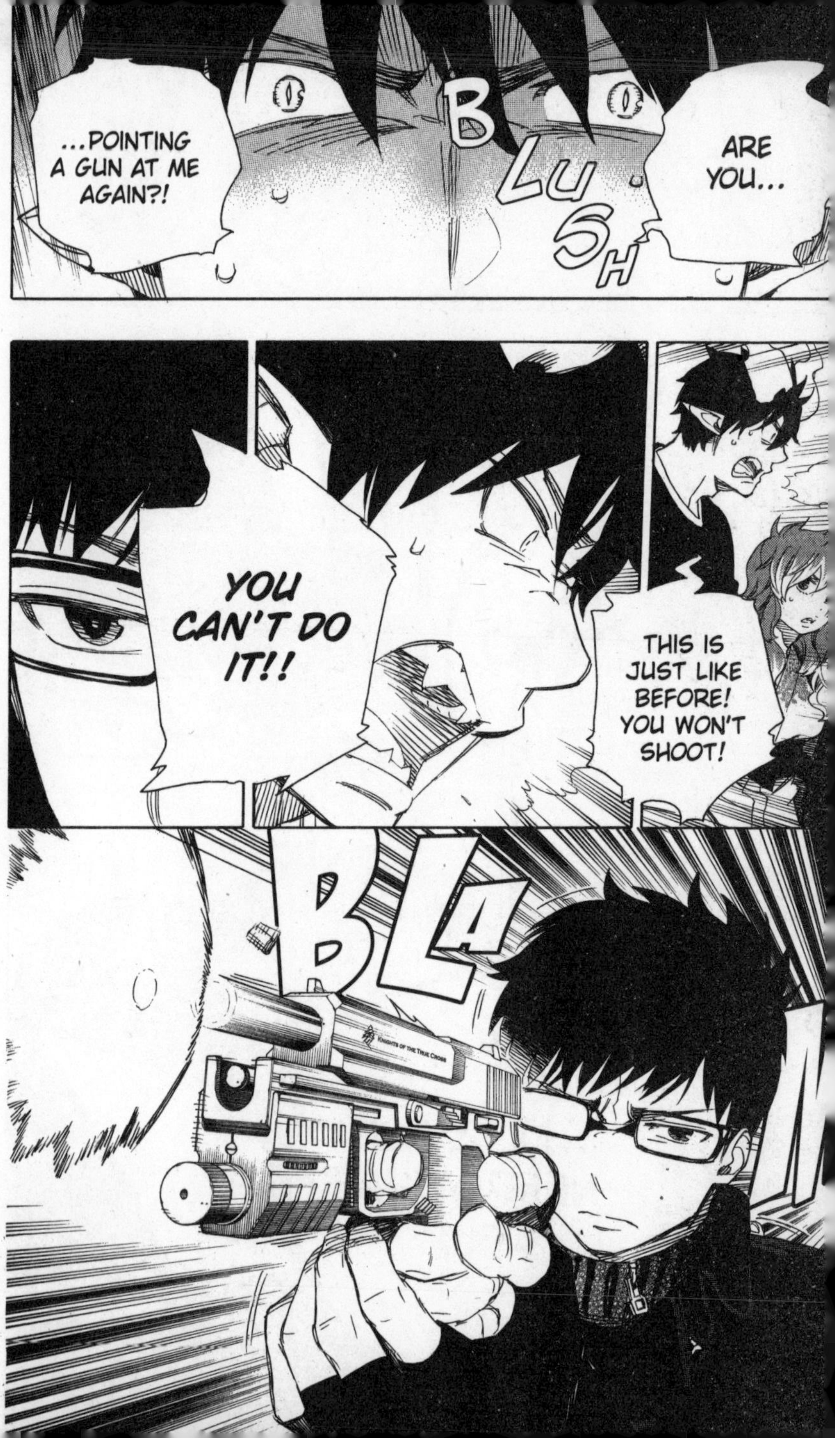
ARE YOU...
BLUSH
...POINTING A GUN AT ME AGAIN?!
THIS IS JUST LIKE BEFORE! YOU WON'T SHOOT!
YOU CAN'T DO IT!!
BLA
KNIGHTS OF THE TRUE CROSS

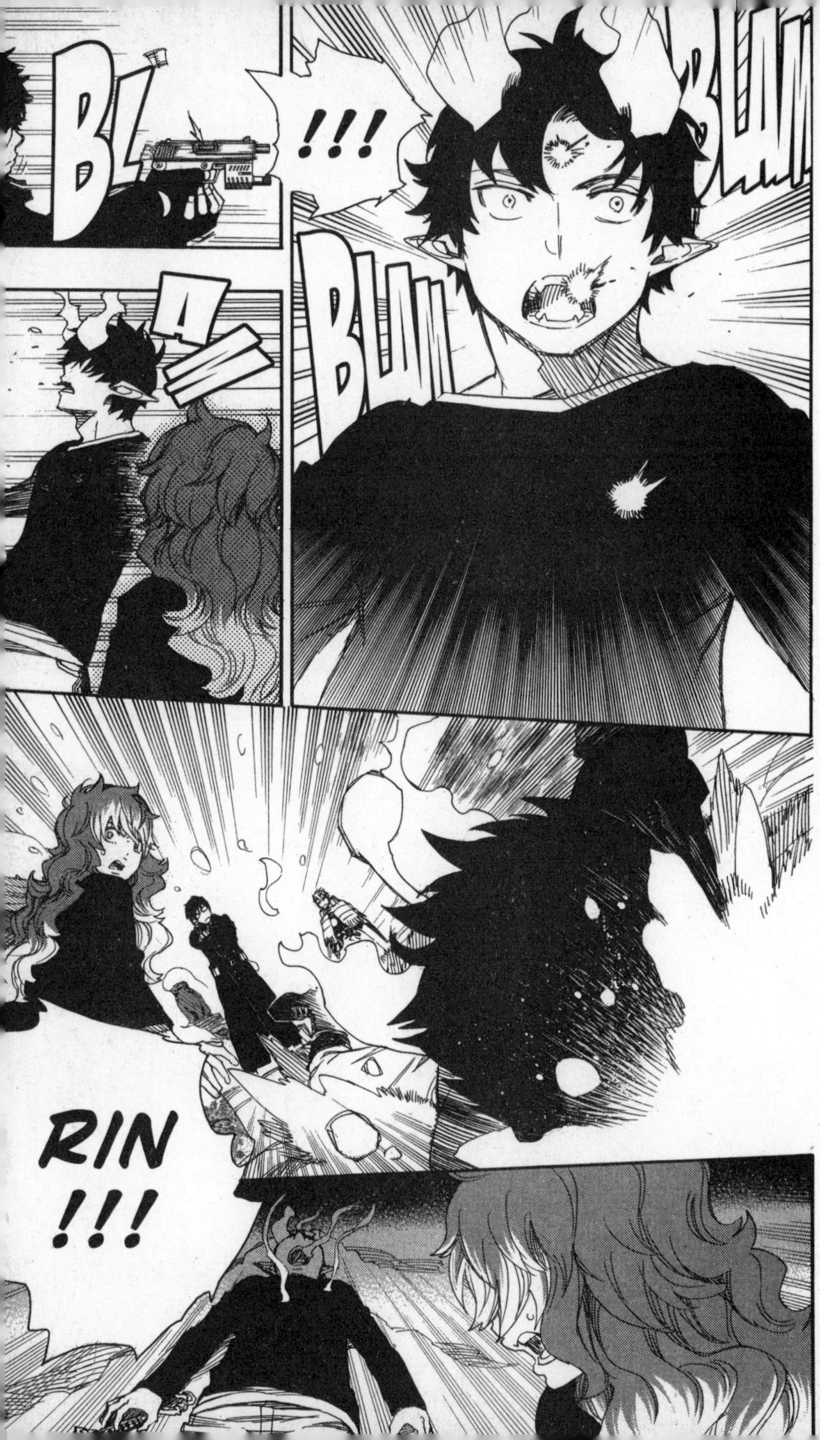
BLAM
!!!
BLAM
BL
A
RIN
!!!

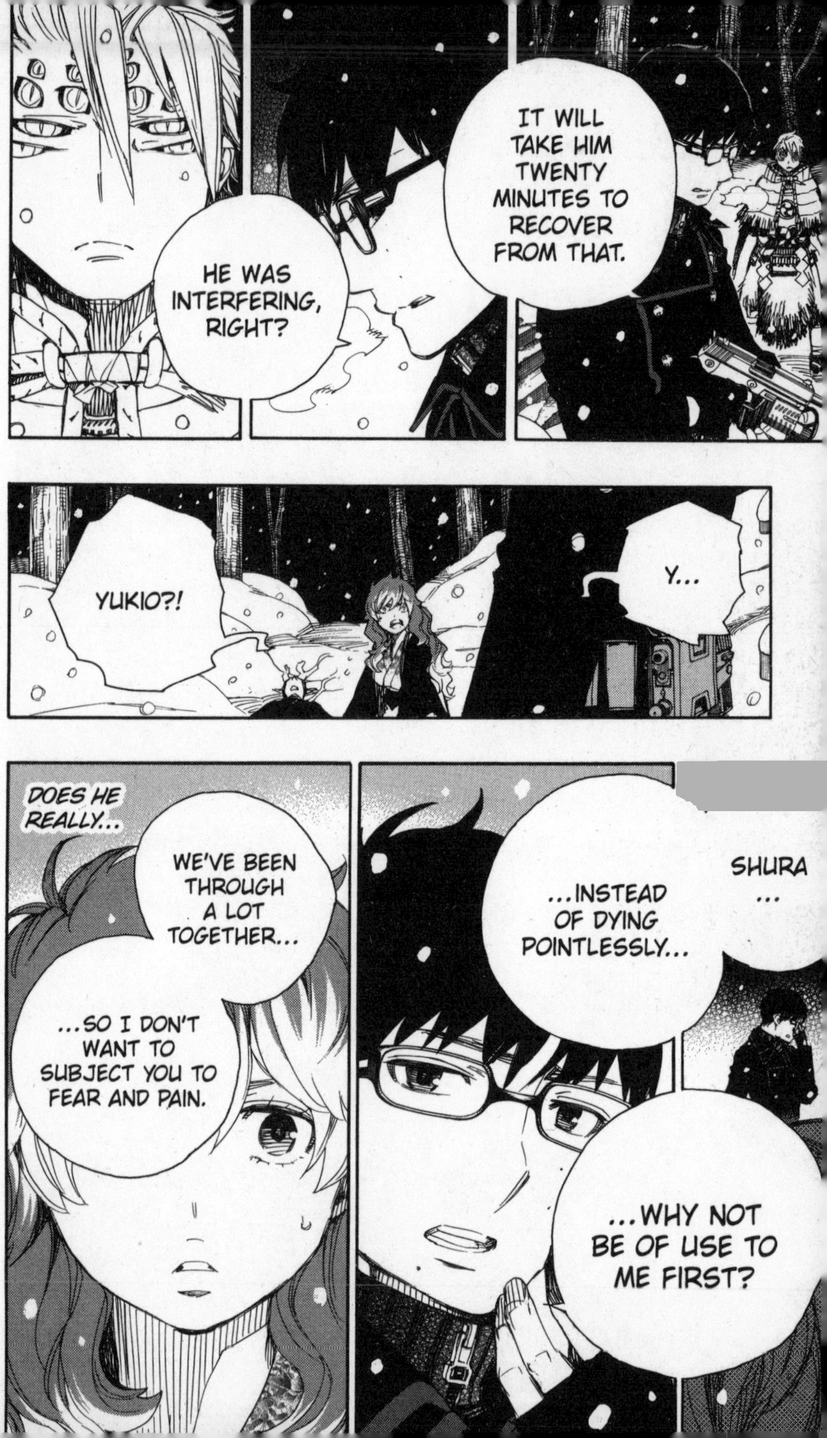
IT WILL TAKE HIM TWENTY MINUTES TO RECOVER FROM THAT.
HE WAS INTERFERING, RIGHT?
Y...
YUKIO?!
SHURA ...
...INSTEAD OF DYING POINTLESSLY...
...WHY NOT BE OF USE TO ME FIRST?
DOES HE REALLY...
WE'VE BEEN THROUGH A LOT TOGETHER...
...SO I DON'T WANT TO SUBJECT YOU TO FEAR AND PAIN.

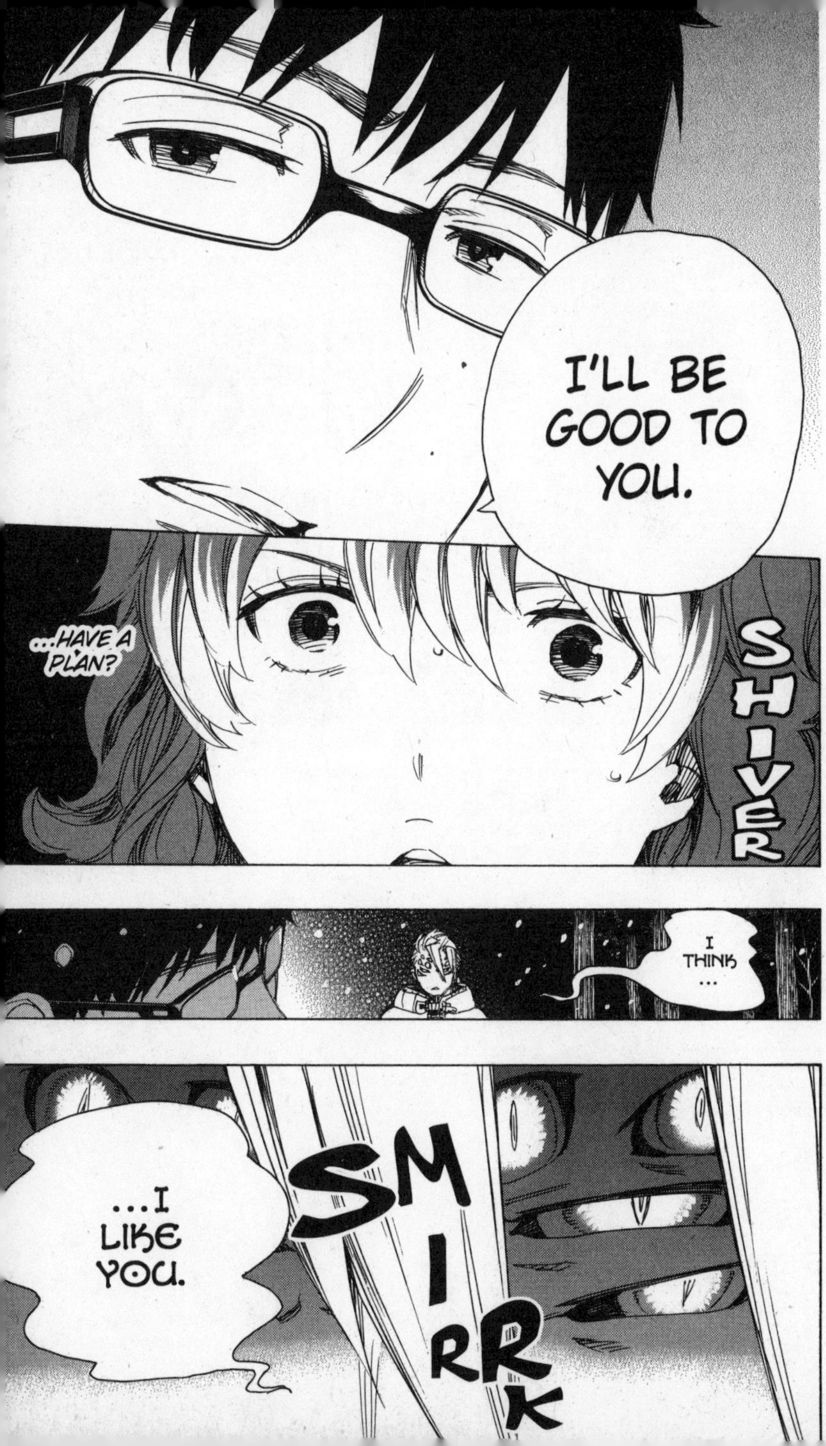
I'LL BE GOOD TO YOU.
SHIVER
...HAVE A PLAN?
I THINK ...
SMIRRK
...I LIKE YOU.

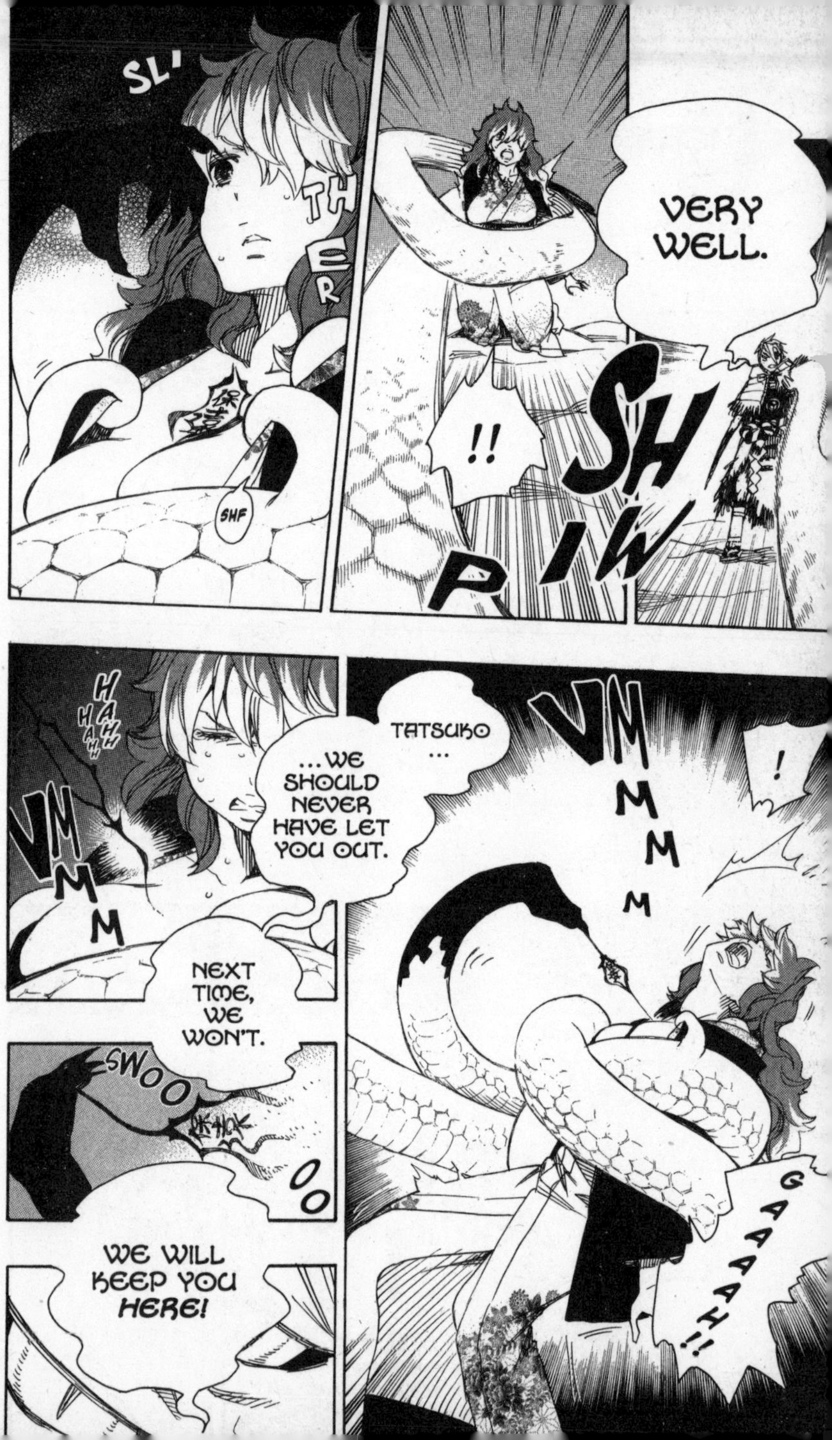
VERY WELL.
SHWIR
!!
SLITHER
SHF
VMMMM
!
GAAAAAH!!
HAHH HAHH
VMMM
TATSUKO...
...WE SHOULD NEVER HAVE LET YOU OUT.
NEXT TIME, WE WON'T.
SWOOOO
WE WILL KEEP YOU HERE!

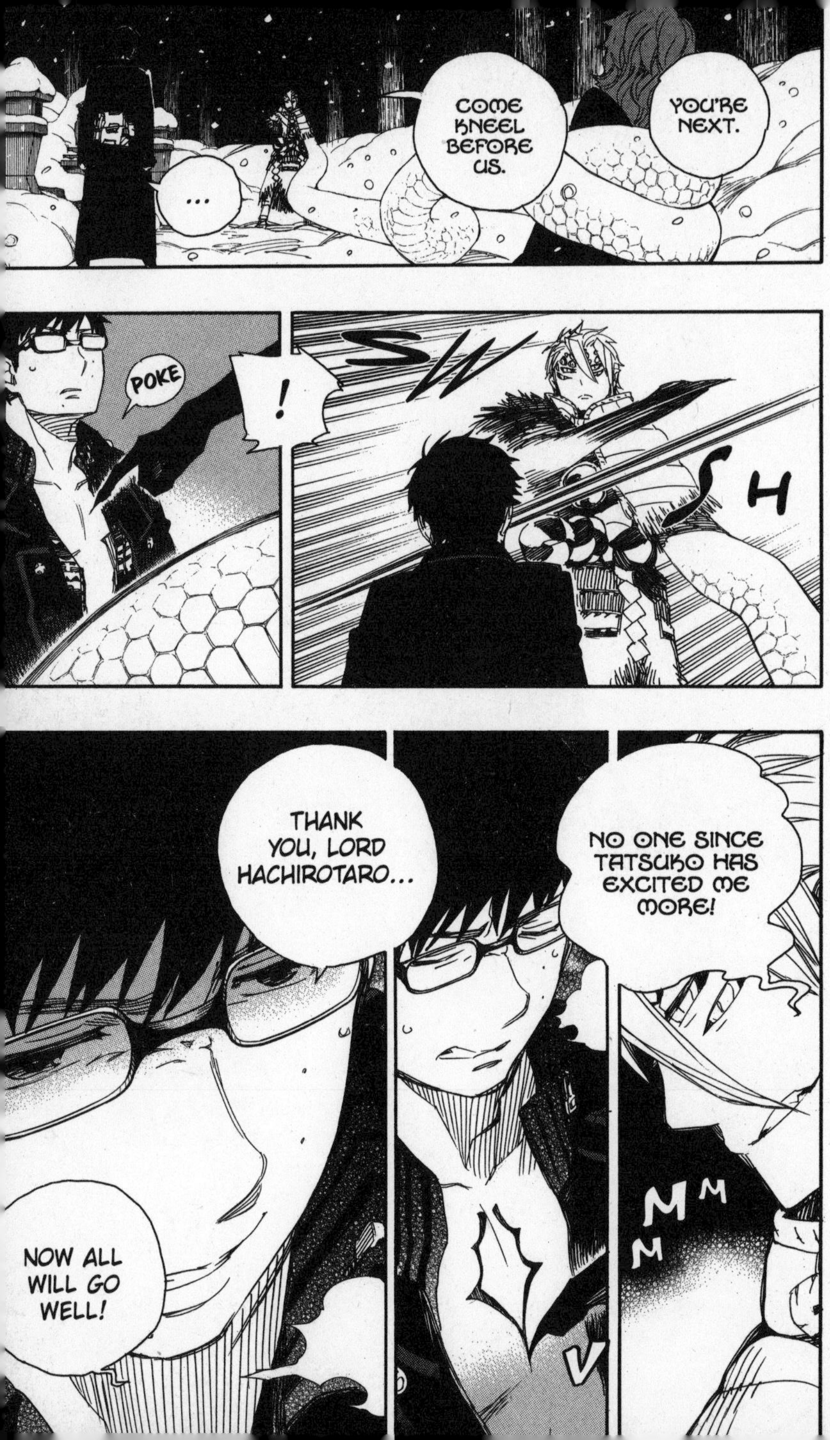
YOU'RE NEXT.
COME KNEEL BEFORE US.
...
SWSH
!
POKE
NO ONE SINCE TATSUKO HAS EXCITED ME MORE!
MMMM
THANK YOU, LORD HACHIROTARO...
V
NOW ALL WILL GO WELL!

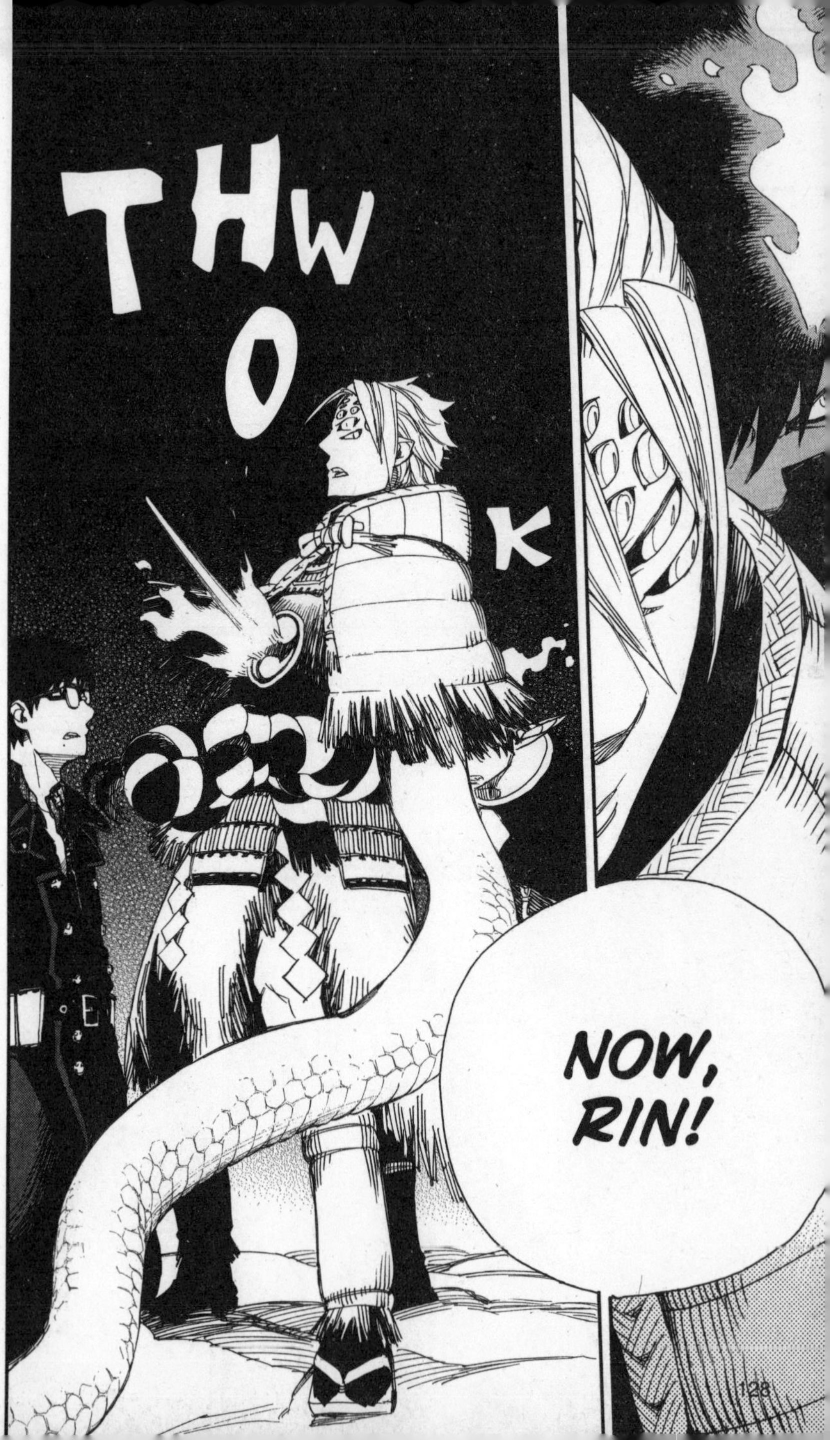
THWOK
NOW, RIN!

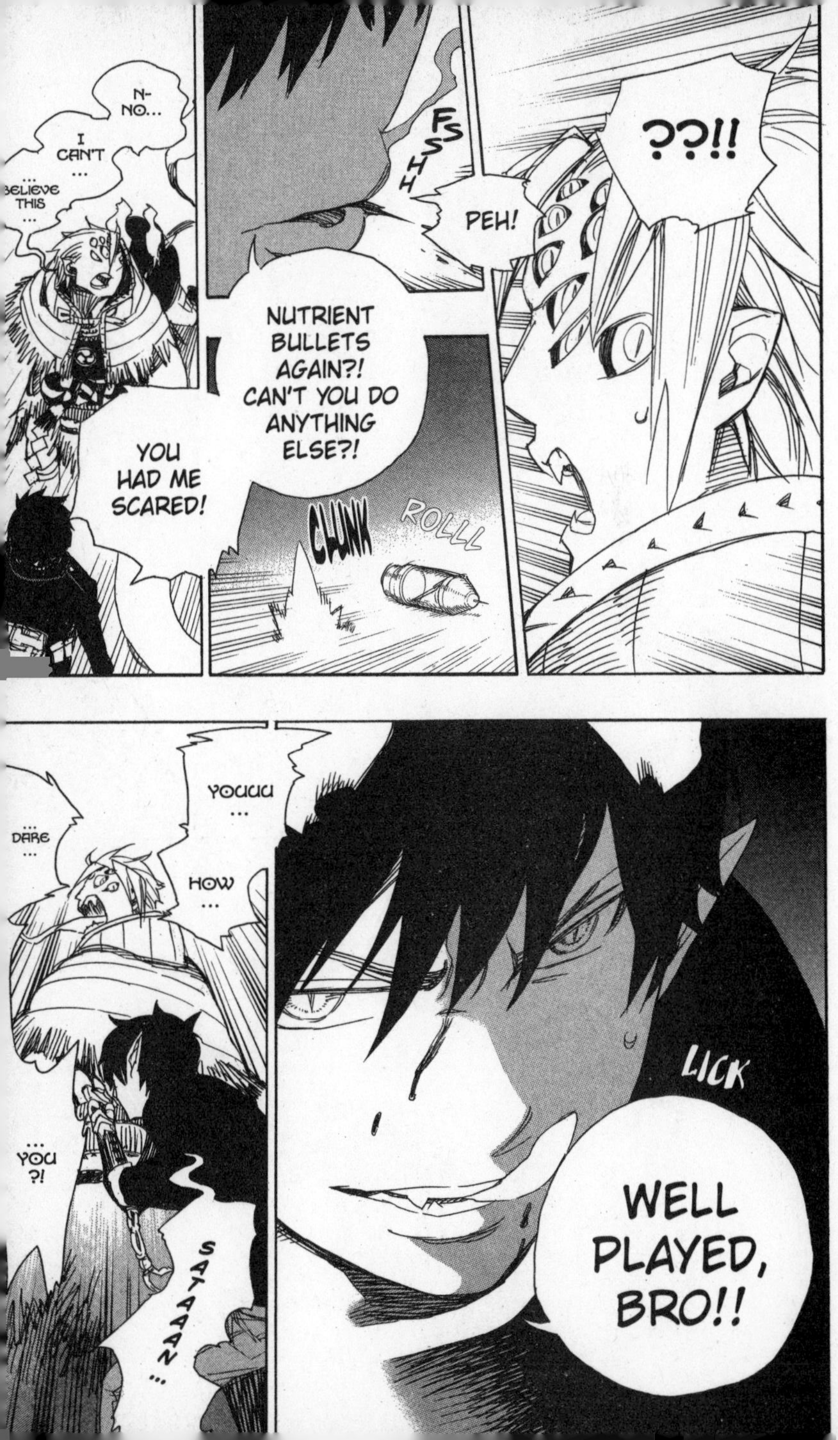
??!!
PEH!
FSSHH
NUTRIENT BULLETS AGAIN?! CAN'T YOU DO ANYTHING ELSE?!
CLUNK
ROLLL
N- NO...
I CAN'T ...
... BELIEVE THIS ...
YOU HAD ME SCARED!
LICK
WELL PLAYED, BRO!!
YOUUU ...
HOW ...
... DARE ...
... YOU ?!
SATAAAAN ...

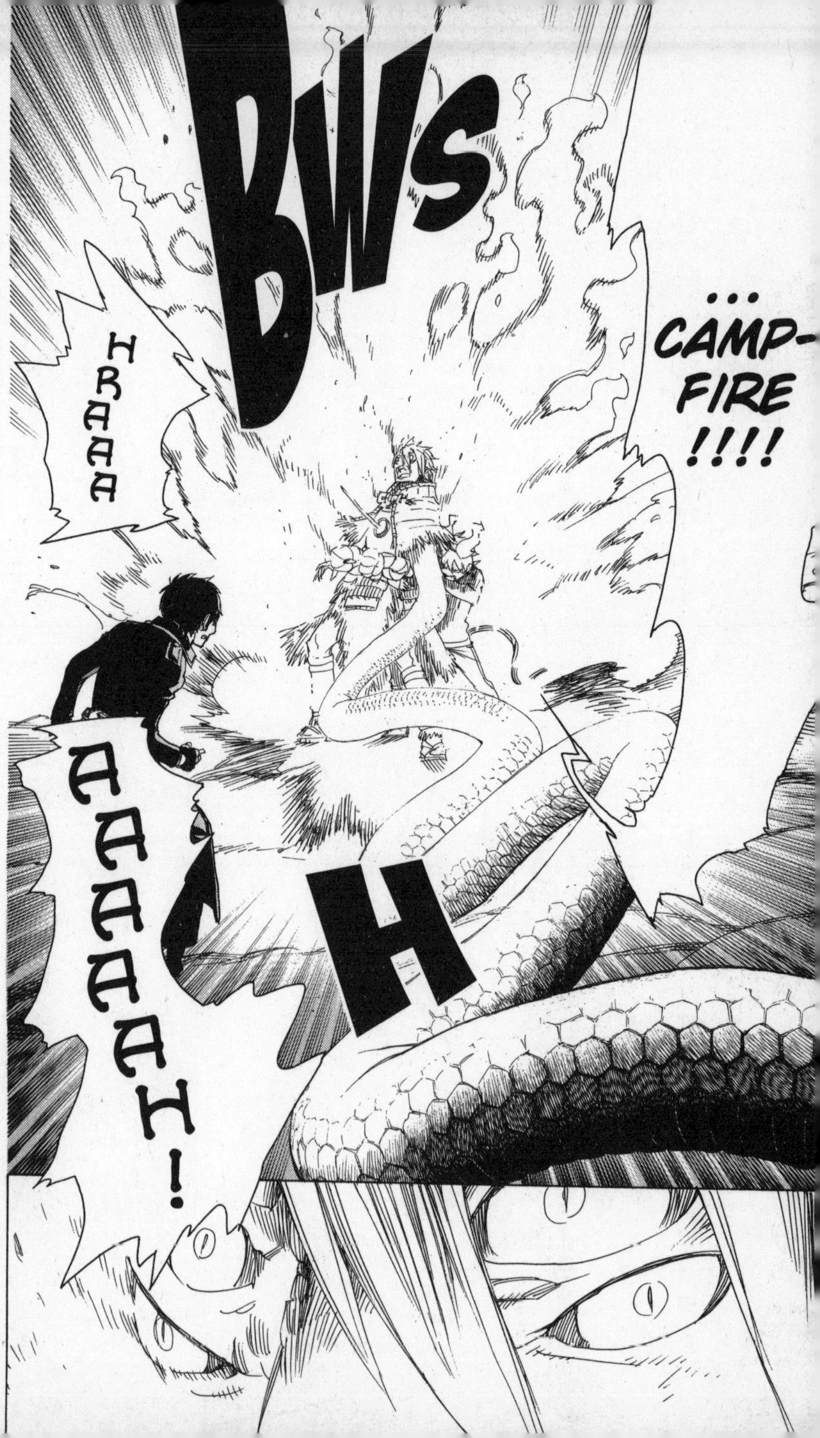
BWSH
... CAMP-FIRE !!!!
HRAAAA
AAAAAAH!

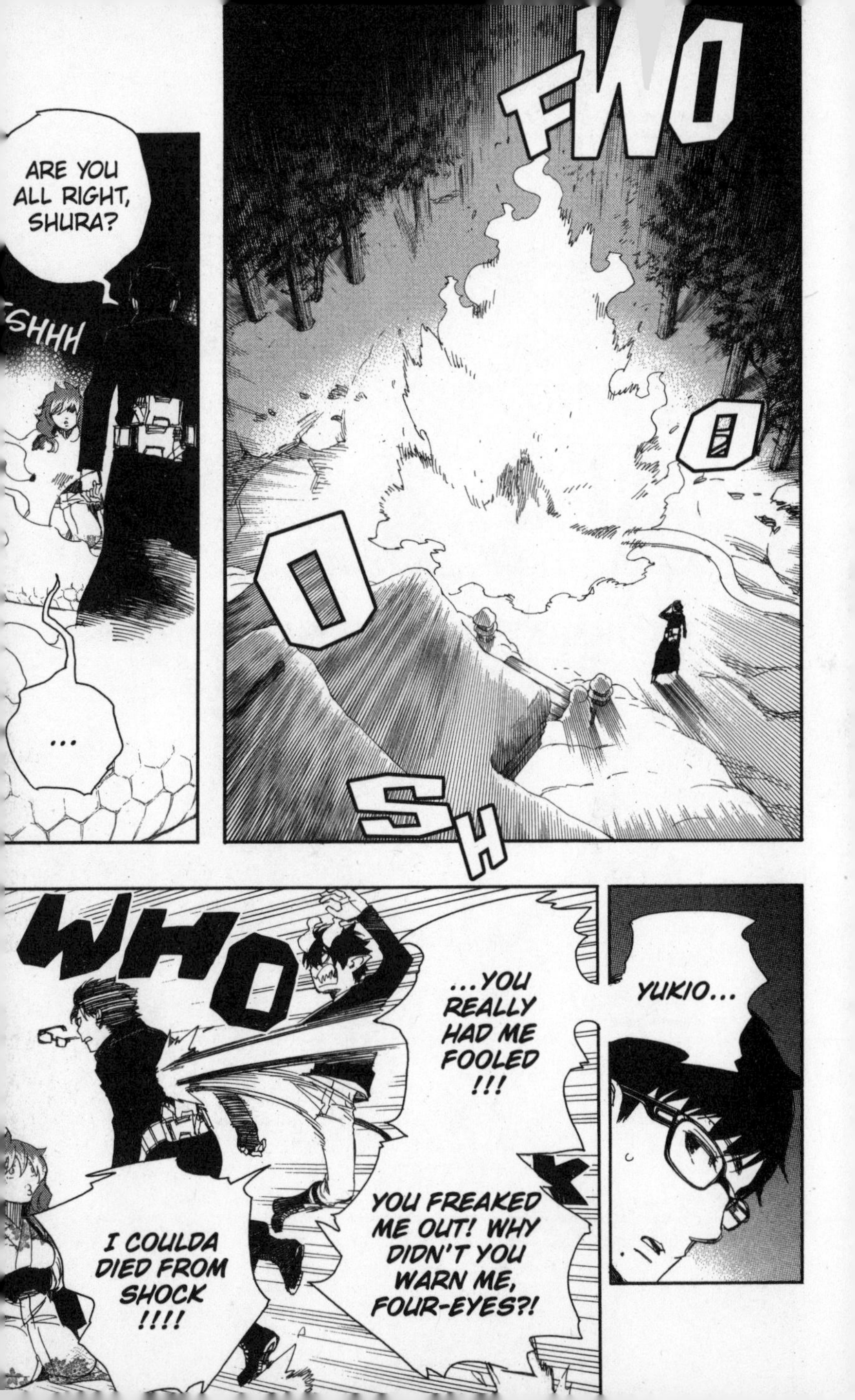
FWO
O
O
SH
ARE YOU ALL RIGHT, SHURA?
SHHH
...
YUKIO...
...YOU REALLY HAD ME FOOLED!!!
WHO
K
YOU FREAKED ME OUT! WHY DIDN'T YOU WARN ME, FOUR-EYES?!
I COULDA DIED FROM SHOCK!!!!

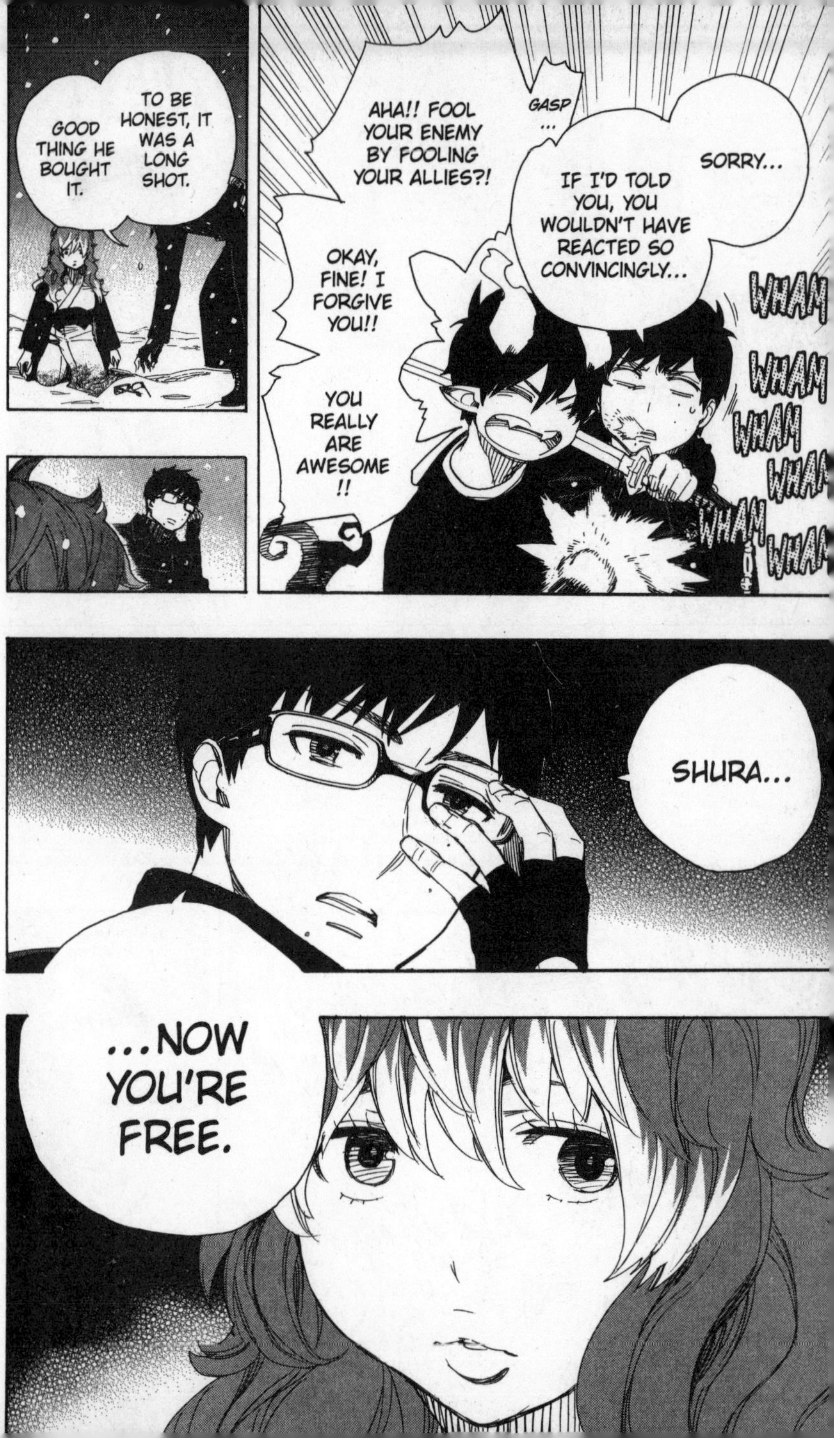
GASP ...
SORRY...
IF I'D TOLD YOU, YOU WOULDN'T HAVE REACTED SO CONVINCINGLY...
AHA!! FOOL YOUR ENEMY BY FOOLING YOUR ALLIES?!
OKAY, FINE! I FORGIVE YOU!!
YOU REALLY ARE AWESOME!!
WHAM
WHAM
WHAM
WHAM
WHAM
WHAM
TO BE HONEST, IT WAS A LONG SHOT.
GOOD THING HE BOUGHT IT.
SHURA...
...NOW YOU'RE FREE.

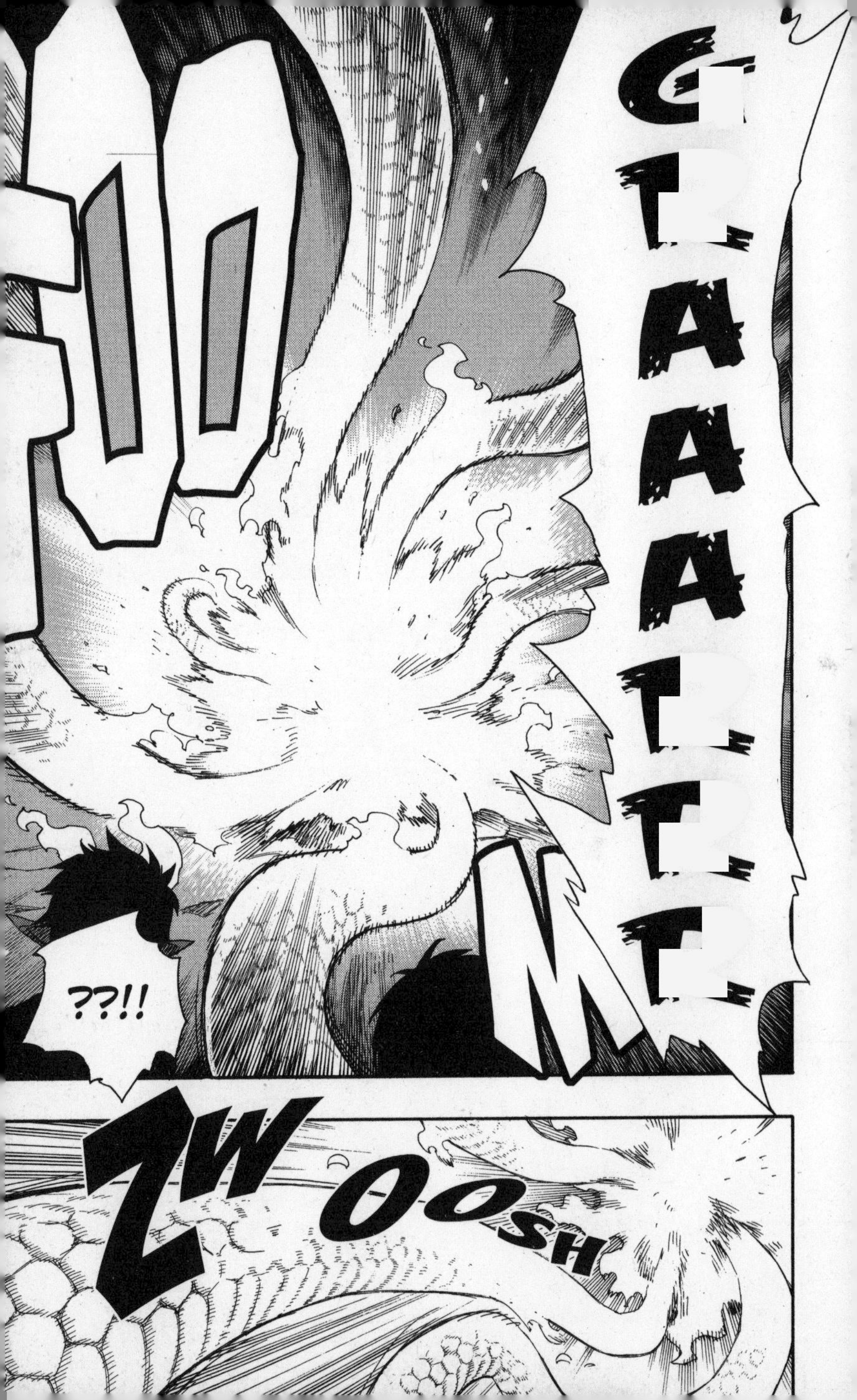
??!!
ZWOOSH

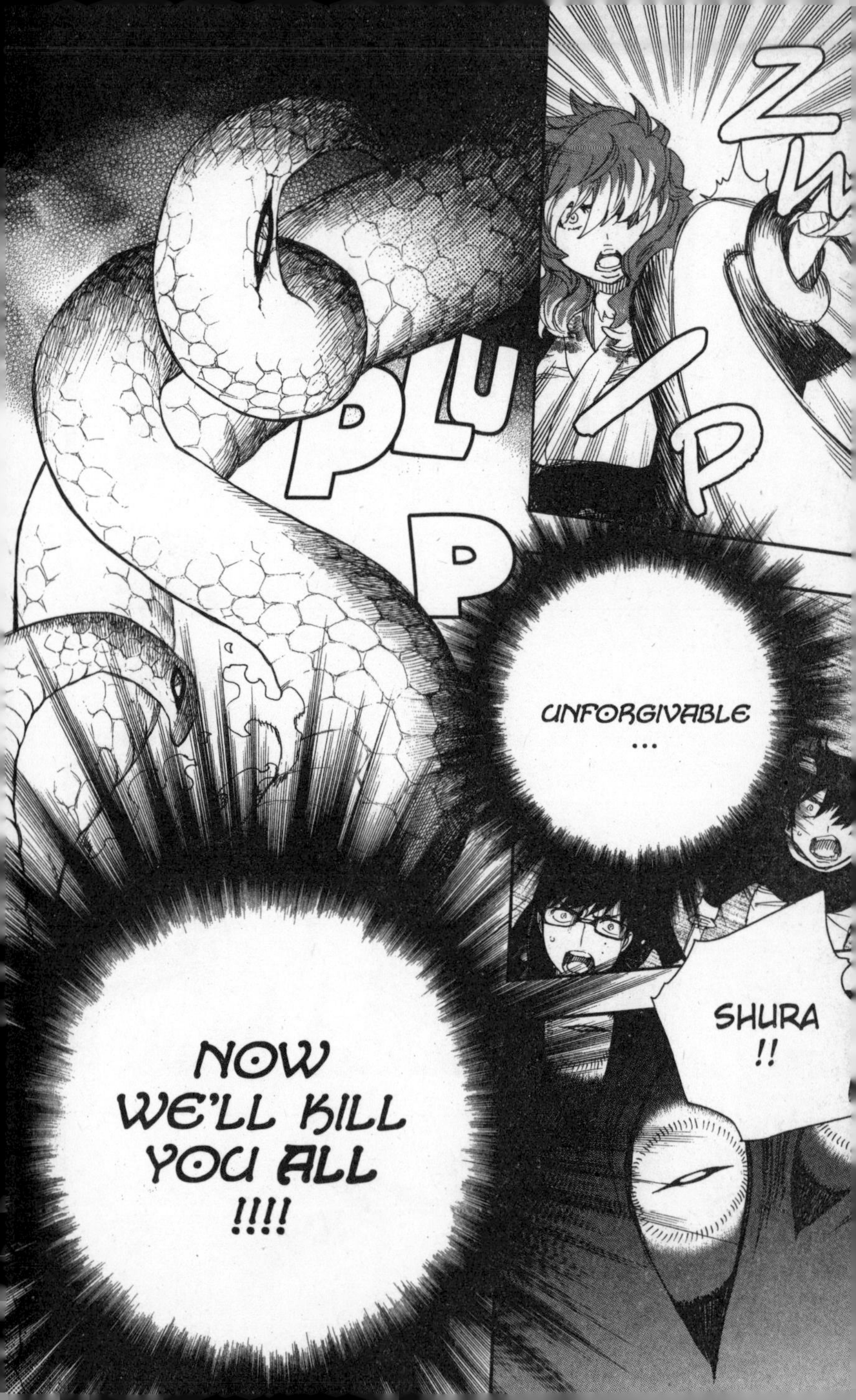
ZWIP
UNFORGIVABLE ...
SHURA !!
PLUP
NOW WE'LL KILL YOU ALL !!!!

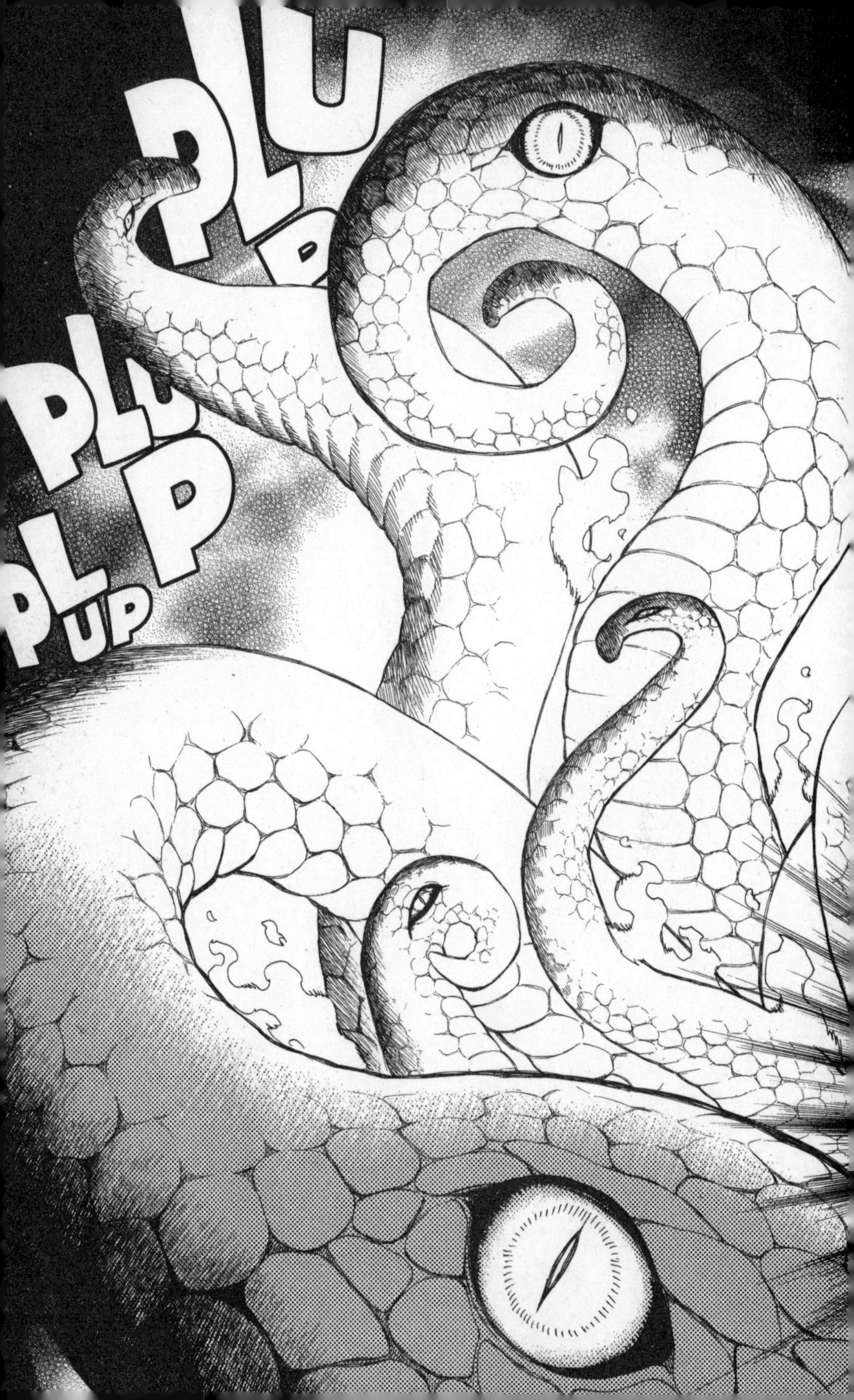
PLUP
PLUP
PLUP

Blue Exorcist Chapter 77: It's All Right If I Don't Go Back

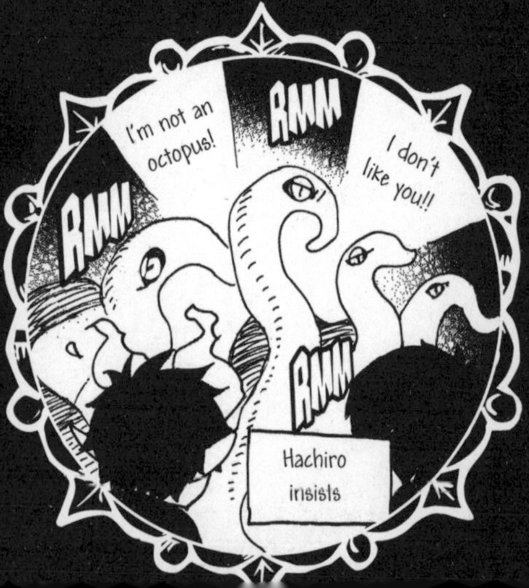
I don't like you!!
RMM
I'm not an octopus!
RMM
RMM
Hachiro insists

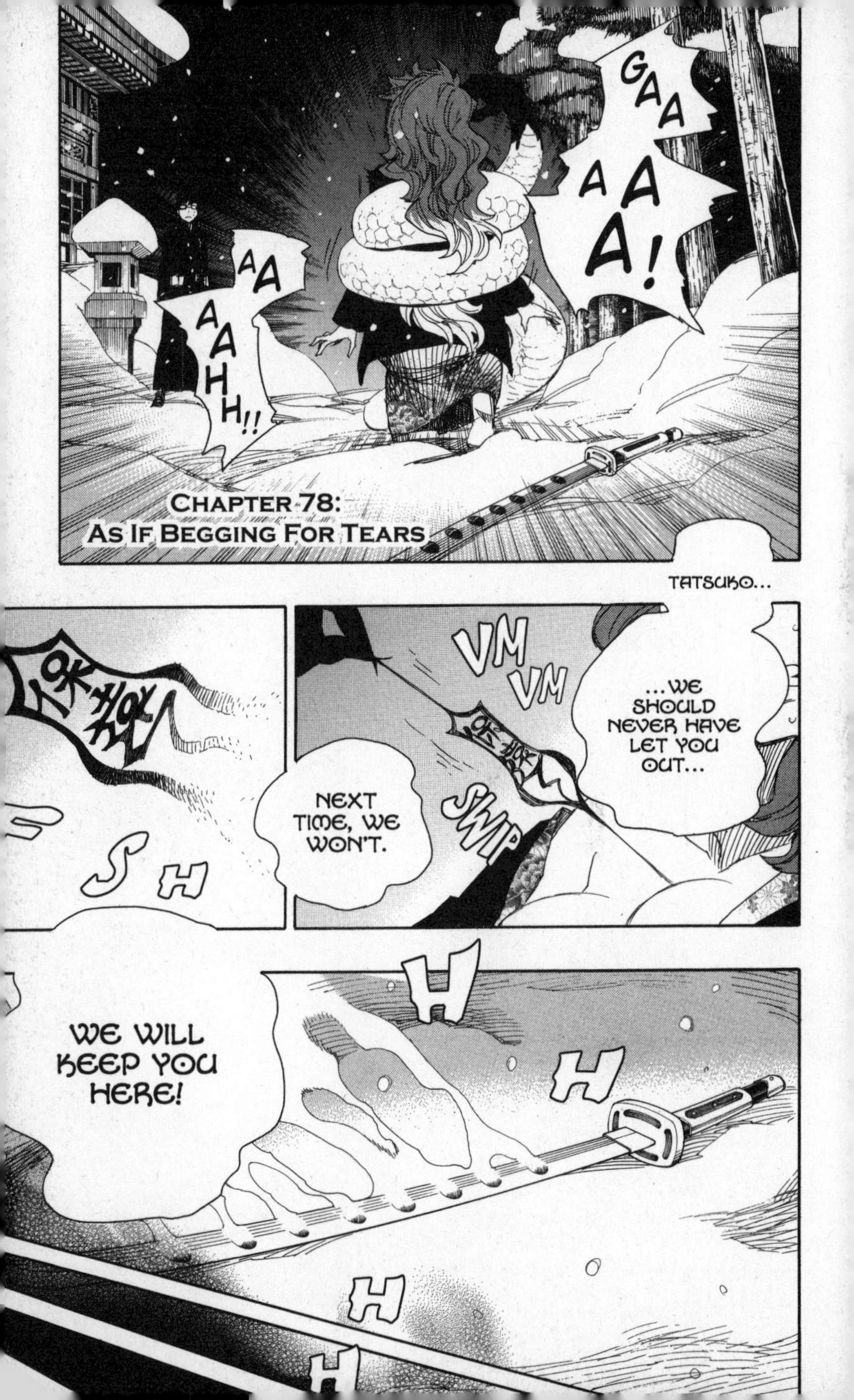
GAAAAA!
AAAAHH!!
Chapter 78:
As If Begging For Tears
TATSUKO...
...WE SHOULD NEVER HAVE LET YOU OUT...
VM VM
SWIP
NEXT TIME, WE WON'T.
SH
WE WILL KEEP YOU HERE!
H
H
H
H

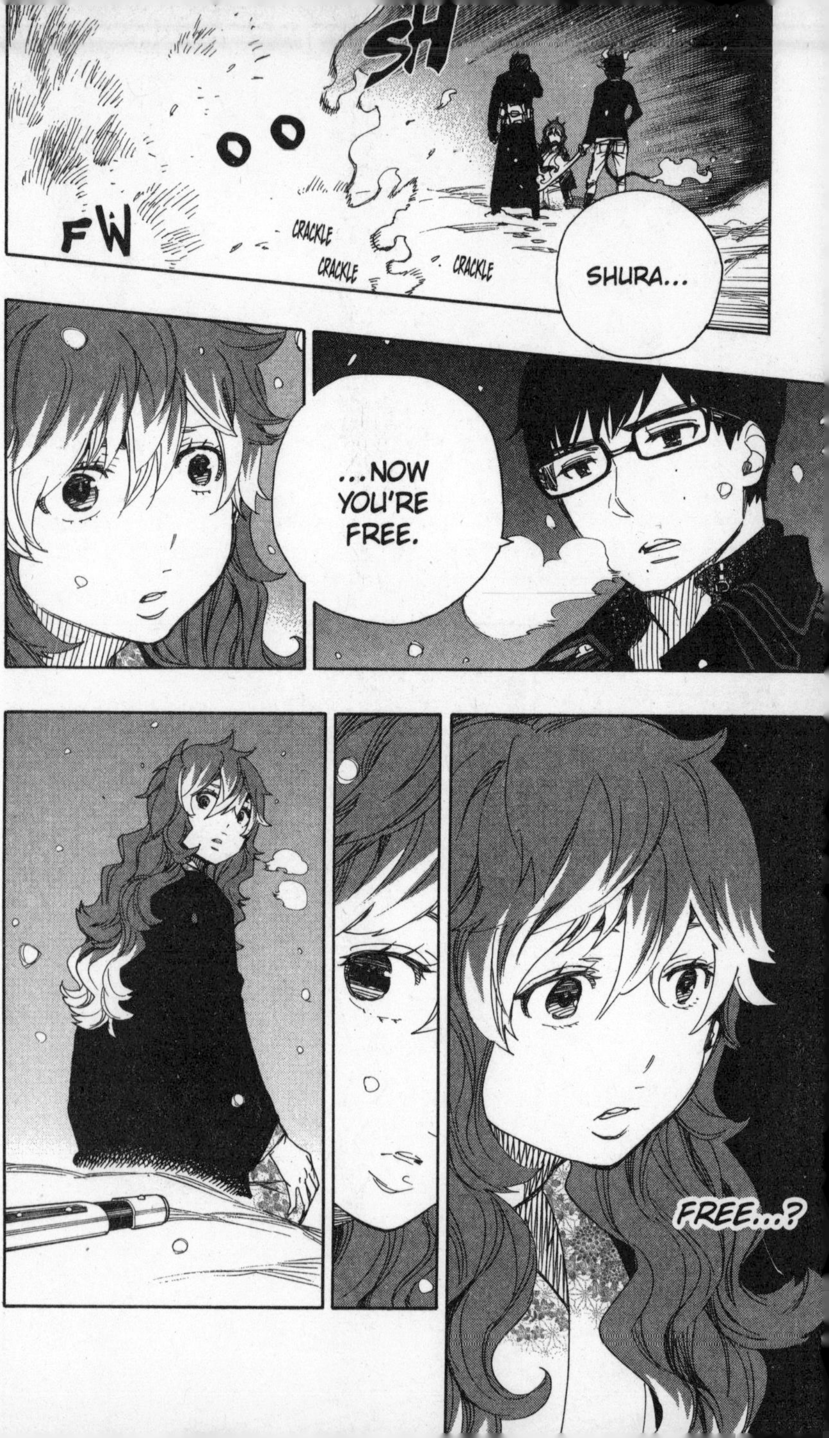
SH
SHURA...
CRACKLE
CRACKLE
CRACKLE
OO
FW
...NOW YOU'RE FREE.
FREE...?

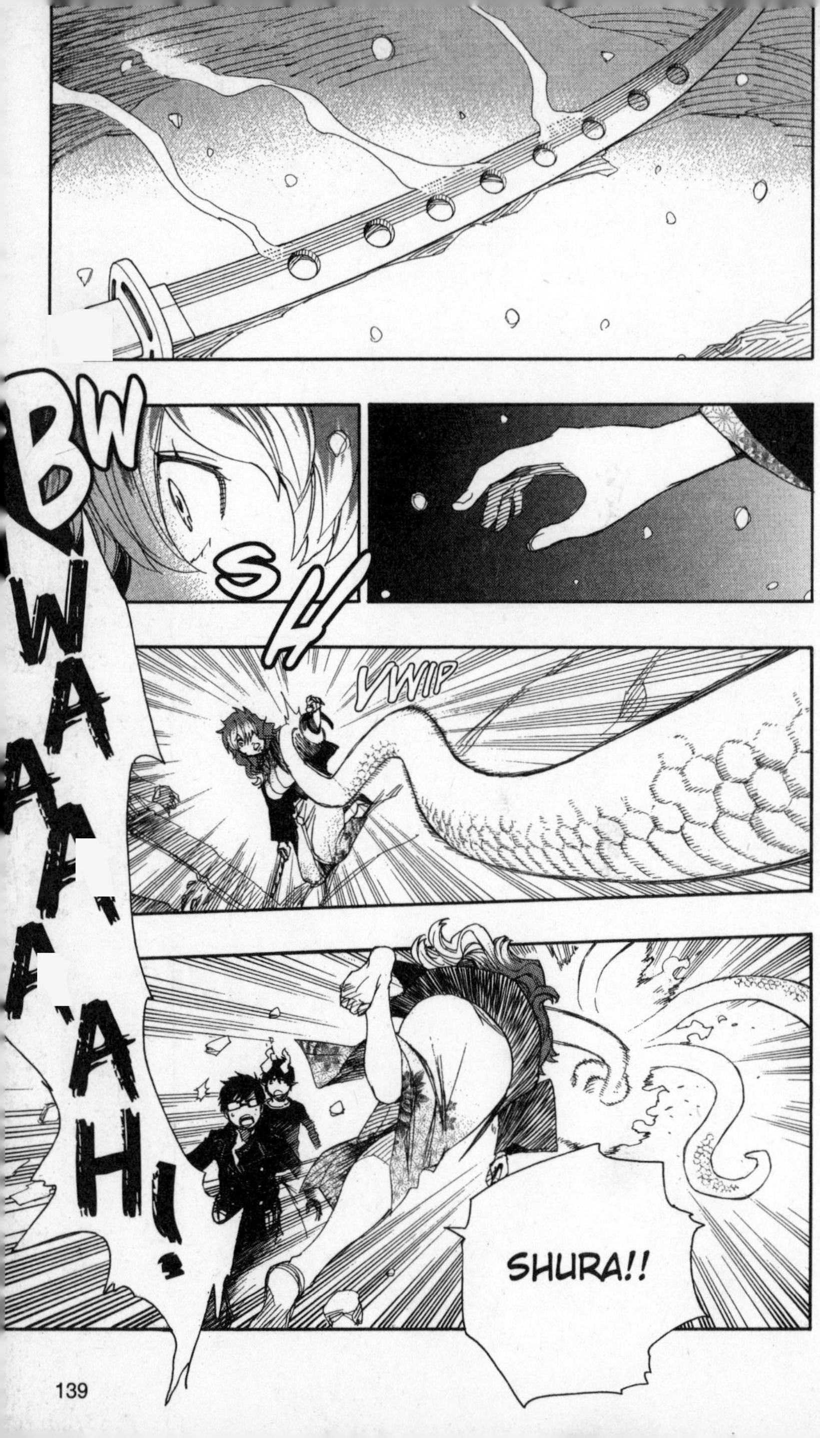
SH
BWAAAAAH!
VWIP
SHURA!!

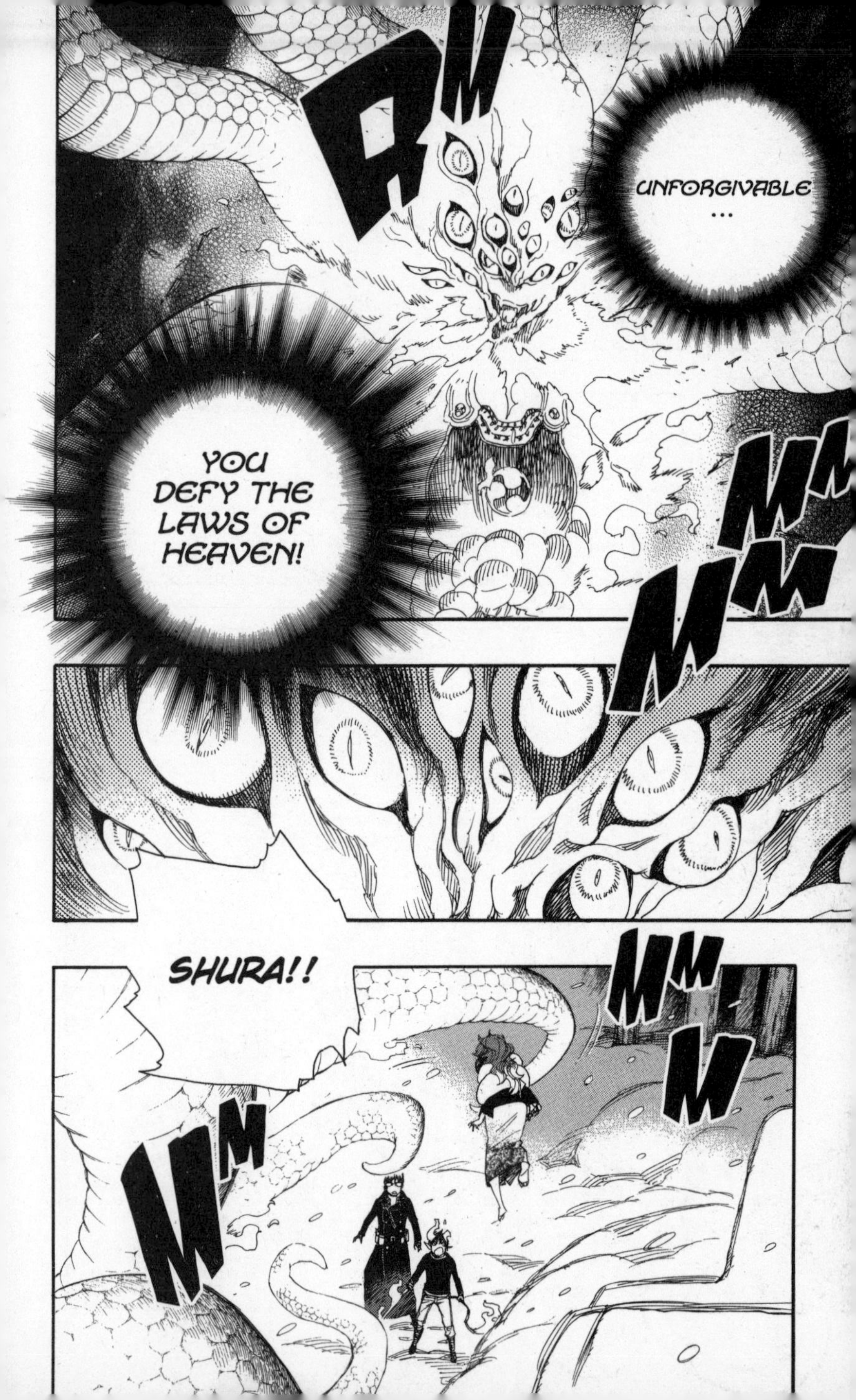

RUMMMMMM
UNFORGIVABLE
...
YOU DEFY THE LAWS OF HEAVEN!
MMMM
SHURA!!
MMM

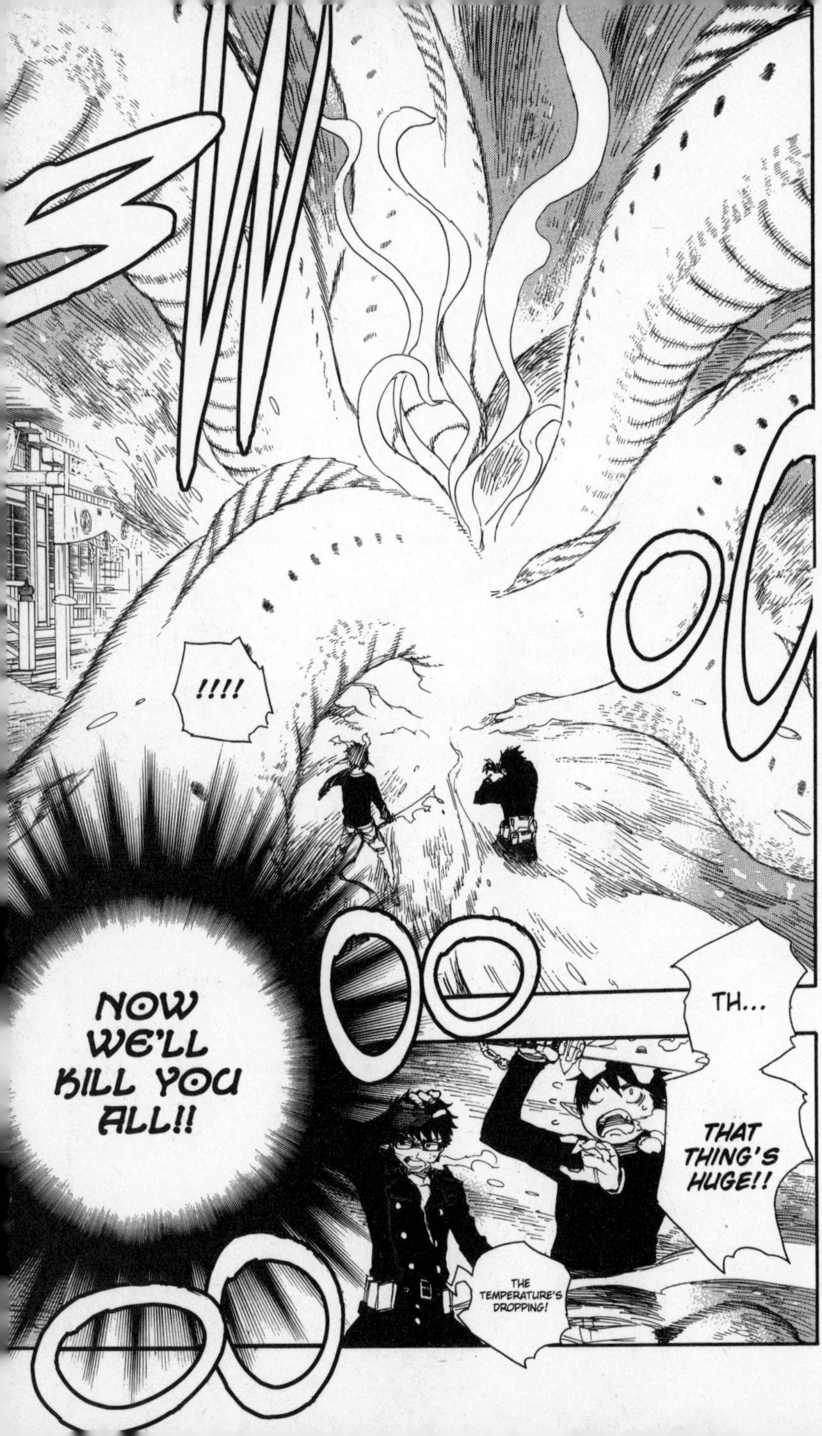
!!!!
TH...
THAT THING'S HUGE!!
THE TEMPERATURE'S DROPPING!
NOW WE'LL KILL YOU ALL!!

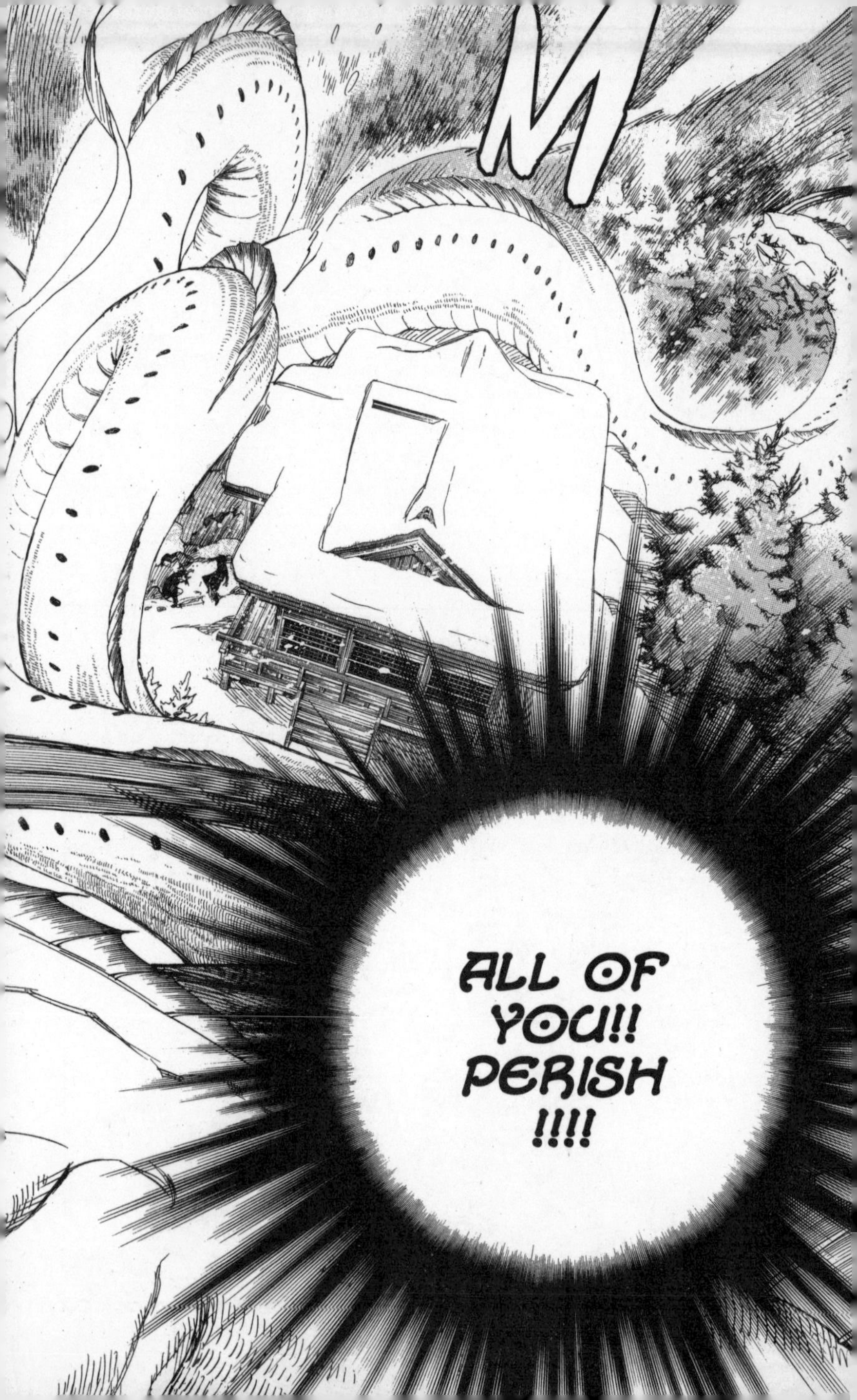
M
ALL OF YOU!! PERISH !!!!

Chapter 78: As If Begging For Tears

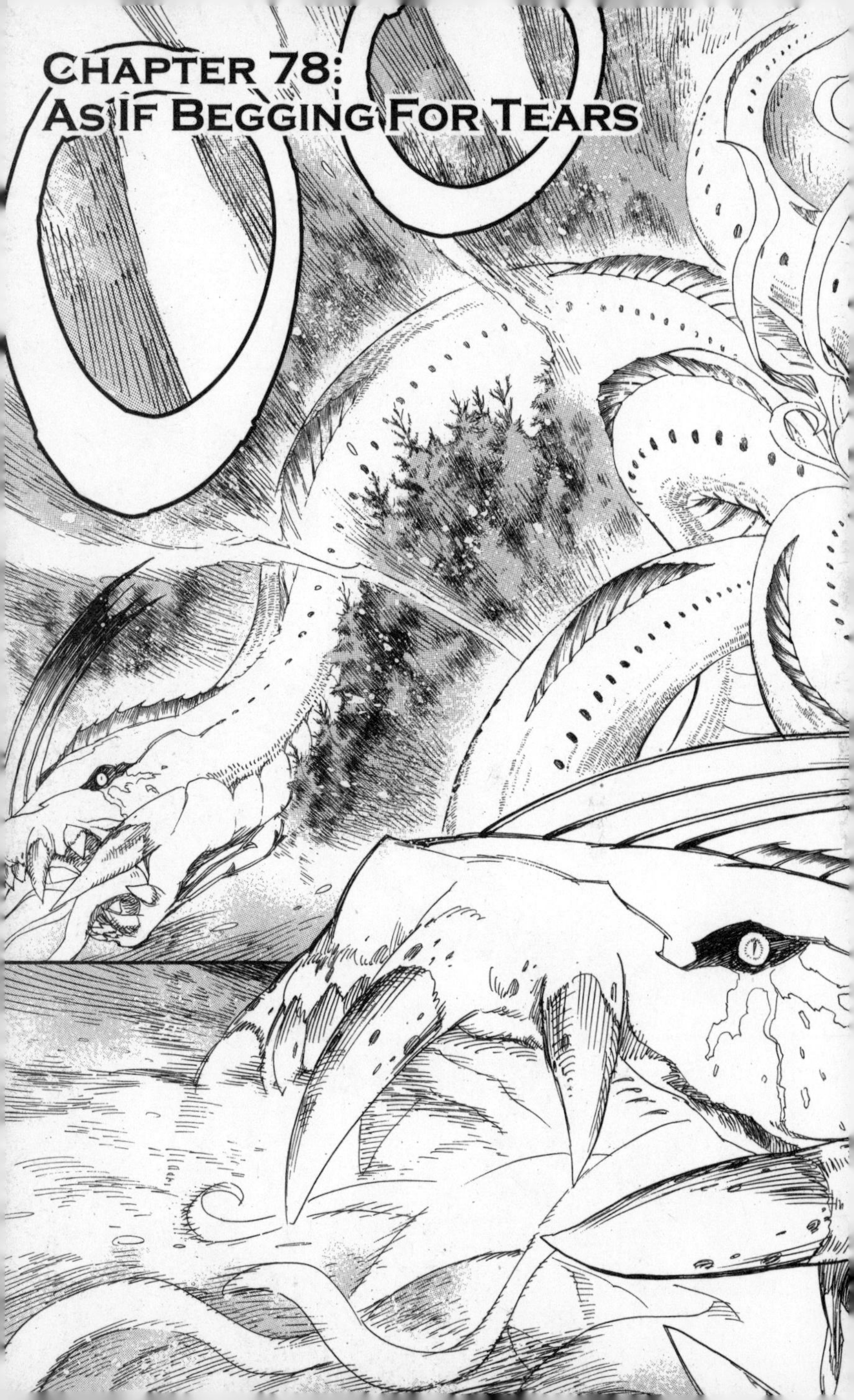

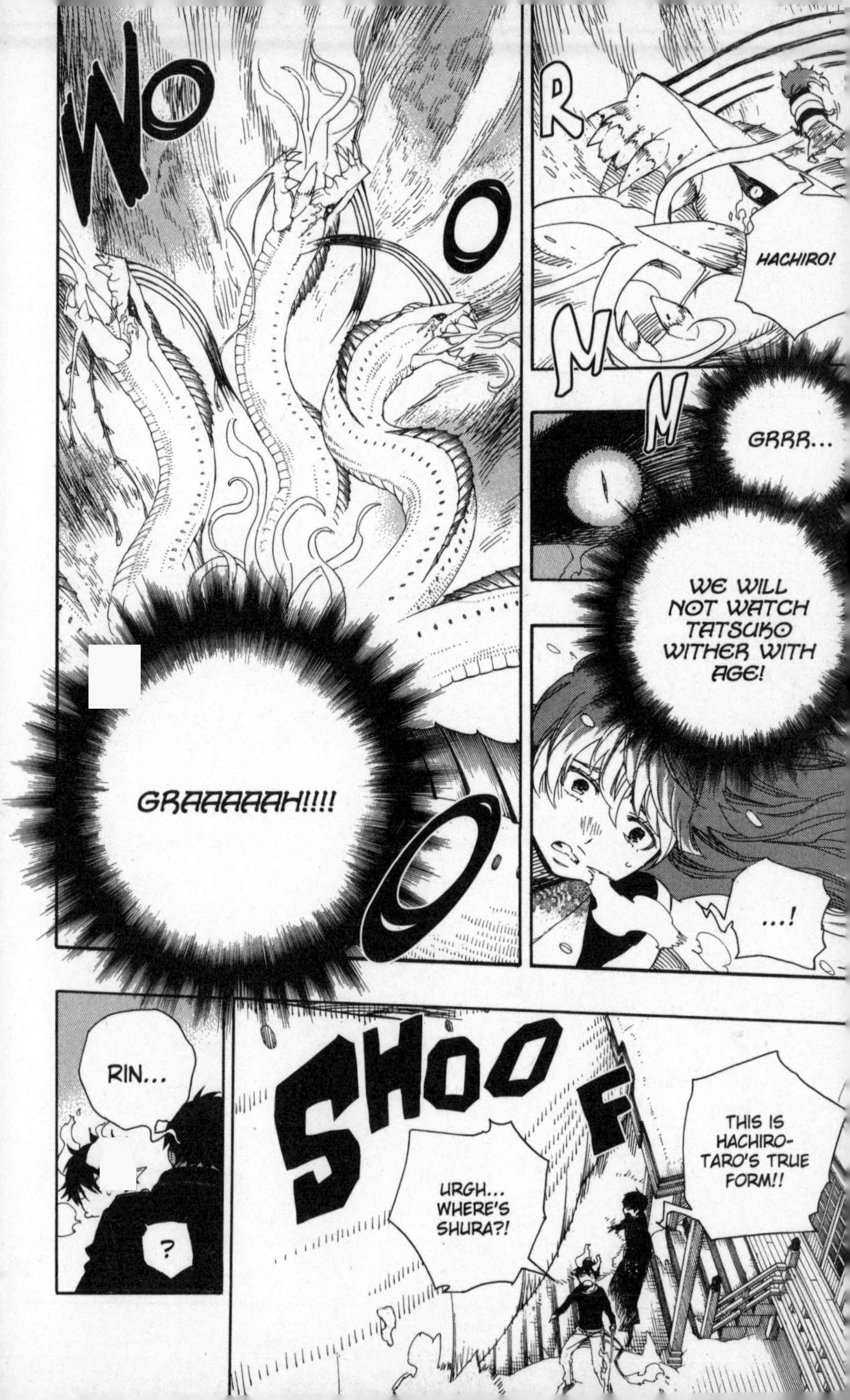
R
HACHIRO!
MN
GRRR...
WE WILL NOT WATCH TATSUKO WITHER WITH AGE!
...!
WOOOO
GRAAAAAH!!!!
THIS IS HACHIRO-TARO'S TRUE FORM!!
URGH... WHERE'S SHURA?!
SHOOF
RIN...
?

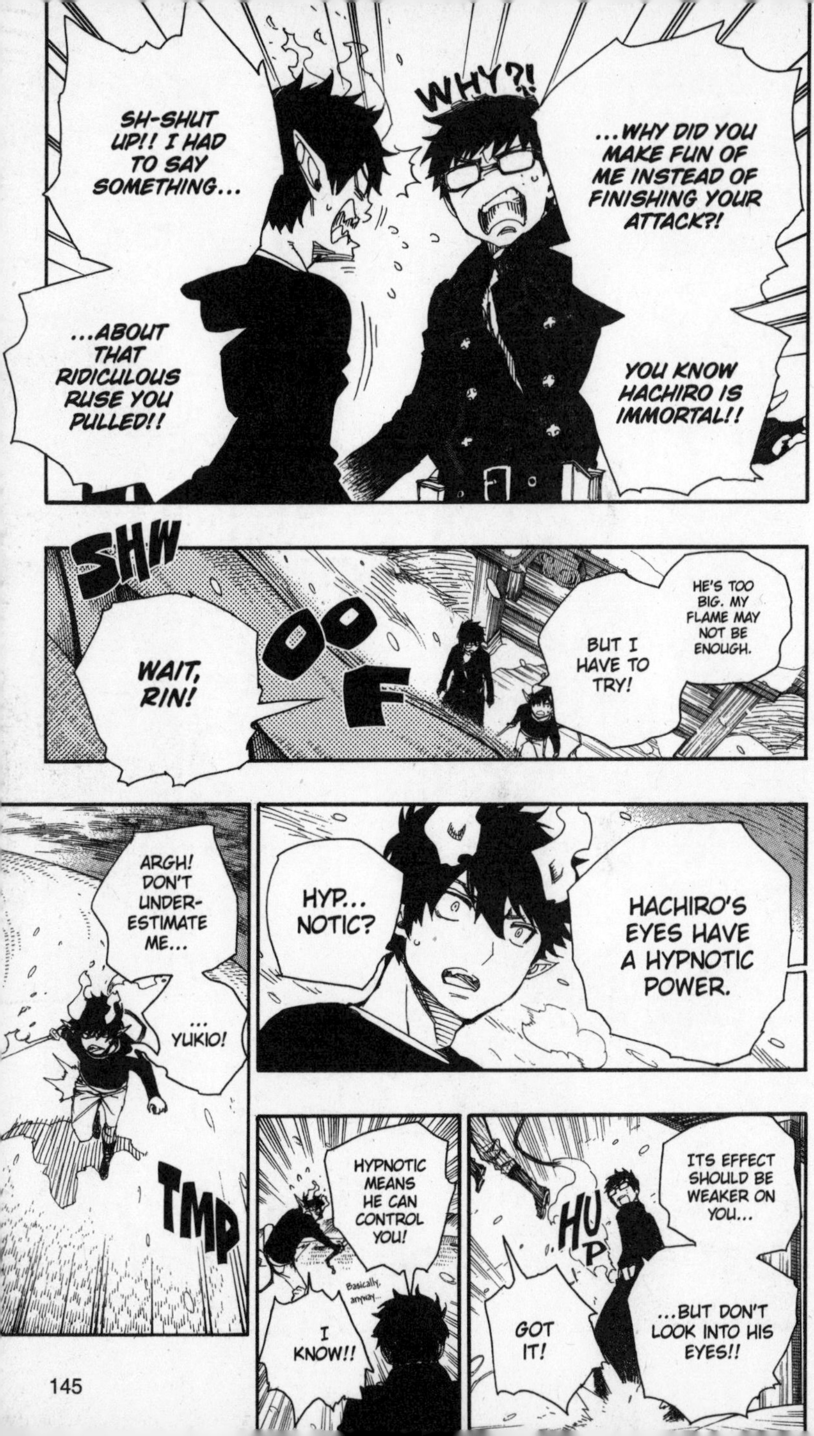
WHY?!
...WHY DID YOU MAKE FUN OF ME INSTEAD OF FINISHING YOUR ATTACK?!
SH-SHUT UP!! I HAD TO SAY SOMETHING...
...ABOUT THAT RIDICULOUS RUSE YOU PULLED!!
YOU KNOW HACHIRO IS IMMORTAL!!
HE'S TOO BIG. MY FLAME MAY NOT BE ENOUGH.
BUT I HAVE TO TRY!
OOF
WAIT, RIN!
SHW
HACHIRO'S EYES HAVE A HYPNOTIC POWER.
HYP... NOTIC?
ITS EFFECT SHOULD BE WEAKER ON YOU...
HUP
...BUT DON'T LOOK INTO HIS EYES!!
GOT IT!
HYPNOTIC MEANS HE CAN CONTROL YOU!
Basically, anyway...
I KNOW!!
ARGH! DON'T UNDER-ESTIMATE ME...
... YUKIO!
TMP

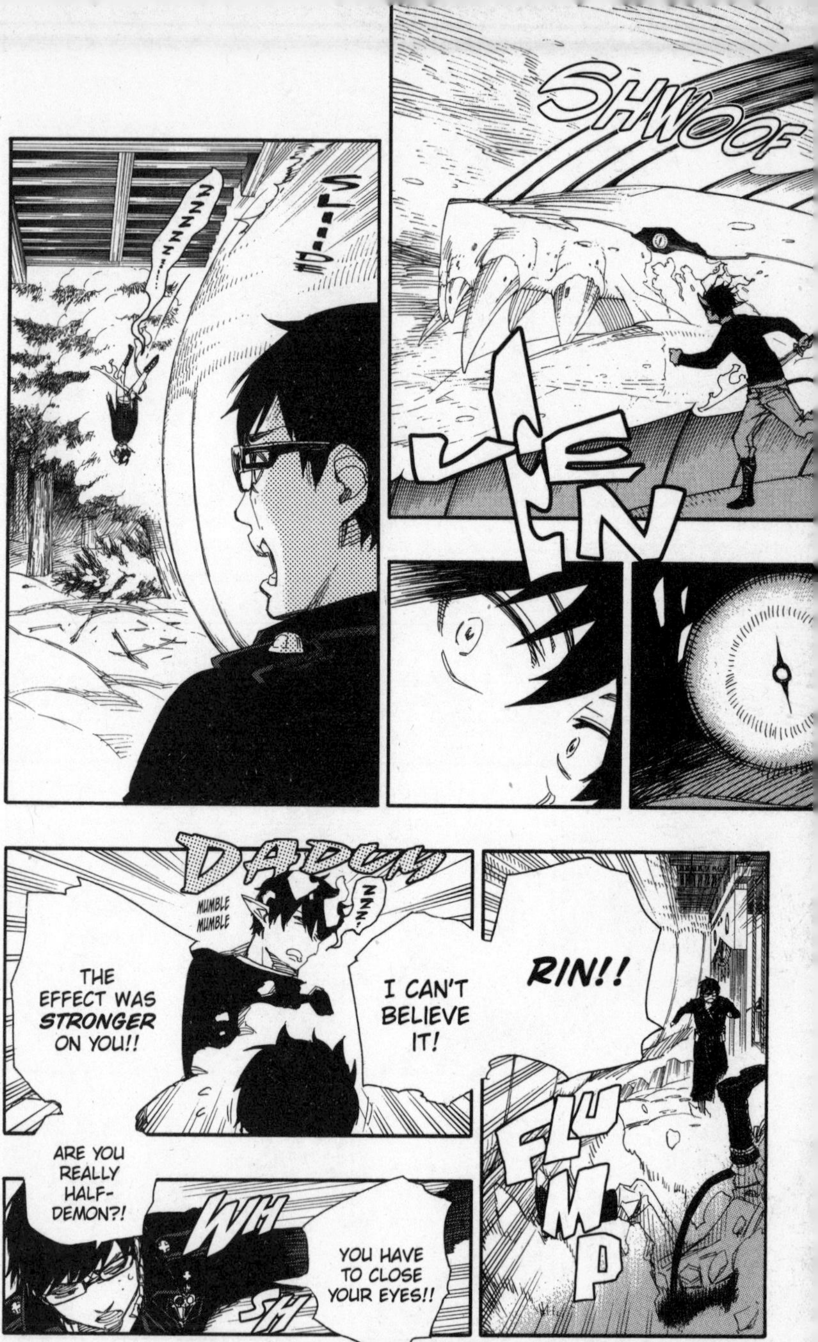
SHWOOF
SLIIID
ZZZZZ...
RIN!!
FLUMP
DADUM
ZZZ...
MUMBLE MUMBLE
I CAN'T BELIEVE IT!
THE EFFECT WAS STRONGER ON YOU!!
WHSH
YOU HAVE TO CLOSE YOUR EYES!!
ARE YOU REALLY HALF-DEMON?!

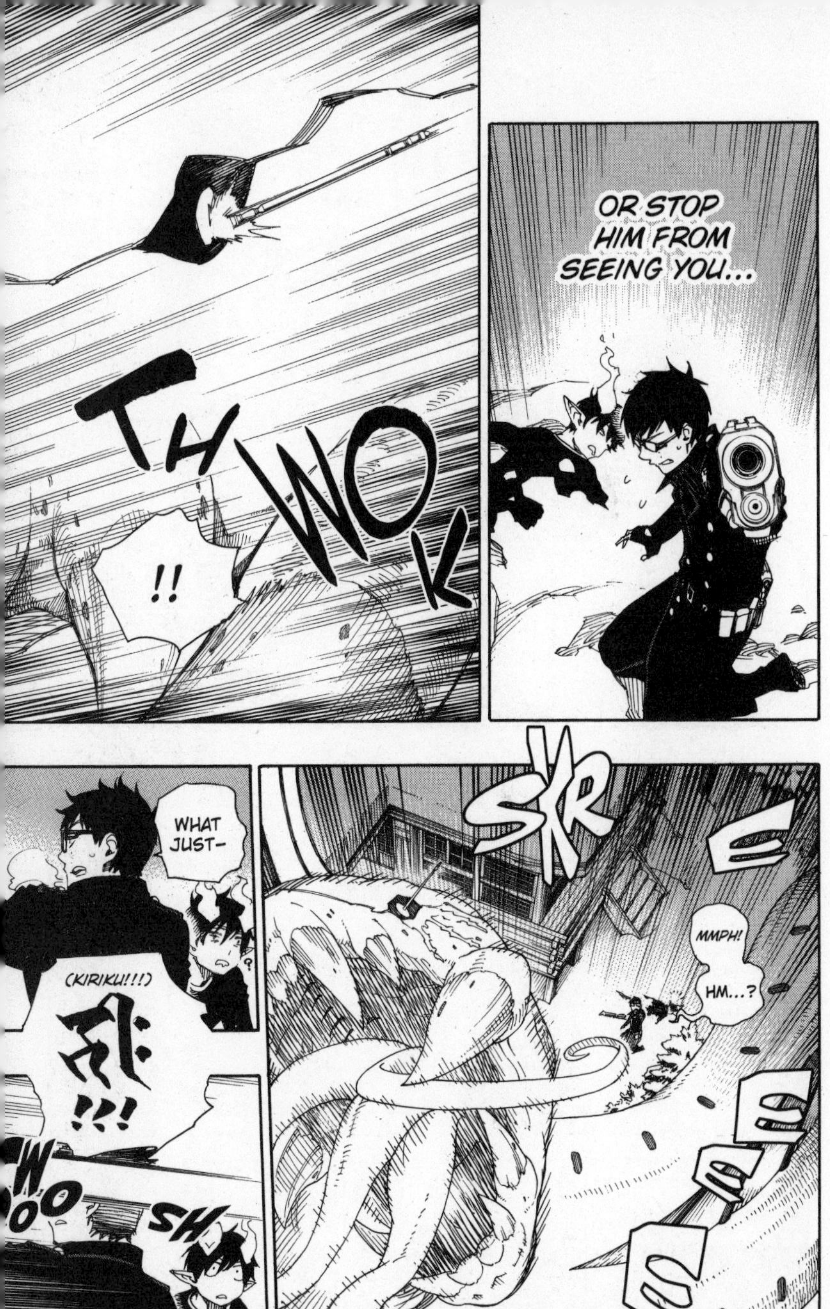
OR STOP HIM FROM SEEING YOU...
THWOK
!!
SKREEEEE
MMPH!
HM...?
WHAT JUST-
(KIRIKU!!!)
!!!
WHOOSH

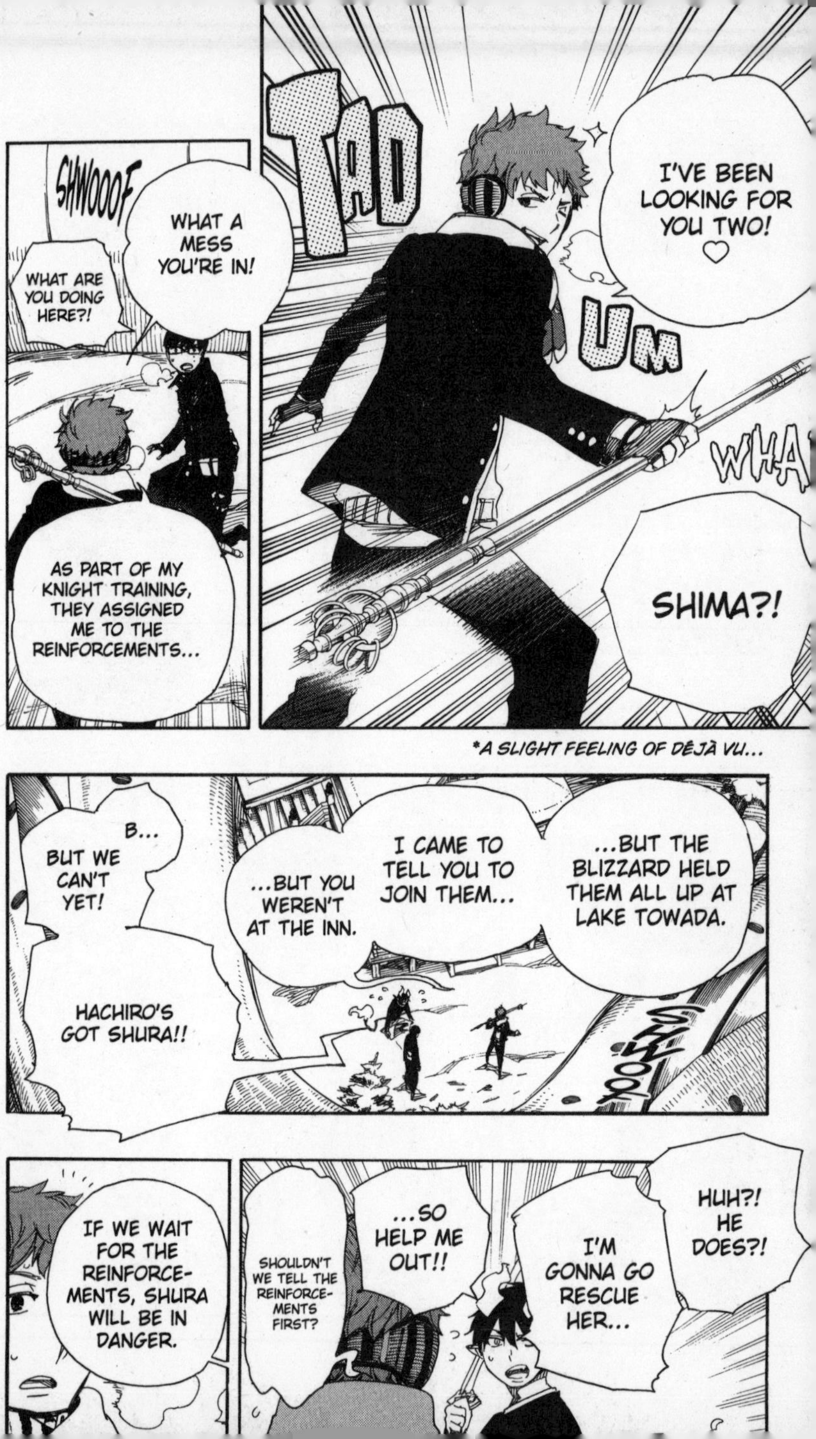
I'VE BEEN LOOKING FOR YOU TWO! ♡
TAD
UM
WHA
SHIMA?!
SHWOOOF
WHAT A MESS YOU'RE IN!
WHAT ARE YOU DOING HERE?!
AS PART OF MY KNIGHT TRAINING, THEY ASSIGNED ME TO THE REINFORCEMENTS...
*A SLIGHT FEELING OF DÉJÀ VU...
...BUT THE BLIZZARD HELD THEM ALL UP AT LAKE TOWADA.
I CAME TO TELL YOU TO JOIN THEM...
...BUT YOU WEREN'T AT THE INN.
SHWOOOK
B... BUT WE CAN'T YET!
HACHIRO'S GOT SHURA!!
HUH?! HE DOES?!
I'M GONNA GO RESCUE HER...
...SO HELP ME OUT!!
SHOULDN'T WE TELL THE REINFORCEMENTS FIRST?
IF WE WAIT FOR THE REINFORCEMENTS, SHURA WILL BE IN DANGER.

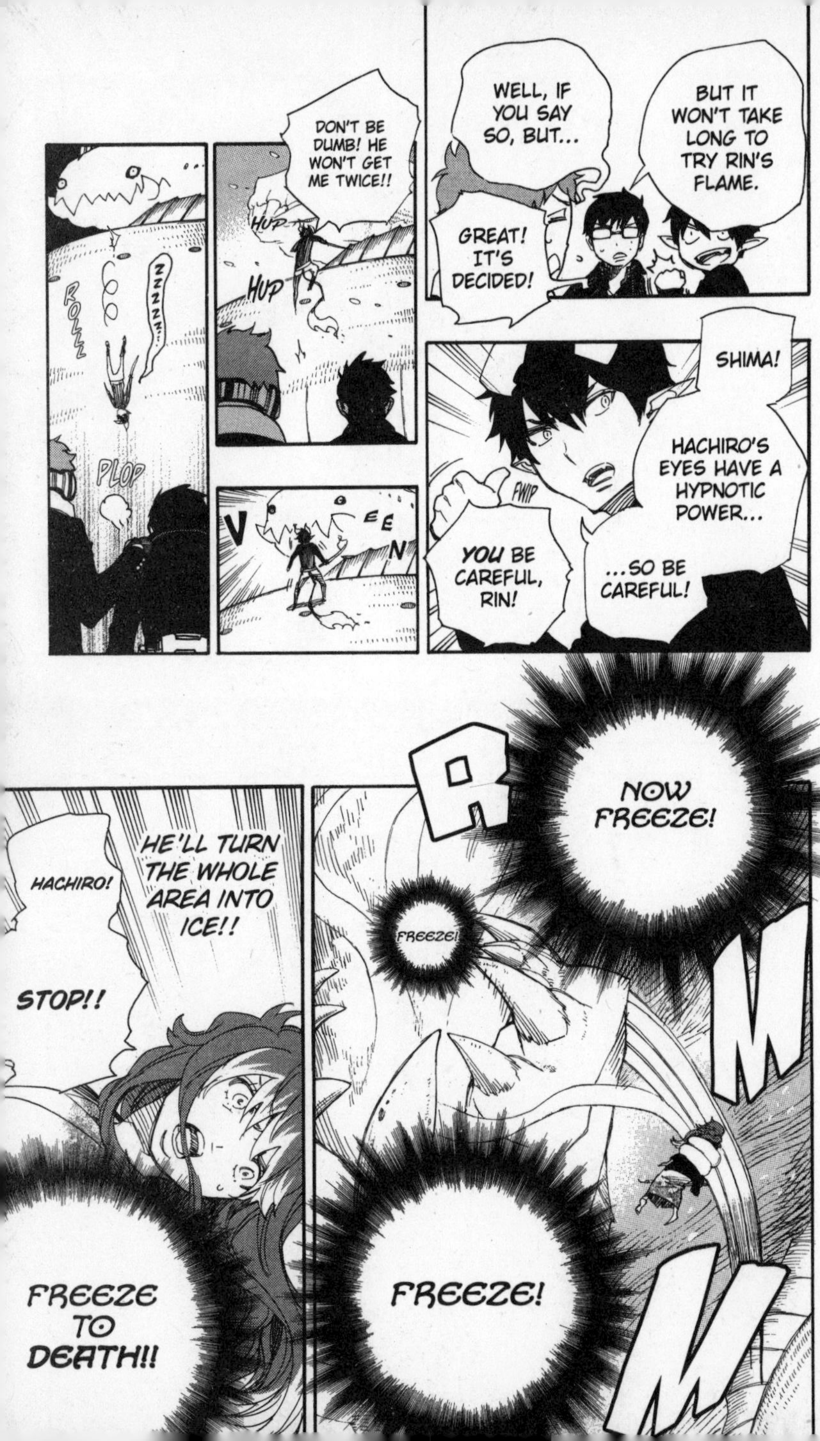
BUT IT WON'T TAKE LONG TO TRY RIN'S FLAME.
WELL, IF YOU SAY SO, BUT...
GREAT! IT'S DECIDED!
SHIMA!
HACHIRO'S EYES HAVE A HYPNOTIC POWER...
...SO BE CAREFUL!
FWIP
YOU BE CAREFUL, RIN!
DON'T BE DUMB! HE WON'T GET ME TWICE!!
HUP
HUP
VEEN
...
ZZZZZ
ROLLL
PLOP
R
NOW FREEZE!
FREEZE!
M
FREEZE!
M
HE'LL TURN THE WHOLE AREA INTO ICE!!
HACHIRO!
STOP!!
FREEZE TO DEATH!!

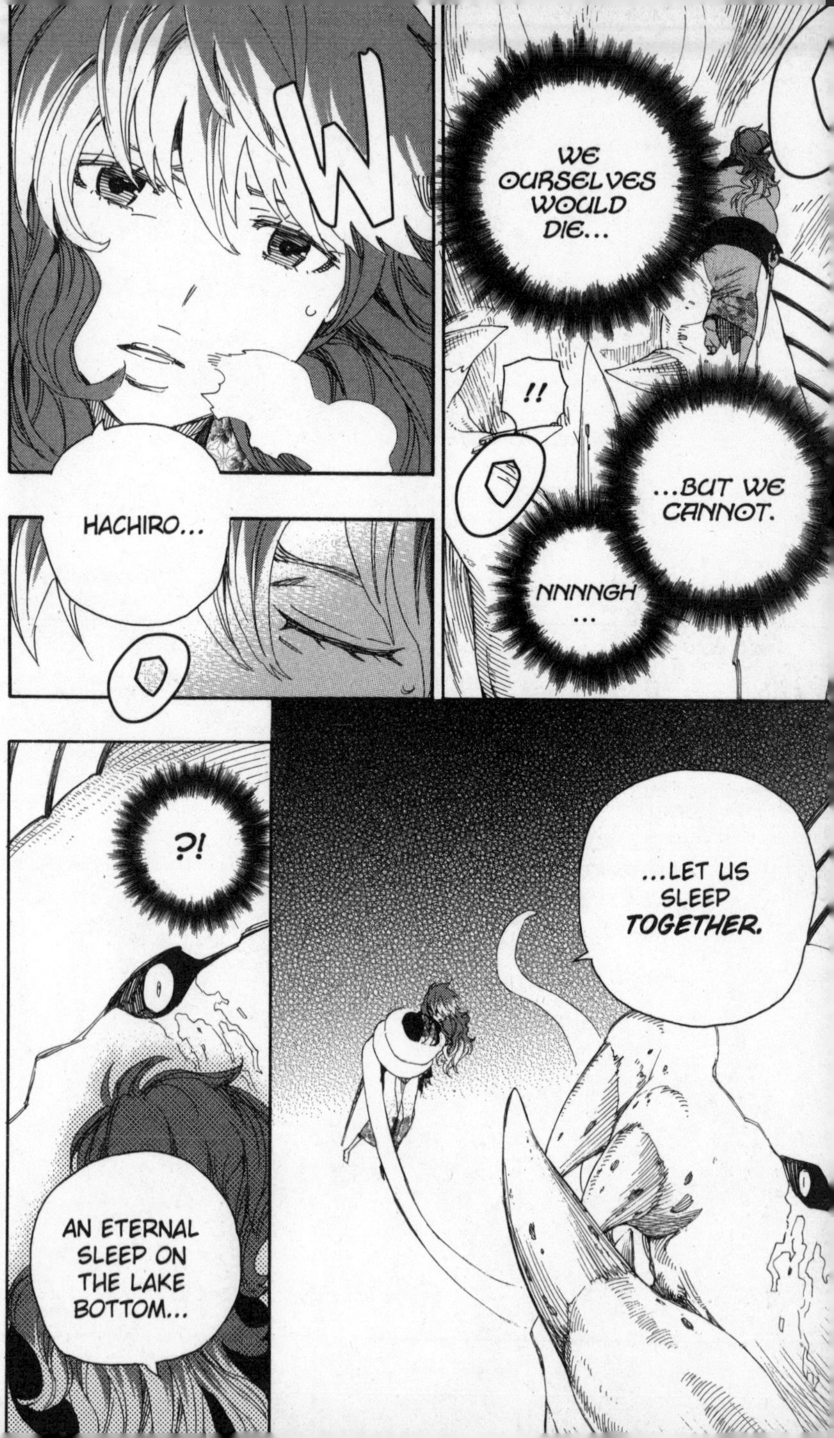
WE OURSELVES WOULD DIE...
!!
...BUT WE CANNOT.
NNNNGH...
HACHIRO...
...LET US SLEEP TOGETHER.
?!
AN ETERNAL SLEEP ON THE LAKE BOTTOM...

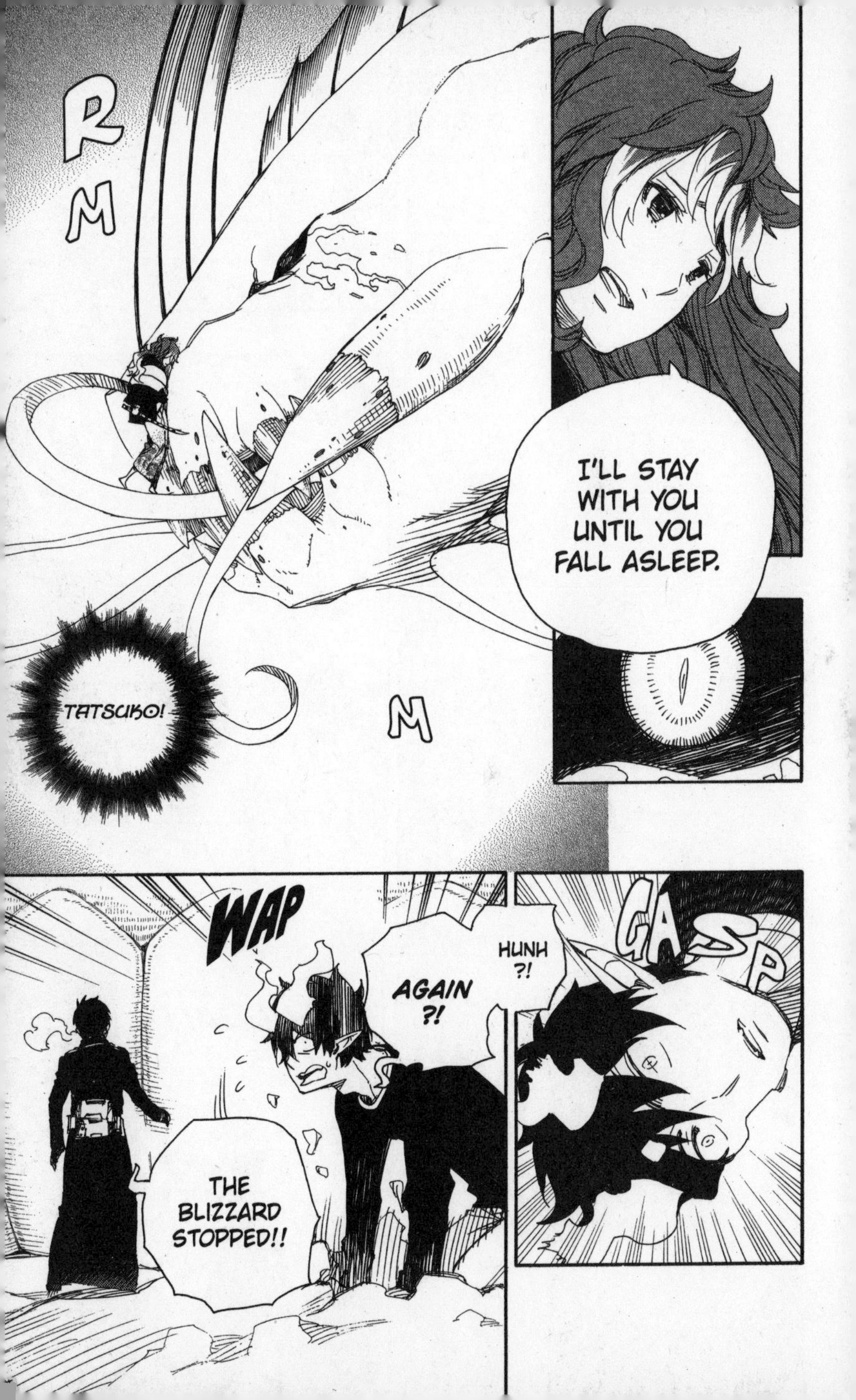
I'LL STAY WITH YOU UNTIL YOU FALL ASLEEP.
R
M
TATSUKO!
M
GASP
HUNH ?!
WAP
AGAIN ?!
THE BLIZZARD STOPPED!!

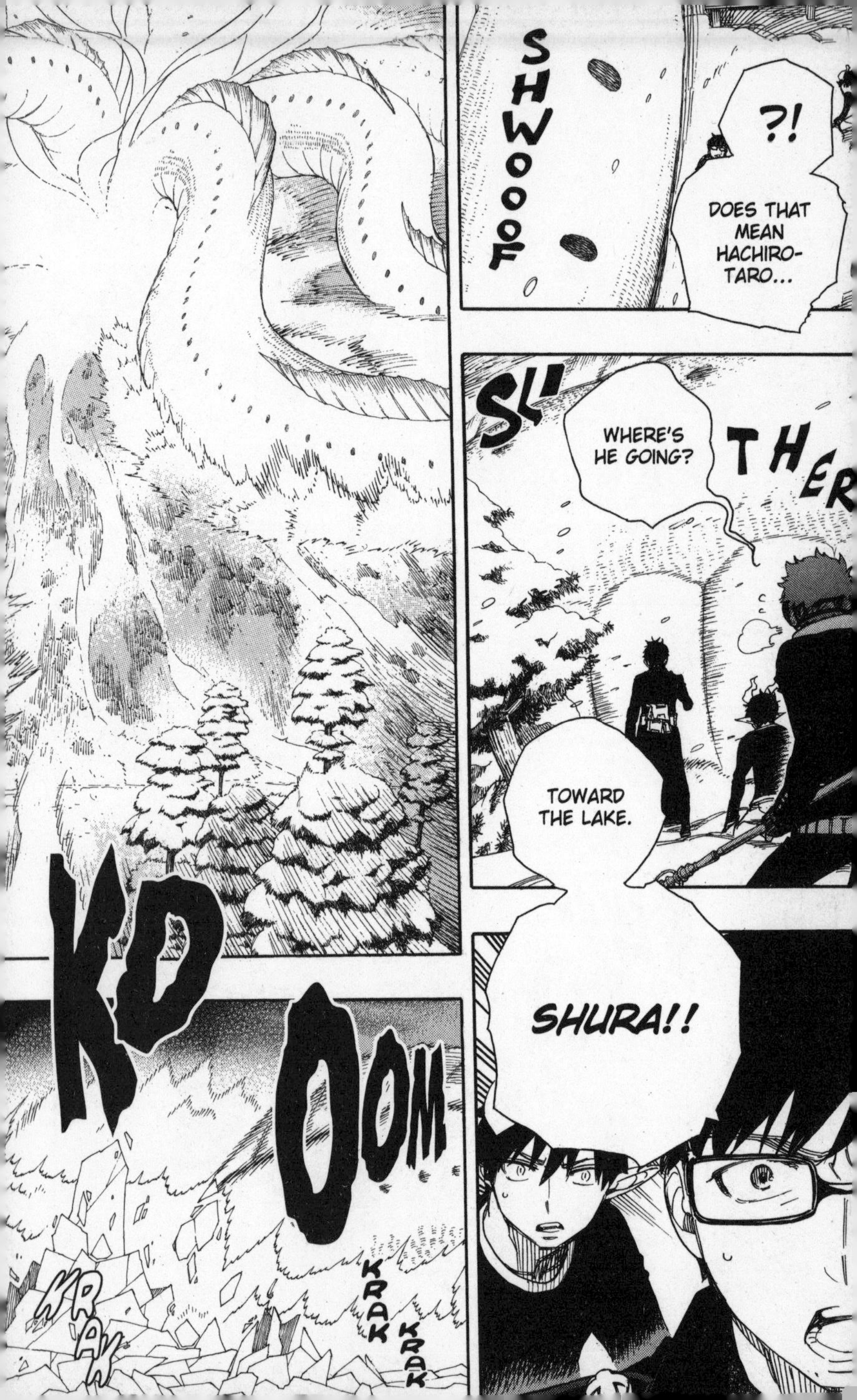
?!
DOES THAT MEAN HACHIRO-TARO...
SHWOOOF
SLITHER
WHERE'S HE GOING?
TOWARD THE LAKE.
SHURA!!
KDOOM
KRAK
KRAK
KRAK

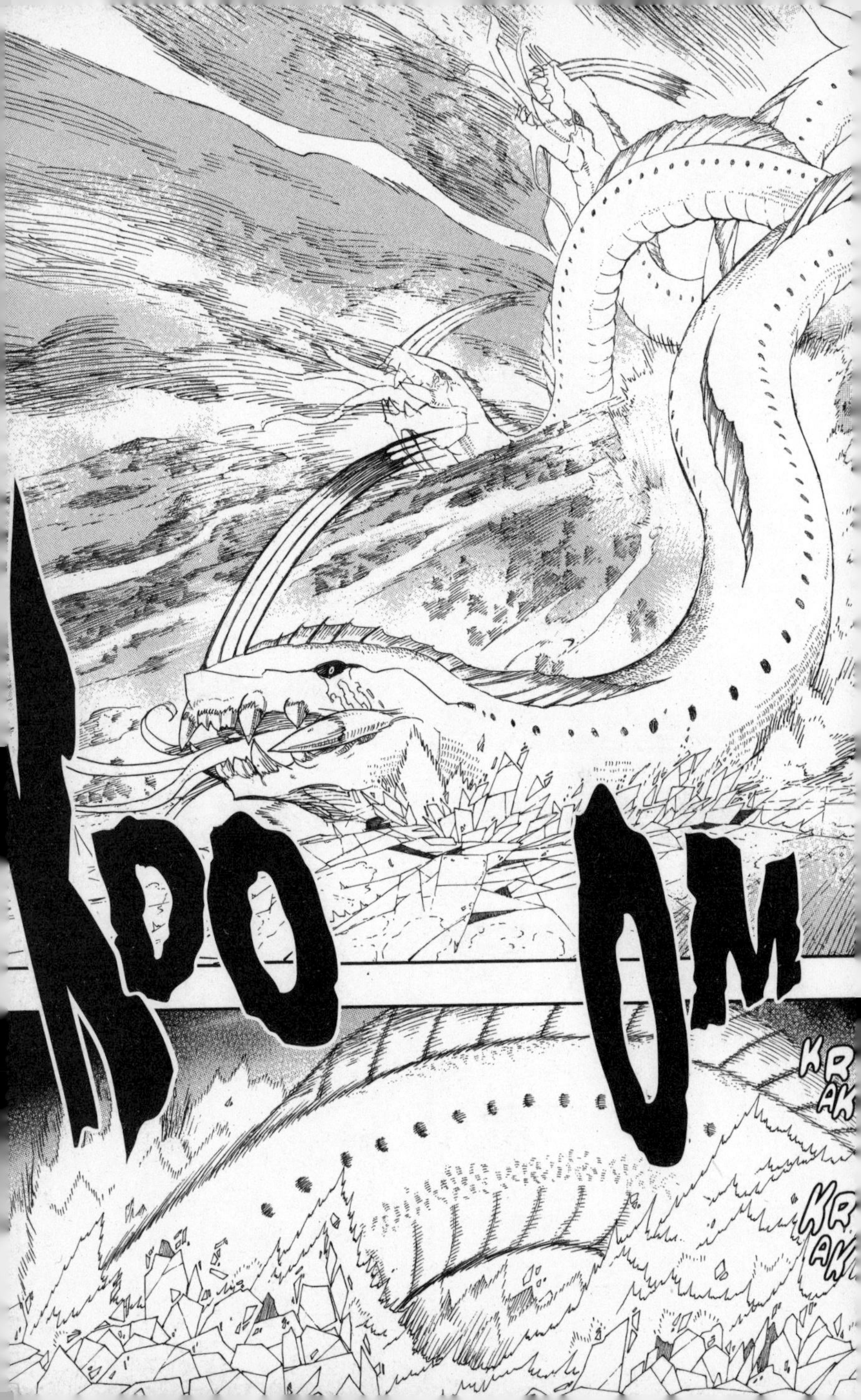
KRAK
KRAK

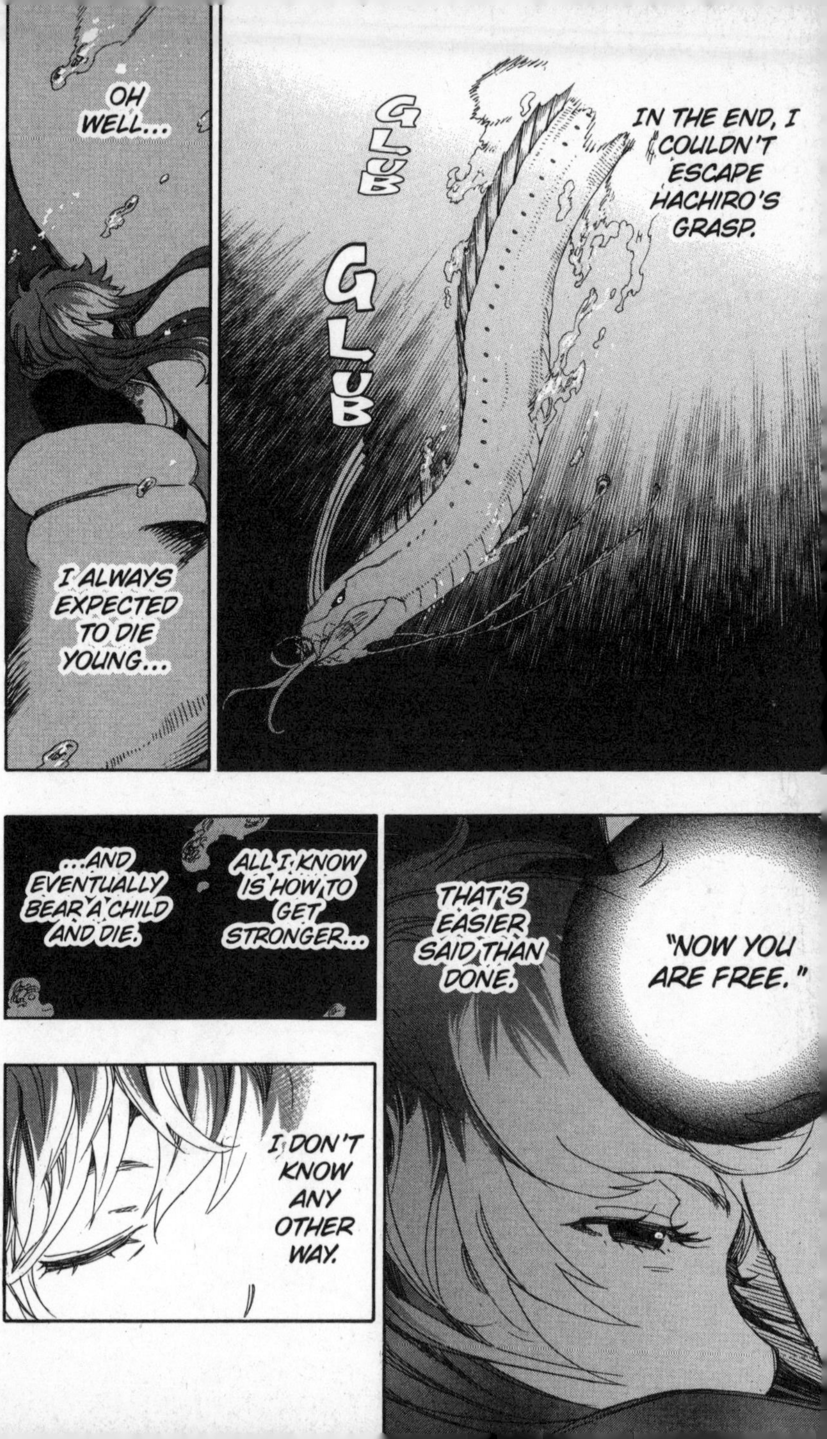
IN THE END, I COULDN'T ESCAPE HACHIRO'S GRASP.
GLUB
GLUB
OH WELL...
I ALWAYS EXPECTED TO DIE YOUNG...
"NOW YOU ARE FREE."
THAT'S EASIER SAID THAN DONE.
ALL I KNOW IS HOW TO GET STRONGER...
...AND EVENTUALLY BEAR A CHILD AND DIE.
I DON'T KNOW ANY OTHER WAY.

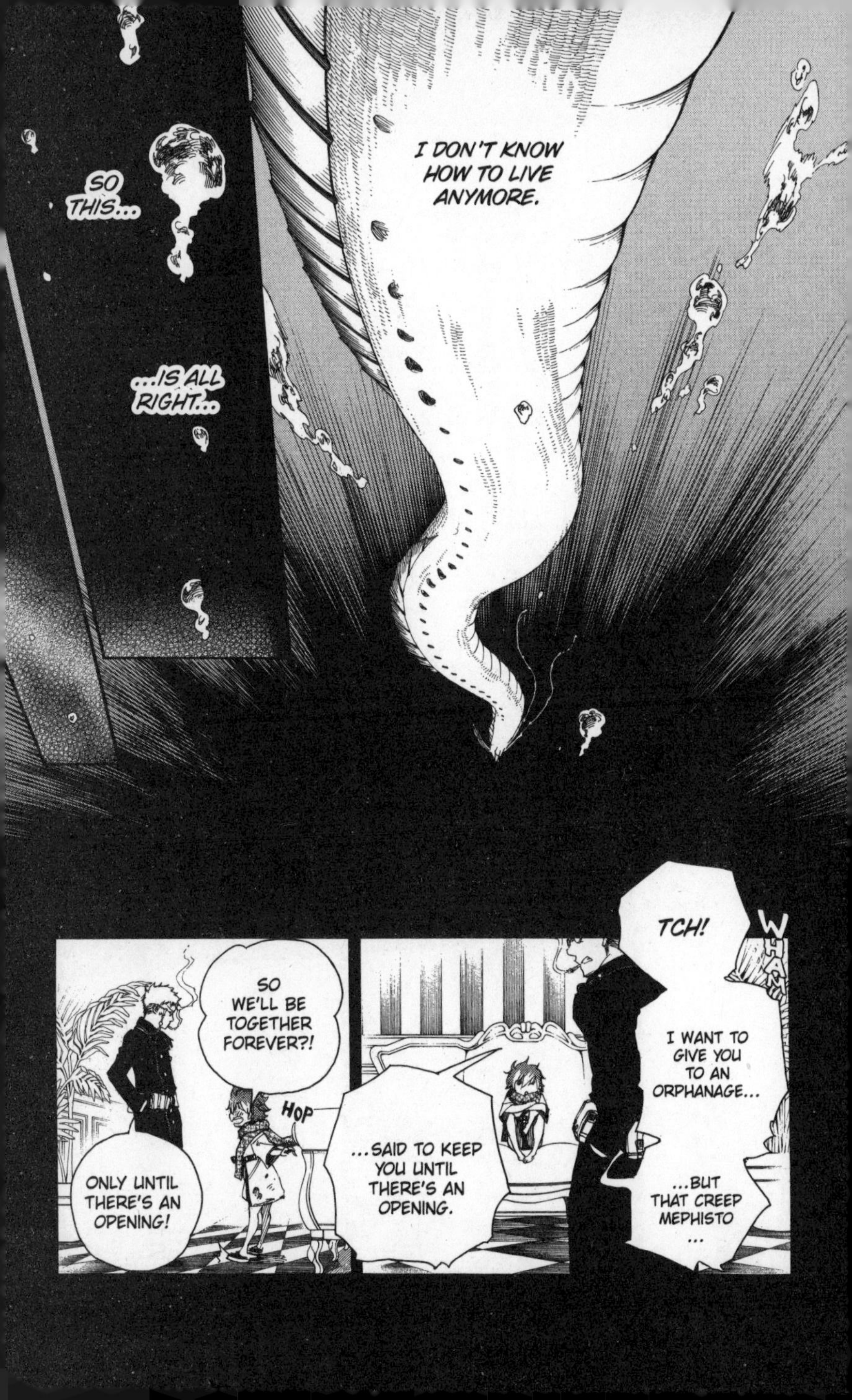
I DON'T KNOW HOW TO LIVE ANYMORE.
SO THIS...
...IS ALL RIGHT...
WHAM
TCH!
I WANT TO GIVE YOU TO AN ORPHANAGE...
...BUT THAT CREEP MEPHISTO ...
...SAID TO KEEP YOU UNTIL THERE'S AN OPENING.
SO WE'LL BE TOGETHER FOREVER?!
HOP
ONLY UNTIL THERE'S AN OPENING!

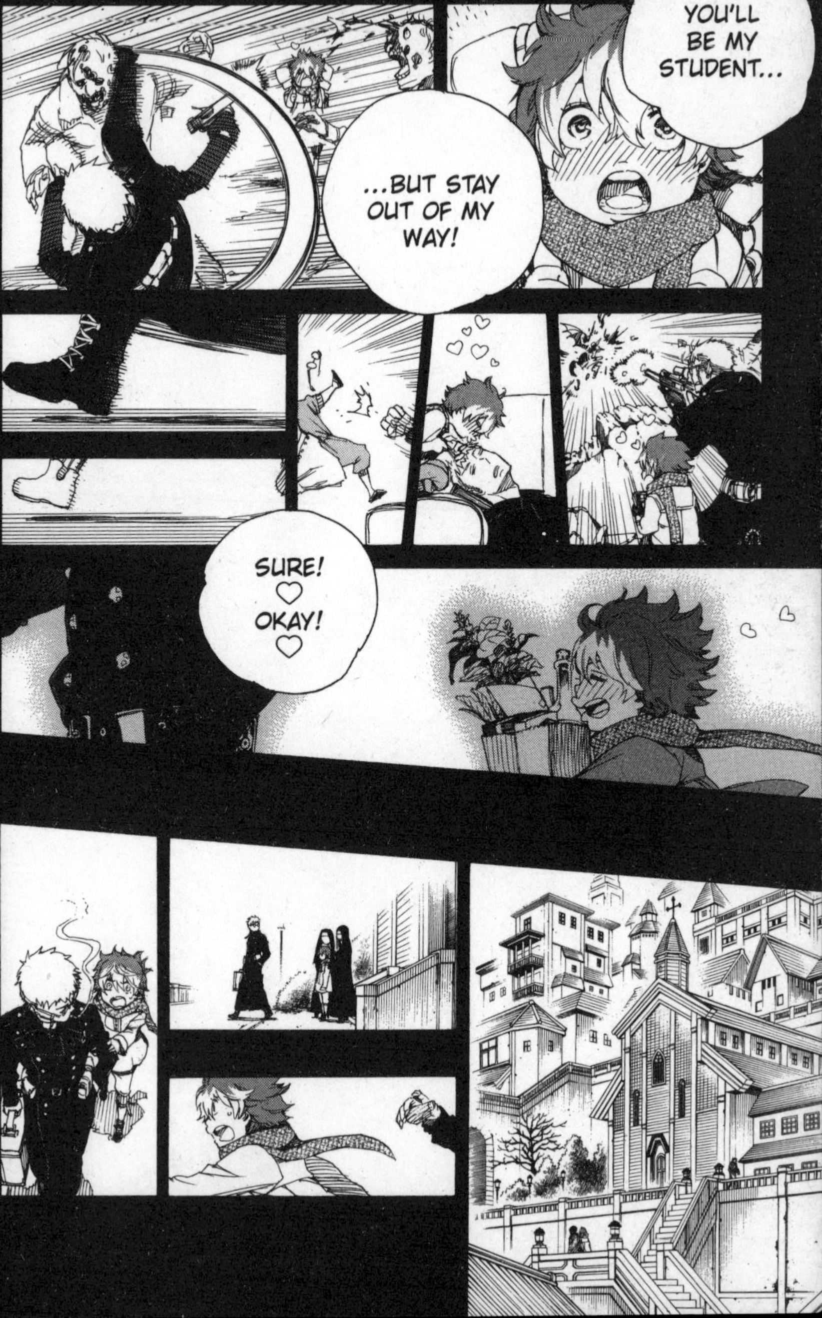
YOU'LL BE MY STUDENT...
...BUT STAY OUT OF MY WAY!
SURE! ♡ OKAY! ♡

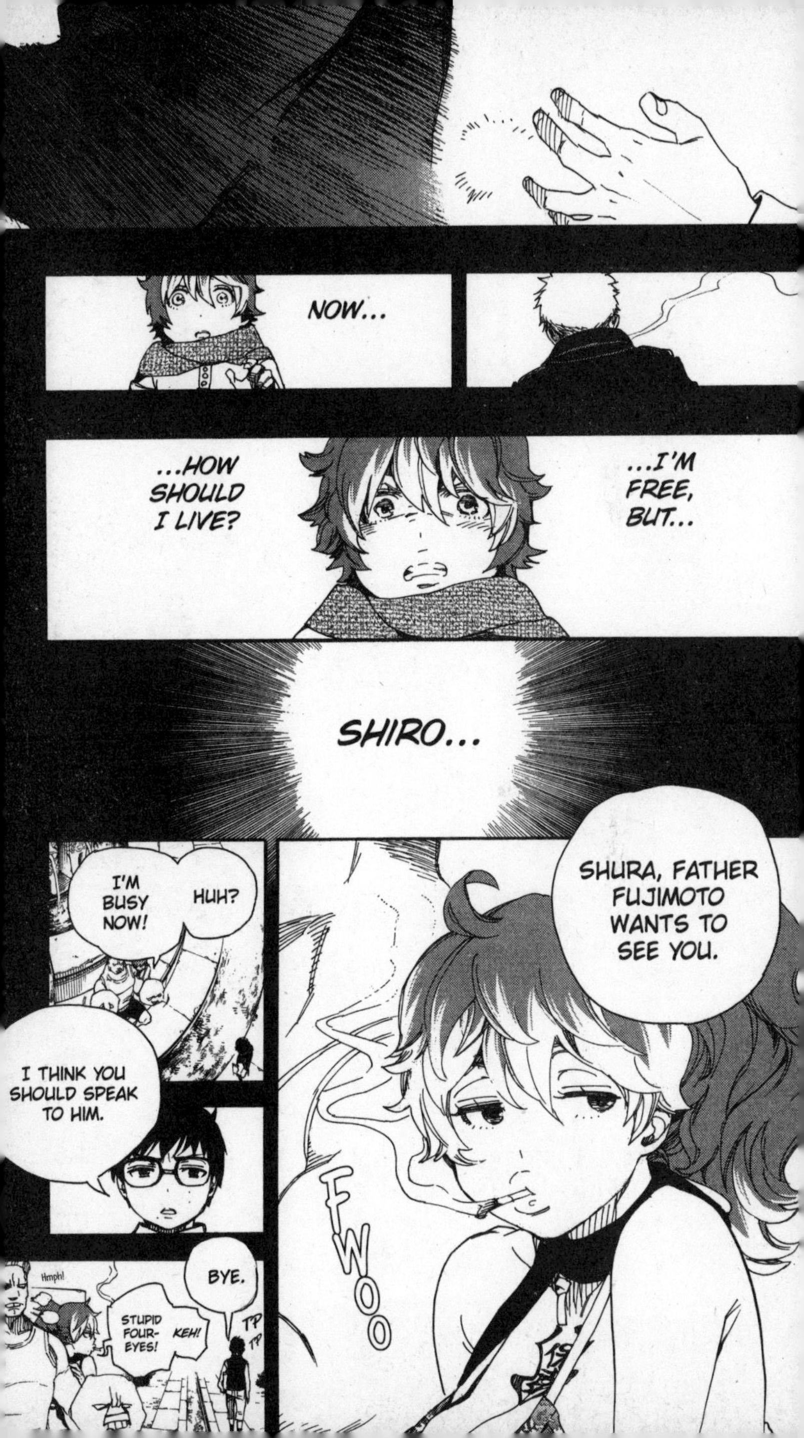
NOW...
...I'M FREE, BUT...
...HOW SHOULD I LIVE?
SHIRO...
SHURA, FATHER FUJIMOTO WANTS TO SEE YOU.
FWOO
HUH?
I'M BUSY NOW!
I THINK YOU SHOULD SPEAK TO HIM.
BYE.
TP TP
KEH!
STUPID FOUR-EYES!
Hmph!

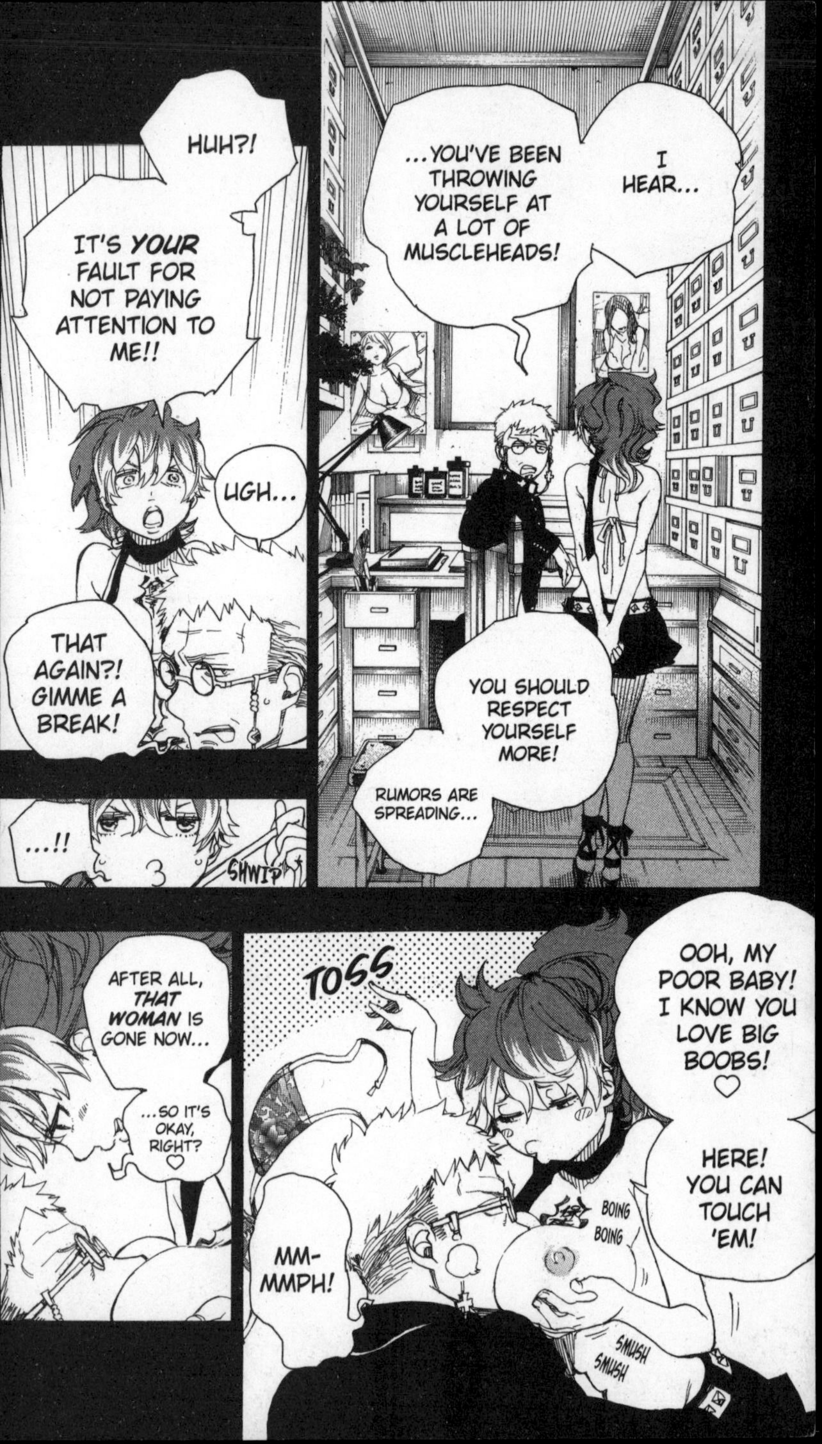
I HEAR...
...YOU'VE BEEN THROWING YOURSELF AT A LOT OF MUSCLEHEADS!
YOU SHOULD RESPECT YOURSELF MORE!
RUMORS ARE SPREADING...
HUH?!
IT'S *YOUR* FAULT FOR NOT PAYING ATTENTION TO ME!!
UGH...
THAT AGAIN?! GIMME A BREAK!
...!!
SHWIP
TOSS
OOH, MY POOR BABY! I KNOW YOU LOVE BIG BOOBS! ♡
HERE! YOU CAN TOUCH 'EM!
BOING BOING
MM-MMPH!
SMUSH SMUSH
AFTER ALL, *THAT WOMAN* IS GONE NOW...
...SO IT'S OKAY, RIGHT? ♡

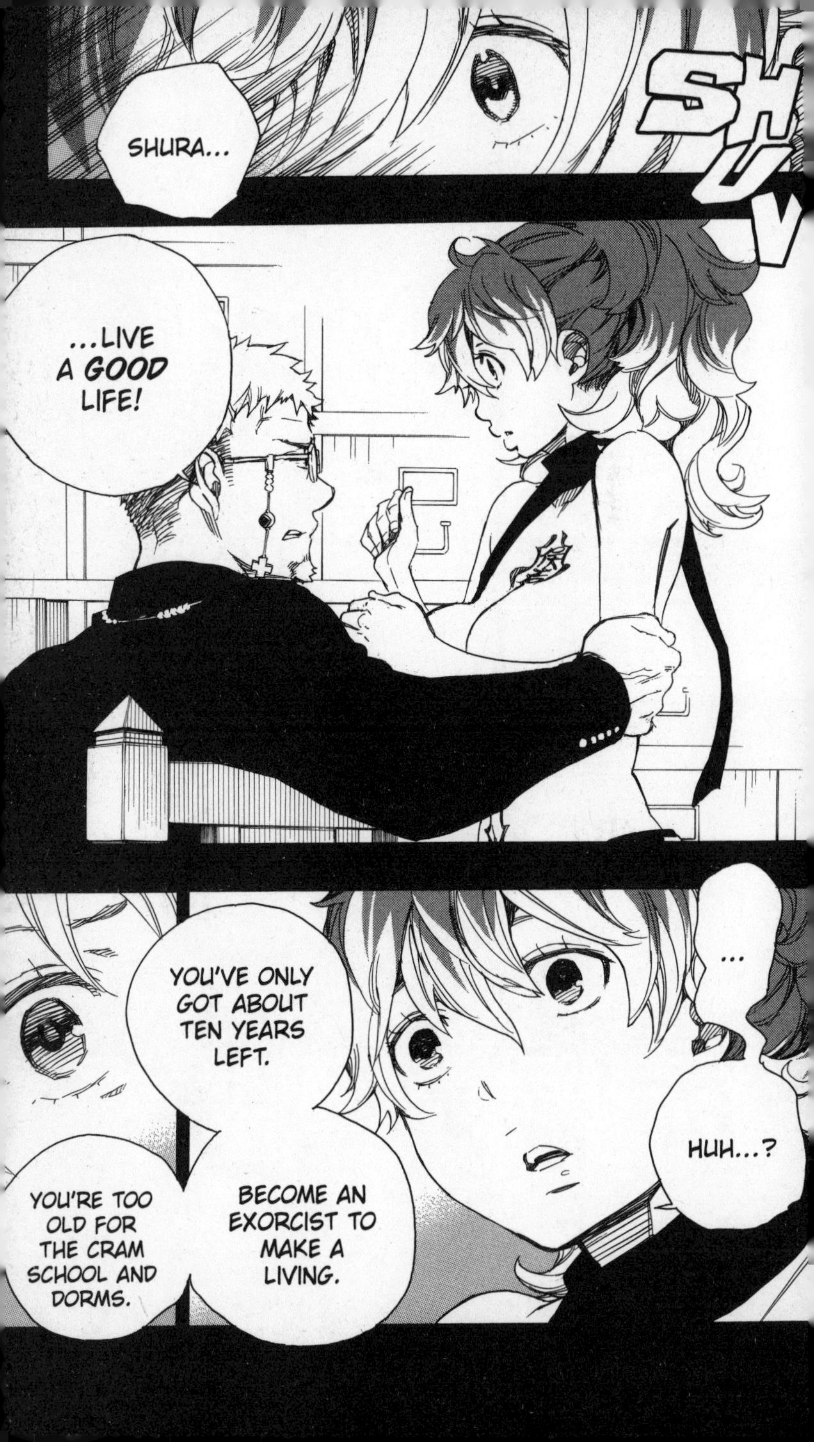
SHURA...
...LIVE A GOOD LIFE!
...
HUH...?
YOU'VE ONLY GOT ABOUT TEN YEARS LEFT.
BECOME AN EXORCIST TO MAKE A LIVING.
YOU'RE TOO OLD FOR THE CRAM SCHOOL AND DORMS.

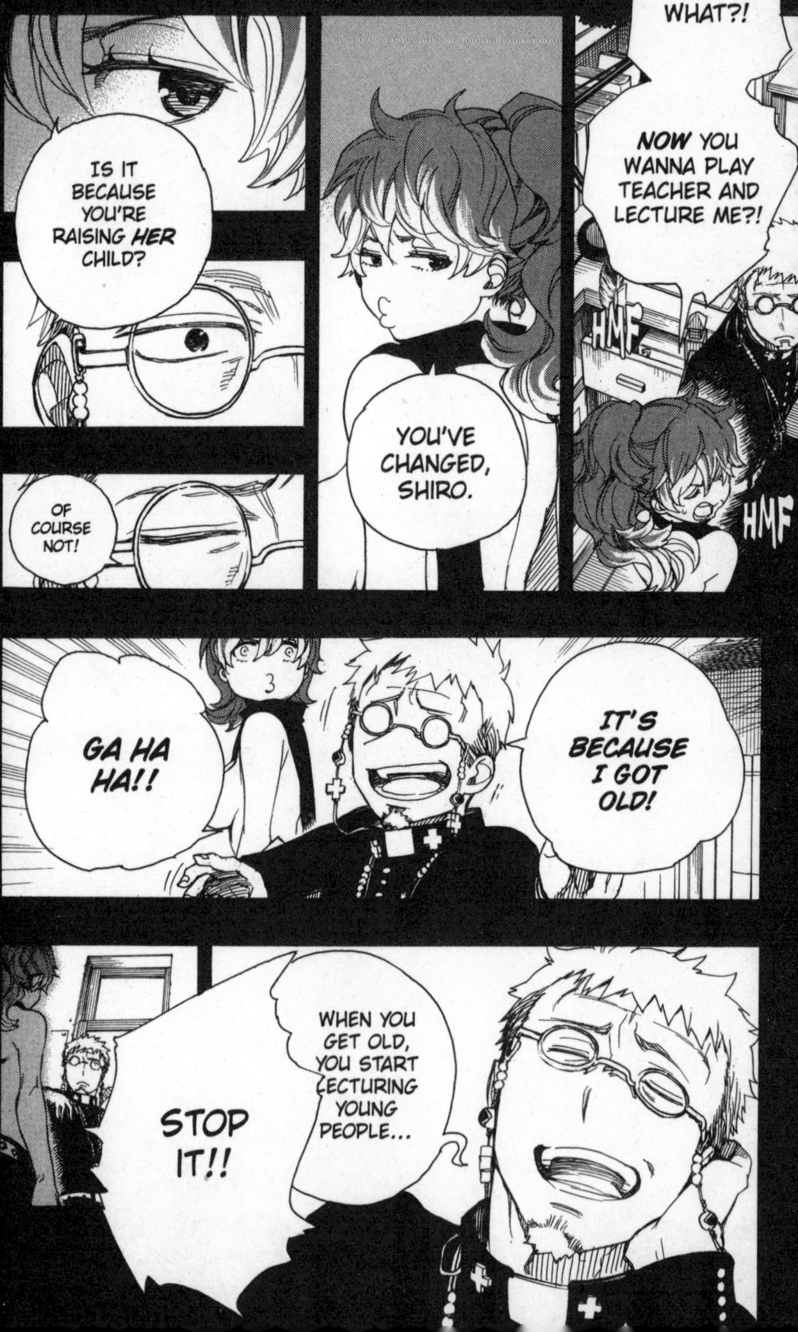
WHAT?!
NOW YOU WANNA PLAY TEACHER AND LECTURE ME?!
HMF
HMF
YOU'VE CHANGED, SHIRO.
IS IT BECAUSE YOU'RE RAISING HER CHILD?
OF COURSE NOT!
IT'S BECAUSE I GOT OLD!
GA HA HA!!
WHEN YOU GET OLD, YOU START LECTURING YOUNG PEOPLE...
STOP IT!!

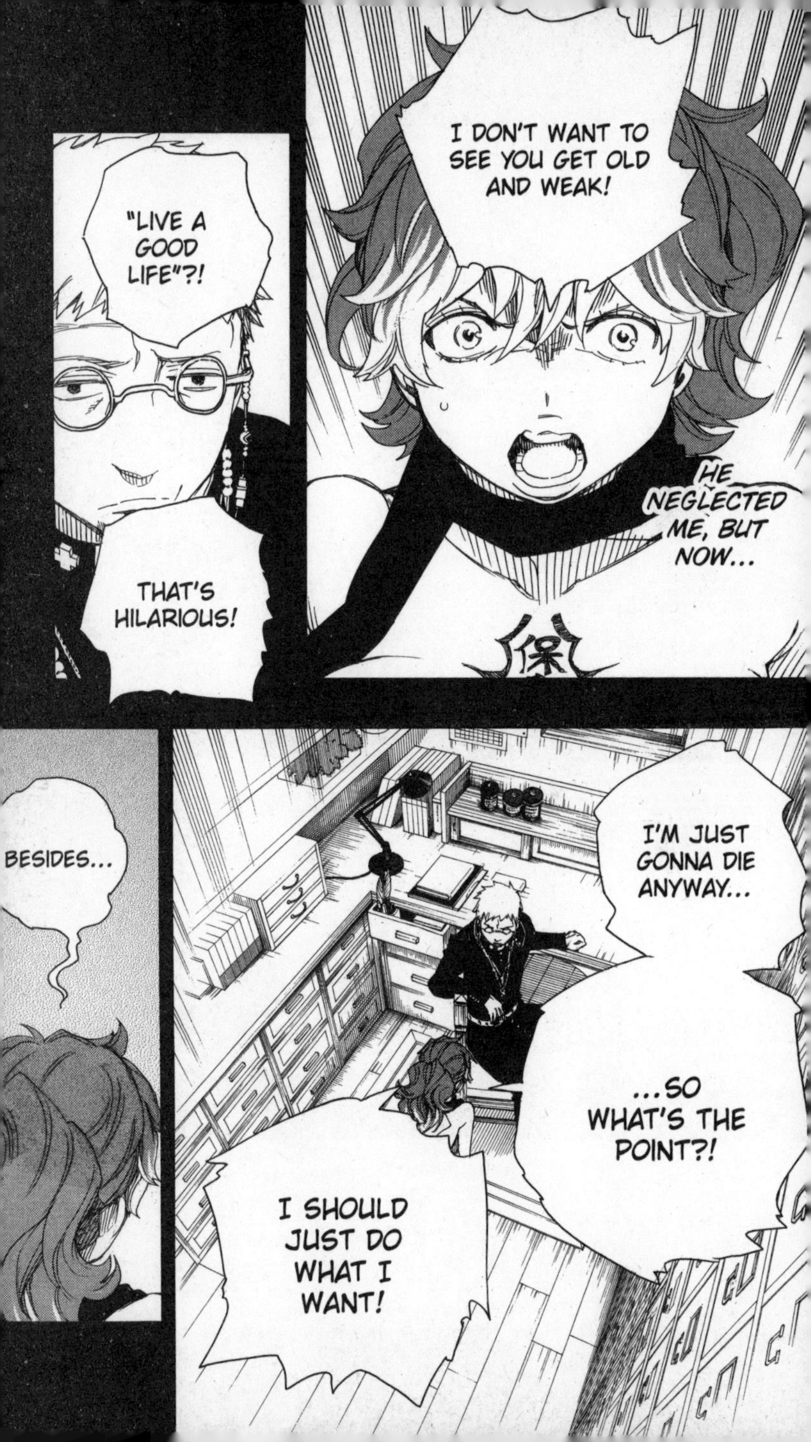
I DON'T WANT TO SEE YOU GET OLD AND WEAK!
HE NEGLECTED ME, BUT NOW...
保
"LIVE A GOOD LIFE"?!
THAT'S HILARIOUS!
I'M JUST GONNA DIE ANYWAY...
...SO WHAT'S THE POINT?!
I SHOULD JUST DO WHAT I WANT!
BESIDES...

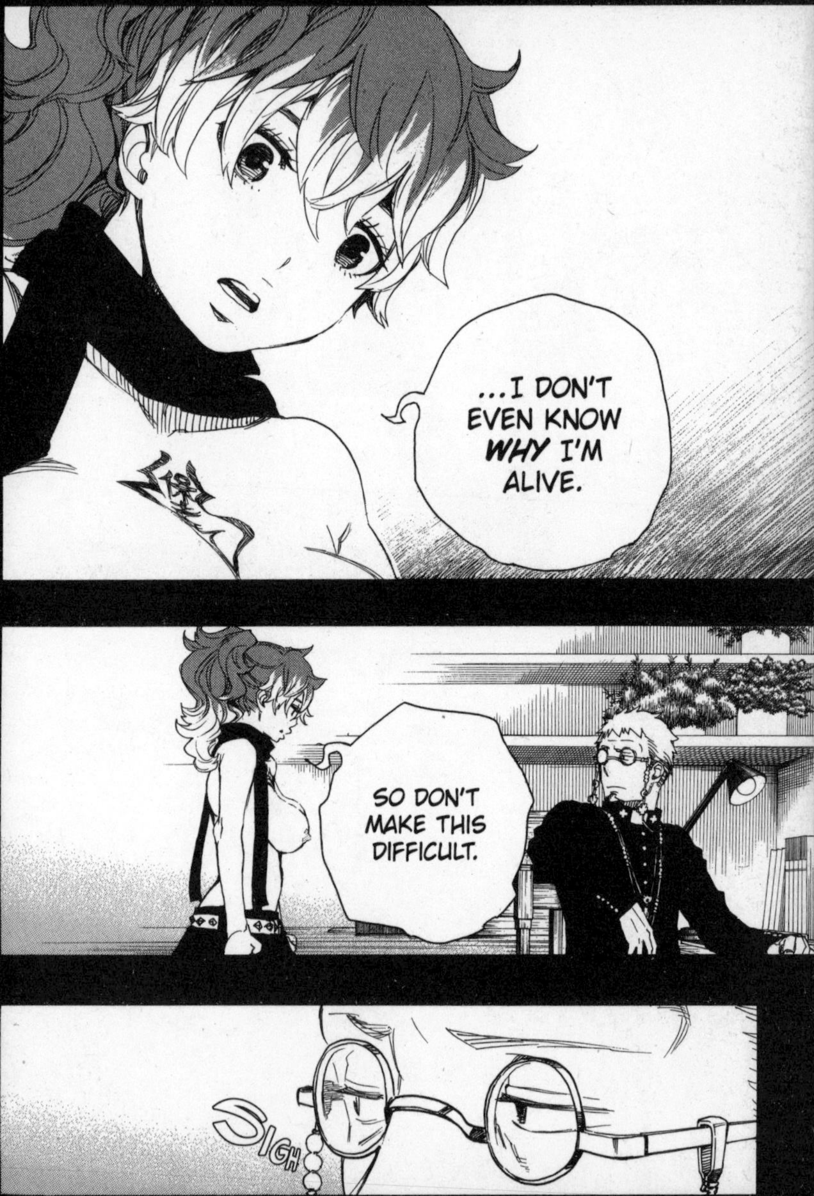
...I DON'T EVEN KNOW *WHY* I'M ALIVE.
SO DON'T MAKE THIS DIFFICULT.
SIGH

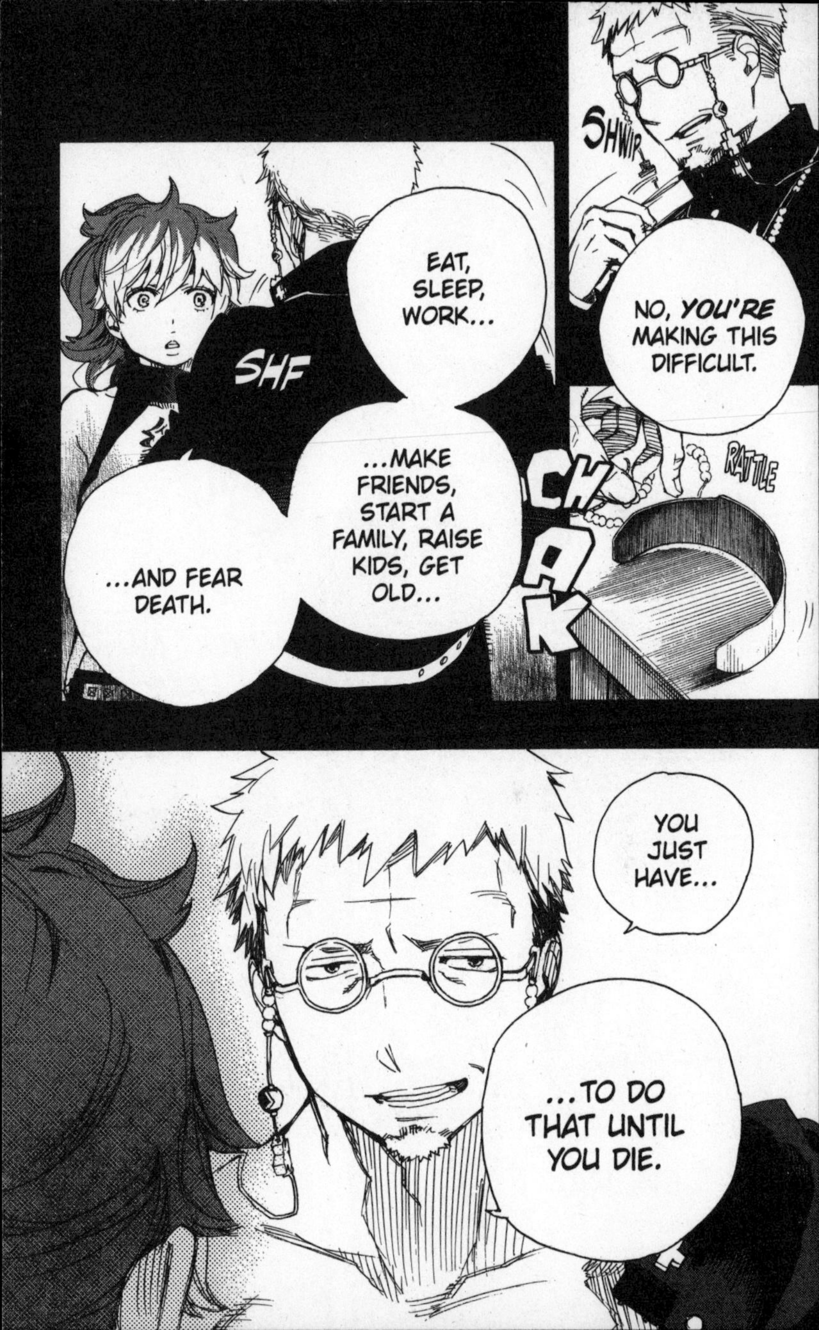
SHWIP
NO, *YOU'RE* MAKING THIS DIFFICULT.
RATTLE
CHAK
SHF
EAT, SLEEP, WORK...
...MAKE FRIENDS, START A FAMILY, RAISE KIDS, GET OLD...
...AND FEAR DEATH.
YOU JUST HAVE...
...TO DO THAT UNTIL YOU DIE.

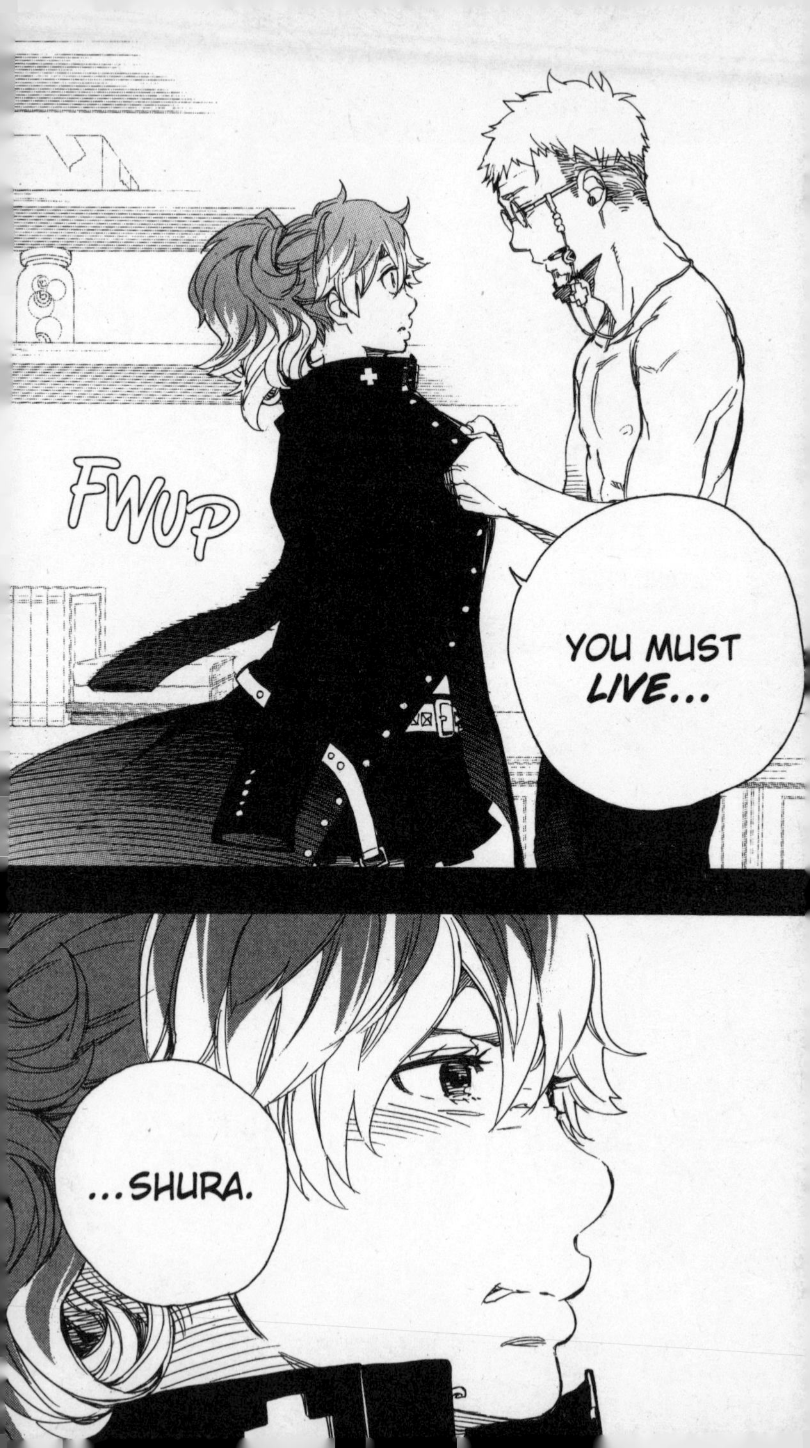
YOU MUST LIVE...
FWUP
...SHURA.

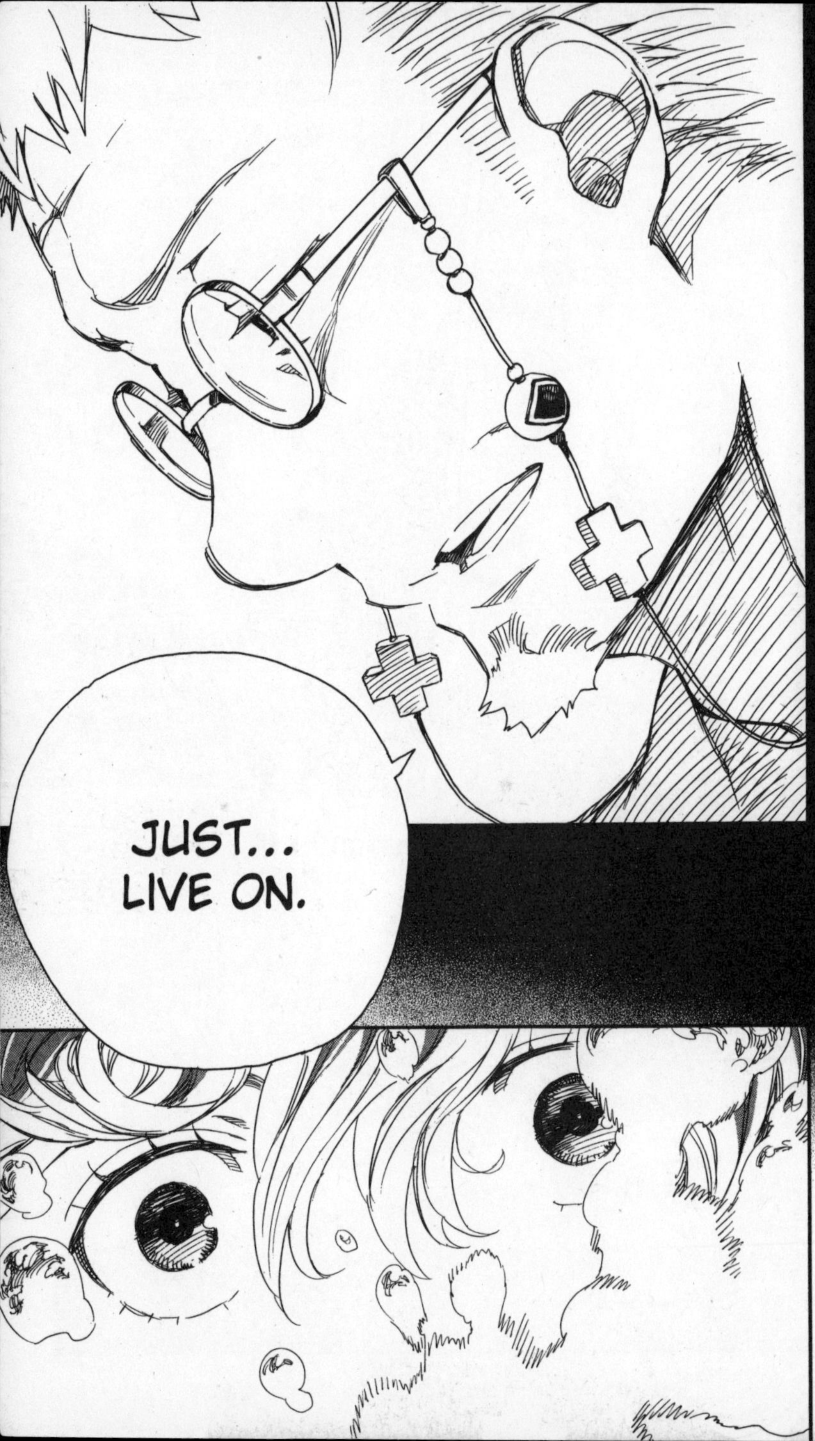
JUST... LIVE ON.

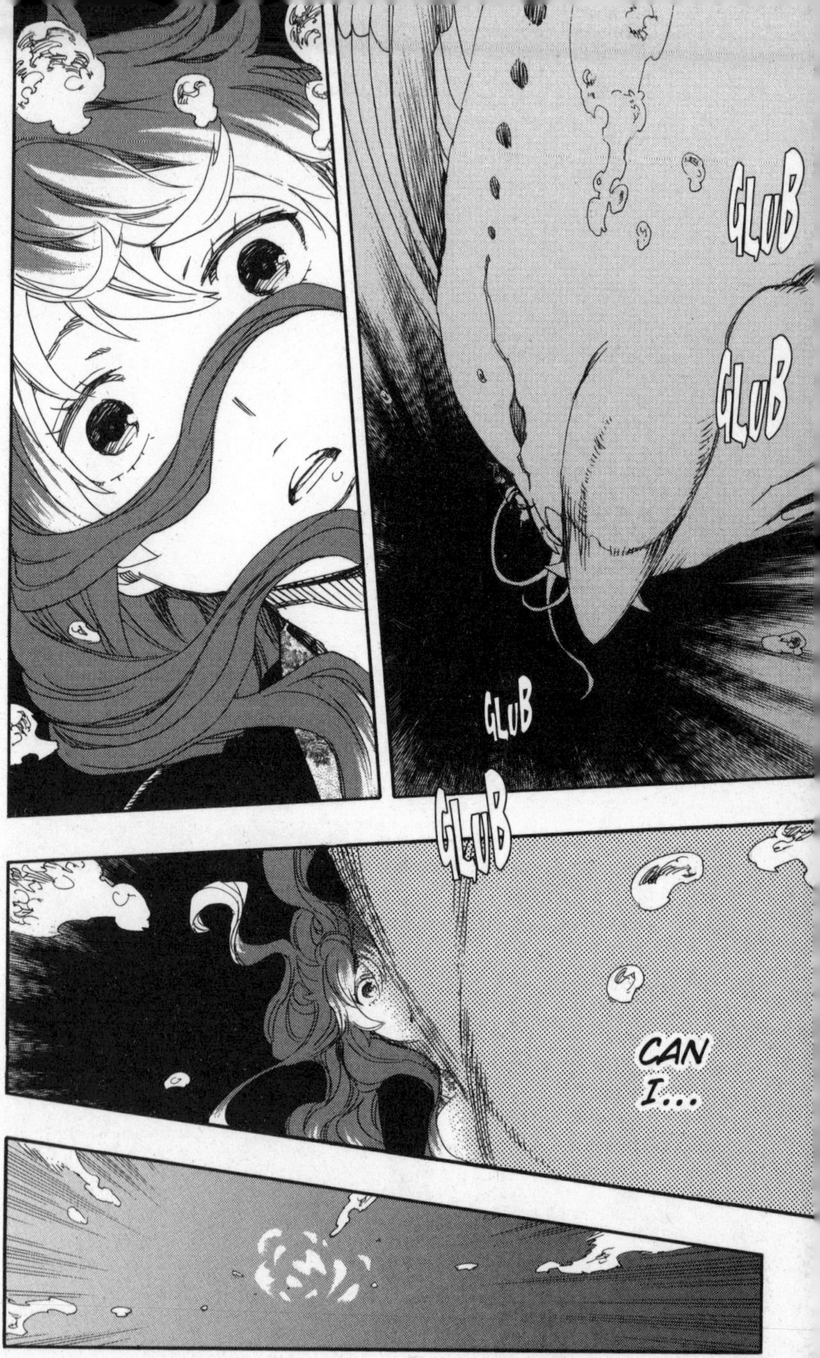
GLUB
GLUB
GLUB
GLUB
CAN I...

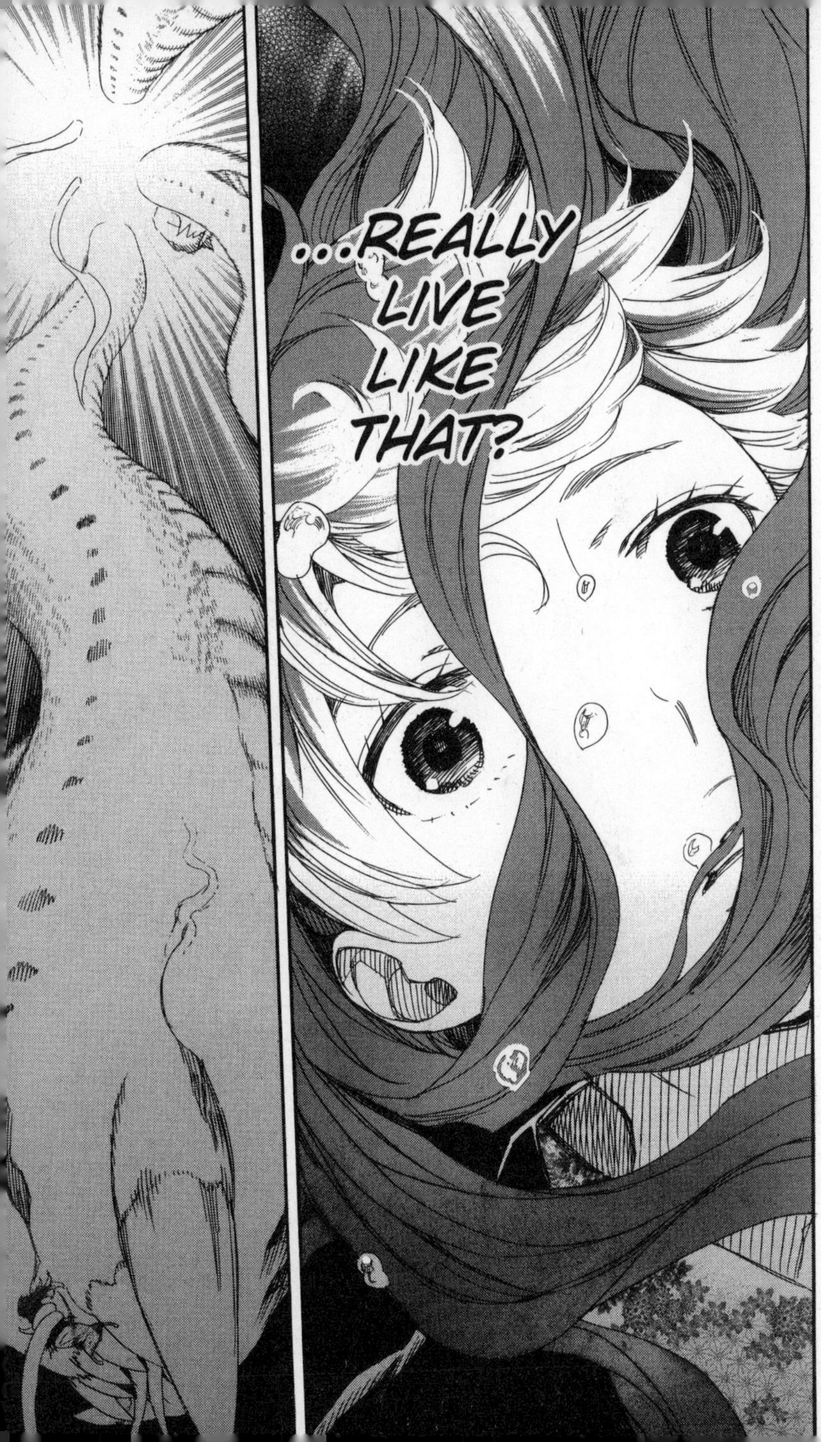
...REALLY LIVE LIKE THAT?

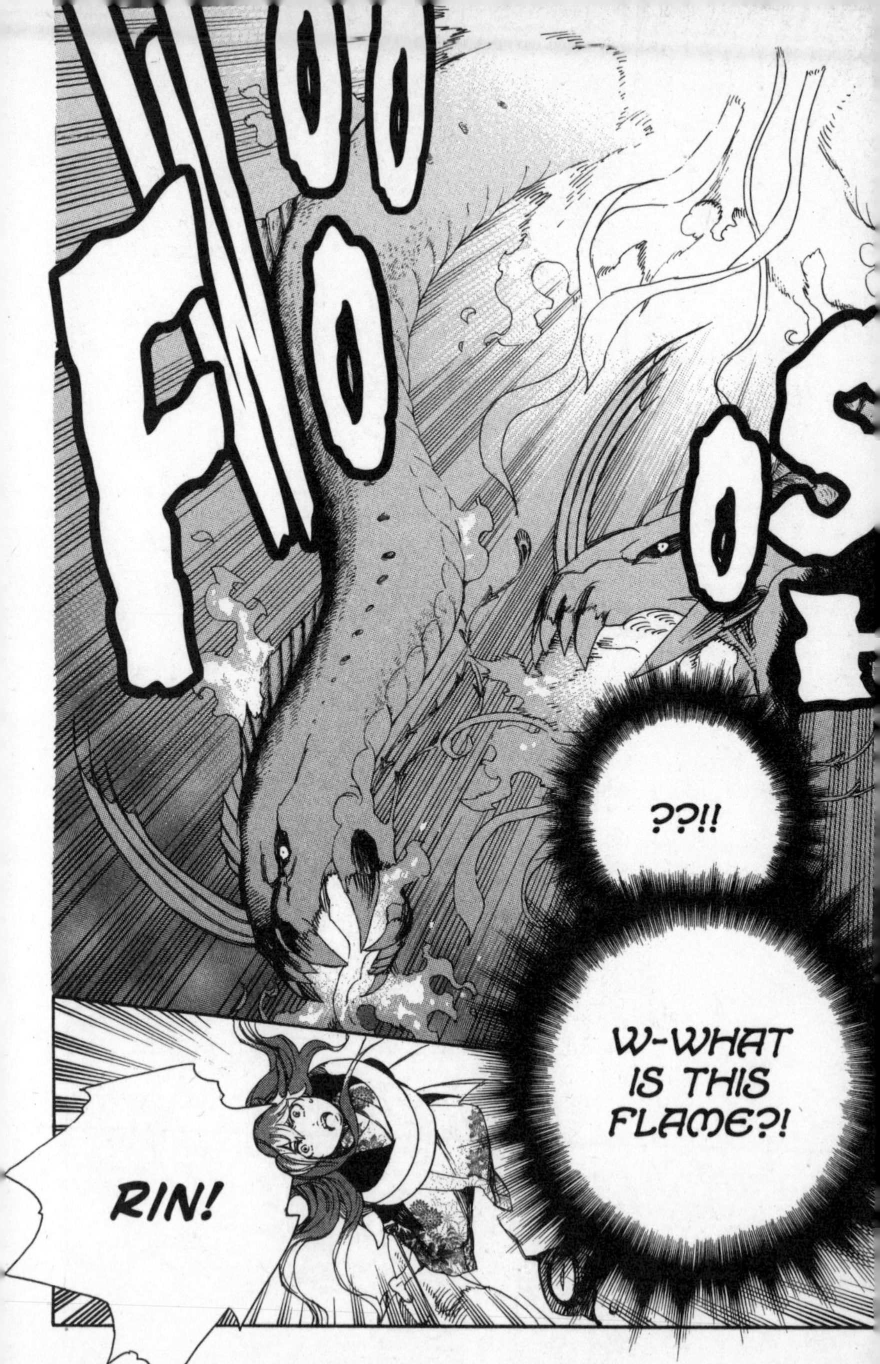
??!!
W-WHAT IS THIS FLAME?!
RIN!

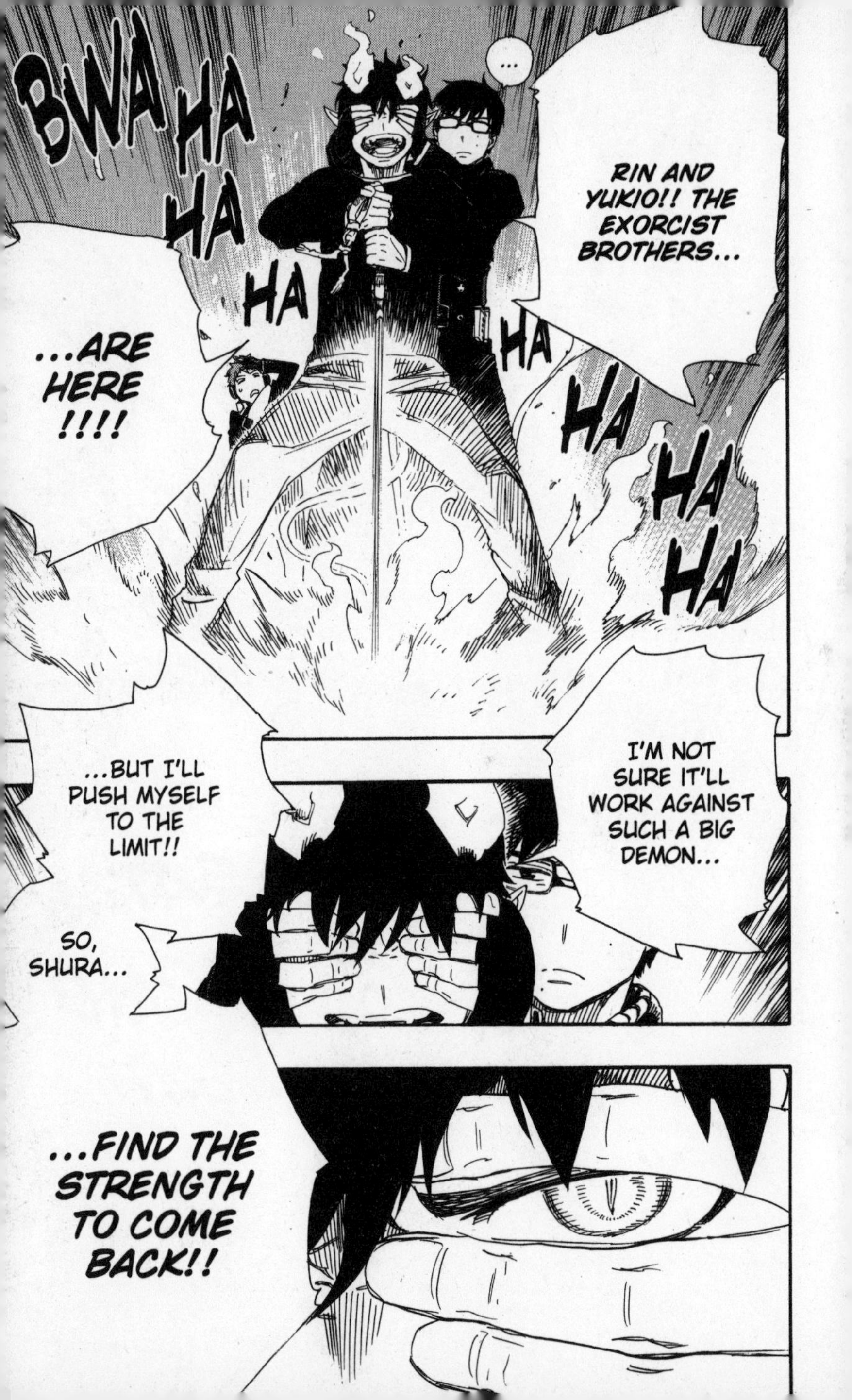
...
RIN AND YUKIO!! THE EXORCIST BROTHERS...
...ARE HERE !!!!
BWA HA HA HA HA HA HA HA HA HA
I'M NOT SURE IT'LL WORK AGAINST SUCH A BIG DEMON...
...BUT I'LL PUSH MYSELF TO THE LIMIT!!
SO, SHURA...
...FIND THE STRENGTH TO COME BACK!!

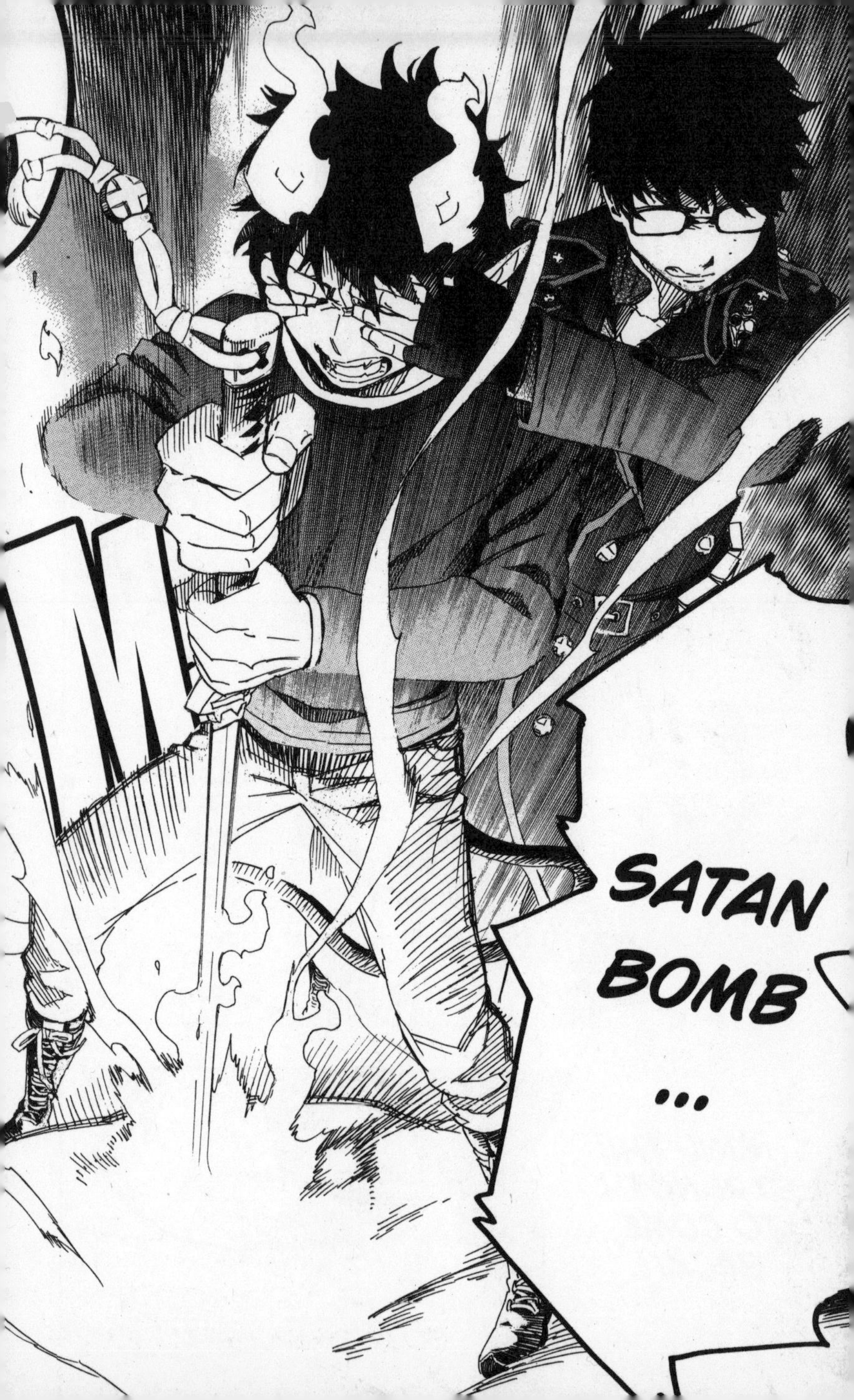
SATAN BOMB
...

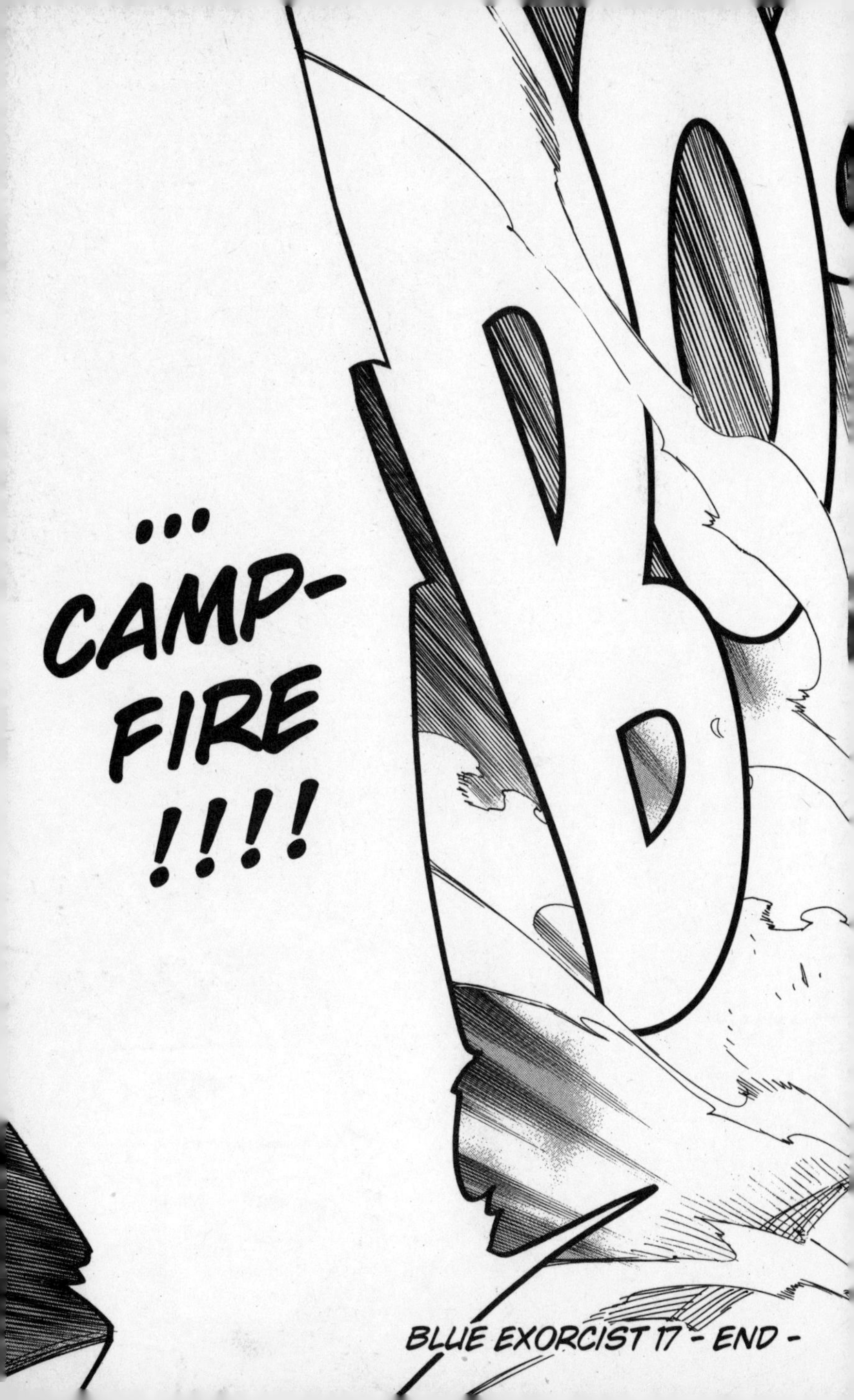
...CAMP-FIRE!!!!
BLUE EXORCIST 17 - END -

Blue Exorcist Chapter 78: As If Begging for Tears

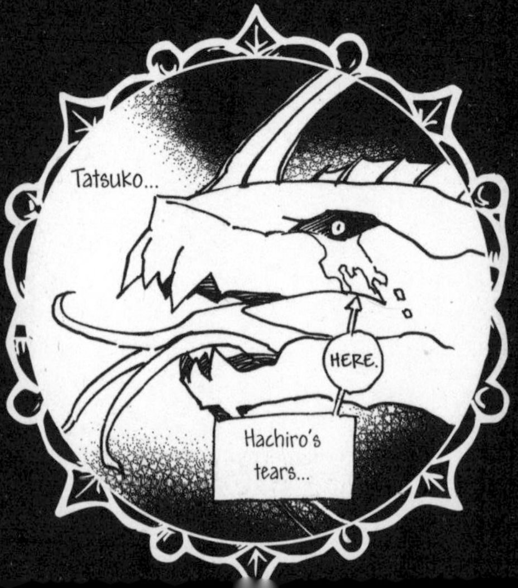
Tatsuko...
HERE.
Hachiro's tears...

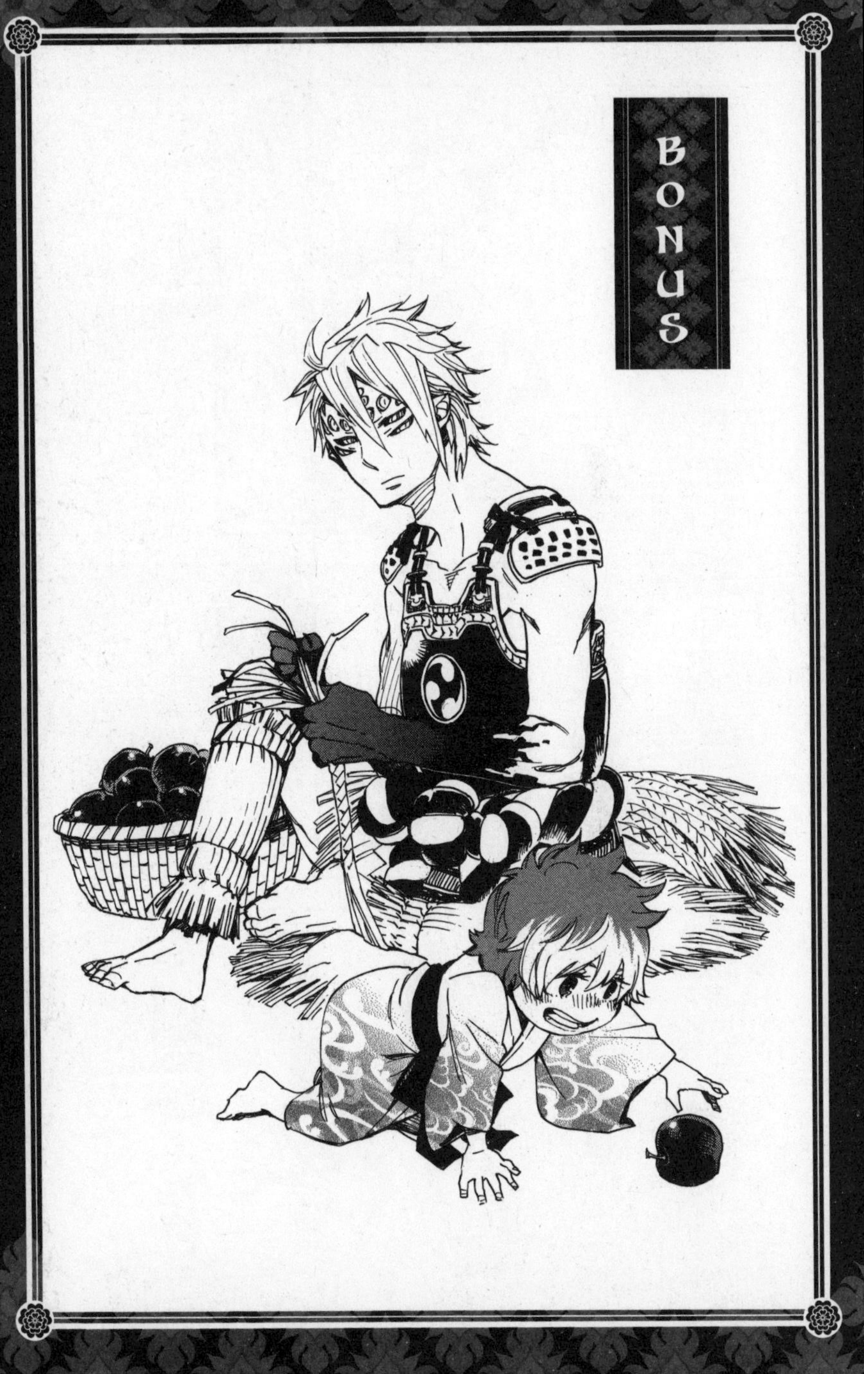
BONUS

BLUE EXORCIST BONUS

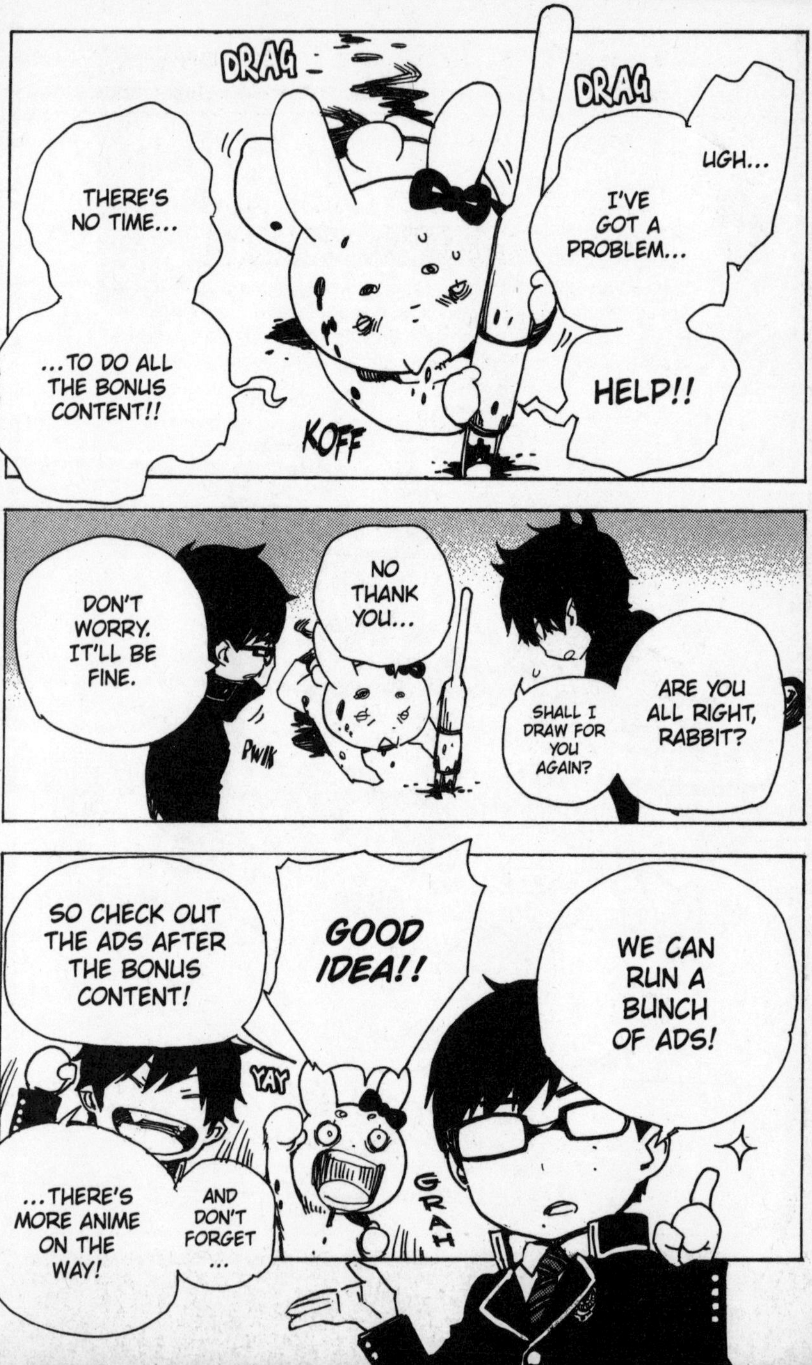
DRAG
UGH...
I'VE GOT A PROBLEM...
HELP!!
DRAG
THERE'S NO TIME...
...TO DO ALL THE BONUS CONTENT!!
KOFF
ARE YOU ALL RIGHT, RABBIT?
SHALL I DRAW FOR YOU AGAIN?
NO THANK YOU...
DON'T WORRY. IT'LL BE FINE.
PWIK
WE CAN RUN A BUNCH OF ADS!
GOOD IDEA!!
SO CHECK OUT THE ADS AFTER THE BONUS CONTENT!
YAY
GRAH
AND DON'T FORGET...
...THERE'S MORE ANIME ON THE WAY!

HACHIROTARO OMIKAMI

FILE 46

HIGH LEVEL

The territory of this particularly strong Hydra is around Lake Towada in Aomori Prefecture and extends to Akita Prefecture. Ever since the Buddhist monk Nansobo sealed him in Lake Towada over a thousand years ago, he has been unable to leave the area and has become the subject of numerous legends.

His regeneration capability surpasses physical constraints to draw upon the atmosphere itself. Thus, he can reconstitute himself despite any injuries or deterioration.

THREE WISE MONKEYS

FILE 47

LOW LEVEL

Kinship unknown. These demons possess images of the monkeys who preach the globally recognized wisdom of see no evil, hear no evil, speak no evil. They reveal the true feelings of those who draw near.

SYLPH

FILE 48

LOW TO MID LEVEL

Kin of Azazel, King of Spirit. This type of Elemental possesses air and manifests as small fairies. They're mischievous, but have the natural ability to purify air.

FURFUR

FILE 49

HIGH LEVEL

Kin of Azazel, King of Spirit. They possess the thunder and plasma in rain clouds and caper around thunderheads. They are extremely skittish and rarely appear before humans.

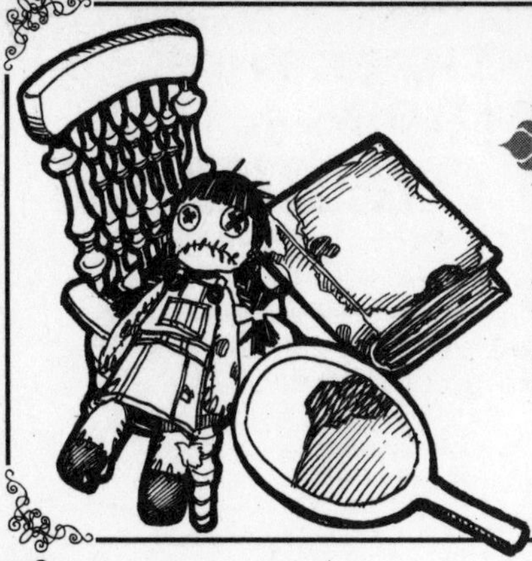

FILE 50

FETISH

LOW TO HIGH LEVEL

Kin of Azazel, King of Spirit. This is a general term for ghosts that possess other objects. The Demon Matching Game is an example of a Fetish. Possessing such an item often brings bad luck.

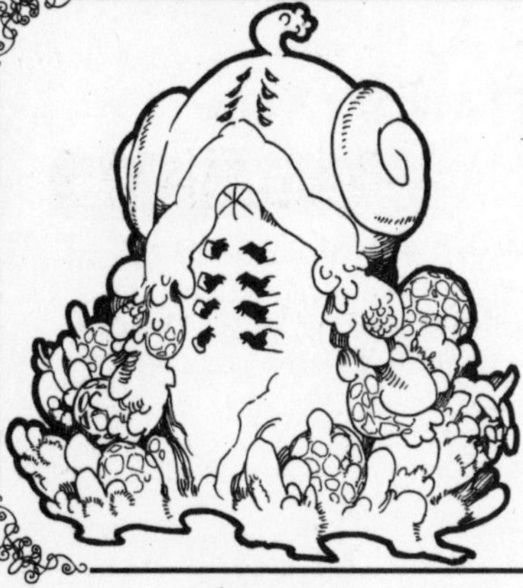

FILE 51

THE IMPURE BARON

HIGH LEVEL

Kin of Astaroth, King of Rot. As a subspecies of the Impure King, his characteristics are similar to that demon. One of the Impure Clan, he is a pet of the King of Rot.

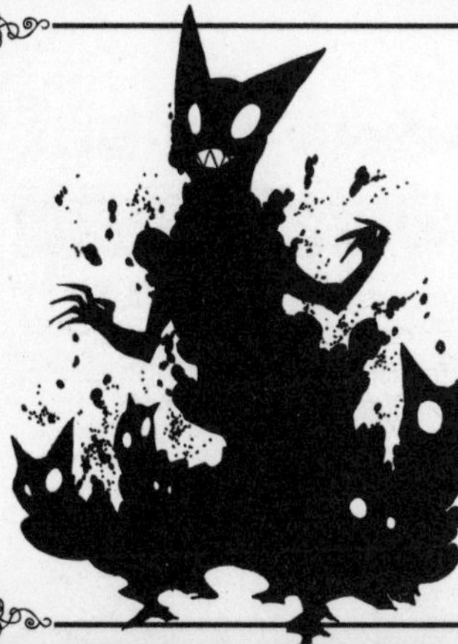

FILE 52

KOKS

MID TO HIGH LEVEL

Kin of Astaroth, King of Rot. This demon possesses fungi and is an amalgamation of Coal Tars. A Koks composed of even the smallest low-level Coal Tars can be a formidable opponent.

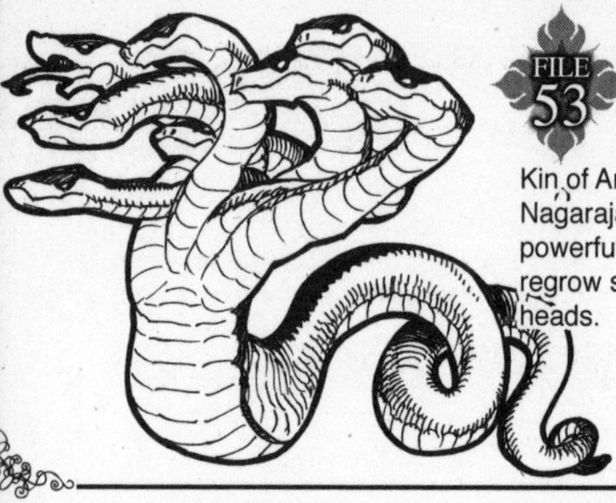

FILE 53 HYDRA

MID TO HIGH LEVEL

Kin of Amaimon, King of Earth. A type of Nagaraja, the king of the Nagas. Due to its powerful regeneration ability, it can quickly regrow severed heads. Noted for its eight heads.

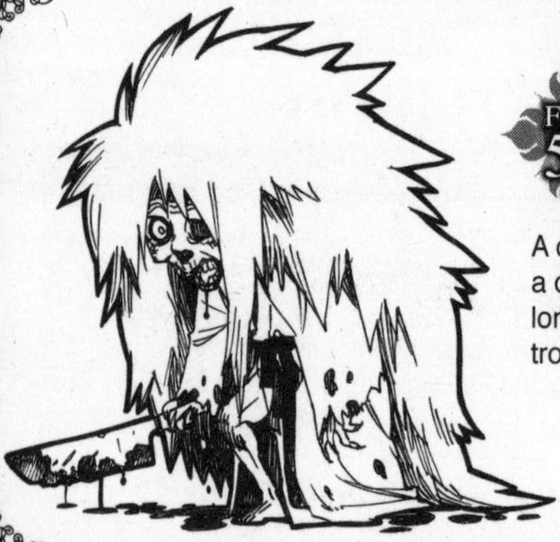

FILE 54 BABA YAGA

LOW TO MID LEVEL

A crone or witch who becomes possessed by a demon due to living in the mountains too long. They come down into villages to cause trouble and cannibalize human populations.

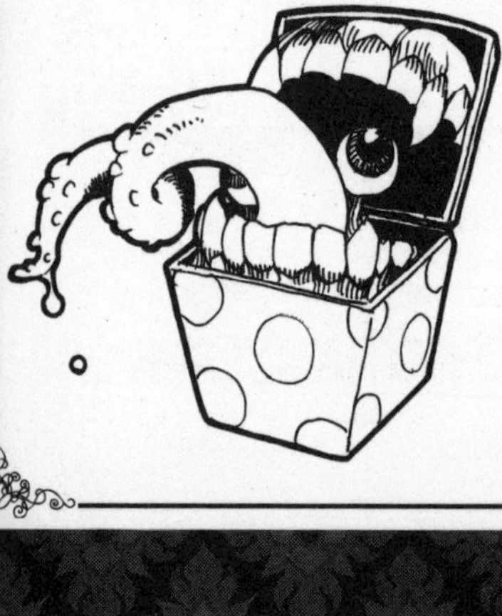

FILE 55 JACK-IN-THE-BOX

LOW TO MID LEVEL

A type of fetish parasitized by a ghost. They pop out of their boxes to scare people and may drag them inside. The powerful ones may even feed on people.

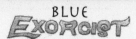

BLUE EXORCIST

Art Staff

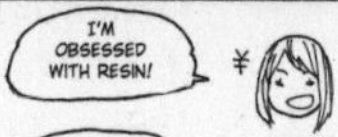
I'M OBSESSED WITH RESIN!
Miyuki Shibuya

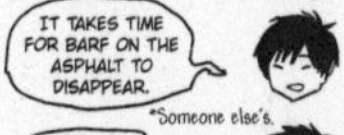
IT TAKES TIME FOR BARF ON THE ASPHALT TO DISAPPEAR.
*Someone else's.
Erika Uemura

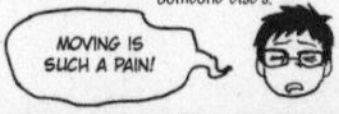
MOVING IS SUCH A PAIN!
Ryoji Hayashi

Art Assistants

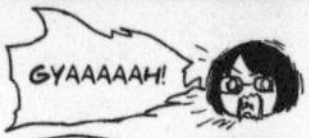
GYAAAAAH!
Yamanaka-san

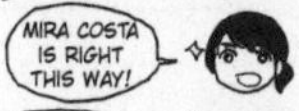
MIRA COSTA IS RIGHT THIS WAY!
Yanagimoto-san

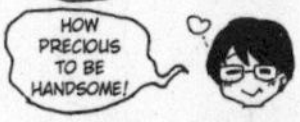
HOW PRECIOUS TO BE HANDSOME!
Yamagishi-san

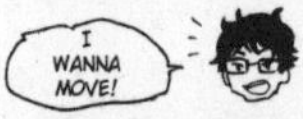
I WANNA MOVE!
Yoshiyama-kun

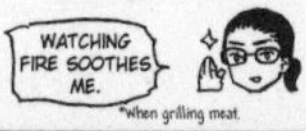
WATCHING FIRE SOOTHES ME.
*when grilling meat.
Obata-san

Composition Assistant

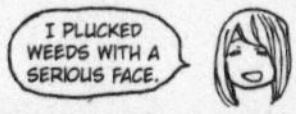
I PLUCKED WEEDS WITH A SERIOUS FACE.
Minoru Sasaki

Editor

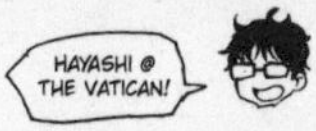
HAYASHI @ THE VATICAN!
Shihei Lin

Graphic Novel Editor

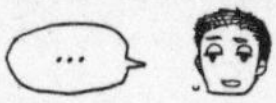
...
Ryusuke Kuroki

Graphic Novel Design

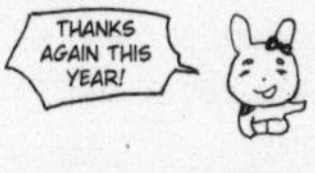
THANKS AGAIN THIS YEAR!
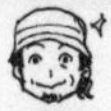
Shimada Hideaki

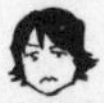
Daiju Asami (L.S.D.)

Manga

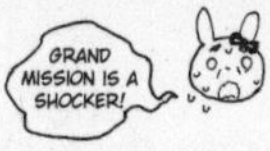
GRAND MISSION IS A SHOCKER!
Kazue Kato

(in no particular order)
(Note: The caricatures and statements are from memory!)

Stick around for volume 18 and check out the anime!!

How Demons Enter the Material World

Basically, there are two ways:

1 Possess an object

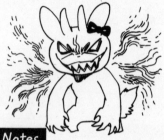

Notes

- Possession of the whole object
- Object's characteristics and appearance change
- Low to high level
- Exorcism is difficult

2 Parasitize an object

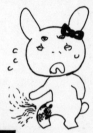

Notes

- Possession of part of an object
- Object's characteristics and appearance don't change much (except when parasitizing the brain)
- Low to mid level
- Exorcism is easy

3 When entering a human brain

Auditory hallucination
Dreams, hallucinations, etc.
Visual hallucination
Olfactory hallucination
Gustatory hallucination
Tactile hallucination

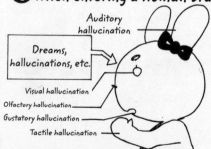

Notes

They say everyone has encountered Gehenna through dreams and such, but research so far is inconclusive.

Magic Sword Types

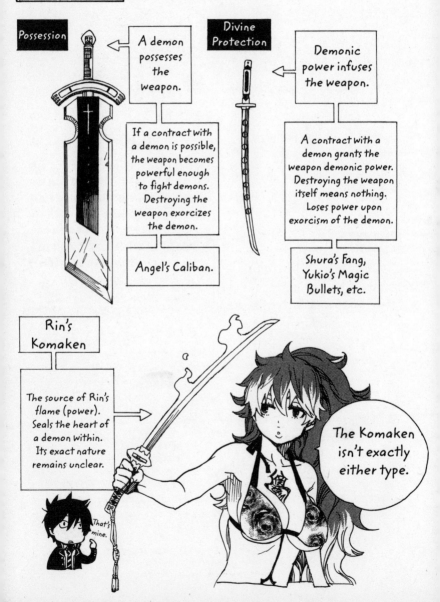

Possession

A demon possesses the weapon.

If a contract with a demon is possible, the weapon becomes powerful enough to fight demons. Destroying the weapon exorcizes the demon.

Angel's Caliban.

Divine Protection

Demonic power infuses the weapon.

A contract with a demon grants the weapon demonic power. Destroying the weapon itself means nothing. Loses power upon exorcism of the demon.

Shura's Fang, Yukio's Magic Bullets, etc.

Rin's Komaken

The source of Rin's flame (power). Seals the heart of a demon within. Its exact nature remains unclear.

The Komaken isn't exactly either type.

That's mine.

...very
well...

SQUINT

I can't
really
wink...

KAZUE KATO

THIS VOLUME BEGINS TELLING
THE MIDDLE PORTION OF
SHURA'S BACKSTORY. SHE'S AN
ADULT, SO I INCLUDED LOTS OF
ADULT TOPICS. YOUNGER
READERS MIGHT NOT ALWAYS
CATCH THE DRIFT...

...BUT YOU WILL
WHEN YOU GET OLDER.

ENJOY VOLUME 17!

BLUE EXORCIST

BLUE EXORCIST VOL. 17
SHONEN JUMP ADVANCED Manga Edition

STORY & ART BY KAZUE KATO

Translation & English Adaptation/John Werry
Touch-up Art & Lettering/John Hunt, Primary Graphix
Cover & Interior Design/Sam Elzway
Editor/Mike Montesa

Printed in the U.S.A.

Published by VIZ Media, LLC
P.O. Box 77010
San Francisco, CA 94107

10 9 8 7 6 5 4 3 2 1
First printing, July 2017

In the next volume...

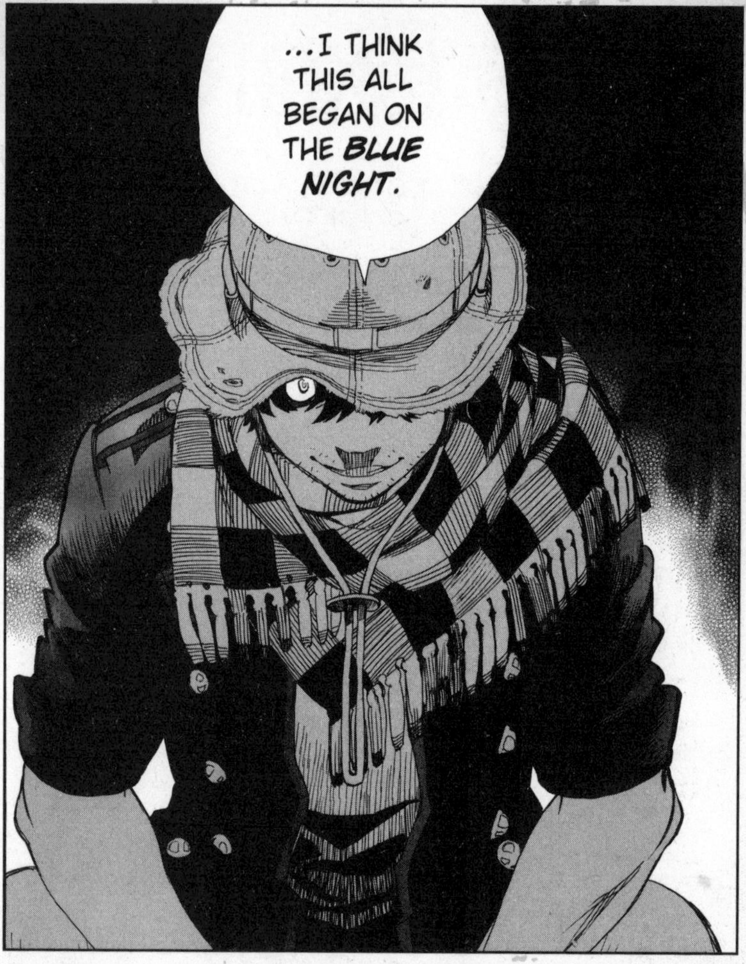
...I THINK THIS ALL BEGAN ON THE *BLUE NIGHT*.

Freed from her curse, Shura returns to True Cross Academy with a new outlook on life and a new appreciation for how far Rin has come (and a new haircut). While Yukio recovers in the hospital, the double agent Renzo Shima is back in action and an old enemy reappears. New plots are being laid and old secrets will come to light. A new phase of the conflict between the Knights of the True Cross and the Illuminati is beginning that will test the Exwires like never before.

Coming Soon!

You're Reading in the Wrong Direction!!

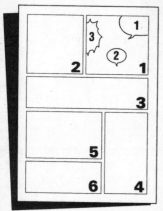

Whoops! Guess what? You're starting at the wrong end of the comic!

…It's true! In keeping with the original Japanese format, **Blue Exorcist** is meant to be read from right to left, starting in the upper-right corner.

Unlike English, which is read from left to right, Japanese is read from right to left, meaning that action, sound effects and word-balloon order are completely reversed… something which can make readers unfamiliar with Japanese feel pretty backwards themselves. For this reason, manga or Japanese comics published in the U.S. in English have sometimes been published "flopped"—that is, printed in exact reverse order, as though seen from the other side of a mirror.

By flopping pages, U.S. publishers can avoid confusing readers, but the compromise is not without its downside. For one thing, a character in a flopped manga series who once wore in the original Japanese version a T-shirt emblazoned with "M A Y" (as in "the merry month of") now wears one which reads "Y A M"! Additionally, many manga creators in Japan are themselves unhappy with the process, as some feel the mirror-imaging of their art skews their original intentions.

We are proud to bring you Kazue Kato's **Blue Exorcist** in the original unflopped format. For now, though, turn to the other side of the book and let the adventure begin…!

—Editor